THE ROMANTIC EXILES

E. H. CARR was one of the most distinguished twentieth-century British historians. After working for the Foreign Office from 1916 to 1936, he became Professor of International Relations at University College Wales, Aberystwyth. He held the post of assistant editor of *The Times* from 1941 to 1946 before becoming Tutor in Politics at Balliol College, Oxford; he was made a Fellow of Trinity College, Cambridge, in 1955. Best known as the author of the classic *What is History?*, Carr was also the author of a multi-volume history of the Soviet Union and a number of other works in the fields of international relations and Russian history. He died in 1982.

BY THE SAME AUTHOR

Dostoevsky, 1821-1881

Karl Marx:
A Study in Fanaticism

Michael Bakunin

International Relations Since the Peace Treaties

Great Britain as a Mediterranean Power

Britain:
A Study of Foreign Policy from the Treaty of Versailles to the
Outbreak of War

Propaganda in International Politics

The Twenty Years' Crisis, 1919-1939

The Future of Nations:
Independence or Interdependence?

Conditions of Peace

Nationalism and After

The Soviet Impact on the Western World

International Relations Between the Two World Wars, 1919-1939

Studies in Revolution

The New Society

German-Soviet Relations Between the Two World Wars, 1919-1939

What is History?

1917: Before and After

The Russian Revolution from Lenin to Stalin, 1917-1929

From Napoleon to Stalin and Other Essays

The Twilight of the Comintern, 1930-1935

The Comintern and the Spanish Civil War

A HISTORY OF SOVIET RUSSIA

The Bolshevik Revolution, 1917-1923

The Interregnum, 1923-1926

Socialism in One Country, 1924-1926

Foundations of a Planned Economy, 1926-1929

The Romantic Exiles

E.H. Carr

Serif
London

This edition first published 1998 by
Serif
47 Strahan Road
London E3 5DA

First published by Victor Gollancz 1933

British Library Cataloguing-in-Publication Data
A catalogue record for this book is available from the British Library.

Library of Congress Cataloging in Publication Data.
A catalog record for this book is available from the Library of Congress.

ISBN 1 897959 35 4

Printed and bound in Ireland by ColourBooks, Dublin

CONTENTS

Preface 9
1 The Departure 11
2 The Promised Land 25
3 A Family Tragedy: I 43
4 A Family Tragedy: II 78
5 The Engelsons 108
6 First Years in London 119
7 Poor Nick: I 137
8 The Recurrent Triangle 164
9 The Great Quinquennium 179
10 Bakunin; or the Slippery Path 192
11 Poland; or the Cruise of the *Ward Jackson* 204
12 Herzen's Last Years 218
13 A Voltairean among the Romantics 242
14 The *Affaire Nechaev;* or the First Terrorist 255
15 The *Affaire Postnikov;* or the Eternal Spy 274
16 Poor Nick: II 291
17 The Last Tragedy 306
Epilogue 320

APPENDIX A: Letter of Herwegh to
Malwida von Meysenbug (1870) 325

APPENDIX B: Letter of Thomas Carlyle
to Herzen (April 13th, 1855) 326

APPENDIX C: List of Addresses at which
Herzen resided in London (1852-65) 328

APPENDIX D: *Bedlam; or A Day of our Life* 329

APPENDIX E: *The Ward Jackson:*
Foreign Office Documents 337

APPENDIX F: Note on Sources 341

PREFACE
to the First Edition of 1933

IN presenting to the reader the story of *The Romantic Exiles*, I have two special debts of gratitude to acknowledge.

Mademoiselle Natalie Herzen, sole survivor of the party which sets out from Moscow in the first sentence of the book, has been good enough to supplement my written sources by drawing on the ample store of her personal reminiscences. The many conversations which I have been privileged to have with her in her home at Lausanne have been of particular assistance to me in the later chapters. She also placed at my disposal the unpublished letter of Carlyle to Herzen which is printed in Appendix B. I desire here not only to thank her warmly for all her kindness, but to apologize for having ventured, throughout the book, to call her by her pet name of Tata (a common Russian diminutive of Natalie). The fact that I already had two Natalies on my hands, and could not conveniently cope with a third bearer of that name, must be my excuse for this otherwise unwarrantable liberty.

My other principal debt is to Monsieur Marcel Herwegh, the only surviving son of George and Emma Herwegh. The unhappy drama which divided for ever the families of Herzen and Herwegh left behind it a lasting bitterness; and Herzen's account of the quarrel – the only account hitherto known – reflects this bitterness to the full. The chapters of Herzen's memoirs which tell the story of the rupture were given to the world by the Soviet State Publishing House in 1919; and from this moment it was inevitable that the copious papers in the possession of the Herwegh family should sooner or later be used to redress the balance and to correct the serious omissions and inaccuracies of the Herzen version. I am grateful to Monsieur Marcel Herwegh for having permitted me to use these papers for this purpose. His generosity has enabled me, in Chapter 3 and 4, to tell the story frankly and impartially with all the documents on both sides before me. In so doing, I have been able for the first time to set the role of George and Emma Herwegh in its true light, and to depict them, not as monsters of iniquity, but as human beings of flesh and blood, whose fallibility (like that of Natalie Herzen or of Herzen himself)

9

does not diminish their claim on our sympathy and our understanding. These papers have now been presented by Monsieur
Herwegh to the British Museum.

It is, however, fair that, in tendering my sincere thanks to
Mademoiselle Herzen and to Monsieur Herwegh, I should make
it clear that neither of them is in any way responsible for any
statement or expression of opinion which may be found in this
book. There may be much in it from which one or both of them
will dissent. I have refrained where possible from judgements of
my own; but I have not been able to avoid giving from time to
time my own interpretations of the situations and events described.
These interpretations are personal to myself. The facts are there;
and the reader can pass his own judgements, which may well be
different from mine.

I have one further apology to make, I am well aware that I
have not done justice in these pages to that amazing energumen of
revolutionary anarchism – a figure at once subhuman and superhuman – Michael Bakunin. His meteoric orbit touches and
intersects at irregular intervals the circle of *The Romantic Exiles;*
and it is these points of contact and intersection which alone are
dealt with here. But Bakunin deserves a volume to himself; and I
plead guilty to an ambition to write it at some future time.

I may add that – the vagaries of Russian being almost as strange
as those of English – the name Ogarev is pronounced approximately A-ga-ryóf. The names of the other principal actors in the
story hold no concealed pitfalls for the Occidental reader. The
standard English transliteration of Russian names has been followed. But variants (particularly -eff for -ev) will be found here
and there in quotations from the French or from older documents.

E. H. C.

CHAPTER I

The Departure

On Sunday, 19 January, 1847, a party of travellers left Moscow in two carriages padded, for protection against the winter cold, with fur. The party consisted of ten persons: Alexander Herzen; his wife Natalie; their three children, Alexander (or Sasha for short) aged seven, Kolya aged three, a deaf-mute, and Natalie the younger, commonly called Tata, aged two; Herzen's mother, Luisa Haag; two female friends and dependants of the family; a Baltic German named Karl Sonnenberg, who had been imported years ago from Reval to be Herzen's tutor, and who now acted as major-domo of his household; and a children's nurse. The terms of Herzen's passport, which was good for six months, showed that he was travelling with his family, for the sake of his wife's health, to Germany and Italy.

A small army of friends, some twenty strong, accompanied them to the first post-station outside Moscow. Its name, which means in translation 'Black Mud', might have held a threat for the travellers at a later season of the year; but now the ground was deep in snow, and the going, for carriages on runners, was excellent. The parting was hearty and convivial. It occurred to nobody that the Herzens were turning their back on Moscow for the last time.

Next day they reached Tver; and Herzen indited a jocular note to Granovsky, one of the friends who had taken leave of them at Black Mud:

As you see, we are making an excellent journey and an excellent meal, namely on sturgeon, in the fair city of Tver. I am writing to you because Jan. 22nd is your name-day. Make my excuses to Liza Bogdanovna [Granovsky's wife] for not calling on that day. The reason is, of course, a paltry one: I shall be in Novgorod. I crave mercy.

We are all well. Sasha is cheerful, Natalie (the second*) is cheerful and Kolya is splendid; he indulges in all the infirmities of nature in the carriage, which does not contribute to the *bien-être* of living in a

* Words added in Natalie Herzen's handwriting.

11

coach with four nags in front and Sonnenberg behind in spinach-green.

Of the farewells on the 18th and 19th I will speak when I have recovered.

The nurse stumbled with Natalie and knocked her head on the floor – which greatly added to the enjoyment of our *partie de plaisir*.

Well, give my greetings to everyone, including Korsh and Co., and my profound gratitude for the thoughts and feelings which I am carrying away with me on the journey. Good-bye. The road is fine . . .

Tell Melgunov that there may really be some element lacking in our friendship – something relating to the feelings rather than to our intelligence or to our sympathy . . . No, I am incapable of expressing myself; I have dined too well on sherry and sturgeon.

Natalie Herzen added a postscript in a similar vein:

Dear, invaluable and incomparable friends! All, all our Moscow friends! I embrace you once more and kiss you all. The mood of yesterday evening lives on in my heart (*notwithstanding twenty-four hours' continuous sickness**), yes, and notwithstanding a terrible headache – as if that mattered . . . I embrace you all once more. Good-bye! Write to Riga. The children are all well and cheerful.

The Herzens, husband and wife, were not only first cousins; they shared the same unconventional origin. They were the illegitimate children of two wealthy brothers named Yakovlev. The Yakovlevs were an ancient family of the Moscow nobility; but they had not for several generations occupied any position of eminence. Self-indulgence had become the family tradition; and it was worthily maintained by the two brothers. Both retired from the public service at an early age to a life of idleness. Both preferred to avoid the restraints and obligations of legal wedlock, and availed themselves to the full of the feudal privileges conferred by the system of serfdom. Their children were all born of irregular unions.

But despite this striking similarity in the conditions of their birth, the upbringing of the two cousins had been widely different. Ivan Yakovlev, Alexander Herzen's father, had served as a captain in the Guards; but he resigned his commission for the more congenial role of a *malade imaginaire*. During a visit to Ger-

* Words added in Herzen's handwriting.

many he carried off with him Henrietta-Wilhelmina-Luisa Haag, the sixteen-year-old daughter of a respectable but undistinguished civil servant of Stuttgart. She became his mistress and, in later years, his nurse; and though he never married her, she came to occupy a recognized position as the head of his household. Alexander, born in 1812, was the eldest child of this union. He received the imaginary surname of Herzen, which was also conferred on a son born to Yakovlev many years before by a serf-woman. The father, never prone to excessive emotion, lavished on his illegitimate offspring the limited degree of affection of which his nature was capable. Alexander, who inherited his father's exceptional intelligence, grew up as the son of the house, and was treated with particular indulgence as his father's favourite child.

At the age of twenty-five Herzen looked back on 'the humiliations and insults of his upbringing', and attributed to them that 'closed and constrained exterior which rarely allows the world to guess what is passing in my soul'. His sufferings, perhaps somewhat exaggerated in retrospect, were moral, not physical. They had their seat in his own consciousness rather than in the attitude of the world around him; but they reacted none the less on his character. The mask of irony, assumed for purposes of defence against the criticism, real or imagined, of his fellow-men, soon became second nature to him.

Really virtuous men [he wrote later] are devoid of irony ... Irony springs from the coldness of the soul – Voltaire, or from hatred of mankind – Shakespeare, Byron. It is a retort to humiliations undergone, a reply to insult, it is the reply of pride, not of the Christian.

In other and more tangible respects, young Herzen had little to suffer. The only recorded complaint against Ivan Yakovlev as a father is that he inflicted on his sixteen-year-old son, who had been caught surreptitiously reading Rousseau's *Confessions*, 'a sermon lasting whole days' – a performance which, however distasteful to the young man, may be regarded as one of the normal prerogatives of orthodox paternity. Russian society was logically tolerant of these accidents of birth, which were encouraged by the existing social system; and there is no evidence that young Herzen ever suffered reproach, or found his career impeded, on the score of his origin. He received the normal education of a young Russian

13

aristocrat, and in 1829, being then seventeen, he entered Moscow University.

Young Alexander Herzen had not awaited the age of seventeen to imbibe the radical ideas which, in the early years of last century, spread eastwards over Europe from the seed-bed of the French Revolution. The first revolutionary outbreak in modern Russian history took place in Petersburg, on the accession of Nicholas I to the imperial throne, in December 1825; and these high-minded but unpractical conspirators have been honoured by posterity under the name of the 'Decembrists'. The rising was suppressed with the greatest ease by the local troops. Five of the insurgents were hanged, and many more sent to Siberia for life. These events, which occurred in his fourteenth year, made an enormous impression on Alexander Herzen; and he and his friend Nicholas Ogarev, a boy two years younger than himself, stood side by side on the Sparrow Hills outside Moscow and solemnly swore to give their lives to the service of the sacred cause in which the Decembrists had suffered.

At the University of Moscow, whither Ogarev soon followed him, Herzen found an outlet for these juvenile ambitions. The Russian universities, in contrast with the Anglo-Saxon tradition, have always been the home of 'advanced' ideas. In the intervals of studying physics and mathematics, Herzen and Ogarev gathered round them the cleverest and most enterprising of their contemporaries; and in the year 1834, at the age of twenty-two, Herzen was arrested, together with several of his friends, for alleged complicity in the 'conspiracy' of a student named Sokolovsky. The 'conspiracy' does not seem to have gone further than hot-head discussion of the theories of socialism and the circulation of lampoons which treated the person of Nicholas I with insufficient respect. But the authorities took no risks; and heavy sentences were passed on the principal 'conspirators'. Herzen's role in the affair, such as it was, was altogether insignificant. But after nearly nine months' imprisonment, he was banished to the distant provincial capital of Vyatka, half-way across to the Urals, where he was given a minor post in the local administration. It was more than three years before he was allowed to return to Moscow.

In the meanwhile Natalie's sufferings had been of another kind. The character of her father, Alexander Yakovlev, was cast

14

in a stronger, coarser mould than that of his brother Ivan. He had for a short time served under Alexander I as Procurator of the Holy Synod. It was a singular office for one who lost no opportunity of displaying his contempt for orthodox religion and orthodox morality; and he did not hold it long. Like his brother he preferred retirement to the cares of the public service; and after his resignation he spent his time in quarrels with his relatives and in the enjoyment of a harem of serf-women, whom he kept in the servants' wing of his big Moscow house. The mother of Natalie was one of these concubines. Tatyana Passek, a cousin of Herzen's who has left us, in letters and memoirs, many details of his earlier years, remembered her as 'a simple peasant woman, sturdy and uneducated'. The church register of Herzen's marriage describes the bride's mother as a 'foreigner'. But this is clearly a harmless fiction, suggested by the similar origin of Herzen's own mother. It cannot have been pleasant for Natalie to reflect on her parentage.

Natalie was born in 1817, and spent the opening years of her life in the company of half a dozen other children whose origin was similar to her own. It was a curious whim of her father's to keep his illegitimate offspring in the part of the house which he himself occupied. The mothers remained in the wing reserved for the seraglio, and did not see the children except on holidays. Such were the conditions of Natalie's earliest childhood. But when she reached her seventh year, a series of incalculable freaks of fortune settled her future on altogether unexpected lines.

In that year, her father, who had just removed his establishment from Moscow to Petersburg, was stricken down by a fatal illness. Conscious that his end was near, Alexander Yakovlev regarded with growing aversion the prospect of leaving his worldly possessions to relatives whom he had for many years treated with contemptuous indifference. A malicious impulse decided him to cheat them of their expectations. He adopted the simple expedient of marrying the mother of his eldest son Alexis, and made the young man, who was now of age, his legitimate son and sole heir. Having savoured this last and subtlest of all his pleasures, the old epicurean expired; and Alexis succeeded to an ample fortune. He was a serious young man, and was known in the family, from the bent of his studies, as 'The Chemist'. Not the least embarrassing item of his inheritance was a bevy of half-brothers and half-sisters of various ages who, together with their mothers, were left at his absolute disposal.

It would have been too much to expect from Alexis a sentimental interest in this part of his property. He decided to dispatch the whole troop to one of his distant estates, where they would find their level naturally enough among the other serfs, and trouble him no more. Such was the destiny which Natalie narrowly escaped; and we are left to wonder whether it was a fortunate or unfortunate star which reserved her for another fate.

The Yakovlevs had a sister, the Princess Maria Khovansky, a wealthy widow. This lady, from motives of kindness or curiosity, so far interested herself in her brother's relicts as to send her companion to visit them on their passage through Moscow; and the companion brought back two young girls for her inspection. One of them, the seven-year-old Natalie, pleased the great lady by her pale and delicate complexion, her dark blue eyes and her shy demeanour. The Princess had no children; and she resolved to gratify a passing caprice by taking the attractive little orphan into her home.

Princess Maria shared to the full the self-indulgent qualities of the Yakovlev character; and her interest in her *protegée* remained superficial and intermittent. Natalie had a maid to look after her, and the proper number of tutors and teachers; but not much personal affection was lavished on her. Life in the big house was lonely and monotonous; and she afterwards filled many pages of her diary with reflexions, in the best romantic vein, on her unhappy and unloved childhood:

It always seemed to me that I had strayed into this life by mistake and should soon return home. But where was my home? My childhood was the gloomiest and bitterest imaginable. How often did I shed tears that were seen by none! How often, not yet understanding what prayer meant, did I get up in the night secretly (not daring even to pray except at the appointed time) and ask God to send someone to love and fondle me! I had no toy or plaything to divert or console me; for if they gave me anything it was with words of reproach and with the inevitable comment: 'It is more than you deserve.' Every trifle they gave me was bathed in my tears.

Natalie's cousin, Alexander Herzen, who was five years older

16

than herself, was a frequent visitor at the Princess Maria's house during his time at the university. The pair were young and romantically inclined, and the circumstances of their birth created a bond of sympathy between them. Their first relations were those of brother and sister. Indeed, Natalie even made Alexander the confidant of her first calf-love for a young man named Biryukov. But the letters which passed between them during Herzen's imprisonment and exile gradually assumed a different tone. It was a case of love by correspondence; and at the beginning of 1836, more than two years after they had last met, they plighted their troth by letter.

The correspondence between Alexander and Natalie during these years has been preserved, and provides for posterity an instructive example of the literary style in which intelligent young people of the 1830s conducted their affairs of the heart. The lovers move on a uniformly exalted plane, and the atmosphere in which they exchange their transports may, to the more material tastes of a later age, seem rarified and unreal. Natalie in particular has absorbed to the full the current romantic idiom. Terrestrial love is a reflexion of celestial love – sometimes, it would seem, scarcely more than an irrelevant excrescence.

> I felt that I was your sister and thanked God for that [she writes]. Now God has deigned to open to me another heaven, to show me that the soul can support a greater happiness, that there is no limit to the happiness of those He loves, that love is above friendship ... Oh, Alexander! You know this paradise of the soul. You have heard its song. You have sung it yourself. But for me this is the first time that the light illumines my soul. I worship. I pray. I love.

A little later she envisages love under another religious aspect:

> You will present me to God as He desires me to be. If I had not this faith, however great my love I would not give myself to you.

And at one point she breaks into verse to celebrate the 'heavenly vocation' and 'god-like dreams' of 'sacred love', and explains that she has lost her taste for 'the embraces of heaven' since her beloved has revealed to her 'another heaven, another paradise'. The language of the poem may seem at first sight inconsistent with the specifically devotional character of the above-quoted letters.

17

But the inconsistency is merely apparent. Her love and her religion are one; and it makes little difference which member of the equation is put first.* Page after page, these and like phrases flow from Natalie's pen with the tireless reiteration which often makes love-letters dull reading for posterity.

Herzen replies manfully, but with a less marked addiction to hyperbole and to religion. Once or twice, indeed, he is taken to task for the too frankly terrestrial quality of his passion; and when he signs himself gaily 'Yours till the grave', he finds himself gently reminded of that 'aspiration for the Beyond', which Natalie had conceived in the Princess Khovansky's gloomy palace, and which had remained one of the deepest longings of her nature. Herzen is in love and he makes an effort to attune himself to this exalted mood. He takes to church-going, and signs himself (still with a faint suspicion of jocularity) 'Yours even beyond the grave'. He declares that Natalie is for him what Christ was for mankind; compares the stony-hearted relatives who would have hindered their marriage with the betrayer and crucifiers of Christ; and even writes, with some show of conviction, of the happiness of dying after a single kiss. He yields not ungraciously. But we feel that these concessions to romantic mysticism are foreign to his nature and will hardly survive the first ecstasies of passion.

There were other incompatibilities, perhaps more profound than those of religious feeling. Natalie brought to her betrothed the virgin offering of first love. Herzen was a vigorous, good-looking and intelligent young man. He had made conquests and enjoyed them. At Vyatka he had consoled the charming and passionate young wife of an elderly invalid. The gradual decline of his infatuation for this lady kept pace with the growth of his love for his young cousin; and his earlier letters to Natalie are full of frank references to the affair. It is an odd coincidence that his first declaration of love to Natalie was penned on the very day that the elderly husband succumbed to his malady; and the unkind commentator may nourish a suspicion that the declaration was hastened by a desire to erect a defensive bulwark against the too ardent pursuits of his now unencumbered *inamorata*.

* Novalis, the most typical of the German Romantics, declares that his feeling for his Sophie is 'not love, but religion'; and after her death he writes a poem in which he identifies her with the Virgin Mary.

I held out to her the hand of a friend [he writes to Natalie]. Several times I spoke to her of you quite openly. I showed her the bracelet, the medallion.

But the lady refused to understand these timid allusions.

The worst of it is [continues Herzen a few weeks later] that I have not the courage to tell her frankly about you. A thousand times I have been on the point of doing so, and could not. What does my role look like now, the role of a man whom you call perfect, divine? But there is no choice; I must either kill her with a single word or, by silence and half-truths, play the coward and let time do its work.

It is perfectly human and natural, this careful damping down of the flames of a discarded passion. But it is decidedly not romantic. Herzen returned Natalie's love; but he could not, in the nature of things, return the pure uncalculating innocence of her infatuation for him.

There was a no less marked discrepancy in the attitude of the lovers to another aspect of married love. Herzen was by temperament expansive. He was a man of social inclinations, of political ambitions, and of keen and varied intellectual interests. Natalie on the other hand was purely intensive. She lived by the heart alone; she declared herself, first and last, as one whose only talent and only ambition is to love. Other interests she had none. But this diversity, felt and recognized from the outset, seemed at this stage merely to cement their union. 'My soul has lost itself in you', exclaims Natalie, 'as a star in the sun.' Her passionate nature demanded as yet only to be swallowed up in the beloved object; and Herzen was ready enough to accept this diagnosis of their relationship. He even explained to her at some length his philosophy of the matter:

Your life has found its goal, its destiny; your life has fulfilled its circuit of the earth. In my embrace your separate existence will disappear, in my love all your needs all your thoughts will be drowned. In a word, your soul is part of my soul; it has quickly returned to its whole, and its separate existence is ended. Thus love was destined to complete and develop your soul. Love was destined to bring you to me, and love will bring you to God. But my life is not yet full; it is the life not of a part, but of the whole. Over and above my private life, there is laid on me the obligation to partake in the common, universal life, in the common activity for the good of mankind; and feeling alone would not

19

satisfy me . . . You are *I*; Alexander and Natalie do not form a *WE*, but only my own *I*. My *I* is full, for you have been completely swallowed up; and *you* no longer exist.

The familiar Byronic text

> Man's love is of his life a thing apart,
> 'Tis woman's whole existence

has seldom been more perfectly – one had almost said, more naïvely – expounded. But Herzen might well, if infatuation had not replaced reflexion, have paused to ask himself whether Natalie at thirty would be as eager to accept this exposition as Natalie at nineteen.

It would be pedantic to insist further on these germs of potential discord. Such seeds have been latent in many marriages where they have never come to flower. Alexander and Natalie were passionately in love; they were, save for their enforced separation, ecstatically happy; and the *dénouement* of their epistolary wooing was as dramatic as the heart of romantic maiden could desire. In March 1838 Herzen, whose place of exile had been changed from Vyatka to the less distant Vladimir, came secretly to Moscow on a false passport to visit his betrothed. He learned that the Princess was trying to marry her to another suitor. The position of the orphan, face to face with an imperious benefactress unaccustomed to be crossed by her dependants, was impossible. Herzen laid his plans. A few weeks later he came to Moscow again, this time with a double motive for secrecy. Natalie was ready. 'Letters pale before union,' she wrote to him on the eve of the elopement, 'as stars before the sun. Quick! Quick!' The gallant lover was not deaf to so winning an appeal. He carried off Natalie with him to Vladimir, and married her there in the early days of May.

The full fragrance of romance surrounds the first months of their married bliss.

Well, what shall I say of myself? [wrote Herzen to a friend in July]. I am happy, happy as a man can be on earth, happy as a man can be who has a soul that is open to the bright and good, that can sympathize with the suffering of others.

Natalie is an ethereal, an unearthly poet; everything about her is unique. She is shy, she fears the multitude, but with me she is always noble and delicate.

20

And his Diary of the following January finds his enthusiasm unabated.

> Our dream has been realized, realized in all its immeasurable fullness. We wanted to be together. Providence has united us and left us *alone*; on this side, we two; on the other, the world. We belong one to the other, and around us is drawn a line which no one crosses.

And he concludes that he will never know a better year in his life than 1838.

The prophecy was in the main fulfilled. For though some of the glory of 1838 brimmed over into the following year, the drab colours soon begin to predominate. Early in 1840, Herzen obtained, through his father's influence, a post in the Ministry of the Interior at Petersburg. It is doubtful whether his restless and inquiring spirit would in any case have found lasting satisfaction in the routine of the civil service. But he had not served for more than six months when a characteristic incident terminated his official career. He happened to write to his father that a certain spot in Petersburg, near the so-called Blue Bridge, had recently been the scene of six successive murders. It was a banal topic, and he added the banal comment: 'So you can judge what sort of police we have here.' Herzen had not paused to reflect that the correspondence of a former political offender was particularly liable to attract the attention of the censorship. His letter was opened; and it was reported to the Tsar that an official in the Ministry of the Interior, once already condemned for subversive behaviour, had cast aspersions on those loyal and effective defenders of autocracy – the Petersburg police. The Tsar took a serious view of this breach of discipline. It was ordered that the offender should be dismissed from his post and exiled for one year to Novgorod, where he might learn respect for the established institutions of his country.

Herzen was now a married man of nearly thirty; and this comparatively lenient punishment stung more keenly and rankled more deeply than the far severer sentence of six years before. He spent the year morosely in Novgorod and came back to Moscow an embittered man. His political opinions, hitherto the expression of a vague and undefined idealism, crystallized into a bitter, life-long hatred of the Russian autocracy. His character soured.

Middle age succeeded youth, and cynicism replaced romance; and friends began to complain that he was self-indulgent and self-opinionated. Restlessness overtook him; and when in 1846 his father died, leaving him a large fortune, he saw for the first time the possibility of escaping, at any rate for a few months, from the tense and stifling atmosphere of the Russia of Nicholas I. The fresh air of western Europe, where opinion was free, where democracy was practised, and where the discussion even of socialism was not a criminal offence, would provide a magic and infallible cure for all his ills.

To Natalie, too, these years had brought her share of trouble and disillusionment. The delicate complexion which, by pleasing the exacting Princess, had played a decisive role in her life, was not the mark of a robust constitution; and her health did not resist the successive pregnancies which followed her marriage. Besides the three children who survived to accompany their parents abroad, there had been three more who died in infancy. These were sore blows, and they relaxed, instead of strengthening, the bonds of affection between Natalie and her husband. Herzen had never, even in the first blind moments of passion, quite shared Natalie's conception of the married pair as 'hermits living in a forest and holding no converse with their fellow-men'. He had long crossed the line which, in the days of their honeymoon at Vladimir, had separated Natalie and himself from the rest of the world. Life claimed him; and the bedside of a perpetually ailing wife could not absorb his energies. He overflowed with vigour and indignation and high spirits, while she wrestled listlessly with the alternate agonies of childbirth and death. There was worse still in store. The discovery, which followed one of her pregnancies, of her husband's passing infidelity with a pretty housemaid, one of his father's serfs, rudely tore down the romantic halo which had hitherto invested their marriage; and the offence rankled in Natalie's introspective mind long after it had been confessed and condoned.

Natalie's love for her husband, tempered in the furnace of many bitter moments, survived the ordeal. But a change came over its spirit. She told herself that she was happy in her affections. But she, like Herzen, became uneasy and restless; she too began to long for another climate. Her disillusionment, though less openly expressed, was no less profound than that of her husband.

It may even have been deeper. For Natalie had seen little of the world; and she had in her composition none of that ironical detachment which became, more and more, Herzen's favourite defensive weapon. There are extant two curious letters written to her husband in the autumn of 1846, in which she seems to be arguing not so much with him as with herself, to be seeking by all the resources of reason to convince herself of her own unclouded happiness:

> Yes, Alexander, I clearly feel that maturity has descended on us; romance with its vague longings, its glance fixed on the misty distance, its striving to some other bourne, its throbbing, aching love for all mankind, has left us – and for ever. I see how much common sense these last years have brought into our life, and I see that common sense does not dry up the soul – all that is nonsense . . .

> Yes, it is maturity, not weariness, not resignation – I can feel it at every step. It was good to live in those days when your heart fluttered without ceasing, when you were unceasingly impelled hither and thither, when you were full of desires – whereas now you can scarcely cope with what you already have. But it is good to reach the haven . . . Yes, Alexander, romance has left us, and we are no longer children but grown-up people; we see more clearly and more deeply, feel more clearly. It is not the exalted enthusiasm of yore, youth intoxicated with life and worshipping its idols – all that lies far away, behind. I no longer see the pedestal on which you used to stand, or the halo round your head. I no longer believe that you are thinking of me and looking at a star at the same moment as I am looking at it and thinking of you; but I see clearly and feel deeply that I love you very much, that my whole being is full of this love, is made up of it, and that this love is my life.

It is admirably done; and the reader who was unacquainted with Natalie's earlier love-letters might well be deceived. But Natalie's heart had fluttered too wildly to the music of Alexander's wooing to be thus easily and quickly tamed into drab acquiescence. This cool, unemotional young wife protests too much. She may have persuaded herself; but she does not convince us. The eulogy of sense is less moving than the funeral oration over the grave of sensibility; and beside these letters to her husband we should place another letter written just afterwards to her husband's friend Ogarev:

> It used to be better. For a single word, a single thought, one was

23

ready to crucify a man or to be crucified for him. Now one has grown used to everything. Your cheeks do not burn; your heart does not burst from your chest; a sort of poison flows through your whole being, and you suffer quietly or – how shall I put it? – submissively, dumbly without the slightest desire either to save or to sacrifice yourself.

Natalie was not yet thirty. In the depths of her sentimental soul she could not bring herself to believe that her life was already over, and that the bright vision of celestial love had faded for ever from her firmament. She scarcely knew, as Herzen himself scarcely knew, what she wanted or what she missed. But both these disillusioned, precociously mature, young people knew that something was wrong; and both believed, consciously or unconsciously, in the curative properties of a foreign pilgrimage. The French capital, which was their chosen destination, was the home not only of Louis-Philippe and Guizot, but of George Sand and Musset. For Herzen, the horizon of western Europe was bright with the mirage of Political Liberty; for Natalie, with the not less elusive lodestar of Romance.

CHAPTER 2

The Promised Land

THE collocation of Romanticism and Revolution sounds forced and rather unreal to most English ears. In England, the Romantic movement remained (except for Byron and in part Shelley, who became, in virtue of this exception, spiritual outcasts) a movement for the worship of Nature and the liberation of literature from the dead hand of convention. In Europe, it was a movement for the worship of Human Nature and the liberation of the individual from the yoke of moral and political absolutism. It was not, in its first and most characteristic phase, a movement against religion and morality as such. It did not occur to the assailants of conventional morality to deny the existence of moral sanctions. The worship of human nature came to fill the gap; and they founded the new code of morals, like Rousseau, on the apotheosis of the feelings, or like George Sand, on the religion of love. It did not occur to the deniers of the divine right of kings to deny divinity; they merely substituted for the divine right of kings the divine right of the people. Romanticism covered every phase of human thought. Its metaphysical counterpart was the Idealism of Fichte, Schelling and Hegel – 'Romanticism for the heart', as Herzen put it, 'and Idealism for the head'. Its supreme political expression was the French Revolution. The Romantic movement, from the seed sown by Rousseau, spread over Europe, flowered, decayed, and finally faded away (subject to sporadic revivals in later years) after the ineffective revolutions of 1848 and 1849. Beyond the Vistula and the Niemen, its timetable was perceptibly later. It scarcely reached Russia before 1830; it bloomed there in the thirties and forties, and lingered feebly on until, at the beginning of the sixties, reaction and nihilism joined hands to give it the *coup de grâce*. It is this last, and specifically Russian, efflorescence of Romanticism – the generation of the thirties and forties – which is here represented in the persons of the Romantic Exiles.

It was at the end of March 1847 that the pilgrims, after a journey of sixty days, reached at last the promised land and drove up to the doors of the Hôtel du Rhin in the Place Vendôme. On the same day, without waiting to feast his eyes on the wonders of the capital, Herzen performed the first essential duty of the Russian tourist arriving in Paris. He went to call on Paul Annenkov. Annenkov was by birth a wealthy Russian landowner, and by choice a globe-trotter – in an age when the globe was synonymous, for these purposes, with the Continent of Europe. For the past year he had been living in a luxurious flat in the Rue Caumartin. It was a period when every Russian aristocrat made, sooner or later, the grand tour of Europe; and Annenkov perfectly combined, before either of these institutions existed, the functions of a tourist agency and a society journalist. He delighted to tell you where to go, and what to see, and whom you would find there. He knew the present whereabouts and the future plans of everyone who counted. He shared none of the narrow prejudices of his class. He rubbed shoulders not only with his fellow Russian serf-owners, but with liberal French politicians. He knew Karl Marx, a journalist who had been expelled from Germany for his revolutionary opinions and had taken refuge in Paris; and he had met Weitling, the tailor from Magdeburg, the first working-man communist. Annenkov moved in every circle. Yet so transparent were the extent of his honesty and the limits of his intelligence that, living in the midst of intrigues of every kind, he was never suspected either by the Russian Government of being a revolutionary, or by the revolutionaries of being a secret agent of the Russian Government. His was the inquisitive temperament of a man made by nature to observe and not to reflect. He has left an admirable picture of Herzen during his first days in Paris, fresh from his Moscow tailor, wearing a long frock-coat which seemed to get in his way as he walked; and it is he who records the rapid transformation of Herzen into a citizen of the world 'with a dandified beard which quickly assumed the correct outlines, and a jacket of free and elegant cut', and of the simple, domestic Natalie into a 'brilliant tourist completely fitted to occupy a place of honour in the great world capital'.

It is now many decades since France was commonly regarded in Europe as the spiritual home of revolution; and we find it hard to share the particular emotions which the view of Paris excited in the breasts of our romantic travellers. There was, perhaps, in the forties of last century, far more real democracy in English than in French institutions. But little was known about English democracy in the rest of Europe, and nothing at all in Russia. It was tradition that counted; and in 1847 the French Revolution was still a living force. It was fifty years since Napoleon had stamped out the embers of that mighty conflagration; but it still had power – in Russia, at any rate – to kindle in men's hearts the emotions of hope and fear. A recent Russian writer scarcely exaggerates when he compares the reputation enjoyed among the subjects of Nicholas I by the Paris of Louis-Philippe with the position of present-day Moscow in the eyes of western Europe. The Paris of 1847 was the bugbear of the conservatives and the Mecca of the extremists.

We had been accustomed [writes Herzen] to connect the word Paris with memories of the great events, the great masses, the great men of 1789 and 1793, memories of a colossal struggle for an idea, for rights, for human dignity . . . The name of Paris was closely bound up with all the noblest enthusiasms of contemporary humanity. I entered it with reverence, as men used to enter Jerusalem and Rome.

It was from Annenkov that Herzen learnt of the presence in Paris of his old friend Sazonov. Herzen and Sazonov had sat side by side at the age of nineteen studying physics and mathematics in the University of Moscow. Their feelings for each other retained the romantic hue of youthful comradeship; and when Herzen in later life came to write his memoirs (under the title *My Past and Thoughts*) he consecrated a long obituary chapter to this early friendship. Sazonov was one of the most brilliant and daring members of Herzen's group in Moscow; and nobody would have doubted that he was destined to make his mark in the world. He had been as much involved as any of them in the Sokolovsky affair; and if he escaped arrest, it was only because he had the habit of 'talking much and writing little', and had therefore few incriminating papers to fall into the hands of the police. The arrest and exile of his friends deprived him of any visible occupation in Moscow, and he drifted aimlessly to Paris. He was probably under the impression that some congenial occupation would inevitably present itself in that home of seething revolutionary activity.

Sazonov was one of those gifted young men whose brilliant future recedes imperceptibly into the past without ever having been realized in the present. He found that Paris offered no more immediate outlet than Moscow for his revolutionary ardour. But it provided the youthful possessor of a large fortune with unequalled opportunities for dissipation; and of these Sazonov fully availed himself. Such indulgences made rapid inroads into his substantial monetary resources. But they did not lessen his faith in the turn of the wheel which would one day set up constitutional government in Russia, and confer on him an important portfolio in the first Russian liberal ministry. He maintained both his illusions and his disreputable manner of life for some fifteen years; and if his amusements became, with the passage of time, somewhat dowdy and faded, his hopes were evergreen. He greeted Herzen with enthusiasm, clamoured for the latest news from Russia, and was disgusted at the cynicism of his visitor, who assured him that the Russian Revolution was more distant than ever.

The rest of Sazonov's story is a record of continuous decline. The European revolutions of 1848 seemed for a moment to justify and flatter his ambitions. He founded an International Club which published a programme, held one meeting, and then collapsed. He indulged in one or two short-lived journalistic enterprises. But nothing helped; Sazanov went ever more rapidly downhill. At one moment he was in prison for debt; then the French authorities expelled him and he went to Geneva. He was accompanied by an Italian mistress whom he married and then deserted. He died at Geneva some years later, forgotten by all his old friends; and Herzen records, as a culmination of his tragedy, that not a single Russian attended his funeral.

It is unnecessary to pursue the catalogue of former acquaintances who once more crossed Herzen's path in Paris. But one of them will occupy too conspicuous a place in this portrait-gallery of Romantic Exiles to be passed over here. Herzen spent many of his first days in Paris in pilgrimages to the Palais-Royal, the Bastille, the Panthéon, the Champs-Elysées, and a dozen other historic sites whose names were as much household words to him as the Nevsky Prospekt in Petersburg or the Arbat in Moscow. It was on one of these expeditions that he saw, at a street-corner, the familiar gigantic form of Michael Bakunin, dressed

28

in a fashion that contrived to be both dandified and untidy, brandishing a cigarette and discoursing to a group of admiring friends on the problems of philosophy, precisely as he had done seven or more years ago in the streets and drawing-rooms of Moscow.

The previous friendship between Herzen and Bakunin had been of short duration. But few who had known Bakunin and tasted the flavour of his dominating personality ever forgot him. Herzen met him in Moscow towards the end of 1839, engaged, like the other young intellectuals of the day, in passionate debate on the political implications of the Hegelian philosophy. They ranged themselves in opposite camps; and the impression on both sides was both vivid and lasting. Next spring Bakunin had found occasion to renew the acquaintance. His ambitions centred on a journey abroad; and his relations with his parents were such as to deprive him of all hope of defraying the cost from family funds. He asked his new friend for a loan. Such requests were commonly addressed by Bakunin to new friends; for his old friends had generally exhausted either their funds or their patience. There is extant a letter of April 1840 in which Bakunin asks Herzen for a loan of 5,000 roubles, of which 2,000 were to be paid at once and the balance during the two ensuing years. Herzen cautiously offered 1,000 roubles, and in July saw his friend off at Petersburg on the Stettin boat. It is improbable that he ever saw his money again; for Bakunin remained faithful, throughout his chequered career, to his own peculiar interpretation of the word 'loan'.

In Moscow days Herzen had been far more of a radical than Bakunin; for the future anarchist was still under the sway of the famous and equivocal Hegelian dictum, 'Everything that is, is rational'. But Bakunin had travelled a long way since. He had imbibed in Berlin the doctrines of the new school of radical philosophers known, in the jargon of the day, as the 'Hegelian Left', and had become a passionately convinced materialist. In Dresden he had associated with Arnold Ruge, the publicist of the school, and had contributed inflammatory articles to his journal, inventing the famous phrase which became the text of all his subsequent activities: 'The passion for destruction is a creative passion.' He had fled from Dresden, under the threat of police persecution, in the company of the young German radical poet, Herwegh. In Switzerland he had consorted with Weitling the communist. Expelled thence by the police, he had taken refuge, first in Brussels, and then in Paris, where he was the constantly shifting centre of a multifarious circle of political refugees and agitators, chiefly belonging to the minor Slav races.

Herzen had watched with admiration the evolution of Bakunin, under western influence, into a fighting revolutionary. It is true that his enthusiasm did not blind him (it is one of Herzen's weaknesses that he was seldom blinded by enthusiasm) to the rather conspicuous failings of his friend. In his diary for 1843 he had already summed up his judgement of Bakunin in the curt phrase 'great ability and a worthless character'. But later on he recorded in the same place that Bakunin was 'redeeming his former sins'; and the joy of seeing a familiar Russian face in the streets of Paris would have made Herzen welcome a far less congenial companion. Bakunin introduced him to the poet Herwegh, who was destined a few years later to play a fatal role in his life.

But neither the revolutionary prestige of the French capital, nor the familiar faces of his Russian friends, nor the new acquaintances made among the *émigrés* of other nationalities, could long satisfy the critical and exacting Herzen. He soon perceived that the Paris of reality bore very little relation to the Paris of the romantic Russian imagination.

We know Europe from school, from literature, that is to say we do not know it, but we imagine it from textbooks and pictures, as children imagine the real world from their *Orbis Pictus*, and suppose that all the women of the Sandwich Islands hold their hands above their heads and carry tambourines, and that wherever there is a naked savage you are sure to find five yards away a lion with flowing mane or an evil-eyed tiger.

The French *bourgeois* monarchy represented nothing but a 'seventeen-year-old creed of crude egoism, of the unclean worship of material gain and tranquillity'. The Paris in which Herzen found himself was not the Paris of his dreams, the Paris of revolution and of the rights of man, but the Paris of Figaro, of the triumphant shopkeeper, the Paris of the king who carried an umbrella, of the crude, long-winded novels of Eugène Sue, and the tedious middle-class comedies of Scribe. The heroic age was decidedly a thing of the past.

Material interests have become the obsession of every class and have stifled all other interests. Great ideas, words that so lately shook the masses, making them leave home and kin, have disappeared, or are repeated, just as poets invoke Olympus and the Muses, or deists 'the Supreme Being', from mere habit and politeness.

The dreary pallor of death lay on everything he saw around him.

Death in literature, death in the theatre, death in politics, death in the Chamber – on one side Guizot, a walking corpse; and on the other, the childish babble of a senile opposition.

Romantic hopes had given place to romantic disillusionment; and after six months in Paris the Herzens, still in search of the promised land, moved on to Italy.

The journey, the oppressive atmosphere of Paris once left behind, was an enchantment. Already at Avignon these natives of a severer clime were conscious of the smiling south. The Italian towns through which they passed – Nice, Genoa, Leghorn, Pisa – remained in their memory as so many 'points of light'; and on the last day of November they reached Rome. 'There is one country in Europe,' Herzen wrote soon afterwards to his friends in Moscow, 'which is capable of soothing and refreshing you and making you shed tears, not of disgust and disappointment, but of delight – and that country is Italy.'

But the enjoyment of soft southern nature would not long have sufficed by itself to charm and re-animate our stern and sceptical traveller. The transformation of his mood must be attributed to political rather than climatic causes. He had been singularly fortunate in the moment of his journey. For the first time since the Middle Ages, the much divided and much harassed peninsula had, in these closing months of 1847, placed itself in the van of European politics. While the rest of Europe still slumbered, popular movements sprang up all over Italy. By accident or design Pope Pius IX had revived a medieval tradition of the Papacy as the champion of the Italian people against the oppression of the secular Empire. His enthronement in 1846 had been marked by an unusually liberal political amnesty throughout his dominions; and in 1847 he had entrusted the administration to an advisory council – a measure which everyone regarded as a first step towards constitutional government. The leaven of the Papal example worked throughout Italy. The Austrian provinces seethed with unrest. In the independent states, the people demanded constitutions and created civic guards.

These excitements, witnessed by Herzen on his journey southwards, provided the tonic he so badly needed. He had found at last the Europe of his dreams – a Europe ready to boil over with divine demociatic discontent. 'These recollections,' he wrote after his arrival in Rome, 'are sacred. They are bound up with my moral recovery, for which I am immensely grateful to Italy.' In his enthusiasm, he discovered a mystical affinity between the Italian and the Russian peasant.

Nowhere except in Central Italy and Great Russia have I seen poverty and toil pass so pitilessly over the face of the people without distorting the noble and manly lineaments. Such people have a hidden power of thought, or – to express it better – a principle of self-dependence, a principle often not understood by themselves, which imparts to them a power of self-preservation and a resistance in suffering, which throws off, as from a rock, anything which threatens to destroy its independence.

After the Herzens had established themselves in Rome, events moved still more rapidly. On 2 January 1848, they witnessed from their windows on the Via del Corso a huge popular demonstration, in which the crowd, without any sense of incongruity, mingled cheers for Pius IX with cries of 'A free press!' and 'Down with the Jesuits!' Ten days later, revolution broke out in Palermo, and in a fortnight swept the Neapolitan garrisons out of Sicily. King Ferdinand of Naples (nicknamed 'Bomba' for his alleged addiction to the bomb as an administrative weapon) was frightened into granting a constitution. Herzen visited Naples in February, and was in time to see King Bomba on the balcony of his palace, raising his hat and bowing – 'bowing literally to the waist' – before his loyal and applauding subjects. The Neapolitan example was infectious; and within the next few days Pius IX, Leopold of Tuscany and Charles Albert of Piedmont all proclaimed constitutional governments in their respective dominions.

I love Piedmont [wrote Herzen shortly after]. These folk seem younger. It is their honeymoon with free institutions, and the King wears such long moustaches and such a magnificent beard that he is willy-nilly on the side of progress.

It required indeed an orgy of enthusiasm to transform the vacillating Charles Albert into a national hero.

Then, in the midst of this débâcle of absolutism, came the news of the revolution in Paris and the abdication of Louis-Philippe. The excitement of Herzen rose to fever-heat. Letters of two and three months ago seemed, when he re-read them now, to be two hundred years old.

They have acquired [he writes ecstatically] an historical interest. They preserve the memory of a time which has suddenly moved away from us, moved away so far that it is scarcely visible. We begin to forget the very features of the old France and adolescent Italy, now that the former has given her soul to God and the latter grown to manhood.

But between the two revolutions, Herzen found no difficulty in choosing. He had sought passing consolation in Italy. He had sunned himself in her beauty, and had raved over her democratic ideals. But he was thinking all the time of the faithlessness of his first love. His heart was in Paris; and now that France had repented and turned to the light, his place was there. He stayed on in Italy, more and more impatiently, till nearly the end of April. Then the party retraced their way northwards, embarking at Civita Vecchia for Marseilles.

*

The Herzens were no longer travelling alone. In the middle of January they had been joined in Rome by a Russian family of the name of Tuchkov, consisting of father and two daughters, Elena and Natalie, aged nineteen and eighteen respectively. Alexis Tuchkov was a landowner of vaguely liberal aspirations. He was an acquaintance of Herzen, and a neighbour, in the government of Penza, of Herzen's dearest friend, Nick Ogarev. Acquaintanceship at home ripened, as frequently happens, into intimacy abroad. The Tuchkovs shared the excitements and hopes of the Herzens' sojourn in Italy and went on with them to Paris, where both families took apartments on the Champs-Elysées, the Tuchkovs near the Rond-Point, the Herzens higher up towards the newly completed Arc de Triomphe.

B

33

The arrival of these friends from Russia was a welcome event for Herzen. The new companions, Russian and foreign, whom he had met abroad, did not replace the social life he had known and loved in Petersburg and Moscow. There was in Herzen, despite his opinions, a good deal of the fastidious aristocrat; and he had in mixed company that fund of shyness which commonly goes with a sceptical disposition. He did not, like Bakunin, feel himself instantly and automatically at home in any international gathering of impecunious adventurers; and novelty was not for him an unfailing social attraction. Alexis Tuchkov was in no way remarkable or distinguished. He was lazy by nature, and not particularly intelligent; he was, both in years and temperament, decidedly middle-aged. But he brought to Herzen, while wandering in foreign lands, the full and satisfying flavour of his native land and caste. He was a comfortable, if not a stimulating, companion.

But if the arrival of the Tuchkovs afforded Herzen a pleasant diversion, it meant for Natalie Herzen something far more fundamental. Natalie had none of her husband's class-consciousness – the circumstances of her upbringing forbade it; and she was not subject to his intermittent attacks of homesickness for Russia. But she was, though she scarcely knew it, the victim of a profound *malaise*. She had come to Europe, like Herzen, full of hopes and ambitions; but she had not Herzen's clear-cut vision of what she was seeking. She experienced in Paris the same sense of disillusionment as her husband. She felt, like him, the soft healing influence of Italian skies. She greeted with him – though her raptures were perhaps less spontaneous and less heart-felt than his – the dawning light of political freedom. She was a good wife and a doting mother. But there was still something which she missed, something the lack of which left her restless and unsatisfied – as restless and unsatisfied as during the last year of her life in Moscow. In other ages, her need might have expressed itself in other forms. But Natalie was a true daughter of the Romantics. She was simple and honest and naïve. She pined for more passionate friendships, more palpitating emotions, more elevated sentiments – in a word, for a richer and more exciting life of the heart.

It did not at first sight seem probable that the Tuchkov family could supply this need. Natalie Herzen, mother of three children, had just passed her thirtieth birthday. Neither Elena nor Natalie Tuchkov had yet reached her twentieth. But Natalie Herzen had remained young. She was in most respects the opposite of her husband; and she had not in her composition one particle of that leaven of scepticism which hastens, and renders tolerable, the advance of middle age. Her emotions were still fresh, her illusions verdant. The difference of age did not make her sensible of any incompatibility between the Tuchkov girls and herself; and there seemed no reason why they should not satisfy her thirst for sentimental companionship. At first she scarcely differentiated between the sisters. But gradually the younger and livelier of the two began to absorb more and more of her consciousness. A few weeks after the meeting in Rome, Natalie Herzen was – using a phrase with due regard to its full emotional content – in love with Natalie Tuchkov.

Natalie Tuchkov, now on the threshold of an eventful life which lasted till 1913, possessed a striking and attractive personality. She was not good-looking. Her features were insignificant, her figure squat; and in later years she used to refer to herself as a 'monstrosity'. Her intelligence was lively but superficial; and she had no serious education. She was one of those whose appeal lies in the direct and unfettered expression of her emotions – a quality which may, in mature life, develop into hysterical self-assertion, but which, at eighteen, carries with it all the charm and grace of untutored frankness and simplicity. She, too, was romantic and her restless emotions were ripe for an outlet. Spark answered spark; and a flame was kindled which, for several months, carried the two Natalies far above the humdrum earth into a romantic dreamland whose very existence neither of them had hitherto suspected.

For the girl of eighteen, this queer affair was no more than an unconventional interlude in a normal emotional development. For the woman of thirty, it was a fateful turning-point in her life – 'a second youth brighter, richer and more real than the first'.

I have never seen so attractive a woman as Natalie Alexandrovna [writes the younger Natalie of the elder]. A beautiful open forehead, thoughtful, deep, dark blue eyes, dark thick eyebrows, something quiet, rather proud in her movements and, with it all, so much womanliness,

35

tenderness, gentleness ... I am astonished that most of our acquaintances thought Natalie cold; I found her the most passionate, burning nature in a gentle, delicate frame.

There is ample evidence of Natalie Herzen's reputation for 'coldness'. Herzen himself, when he had first seen her as a child in the house of Princess Khovansky, had called her '*une froide Anglaise*'. Since her marriage, the more critical of her Moscow acquaintances had found her prim, unresponsive and self-satisfied. She seemed all head and no heart, and looked on the world with an air of aloofness and disapproval, from which none but her husband and children were excepted. But the ice had suddenly melted under the dynamic rays which emanated from her new friend. The barriers were down; and Natalie Herzen, with a new sense of release and self-fulfilment, and with all the force that comes from long-accustomed self-denial, abandoned herself to the delicious sensation of an unrestrained yet innocent passion.

The effective duration of this sentimental friendship did not exceed seven months – from January, when the two women first met in Rome, to August, when the Tuchkovs left Paris to return to Russia. Of the correspondence which passed between the lovers, the letters of the elder to the younger Natalie alone survive. Some of them date from the time when they were living side by side in Italy or in Paris and meeting several times a day; for letter-writing was an essential convention of romantic passion. The rest were written after the younger Natalie's departure. The tone does not vary greatly from first to last; for the infatuation was sudden and complete.

Since I have come to know you [runs one of the earliest] your existence is on the same footing as the most intimate and vital objects of my thought. A day rarely passes – indeed I do not know whether there has been a day – on which I have not thought of you as I fell asleep and again as I waked. The feeling of emotion which enters into my love for the children has entered into my love for you. It has become an essential element of my life and will, I think, remain so to my life's end.

My meeting with you has brought so much beauty into my soul, has made me so much better. Yes, yes! Do not laugh at this, I have not succumbed to the disease of paying compliments; or if it is a disease, it has been going on so long that I must regard it as my normal condition.

and I repeat a thousand times that your coming, the feeling which you have awakened in me, has given me an infinity of delight. Often, when I feel most gloomy and oppressed, the thought of you calms me, restores my powers, and I begin to live again with a new energy.

They placed themselves under the patronage of that pattern of romantic womanhood, George Sand; and Natalie Herzen called her beloved by the name of one of George Sand's heroines, Consuelo. The following letter was written soon after the parting:

Now it is your turn, my Tata, my wonderful Consuelo di mi alma! I wanted to write to you last of all, I don't know why. How much I feel that you are not with me. But I feel clearly that you are there. How much fuller, how much more harmonious my life has become since it was blended in yours, and you became one of its most vital strings. My life, you know, is varied in hue; but you shine in it as one of its brightest threads . . . Since your departure my soul feels as the body would feel if a limb were cut off – a dull, stupid, senseless, dumb ache. If an arm were taken away, habit is so strong that you would be constantly wanting to move it and there would be nothing there. But the trouble is that you cannot amputate limbs from the soul; they can only live and die with it.

In October she continues in the same strain:

I am often with you. You are sometimes like the sun on a cloudy day: I think and think of you and it warms me, so that everything which separates us seems not to exist . . . I see you, I feel your breathing, I yearn to embrace you and squeeze you tight – or is this only a sheet of paper, and instead of your hands am I clasping only a pen which I squeeze and crush and throw away?

And another letter, written in the last month of the year, reaches a climax of romantic hyperbole:

Consuelo di mi alma, dear child, my beloved, my Natalie! I say it from the depths of my soul, with all my strength, all my fullness, all my passion. Yes, I love you terribly! Your letters illuminate my love for you. It makes me happy, and it would make me happy even if you did not love me too. In Italy I was born again. How beautiful was that time, how I would love to live it again! I would love the sun, the warmth, the mountains around, the distant horizon, the sea; and I would press you to me and be borne with you far, far away, and borne aloft a long, long time . . . and then I would return home, and at home all would be beautiful. I am raving, Natalie, and I am sending you my ravings, and if you were with me you would be sitting here beside my bed . . .

Natalie Herzen spent the greater part of the year of Revolution 1848 in a dangerous paroxysm of erotic excitement, a reaction against the too purely cerebral contemplation of the romantic ideal.

*

When the Herzens and the Tuchkovs, travelling together, reached Paris on 5 May, the first bloom of spring was over, and the laurels of the revolution, now ten weeks old, were already dusty and bedraggled. The initial enthusiasm had abated; riots in Rouen had been put down with bloodshed; and in the Constituent Assembly, which met for the first time on 4 May, the republicans were not only divided against themselves, but were confronted by a powerful and respectable minority of avowed monarchists and reactionaries. Herzen's own revolutionary activities were confined to three or four banquets where he 'ate cold mutton, drank sour wine, listened to Pierre Leroux and Father Cabet, and droned out the *Marseillaise*'; and he reached about the same time as Lamennais, though he did not express it so tersely, the depressing conclusion that 'les républicans sont faits pour rendre la république impossible'. His ardent faith in the revolution survived his return by exactly ten days. On 15 May a procession of unemployed marched across Paris to the Hôtel de Ville, demanding work, singing the *Marseillaise*, and shouting threats against the Constituent Assembly. They were repulsed and dispersed by the National Guard; and several of their leaders – men who had been the heroes of the February revolution – were clapped into prison, unaccused and untried. The revolutionary government showed every inclination to defend itself against the proletariat by force.

But worse was in store. Riots broke out again in Paris on 23 June. The government decided to take the matter fairly in hand. The subservient Assembly proclaimed martial law, dissolved the National Workshops which had been set up after the revolution, and gave General Cavaignac full powers to restore order. Street fighting lasted for three days. On 25 June, Herzen and Annenkov, who had rashly ventured out into the streets, were seized by a detachment of the National Guard, and were hurried from post to post, their fate hanging in the balance, until, some hours after their arrest, they established their identity and were released. Next day the fighting came to an end. The Faubourg St Antoine, where resistance had lasted longest, was half in ruins. The Herzens from their lodgings on the Champs-Elysées could hear the volleys of the firing-squads across the river on the Champ de Mars; and several thousand proletarians who escaped execution were sentenced to transportation for their share in the insurrection. Paris under Cavaignac seemed to Herzen rather worse than Petersburg under Nicholas I; and he declared that 'Cossacks and Croats were meek as lambs' in comparison with the French *bourgeois* National Guard.

The victorious *bourgeoisie* continued step by step to consolidate its gains until, in December 1848, the tragi-comedy of the Second Republic culminated in the election of Prince Louis Napoleon as President of the Republic. Herzen watched the proceedings in agonized disgust. He found some relief for his feelings in letters to his Moscow friends in which he refers amiably to 'the syphilitic Cavaignac' and 'that cross-eyed *crétin* Louis Bonaparte', and compares the French electors unfavourably with orang-outangs. He even discovered the futility of universal suffrage:

> Who that respects the truth would ask the opinion of the first man he meets? Suppose Columbus or Copernicus had put to the vote the existence of America or the movement of the earth?

It was not an original discovery. But it is odd that it should have been made by one who was, and long remained, the foremost Russian advocate of constitutional democracy.

The Herzens now found themselves almost alone in Paris. The Tuchkovs had gone back to Russia in August, and Annenkov in September. Bakunin was stirring up revolution in Bohemia; and of their Russian friends, only Turgenev remained to spend the winter of 1848–9 in Paris. Turgenev was a regular visitor to the Herzens' flat. So long as the Tuchkovs remained in Paris, he had played chess with old Alexis, and paid compliments to Natalie; and now they were gone he continued to discourse to Natalie Herzen on the state of his heart without once betraying the secret – which is still a secret for posterity – of his relations with Pauline Viardot. But despite his visits the winter was one of unrelieved gloom. The four-year-old Tata caught typhoid fever, and for days her life hung in the balance. Anxiety and isolation intensified Herzen's mood of apathy and blank despair.

It was too late now to dream of a return to Russia. In Italy he had sometimes thought and spoken of going back. But the enthusiasm with which he had greeted the new French Republic was well enough known to the Russian authorities; and since he left Italy he had not troubled to renew his Russian passport. If he returned now it could only be as a repentant backslider; and considering his past record, he could expect little mercy if he put himself within the reach of the gendarmes of Nicholas. He knew now that he made himself an exile and an outcast from his country for ever – or until such time as the Russian Revolution should take place. He occupied himself during the winter of 1848–9 in transferring his considerable fortune from Russia and investing it, on the advice of James Rothschild, in American bonds and freehold property in Paris. He had scarcely completed the transaction when a decree was issued in Petersburg placing an embargo on the possessions of himself and his family. His mother's property was only saved by a fictitious sale to Rothschild who, dealing with the Imperial Government as one great power with another, succeeded in obtaining its release. Herzen the revolutionary was a good business man, and knew how to make friends of the mammon of unrighteousness.

The reaction of Herzen's feelings in the latter half of 1848 was far profounder and more fundamental than the disappointment which he had experienced when he first came to Paris in the preceding year. The pessimism engendered by a revolution which had failed to materialize was nothing to the despair of a revolution which, having once materialized, had betrayed its own hopes and ideals. He began to wish that he had died, rifle in hand, on the barricades. Then, he told himself, he 'would at least have carried with him to the grave two or three convictions'. Now he had lost belief in himself and in others. Herzen resorted freely during the next few years to the pastime of analysing his own sensations. He felt himself something of a Byron. The tragedy of Byron had been 'not that his demands were false, but that England and Byron belonged to two different ages and two different cultures'. He, Herzen, like Byron, had been born out of due time. He had found himself in disharmony not only, as he had once supposed, with his country, Russia, but with his age, the *bourgeois* nineteenth century. He had been born too soon – or too late. The irony and scepticism which had always been latent in his character found an outlet and a justification.

The rationalistic eighteenth century was, as Herzen acutely observed, still an age of faith. 'Was not Father Voltaire, when he blessed Franklin's grandson in the name of God and Liberty, himself a fanatic of the religion of humanity?' Scepticism was the child of Revolution and Romanticism – of the great age which had believed in idealism and in progress, in democracy and in the perfectibility of human nature, and which, by the most contemptible anti-climax in history, had issued only in the complacent triumph of *bourgeois* plutocracy.

We have marvelled long enough [he wrote afterwards] at the abstract wisdom of nature and of the historical process. It is time for us to understand that there is much in nature and in history which is fortuitous, stupid, unsuccessful and misguided . . . Generally, in nature, in history and in life, we notice most the fortunate and successful; only now are we beginning to feel that the cards are not so well arranged as we thought, because we ourselves are a failure, a card that has been played and lost.

Consciousness of the bankruptcy of ideas, of the lack of any controlling power of truth over the world of reality, embitters us. A new kind of Manicheism takes possession of us, we are ready, *par dépit*, to believe in rational (i.e. purposive) evil, just as we used to believe in rational good. That is the last tribute which we pay to idealism.

The pain will pass in time, its passionate and tragic ache will be assuaged. It scarcely exists in the *new* world of the United States. This young and enterprising people, more active than intelligent, is so much occupied with the material ordering of its life that it knows none of our torturing pains. In that country, above all, there are not two cultures. The persons who form the grades of their society are constantly changing; they move up and down with the state of their bank balances. The sturdy race of English colonists multiplies exceedingly; and if it comes to the top, the people belonging to it will be, I will not say happier, but more contented. Their contentment will be poorer, more commonplace, more sapless than that which was dreamed of in the ideals of romantic Europe; but it will bring with it no Tsars, no centralization, perhaps no hunger. He who can put off the old European Adam and put on the new Jonathan, let him take the first steamer to –

41

somewhere in Wisconsin or Kansas. He will be better off there than in decaying Europe.

Those who cannot will remain and live out their time, fragments of a beautiful dream with which humanity lulled itself to sleep. They have lived too much by fantasy and by ideals to enter into the rational American age.

It makes no great odds. There are not many of us, and we shall soon die.

Herzen stayed on in Europe; and his romantic ideals, battered in the political tumults of 1848, were once more exposed to the staggering blow of an intimate domestic tragedy.

CHAPTER 3

A Family Tragedy: 1

ABOUT two years before leaving Moscow, Herzen had written
and published a novel entitled *Who Is To Blame?* In it Dmitri
Krutsifersky, a romantic youth, weds a romantic maiden named
Lyubov, the orphan ward of a heartless *grande dame*. Some years
after the marriage, there appears on the scene a rich, intelligent
and sceptically minded young man named Beltov. Suffering
chiefly from lack of any other occupation, Beltov falls in love with
Lyubov, and she with him; and they are unable to conceal their
passion from her husband. Both are too high-minded for adultery;
and it only remains for Beltov to withdraw. But the damage has
been done; and the author, leaving his three principal characters
to eat out their hearts in sorrow, invites the reader to ask himself,
in the words of the title, *Who Is To Blame?*

Many novelists have drawn inspiration from domestic occur-
rences in which they have participated. But it is rare for a writer
to participate, as closely as Herzen did in *Who Is To Blame?* a
family drama which was to be played out five or more years after
it was written. In one vital respect, however, Herzen proved to
have diverged in his novel from the truth of actual experience.
He had depicted himself, not in the gentle Dmitri who was 'always
ready to weep' and 'liked on quiet evenings to look for a long,
long time at the sky', but in the self-assured and all-conquering
sceptic Beltov. The drama of real life reversed the parts. The
strong sceptic Herzen, cast for the role of husband, found his
happiness destroyed by the romantic and sentimental weakling
Herwegh.

*

The father of George Herwegh was a distinguished *restaurateur* of
Stuttgart, hailed by his grateful clients as the Vatel of Württem-
berg. George was the eldest child and only son of his parents, and
rapidly became his mother's darling. He was unusually good-
looking, intelligent and studious. But his constitution showed

43

signs from the first of a certain instability; and at the age of fourteen his school career was interrupted by a mysterious disease. It was diagnosed as St Vitus's Dance, but yielded to the then fashionable treatment of animal magnetism. Young Herwegh even became a famous case; and a professor of medicine at Tübingen devoted his inaugural lecture to this startling vindication of the science of Mesmer. Encouraged by this remarkable cure, the proud mother (who about this time separated from her husband) destined the boy for the Lutheran pastorate; and he was sent with a scholarship to a theological seminary, from which he proceeded at the age of eighteen to the University of Tübingen. There, however, new influences induced him to abandon the career which had been marked out for him. He deserted theology for the law, and the law for literature. In later life he was a distinguished amateur in more than one branch of natural science, and considered himself qualified, though he had never taken a medical degree, to practise as a doctor. George Herwegh was a dilettante of many parts.

The turning-point in his life came when he was called on to perform his statutory term of military service. Herwegh did not love discipline; and twice in succession he came into uncongenial contact with his officers. On the second occasion he decided to abandon his ungrateful fatherland, and fled across the frontier into free Switzerland. Here he turned his literary talents to advantage, and in 1841 he published at Zürich a volume of political poems. *Letters of a Dead Man*, the cynical reflections of the notorious Prince Pückler-Muskau, had reached about this time the height of their short-lived popularity. Young Herwegh caught the suggestion and, not less appropriately, called his verses *Poems of One Who is Alive*. They echoed the mood of the young Germany in whose hearts the ferment of democracy was already at work; and their spirited versification and revolutionary fervour still give the poet a modest but noteworthy place in the history of German literature.

The spoilt son of his mother became the spoilt child of fortune. *Poems of One Who is Alive* made Herwegh famous in a day. They ran into half a dozen editions in two years, selling the phenomenal total of fifteen thousand copies. Herwegh became the idol of the German democracy. He made a triumphal progress through the country which he had so ignominiously abandoned two years before; and he was received by King Frederick William of Prussia who, in an outburst of eccentric generosity, declared that he respected 'honourable opponents'. The young poet, handsome, romantic and successful, won all hearts; and, among them, the heart of Emma Siegmund, the daughter of a wealthy Berlin merchant, who was a purveyor of silk furnishings to the court of Frederick William, and a baptized Jew. The attraction was mutual; and a betrothal quickly followed the first meeting of the young couple. The bride could not match her suitor in good looks; and her long nose intrudes conspicuously, for the sake of the rhyme, into Heine's well-known lampoon on his brother-poet. But she was intelligent and cultivated; she brought Herwegh a substantial fortune; and as there was no doubt that she was passionately in love with him, he seemed to be assured not only of the material comforts of life, but of the hero-worship which had become equally indispensable to his amiable, self-indulgent nature. When he was once more compelled to leave Germany, Emma followed him to Zürich; and they were married in the little Swiss town of Baden in the spring of 1843. Bakunin was one of the witnesses of the marriage.

The ambitions of the happy pair were not confined to the narrow limits of Switzerland. After a prolonged honeymoon in Italy they migrated to Paris, where Herwegh's romantic mien, democratic convictions and poetical fame, coupled with the fortune and intelligence of his wife, made him a prominent figure in the foreign colony. Herwegh always possessed a distinction of manner which belied his plebeian origin. His character, as one of his friends remarked in later years, 'would have better fitted a Marquis of the Regency than a hero of the Revolution'. He was promptly lionized in French literary circles, where he enjoyed the favours and patronage of that remarkable lady of letters, the Comtesse d'Agoult; and he met in turn most of the Russian visitors to Paris during this time – Turgenev and Annenkov, Ogarev and Bakunin, and finally Herzen. Life flowed on easily and painlessly into the revolutionary year 1848. The Herweghs shared the enthusiasm of the February days in Paris, and listened eagerly to the first rumbling of revolt on the other side of the Rhine. New ambitions stirred in Emma's breast – ambitions, not for herself, but for her adored husband. Had not Lamartine, a poet, been hailed as the father of the French Republic? And might not the coming German Republic vaunt the paternity of another poet? Early in March a committee of German democrats resident in Paris was formed with the double mission of voting a congratulatory address to French democracy and of assisting the cause of revolution in Germany; and Herwegh, though he had recently exchanged German for Swiss nationality, was elected president. The first part of the committee's task was punctually discharged at a monster meeting on the *place* of the Hôtel de Ville, which enthusiastically affirmed the brotherhood of the French and German Republics. Its second duty was more arduous. Plans were set on foot for the organization and equipment in Paris of a legion of German democrats, who would throw themselves into the revolutionary struggles of the fatherland. But the French Government, when appealed to for help, refused arms and offered a subsidy of 5,000 francs – a beggarly gift which betrayed a desire to rid France of a crowd of dangerous hotheads rather than to assist seriously in the promotion of the enterprise. Notwithstanding this discouragement, the legion was formed. Emma Herwegh was a moving spirit in all the preparations. Her fortune proved invaluable in meeting the financial requirements of the legion; and she supplemented her supply of ready cash by selling the family plate. In the middle of April, Herwegh marched boldly out from Strasburg accompanied by his wife in man's clothes and some six hundred legionaries. Their destination was Baden, where local revolutionaries were reported to have already overthrown the Grand-Ducal Government.

Everything that Emma Herwegh could contribute to the success of the expedition had been liberally supplied. But neither poets nor the wives of poets habitually make good generals; and there was a conspicuous absence of military talent. The intention had been to effect a junction with two other columns of democrats which were believed to be equally converging on Baden. But the meeting had not been achieved when news reached the legion of the approach of government troops. A hasty decision was taken to retire southwards in the direction of the Swiss frontier; but while in process of retreat the legionaries were overtaken on 27 April, at Dossenbach, by the regular troops. Some fifty of them were killed, and many more taken prisoners. The remainder took to their heels; and the expedition came to an ignominious end.

The hapless leader was made by popular rumour the principal scapegoat of the disaster. The commander of the regulars, anxious to excuse his failure to capture so important a prize, reported to Baden that Herwegh and his wife had fled 'before the battle, as soon as they heard of the approach of the troops'. Another authority alleged that Emma drove her husband away from the battlefield cowering behind the dashboard of her carriage; while Heine declared that 'our hero could no more bear the smell of powder than Goethe of tobacco', and described with unsavoury coarseness the excretory symptoms of Herwegh's cowardice. These legends, however graphic and circumstantial, must be dismissed as apocryphal. Herwegh and his wife seem to have occupied themselves during the battle with the prosaic but necessary duty of serving out cartridges to the combatants. When the legion broke, they beat a hasty retreat in the rustic cart which had served as their headquarters. The authorities had paid Herwegh the compliment of putting a price on his head. He prudently disguised himself by shaving his magnificent beard and whiskers, and sought concealment in a ditch, whence he was rescued by a friendly farmer and, when the hue and cry was over, smuggled back over the French frontier. It was the first reverse in a career which had hitherto been an unbroken series of triumphs. The poet returned to Paris with his laurels faded and his temper impaired.

It was after this unfortunate episode, during the winter of 1848-9, that the acquaintanceship previously established between the Herweghs and the Herzens ripened into intimacy. It was a difficult moment in the Herwegh *ménage*. Not only was Herwegh embittered by consciousness of inglorious failure and diminished prestige. Financial difficulties had begun for the first time to make their appearance. Herr Siegmund, the court furnisher, had accepted with good grace as a son-in-law a democratic poet at the height of his fame and popularity. But the unsuccessful promoter of active sedition wore a different aspect in his orthodox eyes. The silk merchant had speculated, largely and lucratively, in building property in the west end of Berlin. The revolution, which his daughter and her husband had so rashly fostered, caused a disastrous collapse of values. Herr Siegmund was obliged to sell on a

47

falling market and saw himself reduced, in the course of a few months, from extreme opulence to moderate comfort. He felt no inclination to continue the munificent subsidies which had been, for the last five years, the mainstay of the Herwegh establishment. A taste of poverty would do those extravagant and irresponsible young people no harm, and the poet might even be driven to earn his own living. Emma's heartrending appeals failed to move him. She had hitherto regarded two things in life as axiomatic: that her father's wealth was unlimited and indestructible, and that her husband's needs took precedence over any other claim. It was a shock to discover that the first of these axioms no longer held good, and that there were people wrong-headed enough to deny the second. The luxurious equipment of the flat in the Rue du Cirque remained as a mocking reminder of former affluence, and contrasted sadly with the straitened style in which they were now compelled to live.

It was at this time of political disgrace and domestic embarrassment that Herwegh became a frequent – almost a nightly – visitor at the Herzens' flat near the Madeleine. He was not a man who had within him a sufficient reserve of strength to bear adversity unaided. The humiliation of Dossenbach had bitten deep into his soul and he came to the Herzens above all for consolation and encouragement.

Two years ago [he wrote in the summer of 1850] I was lost, I was disillusioned, I had fallen full length to the ground; I sought, and I found, the one man of whom I was not afraid and to whom I could attach myself.

But he came, for the most part, alone. After six years of married life, Emma's hero-worship had begun to pall. He reflected perhaps that it was her busy and uncalculating enthusiasm which had thrust him into the ridiculous Baden expedition. Emma's affection was demonstrative and untiring. He noticed that her voice was loud and her manners sometimes aggressive; and she was now in an advanced stage of her third pregnancy. He came to the conclusion, as he afterwards told Herzen, that he had 'little taste and less talent' for that 'abominable institution' – family life.* It did

* Jacques, in George Sand's novel of that name, calls marriage 'one of the most barbarous institutions which society has invented'.

not strike him as inconsistent that he should find repose from Emma's exacting devotion in the idyllic calm which reigned at the fireside of Alexander and Natalie Herzen.

Herzen himself encouraged these visits. He had found few acquaintances, and no intimates, among the French; and his Russian friends, with the single exception of Turgenev, had fled from Paris since the revolution. Herzen was still young enough to feel the need of constant society. He thirsted for companionship; and, like many others, he fell in love at first sight with the vivid intelligence and social charm of the German poet. Political affinities sealed the friendship. Herwegh was not merely a democrat, but a martyr in the cause of revolution. Herzen was far at this time from accepting the stories of Herwegh's cowardice at Dossenbach which he afterwards retailed with so much gusto in *My Past and Thoughts*.

His attempt [he wrote four months after the event] was one of those bright dreams which in March seemed so feasible and now in August look like madness.

Herwegh, when he was first admitted on intimate terms to the Herzen household, wore the aspect of a pure, though unpractical, idealist. He affected that lofty indifference to the sordid cares of everyday life which Herzen himself never achieved, but always envied and admired in others. In short, he struck Herzen as an exceptional, almost ethereal being – something far removed from the conventional *bourgeois* world into which he had strayed.

George is the only *Russian* here [he wrote enthusiastically at this time], i.e. the only man among the foreigners here in whom there is none of this western dullness, impenetrable by logic or by feeling, none of this narrowness of human nature in its decline, this cretinism in its death-agony. In a word, he is a personality . . . not a society mannikin like the French, or a lymphatic abstraction like the Germans, or a revolting creature of habit like the English.

There was something even in Herwegh's weakness which had an almost feminine appeal. He stood in such pathetic need of sympathy, counsel and support, and looked up so naturally to Herzen as his mentor and spiritual director.

It seemed to me [Herzen confessed afterwards] – and this was my

worst mistake – that the weak side of his nature was being transformed. It seemed to me that I could help him more than anyone else
could.

The protective vanity of the male was strong in Herzen; and
Herwegh's helpless reliance on him was the subtlest and most fatal
form of flattery.

The initial attraction of Herwegh for Natalie was more com-
posite in character. His fascination for women is attested by the
long list of his conquests. Natalie at thirty had preserved in an
unusual degree the shy innocence of girlhood; but unknown
depths of sensuality lay beneath the unruffled surface. Herwegh
with his flashing eyes and delicate perfection of profile seemed to
embody her ideal of manly beauty;* and his poetic fame completed her picture of the romantic hero. Her maternal instincts
were no less strongly affected; and they went out to the wayward,
irresponsible, trusting Herwegh who seemed so ready to throw
himself on her mercy. To be solitary and to be misunderstood
were the prerogatives of the romantic poet; and Herwegh
answered so perfectly to both descriptions that she could not help
believing in his genius. She accepted at their face value his pro-
fessions of spiritual loneliness. She pitied him (as indeed he was
quite ready to pity himself) for having (so unlike Alexander) a
wife who was incapable of appreciating him. Natalie's intentions,
like those of her husband, were philanthropic. 'The mission on
earth' of romantic womanhood is, as one of George Sand's heroes
remarks, 'to console the unfortunate'. She felt that she and she
alone could *save* Herwegh – save from his own weakness and from
the scorn of a dull disdainful world. She poured out on him all her
unused store of warm-hearted solicitude and affection. And with
the schoolgirl's admiration of the dark and handsome poet, and
the mother's tenderness for the lonely and neglected outcast, there
mingled, yet unperceived by Natalie herself, those erotic promptings which had found so curious an expression in her love for
Natalie Tuchkov. Unconsciously she began to reserve for him
the place in her emotions so lately occupied by her dear Consuelo;

* Herwegh is described at this time by one of his compatriots as 'a remarkably
handsome man – black, silky hair with a touch of grey, a smooth beard, flashing
eyes, a tanned complexion, soft features and small delicate hands'. Bamberger,
Erinnerungen.

and it is significant that, after the spring of 1849, her letters to Natalie Tuchkov grow rarer and less effusive. 'It is good to be with Herwegh,' she remarks in one of the last of them, 'even when we are both silent.'

The triangular intimacy now being established between Herwegh, Natalie and Herzen (with Emma as an awkward and unwanted *quartum quid*) seemed to these votaries of the romantic faith a realization of the loftiest ideal of human friendship. The relationship was perfect. It only remained to find for it a romantic ritual and a romantic terminology; and these were discovered, appropriately enough, in George Sand's most recently published novel. *La Petite Fadette* is one of those pastoral romances of George Sand's middle period which have worn so much better than the more temperamental and volcanic productions of her youth. It is the story of the twin sons of a country farmer. The elder and stronger, Landry by name, is all 'gaiety and courage', and loves 'pleasure and turbulence'; the younger, Sylvain or Sylvinet, is delicate and subtle, and has 'too sensitive and too passionate a heart' for the happiness of ordinary mortals. Sylvinet demands the exclusive and undivided affection of his twin; and when Landry finds other interests, he falls into a fever.

He pretended that nobody loved him, though he had always been more spoiled and petted than any other member of his family.

Only little Fadette, the betrothed of Landry, could calm him; but rather than disturb his brother's happiness, Sylvinet, in a moment of supreme self-sacrifice, leaves Landry and Fadette in each other's arms and goes off to be a soldier.

The application of this harmless story was immediately apparent to these romantic enthusiasts. The cheerful and active Herzen was Landry; the delicate and sensitive Herwegh, so apt to feel that nobody loved him, was Sylvinet; and, since this Sylvinet had no inclination to repeat his unfortunate military experience, he remained to receive, without of course any desire to encroach on Landry's rights, the consoling ministrations of Fadette. It should be said, in justice to Herzen, that he lent himself reluctantly, and somewhat shamefacedly, to this silly game. Herwegh, in the extant remains of their correspondence, constantly addresses him as 'Landry' and 'my twin'; Herzen rarely – and then half in jest

51

– reciprocates the title. But Herwegh and Natalie knew no such restraint. 'My twin' became the recognized mode of address between them, and in moments of stress or emotion passed readily into 'Sylvinet' and 'Fadette'. Natalie, brought up in the Russia of the romantic thirties, suspected no dangers in this passionate friendship. Herwegh, the westerner, may sometimes have had his doubts. In western civilization other conventions prevailed. The triangle was conditioned by a different set of postulates.

Meanwhile the second French Republic had firmly established itself. In the full enjoyment of the recognized prerogatives of authority, it now began to arrest, to imprison, and to transport its opponents, including some of those enthusiastic revolutionaries who, a year before, had triumphantly welcomed its advent. Foreign revolutionaries were particularly suspect; and the house at Ville d'Avray which the Herzens had taken for the summer was searched by the police for wanted persons. Herzen, with or without reason, took fright. In the middle of June, having borrowed a passport from a native of Wallachia, he fled to Geneva, leaving Natalie to follow him as soon as possible with the children. Herwegh saw no reason to suppose himself immune from the dangers which threatened his friend; and he regarded with distaste the prospect of separation from the Herzens. He decided that he too must flee; and what could be more appropriate than that he should escort Natalie and her children on their tedious journey? Just before their departure, there was a family picnic at St Cloud; and it was on this occasion that the lynx-eyed Emma (who had not been invited to join in the flight to Geneva) perceived in her husband the familiar symptoms of a sentimental interest in Natalie. She taxed him with it the same night. He reassured her and called her a 'silly darling'. Two days later, on 7 July, the travellers set forth on their journey; and late on the evening of 10 July, the mail-coach brought them into Geneva in the midst of one of the most magnificent thunderstorms they could remember.

*

The journey to Geneva is the beginning of a story which, from this point onwards, advances with gathering momentum to its tragic end. Next morning Natalie gazed from her window in the

Hôtel des Bergues at the clouds which hid Mont Blanc from view forty miles away, and at Rousseau's island 'bathed in the lake' before her eyes; and having invoked the sentimental mood proper to the newly arrived visitor in Geneva, she wrote a long letter to Emma.

Your darling [ran the passage which perhaps interested the recipient most] was really magnificent. You cannot believe how kind he was to us, particularly to Tata. I am happy to have had the opportunity of getting to know him in this aspect – what a rich nature! I do not say this to flatter you.

Herzen, restored to the highest of spirits by the family reunion, took Herwegh and Natalie to see the sights of the town. He joked about everything; and even the cats and dogs and donkeys of Geneva seemed for some reason supremely amusing. Writing to Herwegh a year later, Natalie recalled the 'mad laughter' of this first excursion together in the city of Calvin – the laughter of undeclared lovers still unconscious of the force which is transforming the world for them. And once more Emma in Paris received, not from her husband, but from Natalie, the naïve and enthusiastic story of the day's doings.

Life in Geneva soon settled down to a regular routine. Herzen, eternally engrossed in politics, was busy conferring with local Genevese politicians and foreign refugees and corresponding with friends in Paris, where he had provided the funds for a new journal of democratic and international complexion, which Proudhon was to edit. Herwegh and Natalie were more interested in self-improvement. Every morning at ten o'clock, Herwegh came to Natalie's room for a Russian lesson. ('I spend half the day learning Russian,' he wrote in one of his rare letters to Emma at this time; 'I have found in it a new source of poetry.') After lunch Natalie went with Sasha to Herwegh for a lesson in botany. The rest of the day was spent in walks or excursions; and Natalie, inspired by the constant view of Rousseau's island, read *La Nouvelle Héloise*. Her heart was full to overflowing; and she continued to pour it out in her letters to the uncongenial and unappreciative Emma.

Nature alone would not suffice. One must live as we are living at this moment; and it is then that one feels one's whole being – the whole

53

creature that is *I* – renewed. Emma, don't be angry, be patient with me. I am too much of a child, I feel the need of pouring out my heart which is too full of all that surrounds it, for all that surrounds it is so beautiful! I think a girl of fourteen would feel like that; never mind, I want to be a little girl – let them laugh at me, let them treat me as such, I don't care, so much the worse for them . . .

It can scarcely have made Natalie's letters at this time more welcome to Emma that many of them were written on George's notepaper bearing the monogram G. H.

In August, Herwegh and Natalie made an excursion to Montreux and climbed the Dent de Jaman. Here Herwegh gave Natalie a sprig of ivy which she put in her hat and kept ever after; here they ate *Vielliebchen** together; and here at length they declared their love. The mountain-top towering over the lake of Geneva remained for the lovers a landmark in their lives and a symbol of their union; and a rude representation of a mountain ∧ became 'our sign', with which Natalie constantly embellishes her letters to Herwegh. Natalie had not yet awakened from the first innocent, unthinking raptures of love to a guilty consciousness of the imperative need for concealment. She took her diamond ring, and with it engraved on three sides of the octagonal handle of Herwegh's crystal seal, first the mountain-sign surmounted with the date '1849', then 'Georges', and finally the cabalistic utterance 'Cela doit être'. But it is in a letter written more than six months later that we find the fullest development of this pictorial symbolism. The mountain summit, marked with a cross, bears the inscription 'Toujours ici avec toi', and far beneath it are the flat waters of the lake – 'C'est le reste de ma vie'. In this exalted and rarified mood Natalie plunged, recklessly and blindly, into the open arms of George Herwegh.

It is seldom easy – and still more rarely worth while – to establish the relative responsibilities of the partners in an illicit liaison. But this delicate question assumed so much prominence in the recriminations provoked by this affair that it cannot be altogether evaded. In his subsequent correspondence with Natalie, Herwegh displays a pathetic, but patently sincere, anxiety lest she should be tempted to place on him the major share of the

* This sentimental name is bestowed by the German language on hazel-nuts with twin kernels.

blame; and in a letter to Emma after the débâcle he becomes still more explicit.

> In things of the heart there is no initiative. Everything happens simultaneously or not at all. But there is an initiative in the outward expression of a feeling. *This* initiative I did not take ... Natalie had first to tell me that she was offering me something which no one else possessed or ever could possess, she had to declare to me that she had never belonged to Herzen.
>
> She did it. She gave me all the proofs that a woman can give. I believed because I felt it; and believing in her immense love I did what I did ... Natalie cannot belong to Herzen when, by her declaration that – for all her gratitude and affection for him – she did not belong to him, she made me throw to the winds the whole world and everything that was dear to me.

The statement, though made for the purpose of self-exculpation, rings true. Of the doubt whether the man or the woman was the prime mover in this affair, the man may claim the benefit such as it is. Indeed, in the whole story of the liaison, Herwegh cuts a pitiful rather than a guilty figure. He never, except perhaps during the first weeks of irresponsible passion, escaped from the gnawing fear of the consequences. He never reached those heights of reckless infatuation and blissful self-oblivion on which Natalie succeeded, almost continuously, in maintaining herself.

In the last days of August, Herzen and Herwegh left Geneva together on an excursion which is described by Herzen in *My Past and Thoughts*. They rode on ponies up to Zermatt, where one of the villagers put up the 'rare travellers' in his house; and from thence they climbed to the Gorner Glacier to survey the magnificent panorama of Monte Rosa and the Matterhorn.

> How melodramatic I should seem [Herzen concludes his narrative] if I completed this picture of Monte Rosa by saying that, of the two travellers suspended on this height, amid this whiteness, purity and calm – of the two travellers who had hitherto reckoned each other intimate friends, one was meditating black treason against the other. Yes, life sometimes has its melodramatic effects, its *coups de théâtre* which seem utterly artificial.

Herzen perhaps never knew (for confessions seldom confess everything) that at that moment the 'black treason' had already been consummated, and that, during the absence of her husband and her lover, Natalie had been busy providing for posterity the first documentary evidence of her guilt. She took a leather note-book belonging to Herwegh. It had been a present from Emma, and bears on the front page the inscription: 'To my darling, for New Year's Day 1849.' The book is half full of verses and other notes in Herwegh's hand, many of them scored through, perhaps by Natalie, perhaps by Herwegh himself. Then follows a series of entries by Natalie:

Aug. 1849.

29 . . . I take up this book as my sole salvation – like your hand, I press it to my heart. Can I read it? Yes, yes, yes, despite everything you are mine. Ah! I have nothing, I feel nothing but you . . .

I put this book under my pillow.

30. You are far away, yet I see nothing, feel nothing, breathe nothing but you, you, you –

You for whom I have been searching since I was a child, everywhere and in everything . . .

1 Sept. . . . Oh – I am afraid – Nothing, nothing, I want nothing, no proof. I would burn even this book if it were mine – nothing, neither writing nor speech. I need nothing.

Only your nearness, your breath.

2 Sept. At last with you! You!

It is midnight, I am in your room alone with you –

How I would that I could break this body of mine that I might be dependent on nothing.

I begin to believe in an immaterial existence . . .

No revolutions, no republics, the world is saved if it understands us. Or even if it perishes, I do not care, you will always be for me what you are.

The next day there is only a single entry in Greek, a reminiscence of Byron's *Maid of Athens*: ζωή μου, σας ἀγαπῶ*; and on the evening of the 4th the mountaineers returned from Zermatt. There are a few more entries, mostly undated ('The reality has surpassed the dream,' runs one; 'What will be – who knows? Ah, why know?' is another); there is a page of childish scrawls, the work of Tata; and finally there appear the further cabalistic signs

* The words as used by Natalie have a special reference to Herwegh. As the author of *Poems of One Who is Alive*, he took the Greek word ζωή (life) as his motto, and used it for the seal described above.

X and O, which, alone or in company with ⋏, will continue to the end to decorate Natalie's correspondence with her lover.

It is not difficult, from the study of this curious confession, and of the mass of Natalie's love-letters to Herwegh, to discern in her passion the peculiar characteristics of the age to which she belonged. The romantic doctrine which caused so much havoc in the family of Herzen sprang, like so much else in the modern world, from the fertile genius of Jean-Jacques Rousseau. It was Rousseau who proclaimed the natural goodness of the human emotions and their sufficiency as a guide to human conduct. He relates in the *Confessions* how he resolved 'to burst asunder the bonds of opinion, to do boldly everything which seemed good to him, and to pay no heed to the judgement of other men'; and he modestly adds that this is 'perhaps the greatest resolution, or at any rate the one most useful to virtue, ever conceived by man'. Immanent morality takes the place of external law; and everything will be perfect in a world where everyone follows the promptings of his own unspoiled nature. But if the author of the romantic creed was Rousseau, its popularizer and vulgarizer was George Sand. The modern reader sees in this remarkable lady only a naïve and ultra-sentimental story-teller, not quite lively enough to be read for amusement, and not quite solid enough to be respected as a classic. But nineteenth-century Europe, and in particular feminine Europe, not only devoured her as a novelist, but worshipped her as a prophet. George Sand practised with consistency, and preached with amazing fluency, a development of the Rousseauistic doctrine which had already been enunciated in its main outlines by the formidable Madame de Staël. If virtue resides in the human emotions, the noblest of these emotions is unquestionably love; and to love must therefore be the supreme act of virtue. In the classical eighteenth century, love had been enjoyed as the most exhilarating of human recreations. It was left to the nineteenth century to make it the crown of romantic virtue and the sacrament of the romantic religion.

Why should it be a sin to abandon oneself to one's own heart? [exclaims the heroine of George Sand's *Jacques*]. It is when one can love no more that one should weep for oneself and blush to have let the sacred fire go out.

57

The new woman blushed for herself, not when she loved, but when she failed to find a lover. No cold and sterile ideal of conjugal fidelity or chaste virginity could satisfy her – any more than it had ever satisfied the man. Before the god of love the sexes were for the first time equal. The sacred flame vindicated its rights over male and female alike. It was irresistible and it was divine; and resistance was as sacrilegious as it was futile. It burned its way through the human heart; and the vaunted fire-proof curtain of matrimony proved to be no more than inflammable tinsel.

The romantic revelation had come to Russia late, and with blinding suddenness. In 1831, when Pushkin published the last canto of *Evgin Onegin*, he could still enunciate in clear and confident tones the classical solution of the eternal triangle. The married woman, whose thoughts had strayed to another man, could find happiness by sacrificing her inclinations on the altar of duty. 'I am given to another,' says Tatyana when she has confessed her love to Onegin, 'and to him I shall be faithful for ever.' But Pushkin had died in 1837; and a few years after his death, George Sand had made Tatyana and Onegin look extinct mammals of the Ice Age. Nowhere in Europe was her influence more potent and more intoxicating than in Russia; and few people were more clearly fated to succumb to it than the gentle, emotional Natalie Herzen. It is no mere coincidence that she bestowed, both on Natalie Tuchkov and on George Herwegh, the names of characters in George Sand's novels, that the one became 'Consuelo' and the other 'Sylvinet'. The confession of her faith had already been consigned to the pages of her Diary two months before she left Russia:

Oh great Sand! How profoundly she has penetrated human nature, boldly carried the living soul through sin and debauchery and brought it unscathed out of this all-devouring flame! Four years ago Botkin remarked of her that she was a female Christ. It sounded comical, but there is much truth in it. What would you have done without *her* to poor Lucrezia Floriani, who at twenty-five already had four children by different fathers whom she had forgotten and about whom she had no desire to know even where they were? Even to speak of her would have seemed a sin; but now you are ready to fall on your knees before this woman . . . Oh, if there were no other way I would rather a thousand times that a daughter of mine should fall, I would receive her with the same love, the same respect, if only her soul remained alive. Then everything passes through the fire, all uncleanness is burned away, and what is left is pure gold.

The divinity of love was, for Natalie as for Madame Dudevant, the one essential article of religion; and both believed that articles of religion are made to be translated into practical life. It could not be wrong to love; and love, being divine, must shed happiness not only on those in the immediate enjoyment of it, but on the world around.

I love my husband, my sister Sylvia, my children more than ever [wrote the heroine of *Jacques* to her lover]. And for you, Octave, I feel an affection for which I will not seek a name, but which God inspires and God blesses.

The heroine of real life is even more lyrical.

I transport myself into the future [writes Natalie to Herwegh] – all, all will be happy, we shall have made everyone happy, harmony and serenity in our circle – the children gay, sympathy even between them – how we shall grow in that atmosphere of tranquillity and perfection – the beauty of nature – and on this azure background *those* moments that blaze like stars.

When Natalie wrote to Emma Herwegh begging her to join the happy band in Geneva, Emma regarded her letters as the supreme proof of her hypocrisy. Never in fact was she more sincere. She refused to accept, refused to face, the possibility of exclusive rights in love; for to exclude was necessarily to detract from its divine properties. It was incredible to her – too bad to be true – that domestic harmony tempered by adultery should be an unrealizable ideal; and the bitterest experience failed to disillusion her on this point. If things went wrong, it was that others had fallen short. It was that George did not love her enough, or that Alexander failed to understand; and it was her inner conviction that Alexander *would* fail to understand which plunged her into the sophistry of deceit. To the last she believed profoundly in the purity of her motives and of her conduct. When all else failed, her faith in love remained intact. 'I want to live,' runs the pathetic peroration of one of her last letters to Herwegh, written a few months before her death, 'in order to love, to love, to love . . .'

59

There are no documents in existence on which we can determine, with equal precision, the state of mind of Natalie's lover.
Herwegh's love-letters were destroyed, as a measure of precaution,
by Natalie herself, and if he followed in them the maxim which
he laid down in his correspondence with Madame d'Agoult ('I
have never put the most passionate things on paper'), they would
have been less valuable as evidence than those of Natalie. Herwegh was too much of a man of the world to believe in adultery
as a source of universal felicity; but in a letter which he wrote to
Herzen after the débâcle he affirms the sanctity of love in terms
which might have been, which perhaps were, borrowed from
Natalie herself:

Everything between N. and me is sanctified by a complete abandon-
ment of one to the other, a losing of soul in soul, up to a point where we
could meet in regions unsullied by any human breath, in regions where
the individual stands trembling before himself, where he will not confess even to himself, but where he may be divined by another, by one
sole being in the universe – there I met Natalie. How often did we
exclaim: If Alexander understood! If he understood! He would fall
and worship!

And he supplements this defence, not unskilfully, with an appeal
to that other romantic tenet – the irresistibility of love:

The irresistibility of an attraction rooted in the essence and quintes-
sence of our two natures, Natalie's and mine, the necessity which rivets
our two souls together – Alexander, I had neither the power nor the right
to flee! And indeed, does one flee from oneself? Yet I would have fled,
had I, by any act of mine, awakened or provoked that feeling in her, if
there had not been reciprocity, simultaneity as of a lightning-flash . . .
Love was there – stronger than ourselves.

The autumn of 1849 slipped peacefully away at Geneva, the
lovers sunk in their surreptitious raptures, and Herzen in his
political and literary occupations. Herzen's one important literary
work of these months, a pamphlet in French On Russia, appeared
with a dedication to 'G. H.'. Only Emma half suspecting, half
refusing to suspect, the course of events, sat restless and unhappy
in Paris. There was talk of Herzen and Herwegh obtaining the
permission of the French authorities to return to Paris. There was
talk of Emma's coming to Switzerland with her children, and of

the two families being united at Veytaux at the upper end of the Lake of Geneva. But neither of these projects was realized. In October Natalie discovered that she was pregnant. In November she had a miscarriage. It seems to have been assumed by Herwegh that the child was his. The fact that Herzen's suspicions were not aroused is sufficient proof that there can have been no certainty; and Natalie, whose opinion alone might have been decisive, has remained silent. Natalie rapidly recovered. The incident had no sequel. But it gave Emma the opportunity for declaring, long afterwards, that Natalie had, during this autumn of 1849, written amiable letters to the wife of the man whose child she was carrying beneath her heart.

Early in December the party at Geneva broke up. The Herzens moved to Zürich, where the deaf-mute Kolya had been placed in a special school; and Herwegh went on a visit to Berne. Just before Christmas, Herzen left Zürich with his mother for Paris, in order to conduct with the house of Rothschild the complicated negotiations for the transfer of her considerable wealth from Russia. On the way, he spent two days at Berne with Herwegh, and the two men took an effusive farewell of each other. 'That was the last time I ever loved this man,' wrote Herzen afterwards in *My Past and Thoughts*; and though the statement is scarcely borne out by the affectionate tone of some of his letters from Paris, it is perhaps the last occasion on which he trusted him unreservedly. The departure of Herzen for Paris opened a new and critical period in their relationship.

*

Opinions differ as to the effect of absence on love; but there is no doubt of its capacity to stimulate the hardier passion of jealousy. Herzen was, like Othello,

> one not easily jealous, but being wrought,
> Perplex'd in the extreme.

In Geneva he had tolerated, without a moment of anxiety or misgiving, the close and continuous association between his wife and his friend. In Paris he visited Emma Herwegh, and heard for the first time her bitter reproaches against her husband: how he had almost ignored her existence throughout the autumn, how he had forgotten their boy's birthday, and how even now he was writing long letters to his friend, but not a word to his wife. Herzen had hitherto probably never given a thought to Emma's position. But now he was touched; and he began to write letters to Herwegh angrily reproaching him with his neglect of his wife. The dispatch of these missives coincided with the arrival of letters from Natalie expressing for Herwegh the gushing enthusiasm which had become the normal mode of intercourse between the 'twins'. Now for the first time the familiar note jarred. Herzen thought of Natalie and Herwegh in Zürich and himself in Paris; and he had a sudden intuition of something wrong – something which he scarcely dared to name even to himself. The seed once sown sprouted with terrifying rapidity. He could not rest until he had had an explanation, and he chose perhaps the worst medium for such an explanation – a written remonstrance. On 9 January 1850, barely a fortnight after his arrival in Paris, he wrote his wife a letter, which he describes as 'gloomy but composed', begging her to examine her heart attentively and to be perfectly frank with herself and with him.

Natalie read the letter with consternation. It drove her one step further on the road of deception.

I have received your letter of the 9th [she wrote back], and I too can only sit and think: why? And weep and weep. Perhaps I am to blame for everything: perhaps I am unworthy to live. But I feel as I felt once when we were sitting alone in the evening. I am pure before myself and before the world, and bear no reproach in my own heart. I have lived in my love for you as in God's world; if not in my love, it seems to me that I have had no life. To cast me out of that world – where could I go? It would mean being born over again. I am as inseparable from my love as I am from the world of nature; I leave it only to return to it. Never for a moment have I felt otherwise. The world is broad and rich. I know no world richer than the world of the heart. It is perhaps too broad; perhaps it has enlarged too much my whole being and its needs. For in this fullness there have been moments – have been, ever since the beginning of our life together – when imperceptibly, down at the very bottom, there has been something, the most delicate thread, which has troubled my soul, and then all has been bright and clear once more.

This pathetic document, a naïve rather than a cunning blend of truth and falsehood, did nothing to calm the overwrought husband. He returned to the charge, this time more brutally, more searchingly.

Do not shirk delving into yourself, do not seek for dialectical explanations. You cannot escape from a whirlpool once you are in it; it will drag you under all the same. In your letter there is a new note which is unfamiliar to me, a note not of grief but of something else. . . . The future is still in our hands, and we shall have the courage to go to the end. Remember that once we have brought out into the open the secret which is troubling our heart, either Herwegh will appear as a false note in our harmony or I – I am ready to go with Sasha to America, and then we shall see how things turn out . . . It will be hard for me, but I shall try to bear it; to remain here would be harder still and I cannot bear it.

Natalie's gentle, inconsequential spirit did not deal in dialectical dilemmas; and her husband's brutal 'either . . . or . . .' seemed to her an irrelevant attempt to solve the affairs of the heart in terms of barren logic. She could not dream of abandoning Herwegh; she could not dream of abandoning Alexander and her children. Both belonged equally to that 'broad and rich world of the heart' which seemed to her identical with life itself. If concealment was the only way to keep this world intact, she must continue to conceal; and the only practical course at the moment was to fly to the danger spot where the circle was threatening to break. She packed her trunks, and started with her children for Paris. It may have been fear, or some remnant of loyalty to her husband, which prevented her from disclosing to her lover the true state of affairs. The unhappy woman had already reached a position in which she could no longer be perfectly frank with anyone. She told Herwegh that Alexander was 'ill'; and he never learnt, or learnt only much later, the real motive for her sudden departure.

Natalie's arrival in Paris at once changed the uneasy balance of the quartette. Her susceptible nature, now that proximity had ceased to kindle the flames of physical passion for her lover, passed once more under the sway of her husband. She too, under his guidance, now awakened to Emma's sufferings; and without pausing to consider her own share of responsibility for them, she joined Herzen in his reproaches against Herwegh. The correspondence reveals the piquant picture of the mistress pleading for mercy for the wife.

> I am so much under the impression of Emma's grief [she wrote to Herwegh a few days after reaching Paris] that I can neither thank you for your charming letter nor answer it as I could wish. . . . It is *she* who brings us your letters, *she herself*. Imagine someone dying of thirst, who has to watch others holding a full glass in their hand – what impression would this picture make on you? Now try to judge the feelings of *the person who holds the glass* – it is a torture greater than I can bear.

Meanwhile the reconciliation between Alexander and Natalie was, to all outward seeming, complete. The spell was broken, the jarring note silenced. Herzen felt that his wife had escaped from some 'encirclement of black magic'; and a month later she was again pregnant. Herzen was completely tranquillized. Restored peace of mind, and remorse for those dark moments of suspicion and mistrust, made him for a few weeks unusually gentle and tolerant. The strident correspondence between the two men was succeeded by an effusive – perhaps too effusive – reconciliation; and only the absence of her lover, and Emma's too evident misery, troubled Natalie's vision of universal happiness.

The combined importunities of Herzen and Natalie had not been without effect; and in February Herwegh invited his wife to visit him in Zürich. The six years of Emma's married life had brought with them many bitter experiences; but they had given this resolute and clear-headed woman a perfectly precise philosophy of life and conduct. The marriage was not a year old when, just before the birth of their first child, the young *ménage* made the acquaintance in Paris of the Comtesse d'Agoult, then at the breaking-point of her long and notorious liaison with Liszt. Between the romantic poet and the sentimental blue-stocking there ensued a literary flirtation, which soon ripened into a more intimate relationship; and this was followed, on Herwegh's side, by a series of humbler and still more transient adventures. Emma rapidly took stock of the situation. She resigned herself, as other wives have done, to the loss of exclusive possession; but she was skilful enough to make a virtue of her resignation and to use it to establish her moral supremacy. She uttered no reproaches for these occasional wanderings of his fancy. She tolerated them or even, when the need arose, assisted them. It seemed to her relatively unimportant that her husband should sometimes stray into the arms of strange women; she had the compensating certainty that, sooner or later, he would return to her for comfort, for consolation and – so long as she disposed of that indispensable adjunct of family happiness – for money. In her feelings for him there had once mingled the passion of a mistress, the devotion of a wife, and the tenderness of a mother. She schooled herself now to exalt the third of these emotions. She regarded his failings with maternal indulgence, and claimed from him no longer the fidelity of a husband or a lover, but only the implicit confidence of a child.

The situation which greeted Emma on her arrival in Zürich gave a serious shock to her equanimity. She had not seen her husband since the day, nearly eight months before, when he had left Paris for Geneva in the company of Natalie. She found him 'unrecognizable'. She had been prepared for an admission of physical infidelity, and would have known how to cope with it. But she found something graver; she found a new loyalty which steeled his heart, and closed his lips, against her. For three weeks, bound by Natalie's insistent demand for secrecy, he remained silent. Then at last the stronger personality prevailed. During the last night of Emma's visit, Herwegh confessed everything. He confessed his love for Natalie and the guilty relations between them; he threw on his mistress the responsibility for his lack of frankness; and he pleaded that, however overwhelming his love for her, it did not weaken or diminish his affection for his wife. Falling on his knees, he begged Emma not to betray or abandon him; and he added that, if she did so, he would kill himself – for he could not live without her.

This confession threw Emma into a ferment of conflicting emotions. She perceived in Herwegh's passion for Natalie a new quality of depth and sincerity which distinguished it from his previous light-hearted entanglements. The existence of a deceived husband, and the close friendship between the two families, provided a further complication; and she regarded with horror the prospect of being compelled to live in close proximity and ostensible amity with her rival. But she found consolation in her newly-won victory. Herwegh's entreaties to her to remain at his side, his pathetic assurances that he could not live without her –

were balm to her wounded soul. If her husband had at last opened his heart to her, it proved that the influence of his wife was in the long run still stronger than the influence of the mistress. If she kept her head, all would be well; and when his infatuation for Natalie had spent itself, she could re-enter into the undivided possession of his affections. She decided to return to Paris, to break up her establishment there as soon as the necessary arrangements could be made, and, with the children, to rejoin her husband at Zürich.

Emma's return to Paris placed her relations with Natalie on a new footing. She lost no time in letting Natalie know that she was aware of the truth, and that a word from her could shatter the fool's paradise in which Natalie was entertaining Herzen. But Emma had no intention of speaking that word. She was both too honest and too subtle for blackmail. She offered to serve as a channel for the transmission of her husband's letters to Natalie; and only Natalie displayed some slight repugnance for this arrangement. Emma herself strongly urged it.

I am not an outsider [she wrote to Herwegh]. My role may be humiliating to you both. But at least Alexander is spared.

And she begged him 'not to make Herzen's life and his own dependent on the discretion of a stranger'. Three months before, the mistress had been pleading for the wife; now we meet the still more curious spectacle of the wife seeking to fan the flames of passion between the husband and the mistress. She told Natalie that it was her duty 'either to cure George or to make him happy', and that if she loved him she would abandon husband and children and link her fate irretrievably with his; and when Natalie replied that she would never leave Alexander, Emma cried out in triumph that her feeling for Herwegh was 'mere exaltation, not love'. The tactics followed by Emma were sufficiently astute. But she was too outspoken to conceal the motives for her advice. She did not refuse herself the satisfaction of telling Natalie that she was one of a series of mistresses whose favours Herwegh had enjoyed and then discarded; that he would tire of his infatuation the more rapidly, the more freely it was indulged; and that when he had had enough of her, he would return – as he had always done from his other loves – to the arms of his faithful and expectant wife. Let free rein be given to their passion; and

66

this desirable consummation would merely be hastened. Natalie listened to Emma's words with that mute incomprehension which is the surest armour against a wounding tongue. They had no meaning for her. The George of whom Emma spoke was a perfect stranger to her; he bore no resemblance to *her* George, union with whom was a religious sacrament – a unique manifestation of the divine spirit of love.

Between these two women no accommodation of thought or feeling was possible. Natalie found room in 'the broad and rich world' of her heart for the burning passion of self-abandonment to George and for the tenderness to Alexander which sought to spare him the normal and logical consequences of her behaviour. Both emotions were right in her eyes – for both sprang from love; and she gave herself equally to both. Emma's heart was more of a piece; and it was compact of sound, hard common sense. Where she loved, she loved exclusively and once for all, with a fierce concentrated passion, with a stern disregard of anything save the single object of her love. Natalie was repelled by the hard-headed determination, the cold ruthlessness of Emma's logic; Emma by the moral and intellectual softness, the confused sophistry of thought and action which expressed themselves in the dualism of Natalie's heart. In Natalie's eyes, Emma had no delicacy, no understanding of the finer sides of the human soul; for Emma, Natalie was a sentimental little fool, dangerous only through her dishonesty and her weakness.

It was about this time – probably during her stay in Zürich – that Emma learned of Natalie's pregnancy. The child was not expected until November, and its paternity could not therefore be open to question. Emma hastened to communicate this intelligence to her husband; and she must have been less than human if she failed to impart to the news a certain note of triumph. The impression on Herwegh was much what she expected. The jealousy of the male was kindled; and he wrote Natalie a letter which 'hurt her too much – too cruelly – more than anyone had hurt her in her life'. She replied in a letter full of ingenious argument:

My child, my darling angel, I understand you. If I were a man – you think that – no, I also will speak without blushing, do you remember when you said that I should recognize your child by a little mark which you have on your lower lip? You supposed then the possibility of another child which would not be yours – and indeed without *this* possibility, could the other exist? – George, my love is more independent, greater, more courageous, like the phoenix it always arises *more* alive from its ashes. You said that no one in the world must know that it was your child, not even the child itself – so how could I avoid ...? Have I not told you that I have never given myself to anyone *as I have to you*, I was virgin before I knew you, I still am when you are away, I shall be always, even though I have ten more children – is not that sufficient for you?

The letter just quoted is one of nearly a hundred and fifty written by Natalie to Herwegh during the seven months of their separation from January to August 1850. Some of these were intended for her husband's eye and were sent in the same envelope, or even on the same sheet of notepaper, as his; but the greater part were secret love-letters. They form a complete and intimate record of Natalie's emotional life during this time. The destruction of Herwegh's letters has deprived them of their natural counterpart; but they are sufficient in themselves to reveal many of the uneasy phases through which the correspondence passed. First Natalie provoked her lover's resentment by allying herself with Herzen and attacking him for his treatment of Emma. He wrote inquiring caustically 'why a letter from Paris must be colder than a letter from Zürich', and reproached her, as Emma had done, with her failure to give up all and join him. Then came another letter which called down on his head a spirited and characteristic retort:

You speak on the first page of your letter as if you were trying to *exonerate yourself* for your love of me, as if you were trying to *accuse* me, and me alone, for it – oh, I thank you! Give me everything, I take everything on myself, I want everything, I want to be, myself alone, the cause of my love for you and of your love for me, I want – yes, if that is a crime, I want to be the criminal, I alone! Everything, everything! To deny that would be to deny my own existence!

Yet side by side with these brave words, she reiterates, over and over again, the insistent demand that 'no shadow of what has been done and said and written' must ever be allowed to reach Herzen; over and over again she appeals to him (an appeal which, even eighty years later, makes the reader of these letters feel like an indiscreet intruder) to burn every line received from her:

> Yes, burn if you *do not detest me*, burn everything I have written to you.

Or again:

> Burn above all *this* letter. I would not have *another* hand than yours even *touch it*.

It may perhaps confirm Natalie's supposition of his anxiety to 'exonerate himself' that, instead of burning the letters (though he told her once that he had done so), Herwegh stored them away among his other papers, methodically pencilling the date of receipt on those which Natalie had failed to date herself. Perhaps he thought of them already as weapons for his own defence.*

But the most curious psychological study provided by these letters is to be found in Natalie's attitude to her husband. In the first blind moments at Geneva, sunk in the arms of her romantic ideal, she had almost forgotten Herzen's existence. But now, living with him in Paris, and isolated from her lover, she found herself more and more obsessed with the problem of her double life. On two points she never wavered. She could not leave him, and she could not face disclosure of the truth; and she justified her deceit by the sophistical argument that it was necessary not in her own interests, but in those of her husband and children.

> I shall avoid arousing the slightest suspicion [she assured Herwegh]. It is as much for them as for us. Think, dear angel, of the horror, if . . . oh, but you know everything, I shudder only to think of it.

Every reference to Herzen in the letters breathes the deepest respect and affection. She nowhere utters the slightest criticism of him, and more than once defends him against the criticism of Herwegh; and the reader may be tempted to ask in amazement (as Herzen himself afterwards asked) what demon of infatuation induced her to betray a husband whom she steadfastly respected for a lover whom she so often seemed to despise. But the letters, in throwing this question into relief, help at the same time to provide an answer.

* In after years, he regarded them as 'a weapon against calumny'. A curious letter written by him in response to a request to return them to the Herzen family will be found in Appendix A (p. 325).

When Natalie married Herzen at the age of twenty, she bestowed on him a heart bursting with gratitude and adoration. The shy and unhappy orphan of equivocal origin had looked up with respect to the distant elder cousin; and when the latter appeared first as her wooer, then as her deliverer, her worship of him knew no bounds. She accepted from him with rapture the masterful love of the stronger partner, and accommodated herself, even when their honeymoon of bliss was past, to the role of complete and admiring dependence on his superior will. The role was not unsuited to Natalie's gentle, retiring character. But it left, after the lapse of years, an unoccupied corner in her heart; and Herwegh – the perfect antithesis of Herzen – neatly filled it. Where Herzen had been cold and ironical, Herwegh was sentimental and clinging. Where Herzen was self-reliant, protective, sometimes patronizing, Herwegh made a parade of weakness, threw himself on the mercy of others and proclaimed at every opportunity his inability to live without them. In the whole range of Natalie's love-letters to Herwegh, no single word or phrase can be found expressive of admiration or respect for his character. He draws her not by his strength, but by his helplessness; and she croons to him in the language of a mother worshipping her adored child:

I often take you on my knees, I rock you like a little child, my darling child – and you fall asleep, and I gaze at you, gaze at you a long, long time – and I put you on the bed, and I fall on my knees beside you – and then I cover you with kisses. Dear, dear, dear!! Yes, and then you wake up and we talk and talk and embrace each other.

She had never written or spoken to Herzen like that, she had been afraid to write or speak to him like that. He had always seemed to her so strong and magnificent and overwhelming; she had never felt him yielding and helpless and utterly dependent in her arms. Herzen lacked the faculty of discernment; and he never understood the quality of the new sensations which Natalie sought and found in the embraces of her lover.

But when all is said and done, when all due allowance has been made for the romantic jargon in which Natalie clothed her infatuation, and for the new joys which she experienced with a lover who, instead of dominating her from above, threw himself unreservedly at her feet, the attraction of Herwegh for Natalie was mainly physical. We must accept her assurance, repeated again and again, that she had never belonged to anyone as she belonged to him. She had come to Herzen a shy and frightened girl. She had shrunk, before their marriage, from his too frank interest in terrestrial love, and preached to him the virtues of love celestial. Herzen, essentially decent and considerate, had shown as much forbearance as can be expected from a man passionately in love; and he treated his wife with the tenderness and the reverence which she appeared to desire. He occasionally indulged elsewhere the coarser lusts of the flesh (even at this time in Paris he seems to have had a momentary affair with a ballet dancer named Leontine, a former flame of Herwegh); but he set a deep gulf between the chaste love of the wife and the riotous indulgence of the prostitute. He continued to place his wife on a pedestal of serene and unspotted purity; and neither he nor Natalie knew that at thirty-two she wanted, and could give, more than she had given or wanted as a bride of twenty. The sensual side of Natalie's nature had developed in secret. Herwegh intervened. The barriers of delicacy and reserve which she had erected in her commerce with her husband did not exist for him; and with him she broke through all inhibitions and tasted for the first time the secrets of unrestrained and unabashed sensual enjoyment.

*

The financial affairs which had brought Herzen to Paris kept him there for more than five months, while the correspondence went to and fro between Paris and Petersburg and the Russian authorities tried every means of procrastination to delay the transfer of his and of his mother's fortune. It had already been agreed in February that the Herzens and the Herweghs should once more unite their lot as soon as Herzen could escape from Paris; and Nice (then an Italian town) had been chosen as the place of their future residence. As the months went on, and the tergiversations of the Russian Government still detained the Herzens in Paris, Herwegh's impatience found vent in outbursts of childish petulance.

Seriously, Alexander, finish this farce of francs and centimes. . . . Live on the half million you already have, until you get the other half.

71

Why all this breathless energy, this feverish impatience? Why deceive yourself – and deceive us – yet again? This further fortnight is pure waste. What do you expect to gain in a fortnight? It may last fourteen weeks as easily as fourteen days – or more. . . . You cannot, you will not leave Paris – that is the truth. And in fourteen or in twenty weeks there will be new excuses. Your wife will be unable to travel, your child will have caught another cough, you will be full of laments – and at heart you will be perfectly happy to remain.

These ill-bred jibes excited Herzen's indignation, but never for a moment his suspicions. Since Natalie had rejoined him in Paris, he had put completely behind him the tormenting, momentary doubts of the past winter. His faith in her was once more absolute. It had been reinforced by remorse for the supposed injustice he had done her; and it would have required circumstances far more incriminating than those of the previous December to shake it anew. Full of blind confidence, he planned the reunion at Nice which was to consummate the tragedy.

Many years later, when he wrote *My Past and Thoughts*, Herzen felt the need of explaining to himself and to the reader his conduct at this time.

Why did I go with Natalie to that very town? The question has often occurred to me and to others, but in reality it is a petty one. Not to mention the fact that wherever we had gone Herwegh could have come too, what purpose could have been served – unless it were to wound – by geographical and other precautions?

The romantic theory of the irresistibility of love is invoked by Herzen in his own defence, just as it had been invoked by the other actors in this drama. It did not matter whether he went to Nice, because whatever he did the same result was bound to follow. Fatalism was perhaps the only philosophy which could, in after years, save him from the madness of those who see too clearly that their ruin has been compassed by their own hand. But historically it is a false trail. Herzen did not go to Nice because he thought it a matter of indifference whether he and Natalie lived again with Herwegh or not. He went because it had been assumed by all concerned, throughout the period of their separation, that the two families would, at the first opportunity, resume their intimacy of the previous autumn, and because – except for a few fleeting days of suspicion of which he was now heartily ashamed –

he had never seen any reason to oppose this arrangement. Emma had already moved to Nice with her children at the end of May. In the middle of June Herzen, having triumphantly secured the transfer from Russia of his mother's fortune, followed with Natalie and the children. They moved by easy stages, for the sake of Natalie's health, and took a week on the way. The last part of the journey was by sea from Marseilles, and they reached Nice on 23 June. The stage was set. The *dramatis personae* were all assembled, save one. It only remained for the *jeune premier* to take his cue.

A period of suspense followed. The drama stands still while Natalie awaits her lover in pained amazement. Herwegh had, for months past, been expressing so much impatience for their reunion that she expected – they all expected – the news of their arrival to bring him post-haste from Zürich by the first coach. Herzen took a large house with a veranda on the select, and not yet fashionable, Rue Anglaise facing the sea. He proposed that the Herweghs should rent the upper storey and that, to save expense, the two families should take their meals together. Emma – for reasons which Herzen could not understand at all, and which Natalie understood only too well – regarded the proposal with horror. She tolerated Herwegh's infatuation for Natalie; but to be the unwilling witness of their happiness was beyond human endurance. Financial conditions proved, however, too strong for her. Supplies from Berlin had been reduced to bare subsistence level, and she was still sending money to her husband in Zürich. She wanted, as Herzen remarked, 'a habitation fit for an Indian nabob at 1,200 francs a year'. But this ideal eluded her search; and she found herself compelled to accept the upper storey of the Herzen house, and to eat at the Herzen table, for the modest sum – for the whole family – of 200 francs a month. Nor was this the limit of her obligations. She borrowed from Herzen the sum of 10,000 francs for two years on a note-of-hand. Emma was too single-minded, too exclusively bent on the salvation of her children and the recovery of her husband, to indulge any of these feelings of delicacy about money which another might have felt in the circumstances. She did not pause to reflect that any financial favours received by her, who knew all, from Herzen, who knew nothing, might savour of false pretences. She could never bring herself to regard the loan as an ordinary debt. It seemed to her a trivial compensation for the humiliations which she had undergone.

Still Herwegh tarried. The first explanation of his reluctance seems to have been vouchsafed in a letter to Emma. He told her that he could not bear to see Natalie pregnant by another man; and Emma, whose native frankness did not recoil from a certain measure of vindictiveness, told Natalie. To Natalie herself Herwegh wrote accusing her of coldness and hinting that she did not really want to have him at Nice. Presently – since these were not reasons that could be given to Herzen – he alleged that it was too hot to travel and that he was ill; and Herzen jocularly expressed relief that he had at last received an intelligible explanation of his friend's non-arrival. Unfortunately letters from Madame Haag arriving at the same time, contained many references to Herwegh, but none to his supposed illness. He had not even taken the trouble to lie plausibly. Amid so many false reasons, the real motive of his procrastination remains obscure. Emma, with her knowledge of his character and habits, surmised – and did not fail to communicate her surmise to Natalie – that he had found a counter-attraction at Zürich.

Natalie's anguished suspense during these weeks can be traced in her almost daily letters to her lover. Of all the pretexts for delay, it was the one he had given to Emma which hurt her the most.

I have told you *that Emma knows* why you do not come. If *that* is the reason, I repeat that *I could not* come near you even in letters, *I shall stop writing* even if it costs me my life.

But Natalie had gone too far to retreat. She had staked her whole faith, her whole being on her love for Herwegh. She had to believe in him now, in face of doubt, in face of knowledge.

Everything is as you desire [she writes simply a week later]. My arms are open. I am waiting for you. Come!

Or, in a mood of more exalted passion:

George, my George!
Dear one, darling – all, all, all! Why are you suffering, my child? Why do you still suffer? What can I do for you more, *more?* Does *our*

love leave room in your heart for some further desire? . . . Tell me, tell me. Behold me, all, all yours – do you need something more? Perhaps, my angel, *I* am not sufficient for you – but *in me* there is nothing left that I have not given you. I have loved, oh, I have loved in my life! But as I love you – never. Oh, George! All my life has been only an ascent towards you.

She chose a corner of the garden which she named in anticipation 'our corner'. 'How I shall kiss you here,' she wrote, sending him a pansy culled from the chosen spot; and on the wall above the bench she scratched the secret signs Λ X and O.

Herwegh resisted these passionate importunities no longer. Two months after the arrival of the Herzens in Nice – and two days after Emma had given Herzen her note of hand for 10,000 francs – he appeared on the scene 'looking', as Herzen wrote many years later, 'like Werther in the last stage of despair'. The reunion of the lovers brought the correspondence to an end. 'Our corner' became the sole witness of those transports and reproaches which had hitherto found a more permanent record on the tenuous and crowded sheets of Natalie's writing-paper; and for posterity a veil is drawn over the next three months – the last of Natalie's pregnancy. Herzen, in *My Past and Thoughts*, draws an ironical picture of Herwegh's constant threats of suicide, and of tear-stained confabulations between Emma and Natalie about the poet's unhappy plight. He also dates from this period the re-birth of his suspicions. But he was anxious, when he wrote *My Past and Thoughts*, to attenuate the embittering confession of his own blindness; and all the other evidence suggests that he lived on in false security until almost the end of the year. His blind trust redounds to the credit of his character. But few men care to see their character exalted at the expense of their intelligence; and the realization how long, and how flagrantly, he had been deceived made the humiliation of the subsequent discovery almost too deep to bear.

On 20 November the child – Herzen's younger daughter, Olga – was born. Every day – and often twice a day – for the next fortnight Natalie, grown reckless with long impunity, smuggled out to her lover hasty pencilled notes which Herwegh preserved with the rest of her letters. His bedroom was directly over hers, and it was her consolation to listen to his footsteps overhead.

How I listen when you move [she scribbled on the day after her confinement]. Every step you take – you set your foot on my lips, you sleep on my knees, think of that, my all, my all.

And next day:

You are there, sunk in my breast, firmly embedded there – dear, dear, dear!

Good-bye, good night, do not leave me, stay stay with me, like that – you know *how*. Yours, yours, yours!

Your Natalie!

He came to visit her every day at noon; and she prayed that 'these moments of beatitude' might serve him 'as a coat of mail against bitter moments'. Among the most passionate letters in the whole collection are those which she wrote from her sick-bed in the days which followed the birth of Olga.

The situation was, in fact, not merely embarrassing but ridiculous, as Herwegh had perceived for some time. Natalie's passion had become too fierce and unmanageable for discreet adultery. At any moment her recklessness might betray them both; and if there must be disclosure, Herwegh had the sense to appreciate the tactical advantages of taking the initiative. He besought her, as Emma had so often besought her before, to face the issue and make a clean breast of the story to Herzen. Natalie too professed to be in favour of 'complete frankness', but thought that the moment was 'not well chosen'; and on the latter point, since it was only four days since she had given birth to her husband's child, it is difficult not to agree with her.

I throw myself blindfold upon your heart [she wrote a few days later] with a boundless faith in your sublime love – dear, dear, dear! Let men one day fall and worship before our love, dazzled as at the transfiguration of Jesus Christ. But a *stupid*, undignified explosion – oh George, my George! I beseech you, I embrace your feet, my George, my George. Kill me rather!

In reality, Natalie's objections were not objections of time or place, but were fundamental to her whole character.

I shall love my family [runs the last letter of this period] as long as there is any love left in my heart – I don't know why, or who needs it – it is my nature, I love madly; perhaps the faculty of loving is so great in

me just because I have no other? I love for myself, like an egoist. I live
the life of my children. I seem to follow each one of their movements
even when I do not see them; and to be something for them, to make
their life ever so little more beautiful, is for me I can't say what happiness! I cling to it with every fibre of my being. Then I know what I am
for Alexander. But when I see *you* suffer, it is no longer tears which flow
from my eyes, it is blood that pours in streams from my heart. I tear
myself away from everything – I do not know what I shall do, but I
shall do everything – I fall at your feet.

Physical relations were resumed between lover and mistress;
and for a moment Natalie persuaded herself – it was a false
alarm – that she was pregnant. But the situation remained unchanged. There was no answer to the riddle, and no escape from
the dilemma. Natalie still stood mute and helpless before the insolu-
ble problem of conflicting loyalties and conflicting loves. Herwegh
still hesitated, full of excellent intentions and ever-changing
resolves. Emma still preached courage and the clean cut. Herzen,
more and more morose, wrestled with suspicions which he strove
to dismiss from his mind as unworthy calumnies. All four shrank
from any decisive word or deed which would make the explosion
inevitable. Thus they drifted into the New Year of 1851, the air
heavy with approaching tragedy.

CHAPTER 4

A Family Tragedy: II

A CHARACTERISTIC scene preluded the final explanation between Natalie and her husband.

Just before the New Year she showed him a water-colour of their house which had been painted for her by the French artist Guiaud. It depicted Natalie in white on the balcony, and the children playing with Tata's pet goat in the courtyard of the house. Herzen thought or feigned to think that it was intended for him. It transpired that it was Natalie's New Year gift to Herwegh.

'Do you like it?' asked Natalie.

'So much,' said Herzen with icy sarcasm, 'that if Herwegh permits, I will have a copy made for myself.'

'Take it yourself,' said Natalie with tears in her eyes.

'On no account. Are you jesting?'

Both husband and wife shrank from taking up the challenge and remained silent. The painting was presented and still survives. Underneath it is the inscription in Natalie's hand in German 'And the pale Natalie on the balcony', and then 'N. à G.' and the date in Russian 'Saturday 4 January'. The storm did not break for more than a fortnight longer.

The story is told by Herzen in detail in *My Past and Thoughts*. It was Natalie, compelled by her husband's glowering looks and ironical sallies, who provoked the final explanation. Herzen repeated the offer he had made just a year before – to withdraw himself for ever from her life by going to America or elsewhere. He begged of her only one thing – a final decision; he could no longer bear the suspense. If she chose for him to remain, Herwegh must go.

It was a fine January morning, and the whole party were to make an excursion to Mentone. Herzen's mother came to call for them, and the conversation remained unfinished. When the ladies and children had packed themselves into the carriage there was room for only one more. Herzen elaborately motioned Herwegh to the vacant seat. Herwegh, 'though not generally distinguished by so much delicacy', declined. Herzen slammed the carriage door and told the coachman to drive on. The two men remained alone.

Herzen afterwards wished that he had either insisted on an open explanation or thrown Herwegh over the cliff. In fact, both men contented themselves with vague hints drawn from the commonplace books of Romanticism. Herwegh murmured that it was the lot of the poet to suffer and to inflict suffering on others. Herzen asked whether he had read George Sand's novel *Horace*. The hero of this forgotten romance is a vain and weak-minded adventurer, whose assets are his good looks, a minimum of moral scruple, and an infinity of self-assurance. Herwegh replied that he did not remember, and undertook to get it from the local bookshop. They parted in silence. Such was the undramatic last meeting of the rivals.

When the party re-assembled for dinner that evening Emma brought a message that Herwegh was ill and would not appear. When the meal was over, Emma retired; the children went to bed; and Natalie and Herzen were once more alone. Natalie sat by the window and wept. Her husband strode up and down the room, a prey to nervous irritability and excitement.

'He is going,' said Natalie at last.

'Surely that is quite unnecessary. Surely it is I who ought to go.'

'In God's name . . .'

'I shall go.'

'Alexander, Alexander, are you not ashamed? Listen to me, and save us all. You alone can do it. He is overwhelmed, he is in complete despair. You know what you were to him. His unreasoning love, his unreasoning friendship, and the consciousness that he has brought you pain – and worse . . . But you must not make things too difficult. He is within an ace of suicide.'

'You think so?'

'I am sure of it.'

'He told you so himself?'

'Both he and Emma. He has been cleaning his pistol.'

Herzen roared with laughter.

'Not the one he took with him to Baden? It would need

79

cleaning. It probably trailed somewhere in the mud. You can tell Emma I answer for his life; I will insure it for anything she likes.'

The bitter mockery once more repelled Natalie.

'What will come of all this?' she asked weakly.

'It is difficult to foresee the consequences,' said Herzen incisively, 'and still more difficult to prevent them.'

'My God, my God! What will become of the poor children?'

'The children? You might have thought before of the children.'

On this cruel sally they broke off for a while. Natalie was exhausted; Herzen's rage was inflamed to its highest point. He began again. He demanded to know the whole truth. Natalie, helpless and broken, confessed her guilt. Still he plied her with questions, putting her and himself on the rack. She broke down under the torture; her lips moved convulsively; and the look of dumb pain on her face was that of one who no longer understood what was said and done around her.

Herzen sat down beside her on the divan and took her hand, a prey to sudden remorse. He asked himself how a man of his education, a man professing his liberal and humanitarian principles, could play the inquisitor and the executioner to an unhappy woman whom he had once loved and whom – as his jealous paroxysms suffice to prove – he still loved in his own fashion. A few moments passed; and Natalie threw her arms round his neck sobbing and declared that she would never leave him. Mingling their tears they decided, there and then, to forget the past and to begin a new life. One thing only she asked; an undertaking that Herzen would allow his relations with his rival to 'end without bloodshed'. He promised, provided Herwegh left Nice the next day.

Next morning Emma appeared in Herzen's room as a messenger from her husband.

'He might have come himself if he wants anything,' was Herzen's greeting. 'Or perhaps he has already shot himself.'

The jest rather spoiled the effect of the message, which was that Herwegh begged Herzen to kill him, since he could not live without his friends. Herzen treated the whole proceedings as a comedy, and spoke cuttingly of 'a man who sends his wife to invite you to commit murder'.

'This is a frightful calamity,' she said, 'it has struck you and me equally. But look at the difference between your rage and my devotion.' Unswerving in the line of conduct she had traced for herself, she begged him to allow Natalie to go away with Herwegh. She would remain with him and the children.

Herzen, infuriated by the comparison and by the proposal, laughed wildly. He would not forgive the woman who had been an accomplice in his wife's betrayal, and who had fallen so low as to play the pimp for her own husband. He told Emma to go and ask Natalie. The conversation with Natalie is recorded by Emma herself.

'I cannot leave Alexander like this,' Natalie told her. 'He is threatening to go away.'

'Then let him go,' rejoined Emma curtly.

'I cannot,' said Natalie. 'When I see him as he is now, I know that if he were to go, I should follow him – everywhere.'

'And George? If George perishes?'

'George will not perish,' said Natalie clasping her hands and raising her eyes to heaven. 'God will protect him!'

Then Emma drained to the bottom the cup of self-humiliation. She implored Natalie, since she herself would not go with Herwegh, to beg him not to abandon *her* – to take *her* with him. The mistress promised to intercede for the wife.

When Emma returned to Herzen and confessed her failure to move Natalie, he was once more deadly calm and adopted a lordly tone. His promise to avoid bloodshed, he explained, only held good on the understanding that Herwegh left Nice next morning. They could not, Emma protested, start so soon; for they had neither visas nor money. Herzen undertook to obtain the necessary visas, and to pay the fare to Genoa. There was another difficulty: they owed 500 francs to local tradesmen. Herzen, more and more the *grand seigneur*, told Emma not to trouble. He would settle the bills.

Then Emma too broke down, and begged him not to refuse to take her hand in farewell.

'I have always respected you, and perhaps you are right,' she conceded. 'But you are a cruel man. If you only knew what I have suffered.'

'But why,' said Herzen, taking her hand with a fleeting

moment of pity, 'have you been a slave all your life? You have deserved your fate.'

Natalie's intercession was successful, and the Herweghs left together next morning. For some reason they had to spend two days in Mentone on the way to Genoa. In the evening Emma sent the elder child back to Nice with a request that he might stay with the Herzens for two days. They could not afford a separate room for him at the hotel, and his presence irritated Herwegh. Herzen ruthlessly turned the boy away, and he wandered about Nice until he found an asylum with some other friends.

Next day Herzen learned that Emma had instructed her servant to buy for her in Nice some linen and children's underclothing, and to include it in the bills which Herzen had promised to pay.

Caesar [Herzen sardonically concludes his chapter] could read, write and dictate at the same time; such was the richness of his genius. But to think about children's stockings and the purchase of cloth on economical terms at a moment when families are being shattered to pieces, and men feel at their throats the cold steel of Saturn's blade! The Germans are a great race!

The blow had been a more staggering one for Natalie even than for her husband. It represented for Herzen the shattering of his dearest illusion, the fall of the woman whose devoted love and immaculate purity had been the cornerstone of his faith. But for Natalie it transcended all personal issues, even the most intimate. It meant the collapse of her whole philosophy of life – the ideal of love.

In the time of my isolation from my childhood down to my twentieth year [she wrote to Herwegh] I conceived too high an ideal of humanity, I fostered within myself the love of an ideal which perhaps does not exist. Life has given me all it can give, but I am not grateful to life; I am faithful to my ideal, and no gratitude will force me to recognize it in a nameless monstrosity, which has nothing human about it.

Her ideal had been transformed into a 'monstrosity'. She had planted the seed of universal love, and had reaped a harvest of brutal conflicting egoisms. She had thought to attain, and to confer on others, the secret of infinite happiness; and she had inflicted infinite pain on those who were dearest to her. She was compelled to question the validity of her ideal; for she could not doubt the reality of the pain.

Oh George [she wrote to him three weeks after the catastrophe] you say that we did not mean to hurt anyone. Ah! no, we did not mean to, no, no, no! But we have done it. Everything in Alexander that was light-hearted, care-free, childlike – I have torn it from him like a skin, and left him all raw and bleeding. I am afraid of my very breath touching him; and the least thing which reminds him – ah, it is as if I were pouring poison on the wound.

For the first time in her life, Natalie was able to pity her husband; and a new link was forged in the chain which bound her to him.

For three months the Herweghs remained in Genoa, and the correspondence between George and Natalie continued. She could not join him; she could not 'assassinate Alexander and begin a new life over his grave'. But she could not become suddenly indifferent to the man to whom she had given herself. She could not repent of those glorious moments of her love for Herwegh, or regard them as a passing aberration which she could now put behind her and forget. She would write to him sometimes – every fortnight – when she could – 'since she could not exist otherwise'; and she promised that she would meet him again in a year's time. But now she could do nothing. She wanted rest and peace. She wanted above all to think and understand and explain. She thought of Natalie Tuchkov now living with Ogarev as his wife, 'the one being in the world, who, I think, would understand me, who would understand everything in all its truth, in all its purity'. She even thought of travelling to Russia 'to tell her everything'; but it would have been impossible for the wife of Herzen to get a permit. Natalie tossed helplessly between her love, so passionate and so tormenting, for Herwegh, and her love, so deep and com-passionate, for her husband. Her gentle spirit struggled con-vulsively in the grip of emotions too powerful for her weakness to master and too complicated for her simplicity to unravel.

Recriminations soon began. Herzen wrote to Emma, on the morrow of their departure, that he would hold her responsible for any word that reached the public ear of the causes of the breach between them; for, he added with a cruel reminder of her de-nunciation of her husband in Paris, 'I have reason to know that you are not in the habit of sparing those who are near to you'.

After reminding her of her financial indebtedness, he returned to the insulting comparison she had made between his position and hers:

> You, Madame, were in the secret, as you admitted to me yourself. You pressed day by day the hand of a friend while you were helping to ruin him and losing your own dignity in the process . . .
> No, Madame, the difference between us is immense, even in another respect. My lips have never uttered a word against N.; I have never dragged her through the mud as you did your husband when you talked to me. I have a good memory, Madame; and no word will ever pass these lips, for I love her with a proud and worthy love, and I know that she has a great love for me – and that she remains with me.
> Whereas you are not favoured in this respect.

Undeterred by this bitter taunt, Emma held on her course. She wrote to Natalie begging her once more to give up all and join her lover. The letter reviewed the past in terms of bitter reproach. Under pretext of sparing everyone, Natalie had sacrificed everyone. Her 'sentimental dilettantism' – her refusal 'to be frankly for one or the other' – had brought about a catastrophe which threatened to end in bloodshed. Her lack of courage, her constant tergiversations, were driving George to the verge of suicide. Emma reminded her rival of the obligations under which she had placed Natalie by her long silence.

> And now I come once more [she concluded] to claim from you George's need of happiness at the expense of my own, I come to repeat again: It is only by living that you can pay your debt to life, it is only by making him happy that you can pay your debt to me – a debt that is more than money. If you could restore him to me *the same as* you took him from me, ah yes! But since that is impossible –

Herwegh himself wrote to Herzen a long and eloquent defence of his conduct and repeated the invitation to kill him; but Herzen returned this and other letters from him unopened. Then Emma wrote to Herzen repeating, in substance, the defence which he had refused to read. She dissected the character of her rival with mordant logic and feminine partiality. It was Natalie's egoism which was responsible for the calamity. It was Natalie who had invited George to love her; it was Natalie who had insisted on a policy of concealment and treachery; and it was Natalie, the real

culprit, who had now left George to bear alone the weight of
Herzen's righteous indignation. Herzen's reply – it has not
survived among the Herwegh papers – seems to have been a
reminder that she and her husband had lived for months on his
charity, and that she owed him 10,000 francs.

This correspondence filled Natalie with dull despair. She felt
more and more that she was living in a world of mean and ignoble
slanderers, incapable of comprehending the breadth and purity
of her own ideal. And from this condemnation she could no longer
exempt her lover, the one man with whom she had thought to
attain perfect harmony. George was now once more subject to the
uncontested influence of Emma's mind and will; and since Emma
exonerated him from blame, he was strongly disposed to agree
with her. He wrote to Natalie complaining (it was the counterpart
of Natalie's insistence on Herzen's sufferings) that they had
'crucified' Emma, and reminding her that Emma had 'blessed'
their union. The reply was crushing:

I never asked for her benediction [wrote Natalie] and when did she
bless *you?* Was it when she defended you at the last moment to Alexander by saying that you had always wanted to tell him, but that I had
prevented you? . . . Or did she bless us when she wrote to me and to
Alexander in her last letters that it was only my egoism which was the
cause of everything that has happened, that it was I who incited you
to love me? (I was ashamed, I blushed for you before Alexander, *I*
would rather have cut out my tongue than say such a thing.) . . . I
thank you for this last accusation; at last you do me justice. Yes, yes!
It was I who incited you! It was my love which incited yours! Ah,
should I ever have done what I did for a love which was afraid to take
the initiative? So you have no need to defend yourself, either to me or
to anyone, you need not seek advocates – *I will defend you.*

Natalie was faithful to the romantic tradition; and as Herwegh
had invited Herzen to kill him, so she now begged Herwegh to be
her executioner. If she could not live for him, she could 'die for
him and by his hand'.

You tell me [she wrote] that I am playing a part – well, say what you
like, *I am getting ready to die.* I should be good for nothing, if I lived, not
even for the children, I should teach them to love too much – and to
what end? One must not, in this world, one must not love too much.
Why should one love? In order to suffer so much and to bring suffering

to everything one loves? Life will teach them without my help to become indifferent, and they will be happier without me! Dear little things! Already you are loving too much, already I have spoilt you, ruined you – forgive me, forgive me! You will be cured – perhaps. George, you will be doing a great service to my children by killing me. My blessing on you in advance! Only, dear, you see, I must first find the right place for them, right in every way, a good home, and arrange everything nicely, nicely, to my taste – perhaps my taste is not good, but I know no other and nobody has *ever* helped me over that. . . .

In such passages there breaks through the romantic idiom of Natalie's speech the austere simplicity of the great classics.

Herzen watched morosely, and in agonized suspense, the emotional struggles of his wife; but he was temperamentally unable to share them. Like Emma, whom he resembled in the straightforward, sometimes brutal, directness of his character, he failed to understand the 'dualism' of Natalie's heart. Natalie's contrition – her compassion for him – had been so spontaneous and so heartfelt that he could not doubt the profound sincerity of her repentance. It would have been an insult to ask her whether she repented. He had forgiven her, and the slate had been wiped clean. His one desire was that he should never again hear the name of Herwegh – a common cad who had abused the privileges of friendship and hospitality – and that nothing should ever happen to remind him of what had been. But Natalie, it seemed, neither could nor would forget. She would not even condemn. Herzen knew that she was still writing to Herwegh, though he was unaware of the extent and contents of the correspondence; and he knew that she had promised to meet him again in a year. She no longer loved – she had never, in any worthy sense of the word, loved – Herwegh; he convinced himself of that. But she lacked the courage to put behind her the entangling memories of the past. Herzen began to drink deeply with a new-found Russian acquaintance named Engelson.* The 'new life', tormented by recollections and remorse, did not fulfil the brilliant hopes formed in those first sentimental moments of reconciliation and tears.

More and more restless, Herzen found, at the beginning of June, a pretext for a journey to Paris with Engelson. He visited the opera and heard Alboni; he tried the Bal Mabille and the

* See the following chapter.

café-chantants; he went to the Louvre. But nothing distracted him
long from his gloomy thoughts. Maria Ern, one of the friends who
had accompanied the Herzens when they left Russia four years
before, had just married a German musician living in Paris
named Reichel. Herzen visited the Reichels; but he soon guessed,
from their looks and from 'the way in which they avoided the
slightest allusion', that they knew something. Sasha's birthday, in
the middle of June, made him remember 'the holy and glorious
days of 1839'; and he did not spare Natalie the sour fruit of his
reflexions.

Why did you conceal from me [he asked cruelly] how empty the
past was to you? To me it was always such a shining memory; now it
is all trampled underfoot and I am afraid to pick it up again. Why, I
was so happy then because I believed as firmly in your happiness as in
my own.

He discussed the future and talked of settling in Edinburgh, which
was comfortable and cheap, or on the coast of Cornwall. Natalie
humbly agreed to everything. She would follow him anywhere.
But he could not divert his bitter thoughts.

I want the impossible [he wrote again]. I want the love of 1838, in
which I believed. . . . Yes, I am still young, I thirst for love for myself,
and I shall not find it again. I have got to abdicate; but how hard it is
to lay down the crown after eleven years!

From Paris Herzen went on to Freiburg in Switzerland. He had
felt for some time the need of protecting himself, by process of
naturalization, from the petty persecutions of the police; and the
canton of Freiburg had agreed to inscribe him on the roll of its
citizens. On his way thither, he met in Geneva his old friend
Sazonov, and was amazed to learn from him, over a bottle of
wine, that his family disaster had become a familiar topic of
conversation in *émigré* circles in Switzerland. Herwegh, now
settled in Zürich, had not only related to Sazonov the nature and
cause of his breach with Herzen; he had explained the conduct of
Natalie after his own fashion. It was only, he declared, owing to
'strong moral pressure' placed on her by her husband that she had
failed to accompany her lover; and she had promised to rejoin
him in Switzerland as soon as Herzen had calmed down.
The revelation tore open the unhealed wound to its sorest

depths. His most intimate affairs had become 'a European scandal'. He not only found himself in the ridiculous and contemptible position of a publicly deceived husband; he stood condemned by his compatriots – for Sazonov, at any rate, had in substance believed Herwegh's story – for betrayal of his most cherished principles. He, Herzen, the enlightened liberal, the upholder of the romantic right to love, had used his authority as a husband to coerce his wife, to deny her access to the man of her choice. The romantic doctrine of the rights of husbands was strict and inexorable.

There are men [writes George Sand in *Jacques*] who will unceremoniously cut the throat of an unfaithful wife, after the manner of the Orientals, because they consider her a piece of legal property. Others fight a duel with their rival, kill him or remove him from the scene, and then solicit the embraces of the woman whom they pretend to love, and who either recoils in horror or resigns in despair. Such are, in conjugal love, the most common methods of procedure; and I say that the love of swine is less gross and beastly than the love of such men.

Could Herzen acquit himself of having practised at any rate the second degree of swinishness? As he listened to Sazonov, he was tormented by the gnawing suspicion that the indictment might, after all, be true. It accounted for so much that seemed incomprehensible in Natalie's behaviour – the continued correspondence with her lover, her quiet refusal to put the past utterly behind her. Perhaps Natalie did still love Herwegh. Perhaps it was only a stern sense of duty, or the thought of the children, which had kept her, an unwilling victim, at his side. Perhaps the vaunted reconciliation had been all an elaborate piece of mystification, inspired by pity for his distress.

The thought worked like madness in his blood. He felt 'insulted, wounded, humiliated'; and, 'in a paroxysm of criminal fury', he wrote Natalie a letter which afterwards he described as a 'stab in the back'. It has been preserved, and runs as follows:

Judge for yourself what I feel.
He has told Sazonov everything. Such details that the hearing of them took my breath away. He said that 'he was sorry for me, but the harm was done; you had implored him to keep silence, but in a few months' time *when I was calmer* you would leave me.'
My dear, I will not add a single word. Sazonov questioned me about

it as if you were ill. I was like a dead man when he was speaking. I demand from you an answer on the last point. Sazonov decidedly knows everything. I insist on the truth. Answer at once; I shall weigh every word. My heart is bursting. And you call that 'growing together'.

I go to Freiburg tomorrow. I have never been in such despair. Address your answer Poste Restante, Turin.

Are they really saying that about you? Oh God, God, how I have suffered for my love. What more? An answer, an answer to Turin.

Natalie had drunk too deeply of the cup of humiliation to be able to suffer any more on her own account. She had no pride left, and she cared nothing for the wagging tongues of Geneva or of Europe. She saw in her husband's letter the incoherent ravings of a man driven to despair by the gadfly of scepticism; and she wanted nothing but to restore his broken faith. She not only wrote protesting her invincible determination 'to live or to die for him'. She set out for Turin to meet him there. Before starting from Nice, she penned what was destined to be almost the last in the long series of her letters to Herwegh:

George, I come before you once more as I am. I thought I had found in you the fulfilment of all my dreams, I was dazzled, transported into regions where human imagination can scarcely penetrate. Then we had to part; and though I thanked you and fate for my boundless happiness, I would not return to it, seeing that it could not be reconciled with the happiness of Alexander. . . .

After untold struggles, I saw that I was destroying Alexander's peace of mind without ever being able to satisfy you. I saw that you were incapable of the smallest sacrifice, that you lived only for yourself. . . . My ideal was overthrown, dragged in the dust; all that I held most sacred was despised and trampled under foot, all your promises, all my prayers rejected. You have destroyed me; but Alexander's love grew meanwhile in all its grandeur, its devotion, its immensity – and his sufferings! He and the children prevented me from accepting the death which you brought me, they still hold me back; and if death does not come of itself, or if you, George, do not send it to tear me from my family, I shall not leave my family, I am dissolved in it, outside it I no longer exist.

I suffer with your sufferings, the more so because I am the cause of them – but I can do no more. Here I am – punish me, kill me, if that will comfort you, if you can – I can do no more . . .

The reunion at Turin produced a reconciliation more complete and more lasting than had been achieved in the first bitter moments of revelation and jealousy at Nice. Herzen describes the meeting in terms which prove how much of the romantic sentimentalist survived in him under the protective shell of cynicism. Natalie, travelling from Nice to Turin in the heat of the summer, was dressed in white. Herzen remembered that she had been in white that day when he had crept into Moscow by stealth from Vladimir to visit her, and that she had been married in white a few months later. The reunion at Turin was a 'second marriage, perhaps more significant than the first'. They talked together half the night; and 'setting out afresh on our path, we shared, without any reckoning between us, the mournful load of the past'. Natalie was worn out with the long struggle. There was no strength or spirit left in her for new emotions or for new hopes. She felt herself betrayed by her lover, and betrayed and cheated by life itself. She broke off her correspondence with Herwegh, and told him that she would destroy unread any further letters she received from him. Herzen was the one fixed star in her firmament; and she turned to him in resignation and weariness of heart.

The three days spent in Turin, and the return together through Genoa and Mentone to Nice seemed to Herzen a second honeymoon. If the spontaneous gaiety of youth had gone for ever, there was the maturer, reflective tranquillity of middle life. A note of autumn melancholy blended not unsuitably with the romantic creed of the ennobling value of suffering. It was the Indian summer of their love – the unnatural, deceptive calm which conceals the approach of coming tempests.

Thanks be to Fate [wrote Herzen in *My Past and Thoughts*] for those days, and for the third of a year which followed them; they were the triumphant ending of my personal life. Thanks be to Fate that she, the eternal pagan, crowned the victims destined for the sacrifice with a luxuriant wreath of autumn flowers, and strewed around them, for a brief space, her poppies and her fragrance.

*

The first herald of doom was a sudden, brutal and irrelevant calamity. Herzen's mother, the deaf-mute boy Kolya, and a German tutor who had been engaged for him, had been spending some weeks in Paris. In the middle of November they set out, with a niece of Madame Haag and a housemaid, on the return journey. They travelled via Marseilles, embarking there on a steamer for Nice. During the night, just off Hyeres, in clear and fine weather, the steamer was rammed by another ship and sank in a few minutes. Of the hundred passengers, most of them sleeping in their cabins, only a handful escaped with their lives. The niece and the housemaid were picked up by a passing ship. Madame Haag, Kolya and the tutor disappeared, and not even their bodies were ever recovered. Herzen brought the dreadful news to Natalie in the evening when the house was decorated with flowers to welcome the returning travellers, and the porch was hung with Chinese lanterns.

The horror of this tragedy, following on the emotions and the torments of the past twelve months, fell on the bereaved parents with stunning force; and Natalie, who was now again pregnant, never recovered from the shock. For weeks they lived on mechanically, scarcely conscious of the world around them. On 2 December, 'the eighteenth Brumaire of Louis Bonaparte' portended the coming of the second empire; but the official burial of the last discredited remnant of the revolution of 1848 passed unheeded by Herzen in the midst of his domestic mourning. Then Natalie's enfeebled constitution gave way. On one of the last days of the year she took to her bed and pleurisy declared itself. On New Year's Day, 1852, Herzen wrote to a friend that 'he never wished to see another 1 January, and no longer cared whether he were alive or dead, whether he were in America or in Schlüsselburg' – Schlüsselburg being the famous Russian prison for political offenders on the shores of Lake Ladoga. He felt that he had reached the nadir of despair.

He had no presentiment of what still awaited him. Since the meeting with Sazonov and the reconciliation at Turin, he had heard nothing of Herwegh; and he had no conception of the slow, bitter hatred still accumulating in his rival's heart. Herwegh had stayed with Emma in Genoa for three months after the rupture. Then the society of his wife had begun once more to irk him. At the end of April he himself left Genoa for Zürich (the disclosure to Sazonov occurred at Geneva on the way), and sent Emma back to Nice. The return of Emma, after all that had happened, to the scene of the rupture and the place where the Herzens were still residing, might well seem a striking example either of malice or of insensitiveness. It contained, in fact, elements of both. Of Herwegh's malice his subsequent proceedings leave no doubt; and the trait of insensitiveness, which Emma had already exhibited in her financial transactions with Herzen, permitted her to fall in, not too unwillingly, with her husband's wishes. Having arrived in Nice, she behaved with discretion. She resumed her relations with the common friends of the two families – in particular, with Karl Vogt, a German naturalist who had dabbled in revolution, with Orsini, the Italian *carbonaro*, and with a Pole named Chojecki, better known under his French *nom de plume* of 'Charles Edmond'. But she made no approach to Herzen or to Natalie; and for the remainder of the year 1851 the peace had been undisturbed.

But so impotent a conclusion offered no satisfaction to Herwegh. The state of his mind at this time provides a curious study in morbid psychology. He had slunk away from Nice ignominiously and under the threat of a challenge from the injured husband. It had seemed at the time the only course to take; but now in retrospect it emerged as an egregious error – tantamount to a confession of guilt, if not of cowardice. Then came Herzen's insulting letters to Emma with their ill-timed reminders of past financial dependence and of outstanding obligations which they had no prospect of fulfilling. He had tried to redress the balance by correspondence from Genoa; and his letters had returned to him unopened. The helplessness and the humiliation of his position ground into his soul. The sending back of his letters was 'a brutality which shocked him more deeply than anything in his life'. He had understood Herzen's first paroxysms of jealous fury. He was well used to hot and transient emotions, and had been content to assume that Herzen's hatred of him was one of these. He could have borne anything better than this cold-blooded, contemptuous ignoring of his existence.

From the moment of his arrival in Zürich at the beginning of May 1851, Herwegh's letters to Emma are a shrill crescendo of uncontrolled rage.

Alexander [he writes] has behaved throughout so vulgarly that I feel myself absolved from any consideration for him . . . He is laughing up his sleeve at the way he has managed by his manœuvres to hush it all up. That is what he wanted. But he is altogether *too* sure; I shall *drive* him from *his hiding-place*.

He still protests from time to time that his love for Natalie is intact and pure (though it in no way detracts from his love for Emma); but love has become a secondary consideration. He confesses that he no longer thinks of winning back Natalie. Perhaps she will even hate him. But it is essential to the restoration of his self-respect that he should repay 'humiliation for humiliation', that he should make Herzen suffer as he is suffering himself, that he should shatter Herzen's smug security. He took a cruel pleasure in heaping on his rival and those associated with him the vilest terms of contempt and abuse. Herzen is a 'cowardly hypocrite', a '*bourgeois cocu*'. Madame Haag a 'common bawd with her knowing air of admitting nothing and, in reality, being privy to everything'. Natalie belongs by right, and by her own confession, to her lover, not to her husband. Her resumed cohabitation with the latter is an act of 'prostitution', to which Herzen has driven her by force.* The very thought of this 'prostitution' is poisoning Herwegh's life. He must punish, he must avenge.

As the instrument of his vengeance he designed, appropriately enough, his energetic and faithful wife. The return of Emma to Nice was a barbed shaft driven into Herzen's inmost soul – a living reminder that Natalie had played him false, and that he had still to reckon with a successful and vindictive rival.

The time for showing consideration is over [wrote Herwegh to Emma with the usual copious underlinings]. *You have not*, I repeat, to show consideration *for anyone* . . . Do not spare Herzen's vanity. Remain, remain in Nice, don't let them get rid of you so easily. Remain out of pride, obstinacy and revenge.

But her mute presence was not enough. More and more clearly Herwegh saw that the most effective lash for Herzen's back was 'the truth'. It maddened him that Herzen should have so readily forgiven Natalie and condoned her fault. He knew nothing of

* Herwegh's argument follows the best romantic tradition. 'What constitutes adultery,' explains George Sand's hero, Jacques, 'is not the hour which a woman gives to her lover, but the night which she afterwards spends in the arms of her husband.'

Herzen's inner torments. He did not believe in concealed sufferings; for he never made any effort to disguise his own. He drew
from Herzen's generosity the conclusion that she had not told
him all. Herzen did not know, he assured Emma, 'one third part
of the truth'. He had no idea that adultery had already begun in
Geneva two years before. He never suspected that the child
conceived in Geneva was not his own, but Herwegh's; 'otherwise
the affair would have taken quite a different turn'. Still less did
he know that his wife had written that she had never belonged to
any man save her lover, and that she had 'remained virgin' in the
embraces of her husband. The more Herwegh brooded on these
things, the more bitterly he resented the injustice which exonerated Natalie and made him the sole culprit in the affair. If he
once disclosed 'the truth' (and Natalie's three hundred letters
were there to prove his assertions up to the hilt), Herzen would be
compelled to regard Natalie as an equal partner in the guilt.
Herzen must – to be consistent – treat both alike; either he must
forgive his friend or spurn his wife. Or even if he did neither of
these things, Herwegh could still enjoy the spectacle of his torments when he realized how completely, how ignominiously
Natalie had betrayed him. Nor need the revelation stop there.
Should the whole story leak out – and there was no particular
reason why it should not – Herzen's disgrace would become public
property, and he would have to hide his head for very shame.
Herwegh had less than anyone to lose from publicity; for public
opinion was always kinder to the triumphant lover than to the
erring wife or to the deceived husband. His honour – or at any
rate his *amour propre* – would be saved. He would be able to face
the world once more.

But how was he to bring 'the truth' home to Herzen? He could
write it; but Herzen would return the letter unopened. It was
only through Emma, who was on the spot, that the blow could be
struck. Emma showed no eagerness for the part. Her only desire
was to win back her husband; and she saw nothing to be gained
by the exposure of Natalie or of Herzen. The role of 'avenging
angel', which her husband offered her, seemed uncommonly like
the role of a common informer. She had promised Herzen, at the
moment of the break, that so long as he remained silent, she would
not open her mouth; and Emma was a woman of her word. More-

over, her habitual caution would not allow her to forget the note-of-hand for 10,000 francs; and she looked forward without enthusiasm to the moment when it would be presented by an enraged and implacable enemy. Herwegh understood none of these scruples, moral or practical. His wife's reluctance seemed to him either treason or cowardice, and his insistence grows ever more strident and reproachful:

I appeal to your pride [he wrote during Herzen's journey to Freiburg] *you* are master in Nice. *You* can command, make that clear. Explain that you will not *allow* Herzen to return to Nice, and that you have in your hands the means to prevent his return; for I swear to you that as soon as Herzen returns to Nice, I come too, even if I have to come on foot . . .

All threats to shut the door in your face are ridiculous if you *want* to enter – and you can see Natalie at your feet the moment you wish. . . . Natalie must grovel on her face before you. Let these dogs feel that . . .

But Herzen returned, and Herwegh did not come; and three months later the situation is still the same.

With every weapon in your hands you *will* not do anything. . . . Until you have taken your revenge on Herzen, do not think of our meeting again. . . . If *you* put up with the insolence of a *parvenu* who sits under your very nose, and whom, with his *bourgeois* fear of being known for a *cocu*, you could drive across the ocean – *I* am determined not to put up with it any longer – From today onwards there is *no* means which I do not regard as permissible in order to repay humiliation for humiliation. I can show myself before the world, and *I will show myself*. And *he* shall get as little pleasure from his life as I do . . . I am coming, you can all be sure of that. Then I shall carry out my will, or I shall pull the house down about their ears and about my own . . . I sit here, bound fast, and gnash my teeth – while you have every weapon in your hands to extort satisfaction.

It was a situation which could not last for ever. But it lasted well into the New Year of 1852; and there is no evidence to show what motive eventually impelled Herwegh, who normally preferred words to deeds, to more decisive action. It may have been some circumstance in his life at Zürich, it may have been the rumour which reached him from Nice of another pregnancy of Natalie's, which stung him to a new paroxysm of rage and hatred.

In January 1852, when Natalie was slowly recovering from the crisis of pleurisy, Herzen found one morning on his table a letter in Herwegh's well-known hand. The envelope bore the superscription 'Affair of Honour – Challenge'; and this circumstance caused Herzen to open it. It was, according to his description, 'a disgustingly filthy letter'. It accused him of having poisoned Natalie's mind against her lover, and taken advantage of her weakness to persuade her to turn traitor to him. It contained various 'revelations' against Natalie and concluded with the words:

Fate has decided between you and me, by drowning your progeny and your family in the sea. You wished to end the affair in blood, when I still thought a humane ending possible. Now I am ready and I demand satisfaction.

The original of the letter has not been preserved. Herzen relates in *My Past and Thoughts* that he read it only once, and destroyed it eighteen months later on Natalie's birthday without re-reading it. His recollections cannot therefore have much claim to textual accuracy. But Herwegh's note-book, the same to which Natalie had confided the first outpourings of illicit love, fortunately comes to our assistance. It contains, pencilled in Herwegh's hand, minute and scarcely legible, what is evidently a rough and incomplete draft of this very letter. It sufficiently corresponds with Herzen's account to justify the conviction that it was not materially altered in its final form.

Knowing your brutal methods [runs the draft] I am communicating with you once more through *this* channel. I wish to exhaust all peaceful means – and if these fail, *I shall shrink from no scandal*. I shall be obliged to bring a third party into the dispute. Be assured that my voice will drown the voice of this child of incest and prostitution which you wish to display to the world as a triumphant proof that you are not what people say you are!* There is your greatness of soul – the solution which you seek at the price of the degradation of her whose possession you dispute with me! Yet you know from her *own mouth* that she never belonged to anyone but me, that she remained virgin in your embraces despite all her children – and she remains so still. You know how we were together at Geneva, at Nice, day after day. You have been told of this union of soul and senses, those vows which only the most unspeak-

* The last five words are inserted above the line in place of the single word *cocu* which is crossed out.

able love could transfigure and sanctify, you find her lips still hot with kisses of my whole body; you know that in the transports of her love she conceived a child by me at Geneva; and I shall never believe that you did not even then suspect, like everybody else – you are not so much deceived as you pretend. You know – but you do not under-stand – that she was unhappily compelled to accept another child by you, that she begged my forgiveness for it, that I forgave her, that my friendship for you was then almost as great as my love, that I could not see you suffer, that we took Emma into our confidence, but begged her on bended knees to sacrifice herself in silence. She saw our love; she saw our affection for you; and she was willing that she alone should be unhappy. But you only know how to *insult* women when, by every kind of falsehood, hypocrisy and manœuvre, you have succeeded in driving away the men. You know that the object in life of Natalie and myself was to repair the unfortunate accident at Geneva, that she dreamed and thought only of getting a child by me, that our whole future lay in that hope, that when she spoke to you she thought she had succeeded; perhaps you do not know that I only remained in the neighbourhood because she had sworn that she meant to escape.

Enough! You will not continue this prostitution of a being whom I did not steal from you, but whom I took because she told me that you had never possessed her; at any rate, I shall not survive it if you do. To your gratuitous insults to Emma you have added the infamy of pretending that I seduced your wife. There are enough wrongs to justify me in demanding satisfaction.

This new child must be baptized in the blood of one of us. The other was baptized very differently. *Tempora mutantur.* I await your orders, I make a last appeal to your honour to select the weapons which you prefer. Let us tear each other's throats like wild beasts – since we are to be no longer men – and show for once (if you have it) something else besides your purse. Ruin for ruin! Enough of cool deliberation –

The draft breaks off here. The reference to fate and the drowning of Herzen's mother and son does not occur in it, and must – for Herzen can scarcely have invented it – have been a brilliant after-thought.

Herzen sprang up from the reading of this letter 'like a wounded beast' in fury. He felt that he had never known before what it was to be insulted. Any hope that he would preserve sufficient dignity and composure to ignore it was destroyed by the discovery that the arrival of the letter was already an open secret in Nice. Herwegh had written to Emma that he was sending a 'terrible letter', which would 'throw Herzen down from the pedestal on which Natalie had placed him' and 'cover them with shame'. Emma had told Orsini, Karl Vogt and Chojecki; and Vogt had told Engelson. Herzen developed a feverish and untimely energy. He commissioned Engelson to write a letter to Herwegh denying the right of the latter to issue a challenge, 'and still more to select for the duel a moment when – as you were probably aware – his wife is seriously ill'. He wrote to Sazonov – a strange choice – begging him to be his second if the duel took place. Finally, as the result of a talk with Orsini, he wrote to the Italian revolutionary leader Mazzini (who, like everyone else, had now been initiated into the affair) begging him to constitute a 'court of honour' to judge between him and Herwegh. The 'court of honour' was a recent invention and a favourite hobby of the day. Their principles precluded these romantic idealists from submitting their differences to the established courts; and from whom could one expect justice, and a sense of revolutionary values, if not from a jury of revolutionaries themselves? The idea was naïve. But it was not more naïve than the fashionable prejudice in favour of the duel as an instrument of justice. It persisted as the revolutionary counterpart of the duel; and even twenty years later we find serious revolutionaries like Bakunin and Liebknecht still appealing to 'courts of honour' for the settlement of their disputes.

Herwegh's immediate object had been attained. It was no longer possible to ignore him and hostilities were resumed in their most virulent form. Even Natalie on her sick-bed was made to play her part. Emma wrote her an appeal – which might have been moving, had not its effect been spoiled in advance by Herwegh's letter – to take upon herself her fair share of the burden of guilt.

It is impossible [wrote Emma] that . . . instead of throwing yourself at the feet of your injured husband and not rising until you had obtained his pardon for *both* of you – it is impossible that you should not realize what solution you are offering in return for so many sacrifices, so many torments, so many miseries. In order to avoid a terrible scandal which will bring disgrace on both families, you need only the courage to take a firm, frank, humane decision, to accept sincerely your part of the burden which up to the present weighs on the shoulders of *one man alone, and which cannot be lifted from your shoulders without being lifted at the same time from his.*

There was now no humiliation which Natalie would not welcome in order to vindicate her husband's honour. At his instigation she wrote to Herwegh a letter in which she referred to the 'treacherous, base and Jewish character' of her former lover and declared that her 'unhappy infatuation had served only as a pedestal on which to raise still higher her love for Alexander'.

You have tried [she went on] to cover this pedestal with mud, but you will never shake our union, which is now indissoluble and more unassailable than ever. Your base calumnies and denunciations of a woman have only inspired my noble husband with contempt and disgust for you; you have dishonoured yourself completely by this cowardly act. . . . You have made even the past hateful to me.

It is difficult for posterity to share the admiration expressed by Herzen for this letter, a copy of which he proudly preserved in his archives and reproduces at length in *My Past and Thoughts*. Except perhaps for the last phrase, it contains scarcely a word of the authentic Natalie, and reflects in every line the inspiration of Herzen's masterful pen. But copies of it were shown in triumph to intimate friends; and Natalie's repentance and her devotion to her husband became the *mot d'ordre* in the Herzen circle.

It appears to be known to everyone [wrote Emma sarcastically to her husband] that she was guilty, that she was caught in a spell, but that she is now ready to let anyone spit on her, and prefers to follow her husband like a dog.

Nobody paused to analyse Natalie's feelings. Perhaps even now the worst humiliation was not the public discussion of her guilt, but the treachery of her lover.

Herwegh read her letter without undue emotion. Poor Natalie had become, on both sides, a mere pawn in the game of vengeance and mutual hatred. He scribbled a few words 'intended to express', as he told his wife, 'that the letter must have reached him by mistake'. Then another idea struck him. Herzen had humiliated him by returning his letters unread. He would repay the insult by returning Natalie's letter. He carefully replaced the seals and readdressed it to the sender. But by a curious stroke of naïvety he had inserted in the envelope his own scribbled reply, thereby affording his enemies proof that he had in fact broken the seals and read the letter which he professed to return intact; and this

99

was hailed, when it was discovered some months later, as a fresh proof of his amazing duplicity. Meanwhile he commented caustically to Emma on the tumult of indignation excited by his 'challenge'.

If what I *wrote is filth*, the *reality* was doubly filthy. If the *words* in which I revealed *the truth* were dirty, the deeds were doubly so, and Alexander is doubly a coward and a knave not to demand a reckoning from me, and to continue to live this life of filth with his alleged wife.

Recriminations about the duel continued in a style more suggestive of Bob Acres than of any serious intention to shoot. In fact, neither side meant to fight; but each was profoundly convinced of the other's cowardice, and intensely eager to demonstrate it. Engelson's first evasive answer to the 'challenge' gave Herwegh the chance of denouncing Herzen to all and sundry as a poltroon. But Herzen perhaps neither knew nor cared; and three weeks later Engelson wrote again on his behalf definitely declining the proffered duel. By an unfortunate miscalculation (he learned of its contents, through the usual channels, too late) Herwegh returned this letter unopened; and Herzen and his friends were able to pretend that, by refusing to receive a letter from Herzen's accredited agent, Herwegh had clearly betrayed his lack of stomach for the fight. Then Herwegh wrote to his wife that what he would like best of all was a duel without witnesses; for he was sure that, once alone together, he and Herzen would fall on each other's necks in an ecstasy of mutual forgiveness. Emma retailed this tit-bit to Vogt, and Vogt to Engelson, and Engelson to Herzen; and it was once more proclaimed that Herwegh had proved that he was not in earnest, and that this absurd travesty of a duel had been from the first the object of the challenge. From time to time, in his letters to Emma, Herwegh dropped hints (which terrified the unhappy woman) of 'crime' and 'the galleys'.

I see nothing before me [he wrote once] but madness, crime, debauch, degradation; and at long last you will be compelled to regret that you ever loved me.

Engelson asked Herzen's permission to go to Zürich and kill Herwegh; and Herzen, having magnanimously refused it, inquired pensively why his friend had been so weak-minded as to ask him first. In fact, not one of these professed desperadoes had any intention of taking life or of risking his own. Herzen and Herwegh were not medieval swashbucklers or courtiers of the *Roi Soleil*, but nineteenth-century men of letters. Their weapon was not the sword or the pistol, but the pen; and if for the moment Herwegh outstripped Herzen in the vigour and virulence of his language, it was Herzen who, in *My Past and Thoughts*, ultimately redressed the balance and dealt the shrewdest and most penetrating thrusts at his rival's reputation.

But these things were fast passing – perhaps they had already passed – beyond Natalie's ken. Her power to suffer was almost gone. When her letter to Herwegh came back, a conference was held at her bedside. Among Herzen's new allies was one Haug, a former Austrian officer who had gone over to Garibaldi in 1848 and become a General of the short-lived Roman Republic. His career constituted his credentials as a fire-eater; and when Natalie spoke of her anxiety 'to justify Alexander', he swore loudly that he would not rest until he had read her letter to Herwegh and compelled him to listen. This heroic promise afforded consolation to Herzen, if not to Natalie, and was loudly applauded. In the meanwhile Engelson set the pace by writing to Herwegh a long and abusive letter, a copy of which was added by Herzen to the archives of the affair.

It can only be pleaded in extenuation of these proceedings that, when they took place, Natalie was convalescent from pleurisy and Herzen had no reason to think that she was a dying woman. Throughout the month of March her recovery went on slowly; and it was during this brief respite that she dictated to Herzen her last fond letter to Natalie Tuchkov, whose love had filled her life four years ago.

I am still in bed [she wrote]. I am not strong enough to get up and walk, but my soul teems with life and fullness – I cannot be silent. After sufferings which, perhaps, you cannot measure, I am living through moments full of blessedness; all the hopes of youth, of childhood have not only been realized, but have passed through terrible, unimaginable sufferings without losing their freshness or their fragrance, and have blossomed in new strength and splendour. *I have never been so happy as now. . . .*

How slowly my strength returns! July is not far away, shall I live to see it? Oh, I should like to live, for his sake, for my own; of the children I do not speak. To live for him, in order to heal all the wounds I have dealt him, to live for myself because I have learned to *know* his love for me, and am happy in it as never before . . .

But Natalie's gloomier premonitions were fulfilled. Towards the end of March, a chill brought on a relapse; and fever became an almost continuous symptom. The now advanced stage of her pregnancy increased the danger. For days and weeks, there was no change; and the hopes of Herzen and the doctors ebbed cruelly away. In the middle of April Natalie sent to Paris for Maria Reichel – the only friend to whom, in the absence of Natalie Tuchkov, she would willingly entrust her children.

She knew now that she was dying. She had still one more account with life to close. On 26 April, making a supreme effort, she took her pen and wrote to Herwegh in a clear, steady hand:

' – a sign of life' – and to what purpose? Always *to justify you* by covering myself with reproaches, by accusing myself. Be at ease, though you have desire enough and means enough to succeed in that without my help – be at ease; if ever I speak before anyone who is able to understand (otherwise I shall not speak, otherwise it would be the greatest profanation of what is most sacred to me), it will not be *to justify myself.*

– Have you hurt me? You ought to know that better than I – I only know that my blessings will follow you everywhere, always.

To say more – would be superfluous.

Herzen was not told of this letter. That too would have been superfluous. He would not have been 'able to understand'.

There was indeed no more to be said. On 29 April Maria Reichel arrived from Paris; and later in the day a boy was born, nearly two months before its time. It was already known in the town that there was no hope. The same night Emma, having asked in vain for admission, sent by Orsini the following note:

Natalie! Pardon for everything and for *all*, and *then* let everything be forgotten. I take your hand with all my heart. Adieu!

EMMA HERWEGH

The words were read by Herzen at the bedside. Natalie smiled; but Herzen, still hard and unforgiving, thought he saw a glint of irony in the smile. It is unlikely that Natalie, innocent of irony all her life, should have acquired it at the moment of her death-agony.

The delivery of the child had taken her last remaining strength. She lived on, exhausted and intermittently conscious, for three days. The baby died; but she did not know. She spoke much of the children, and expressed a wish to live until there was time for Natalie Tuchkov to come and take them from her. She called for light, though candles were burning by the bed. Then she became completely unconscious; and on the morning of 2 May she died – child and victim of the romantic age which she had never out-grown.

*

Natalie had been dead for nearly two months when 'General' Haug set out, in accordance with his promise, on the campaign to compel Herwegh to listen to the letter he had refused to receive. Herwegh's position in Zürich was by now an unenviable one. Ever since the revolution of 1848, the subsidies received from the parents of his wife had been sufficient to maintain only a bare existence, not a life worthy of a hero and a poet. Now, since the Herzen scandal and Herwegh's overt separation from his wife, the Siegmund family not only refused to have any further dealings with him, but took steps to ensure that the meagre charity doled out to Emma in Nice should not find its way to Zürich. Emma would have sacrificed herself – and perhaps her children – to her erring but still adored husband. Her devotion, if not her respect, survived even the piteous appeals for money which found a prominent place in every letter he wrote to her. But Emma could not perform the impossible; and these appeals went unanswered, or answered only to an extent which made no perceptible impression on Herwegh's spacious requirements.

The *impasse* was complete, and Herwegh drew the necessary conclusion.

I cannot resist the demoralizing influence of poverty [he wrote to Emma with engaging candour], and this is not the time for an *honest* man to earn money.

He accepted the consoling ministrations of a lady living with her aged mother in the same hotel. The situation was frankly equivocal. The news spread to Nice that Herwegh, once the idol and the spoilt child of German democracy, was being kept in Zürich by *une vieille putain*, an ex-mistress of Louis Bonaparte; and the story in this form was eagerly snapped up by Herzen and his allies. The reply of Herwegh, when his wife questioned him, put a somewhat different complexion on the affair. He assured her that the lady in the case, who was nearly fifty and had a married daughter, was actuated by motives of the purest compassion; and he denied that she had ever been Napoleon's mistress, though she had sometimes been his hostess when, more than twenty years before, he had undergone the rigours of military training in the vicinity of the little Swiss town of Thun. The lady's identity remains unrevealed; and the nature of the entertainment accorded by her to the young Louis Bonaparte may be allowed to remain in the same obscurity which envelops her relations with Herwegh. But the scandal was none the less glaring.

> The individual at Zürich [Vogt wrote graphically to Herzen] has so fallen into general contempt that the very dogs would be ashamed to use his leg as a post.

Orsini begged Emma to forget 'that brigand George' and assured her that 'his actions proved him the biggest scoundrel in the world'; Vogt counselled her to return to her parents in Germany, where her husband could not pursue her; and Charles Edmond the Pole invited her to divorce Herwegh and marry him. Emma reasoned with Orsini, quarrelled with Vogt, and indignantly forbade Edmond to darken her door again. This remarkable woman who by infinite patience, toleration and self-effacement eventually brought her husband back to her, deserves – for all her faults – more than the cold contempt which Herzen pours on her in *My Past and Thoughts*.

It was in these conditions that 'General' Haug arrived at Zürich on 10 July in the company of a Frenchman named Tessier. The pair, seizing their opportunity, burst unannounced into Herwegh's room at the hotel. Ordering Herwegh to sit down and listen, Haug tore open Natalie's letter. It had remained in exactly the state in which it was returned to her. As Tessier began to read it solemnly aloud, there fluttered out from the envelope the note in Herwegh's hand – the proof that he had in fact opened and read the letter before returning it. Haug threw the note in Herwegh's face and called him a blackguard. Herwegh pulled the bellrope and rushed into the corridor shouting 'Murder! Police!' The doughty General, nothing daunted, pursued him and, with the words 'Take that for your police!' smacked him across the face. He then handed Herwegh the visiting-cards of himself and his companion, apologized for the disturbance to the manager of the hotel, and stalked away. Natalie had been avenged. Herwegh had visions of assaults on his life by Herzen's 'Cossack and Polak mercenaries';* and Emma wrote to her husband's unknown patroness begging her to make sure that 'his friends did not leave him alone for a single moment'.

Meanwhile, Herzen could not bear to remain on the scene of so many tragedies. He had left Nice early in June, and spent the next two months wandering aimlessly from place to place in northern Italy and Switzerland. But he found no rest from the torturing memories which obsessed him. Vengeance on Herwegh assumed in his disordered mind the dimensions of a crusade. He penned an appeal *To My Brother-Democrats* in which he explained his refusal to meet Herwegh in a duel, and asked that 'justice might be done on him without prosecutor or gendarmes, in the name of the solidarity of peoples, and the autonomy of the individual'; and a number of his friends, arrogating to themselves the label of 'brother-democrats', issued a 'verdict' declaring that Herwegh had 'forfeited his honour' and that a duel between Herzen and such a man was 'impossible'. Meanwhile an account of the incident at Zürich, evidently furnished by Haug, appeared in the Italian press, whence it was reproduced in the *Neue Zürcher Zeitung* and in the local newspaper at Nice.

The ball which Herzen and his lieutenant had thus set rolling went merrily on. Emma published in *L'Avenir de Nice* a dignified protest against 'the attempt to impart a political character to the attack made on my husband in Switzerland', and explained that the question at issue was 'a fact of an essentially private character arising exclusively from a conflict of passions and far removed from the sphere of politics and of publicity'. Herwegh himself, in

---

* The 'Cossack' was Engelson, the 'Polak' Chojecki. For the modern German, as for the Elizabethan Englishman (cf. *Hamlet*, Act II, Sc. 2) 'Polak' is a contemptuous synonym for 'Pole'.

the *Neue Zürcher Zeitung*, more pungently declared that his two assailants ought to have been dealt with by the health authorities and removed to the madhouse, and that the whole affair had been engineered with 'Russian subsidies'.

This gave the other side too good an opening to be missed. Tessier took a hand, and vindicated his sanity by describing the scene at the hotel in its minutest and most humiliating details; and Herzen published, also in the *Neue Zürcher Zeitung*, a short declaration that 'nobody had ever been "subsidized" by him, except his domestic servants and *George Herwegh himself*, who was even now in possession of a sum of 10,000 francs lent to him without interest two years ago'. Ten days later, there appeared another rambling statement by Herwegh who referred to 'Russian brutality', reviewed at length his relations with 'Baron Herzen' (the title being enough to discredit any democrat) and, recurring to the Zürich affair, declared that, far from having been smacked in the face, he had pushed the intruders roughly downstairs in the presence of a jeering chambermaid.

The Herzen–Herwegh quarrel was rapidly growing from the dimensions of a local scandal into those of a European *cause célèbre*. Herzen wrote long explanations of his conduct, coupled with denunciations of his rival, to such casual acquaintances as Proudhon and Michelet. He sent a letter to a German friend named Müller-Strübing, at this time living with George Sand at Nohant, and begged him to communicate it to 'the highest authority on all that pertains to woman'.

She ought to know this story [he wrote] she who resumes in her person the revolutionary conception of woman.

Rumours of the story even reached London; and Karl Marx, who seldom minced his words, reported to the faithful Engels in Manchester that Herwegh had 'not only put horns on Herzen's head, but milked him of 80,000 francs'. Other complete strangers became involved. Richard Wagner, the composer, who, having played an ignominious part in the Dresden insurrection of 1849, might claim to rank as a 'brother democrat', was approached by Haug with the story of Herwegh's iniquity. Wagner, being at this time on terms of friendship with Herwegh and being about to spend a summer holiday with him in Italian Switzerland, was cautious and evasive. 'While frankly admitting Herwegh's weaknesses and the degeneration of his character under social influences to which, at an earlier period of his life, he had fortunately been a stranger', he knew nothing of the present dispute and had no inclination to pass judgement on it. Polite neutrality gave no satisfaction to Herzen's new fanaticism; and he addressed to Wagner a long and detailed reply pulverizing the character and conduct of his rival.

In Switzerland, in France, in Italy [the letter concluded], he shall never find rest. I swear it, and my friends swear it; and every day brings us fresh proofs that we are supported by all the champions of militant revolution.

Sheer weariness, or a surviving vestige of common sense, delivered Herzen at last from this numbing and degrading obsession. His hope lay in the possibility of beginning a new life in a new country. He had often thought of America; but now, more or less at random, he chose England. Leaving his daughters with the Reichels in Paris, he took Sasha with him and reached London on 25 August. A few days later he looked for the first time from the fourth storey of Morley's Hotel in Trafalgar Square, on the phenomenon of a London fog.*

* Herzen, who was nothing if not a stylist, must take the responsibility for this touch of local colour. A search of the file of *The Times* reveals no trace of so unusual a portent as a 'London fog' in August or September.

CHAPTER 5

The Engelsons

THE figure of Engelson, which has flitted across the dark pages of Herzen's tragedy, is sufficiently curious and characteristic to merit a half-length portrait.

In the thirties and forties of last century a Finn of Swedish extraction, Arist Engelson by name, rose to an important position in the financial administration at Petersburg. He acquired not only dignity but riches. He bought a house in the capital and an estate of nearly 'eight hundred souls' in the country, married a Russian wife and became thoroughly Russian. He brought up his children in the Orthodox faith (he himself was a Lutheran), and christened his eldest son by the old Russian name of Vladimir.

Vladimir Engelson was an intelligent young man. Being the son of a wealthy and indulgent father, he felt neither the necessity nor the inclination to choose a career. He completed in leisurely fashion his studies in philology at the University of Petersburg, and cast about for an agreeable method of passing his time. His pursuit of this objective was at first so unpromising that he decided (it seems to have happened in the winter of 1843-4, when he was in his twenty-third year) to cut the Gordian knot by committing suicide. He selected poison as the most genteel instrument of death; and entering a fashionable café to meditate on his resolve, he picked up a number of a popular radical periodical, *Notes on the Fatherland*. His eyes rested on an article of Herzen's entitled 'Apropos of a Play'. It took the form of a *critique* of a play by two forgotten French dramatists, Arnould and Fournier; and its moral was that, both in love and in the other relationships of life, self-tormenting introspection, instead of being the token of an exalted and sensitive soul, is an offence against 'reality'. Engelson began to read carelessly, then the eloquent phrases of the critic absorbed his attention, and he went on eagerly to the end. Abandoning the thought of poison, he ordered half a bottle of Madeira and read the article right through a second time.* By the time he had finished, his taste for suicide had evaporated; and thereafter, with touching inconsistency, he secretly worshipped Herzen as the preserver of a life for which he could find no use.

The following summer suggested a different cure for his romantic *ennui*. He and a comrade named Speshnev applied for foreign passports for the purpose of visiting Germany, the home of philosophy. It seemed an innocent form of recreation. But Nicholas I liked to pose as the father of his people; and received the young men's application with a paternal shrug of the shoulders.

It is possible [ran the Imperial fiat] to take a course at the university here; and for young men of their age to go roving about the world instead of entering the service is discreditable and unworthy of their rank. But for all that, they may do as they please.

The gracious decision of the Tsar was read personally to the two young men by Count Orlov, the head of the political police. Speshnev, who showed in later life that he possessed unusual determination, stuck to his intention, and received his passport. Engelson, on the other hand, seldom saw any strong reason for preferring one course of action to another; and he allowed himself to be deterred from foreign travel by Nicholas as easily as he had been deterred by Herzen from suicide. He declared his readiness to enter the Imperial service; and at the beginning of 1845 a post was found for him in the Ministry for Foreign Affairs.

The next stage in Engelson's career remains somewhat obscure. In the Petersburg of the forties – one of the most oppressive periods

* The story was related to Herzen by Engelson and appears in a well-known chapter of *My Past and Thoughts*. Herzen places it after the Petrashevsky affair, i.e. in 1849 or 1850. But the critic cannot fail to remark that the article which figures in the story appeared in the issue of *Notes of the Fatherland* for August 1843; and unless we assume that the copy which Engelson found in the café was more than six years old, we are compelled to transfer the story to an earlier stage of his career. Exact chronology was never a strong point with Herzen. Indeed the whole story, told by an excellent raconteur, and recorded for posterity by a first-rate *littérateur*, may perhaps be described as second cousin to the truth.

even in the history of Russian Tsardom – every intelligent youth secretly nursed radical opinions and ambitions; and Engelson, with his quick wit and pliant will, could not escape the prevailing mood. But his customary state of indecision was not affected by his political convictions; and the next landmark in his career was the return to Petersburg, after two years' absence, of his friend Speshnev. His political views developed and matured by his sojourn in Europe, Speshnev now joined the set of radical young men which centred round the person of Petrashevsky. And he carried with him, as a sympathizer if not an actual member of the group, his friend and satellite Engelson.

The attention of Nicholas was soon drawn to the activities – if such they can be called, for they began and ended in talk – of this nest of potential revolutionaries. Recent events in Europe had made him nervous; and in April 1849 the followers of Petrashevsky were arrested and consigned to the Peter-and-Paul fortress. Among them were Speshnev and the novelist Dostoevsky, who both suffered transportation to Siberia for their participation in the alleged conspiracy. It is uncertain how far Engelson had been personally involved. But his association with Speshnev would have sufficed to render him suspect; and in August he too was placed under arrest. The affair passed off without serious consequences for Engelson, whom even the Tsarist police could scarcely have taken for a revolutionary. He was released without being brought to trial. But his official career was at an end; and he was once more face to face with the elementary problem: what to do with his life.

He solved it by engaging in a matrimonial adventure. He fell in love with a woman who was, like himself, of Scandinavian origin and, like himself, had been brought up in Russia. She had married at eighteen an elderly official, and had quickly divorced her husband. When Engelson first met her, she was engaged in an unhappy love affair with a young officer whose passions were divided between his mistress and the gaming-table. The young officer committed suicide; and Engelson presented himself in the opportune role of consoler.

The consolations he administered were at first purely spiritual; but they were of a disturbing kind. The lady, however eventful and restless her life, had hitherto never swerved from the narrow unreflecting path of religious and political orthodoxy in which she had been brought up. She was 'mildly Christian, mildly romantic, mildly moral and patriarchal'. Under Engelson's tuition, she strayed along the dangerous avenues of philosophical and political speculation. She too wanted to become 'a free woman like George Sand's heroines'. She studied Hegel, Feuerbach and Fourier, and became an ardent materialist and socialist. The new faith broadened her outlook, but destroyed for ever her mental equilibrium. Her character, when Herzen met her, was 'like an untidy room in which everything is strewn about at random: children's toys, a wedding-dress, a prayer-book, a novel of George Sand, slippers, flowers and crockery'. She became hopelessly hypochondriacal, and, like all Russian hypochondriacs, she convinced herself that the one cure for her distressed nerves was a journey abroad.

It was, in the middle of last century, neither safe nor seemly for a young widow to travel alone about Europe. In the absence of a more legitimate protector, Engelson once more appeared in the role of *deus ex machina*. Hitherto the object of his affections had accepted him as a mentor, but rejected him as a lover; and Engelson was too delicate or too indolent to press an unwelcome suit. He now proposed marriage and offered to accompany her abroad; but he gave her to understand that he would not embarrass her by claiming any of the rights of a husband. He too would like to travel; and the duties of a *cavalier servant* would give his life the purpose and occupation which it had hitherto lacked. The fair Alexandra (for this was her name) was touched by the proposal; and in accepting it, she decided that she could not decently share Engelson's name and passport without sharing his bed. The marriage was not only celebrated but consummated; and husband and wife set out in the autumn of 1850 for Nice. Here they fell in with Herzen, the object, for the past seven years, of Engelson's secret cult.

The character of Engelson serves Herzen as the text for a famous and brilliant diagnosis of the malady of the Russian intellectual in the later years of Nicholas I – a diagnosis which will strike the reader by its appositeness not only to Engelson, but to Dostoevsky and, particularly in its later passages, to Herzen himself.

A terrible crime must be laid at the door of the régime of Nicholas – moral abortion and the killing of the souls of the young . . .The whole system of public education was reduced to the preaching of a religion of blind obedience, leading to official position as the natural reward. The naturally expansive feelings of youth were roughly driven inwards, and were replaced by ambition and by jealous, spiteful rivalry. Those who did not perish emerged sick in mind and soul. Rampant vanity was combined with a sort of hopelessness, a consciousness of impotence, a weary disinclination for work. Young people became hypochondriacal, suspicious, worn-out before they had reached the age of twenty. They were all infected with the passion for self-observation, self-examination, self-accusation; they carefully studied their own psychological symptoms, and loved endless discussions and stories about their own nervous case-history. In after years, I often had on my hands both men and women belonging to this category. When I looked sympathetically into their confessions, into their psychological self-castigation (which was often a slander on themselves), I came at last to the conclusion that all this was only a form of vanity. Instead of protesting and sympathizing, you had only to take the penitent at his word in order to convince yourself how easily antagonized and how mercilessly resentful are these Magdalenes of both sexes. You are expected to behave to them as a Christian priest behaves to the mighty ones of the earth: you have only the right solemnly to absolve them from their sins and say no more . . .

Their repentances were sincere, but did not preclude repetition of the sin. They had broken the spring which moderates and controls the movements of the wheels; the wheels revolve with ten-fold rapidity, but produce nothing and merely smash the machine. Harmonious coordination is destroyed, the aesthetic measure lost. You cannot live with them, and they cannot live with their own character.

No happiness could exist for them; they did not know how to retain it. On the slightest pretext they reacted inhumanly and dealt brutally with their neighbour. Their irony has been just as ruinous and destructive as pompous German sentimentality. The strange thing is that these people are passionately anxious to be loved; they seek enjoyment, and then, as they lift the cup to their lips, an evil spirit jogs their hand, the wine is spilled on the ground, and the cup, impetuously flung away, rolls in the mud.

Alexandra Engelson was a less typical and more complicated character. Her unfortunate first marriage and still more unfortunate love-affair had sapped the foundations of her self-esteem. The teaching of Engelson had destroyed the simple conventional faith which might have kept her on an even keel; and she was now married to a man for whom she felt affection but not passion, and pity but not respect. His moods of morose introspection, his lack of any consistent taste or occupation, his fits of irresponsible boyish levity, his drinking bouts and his spasms of abject self-reproach – everything about Engelson was sure, sooner or later, to produce an explosion of nervous irritation in his wife. At such times she felt equally disgusted with him and with herself; and the consequence of this common disgust was merely to create between them a new bond of morbid sympathy. By a tragic paradox, the ties which united them were strengthened and intensified by those recurrent emotional storms. The more frequent these mental torments and insults, the more necessary did each become to the other's existence.

The psychological contortions of this strange *ménage* provided Herzen with a new experience.

I often used to find them [he relates], in the big room in the hotel which served them as both bedroom and sitting-room, in a state of complete prostration. She would be in one corner, exhausted, with tear-stained eyes, he in another corner, pale as a corpse, with white lips, distracted and silent. They sat like that sometimes for whole hours, whole days, a few paces away from the blue Mediterranean and the orange groves, where nature was calling – the azure sky and the bright, noisy gaiety of southern life. They did not exactly quarrel; there was no jealousy, or estrangement, or, in general, any tangible cause. He would suddenly get up, approach her and falling on his knees, sometimes with sobs, would repeat: 'I have ruined you, my child, ruined you.' And she cried and believed that he had ruined her . . .

It struck me at times that, by constantly inflaming their wounds, they found a sort of burning voluptuousness in the pain, and that this mutual devouring of each other had become a necessity to them, like vodka or pickles. But unfortunately their constitution was obviously beginning to break down, and they were well on their way to the madhouse or the grave.

It was not possible for Herzen to remain a mere spectator; for both parties in turn, with the natural instinct of the weak, applied to him for sympathy, judgement and mediation. For a time the Engelsons travelled in Italy; but their united misery defied all changes of scene and climate and they returned to Herzen at Nice for fresh advice. Herzen rashly prescribed a temporary separation. Both expressed hearty agreement. But they did not follow his advice (it would have required a strength of will that neither of them possessed); and Madame Engelson at any rate never forgave him for it. The friendship continued. In the tragic years of Herzen's life, Engelson became his confidant and, in moments of depression, his boon-companion. He acted as Herzen's principal lieutenant in the last unseemly exchanges of vituperation with Herwegh; and when Natalie died he appeared, on behalf of his wife, with the proposal that the care of the orphaned children should be entrusted to her. A curious dialogue ensued.

I answered [relates Herzen] that my children, except the boy, would go to Paris, and that I must frankly confess that I could not accept his offer.

My answer hurt him; and I was sorry that he should be hurt.

'Tell me,' I said 'hand on heart: Do you think your wife is capable of bringing up children?'

'No,' answered Engelson; 'but . . . but perhaps this would be a *planche de salut* for her. She really does suffer, and she always has suffered; and this would bring her a new confidence and new duties.'

'Well, and suppose the experiment does not succeed?'

'You are right. We will talk no more of it. But it is so difficult.'

Engelson, who could never conceal anything, repeated the conversation to his wife; and it was a sore which rankled and still further inflamed her resentment against the friend and 'saviour' of her husband.

The Engelsons went back to Italy. Herzen moved to London and for some months lost sight of them. Engelson became interested in aerostatics and the theory of balloon construction. His wife, feeling the need of some spiritual stimulant, took to spirit-rapping.* She could, as Herzen remarks, turn not only tables, but her husband, round her little finger; and she gradually succeeded in inspiring him with the full force of her own hatred of Herzen. In the months which followed Natalie's death, Herzen was as nerve-racked and as irresponsible as Engelson himself; and the two men quarrelled by correspondence, with the shallow, brutal vindictiveness of schoolboys. Herzen harked back gratuitously

* There are several references in Herzen's correspondence to the rage for 'table-turning' which overtook European society in the fifties. It was for him 'a certain token of the depths to which contemporary Europe has sunk'.

enough to the proposal that Madame Engelson should take charge of his children and to her resentment at its rejection by him. 'We know,' he remarked bitterly and, as he presumably supposed, wittily, 'that Saturn *ate* his children; but I have never heard of anyone surrendering his children to his friends by way of gratitude for sympathy received.' Engelson was not to be outdone. Irrelevantly, but with that tiny grain of truth which constitutes the worst of calumnies, he rejoined that Herzen always liked to 'play a part', and that this had been clearly visible in his behaviour over his domestic tragedy. 'Man loves an effective role, particularly a tragic one,' he quoted from one of Herzen's own writings; and, with a sort of ingenious superfluity of malice, he added that he had compared the German and Russian texts of the passage in question (which had originally appeared in German) and that they exactly tallied.

For a year or more, relations between Herzen and Engelson ceased altogether. Then political differences came to reinforce personal animosities. The Crimean War broke out in March 1854. Herzen felt that, in this clash of empires and kingdoms, the true democrat could only remain neutral. Engelson, in common with many other *émigrés* (especially the Poles), thought that Napoleon III was a good enough stick with which to belabour Nicholas I. He offered the fruits of his aerostatic investigations to the French Government. He wrote a number of pamphlets in Russian against the Russian Government and, transferring his residence to London, had them printed at Herzen's Russian press. In July he addressed to the French Ministry of War the following letter, a copy of which he forwarded to Herzen:

YOUR EXCELLENCY,

On 23 May I ventured to address to his Imperial Majesty a letter in which I sketched a plan for the utilization of balloons (aerostats) to assist the artillery. I had the honour to receive an acknowledgement dated 26 June from the Commission of Petitions of the State Council, under no. 10039, bearing the signature of the secretary of the Commission, in which it is stated that my petition to the Emperor has been transmitted to Your Excellency and that *any further petitions or communications on this subject* should be addressed to you, Monsieur le Ministre.

Concluding from the above that my plan has not been finally rejected, I permit myself to address to you the following request:

In the above-mentioned letter to his Majesty I mentioned that the aerostatical apparatus might also serve for the distribution in the central governments of Russia of pamphlets which would explain to the Russian people, who have been deluded by the manifestos of their government, the true causes of the present war.

If the French Government desired, for 'the triumph of the cause of law and civilization' in the war against Russia, to make use of such pamphlets, I propose to prepare as many pamphlets in the Russian language as may be required, of the same character as that which I have the honour to enclose, in a French translation, for Your Excellency's information.

Being the author of the enclosed pamphet, I undertake to supply to the French Government such number of copies as it may require from me, at exactly the cost price to me of the paper and the re-printing. I say 're-printing' as the first edition is already exhausted.

These articles which have been written to counteract the manifestos of the Tsar to the Russian people, could, it seems to me, be distributed through the agency of the aerostatical apparatus described in my above-mentioned letter to his Imperial Majesty, either by placing them in damp-proof tubes or by making the sheets of paper on which they are printed damp-proof.

I base my hopes in this propaganda by pamphlets on the impression which will be produced on a superstitious people like the Russian people by the spectacle of the dropping of the pamphlets from a balloon floating in the air.

Be so good, Monsieur le Ministre, when reading this letter and the enclosed translation, as not to form an impression unfavourable to my ideas from the faults of style which are necessarily found in my writings owing to the fact that I did not enjoy the good fortune to be born in France and have had no time to find anyone to correct them. On the other hand, I venture to guarantee the purity of the Russian *popular* style in which my articles are written.

In the hope that I may be honoured with some answer from you, I have the honour to be, Monsieur le Ministre,

Your Excellency's
Obedient humble servant
VLADIMIR ENGELSON

The brilliant and original project of feeding the enemy population with propaganda from the air appealed neither to Herzen nor to the French authorities; and its adoption was deferred for some sixty years. The cool reception accorded to his ambitious designs embittered Engelson; but Madame Engelson derived consolation from the spirits, who predicted Herzen's early demise. Further consolation was provided by the birth of a child; and the strange pair found new bonds of union in their common devotion to the infant and their common enmity for Herzen.

The family finances were far from brilliant; and it was galling when Engelson found himself obliged to balance the family budget by accepting an offer to give lessons to the Herzen children at four shillings an hour, which was subsequently increased to the philanthropic rate of eight shillings an hour. Such a situation could hardly fail, among such people, to breed a poisonous and fatal sensitiveness. Herzen made fun of their anxiety when they sent for the doctor three times because the child had a cold. 'Is it because we are poor,' rejoined Madame Engelson, 'that our baby must die without medical assistance? And is it you who say this, you, a socialist, a friend of my husband, who refused to lend him fifty pounds and are exploiting him with your lessons?'

The lessons continued a few weeks longer. Then one day Engelson appeared at the house in Herzen's absence, shouted at the astonished children and their governess that Herzen had called him a coward, and produced a loaded revolver with which he intended to shoot him on his return. He was pacified and induced to return home. Next day the incident had already been forgotten. He merely wrote to Herzen saying that he was indisposed, and asking that the children might come to him for their lessons instead of his going to them.

This happened in May 1855, and brought to an end the strange story of Herzen's relations with the Engelsons. They drifted away to Jersey; and there soon afterwards Engelson died at the age of thirty-four or thirty-five. A life-long victim of the fashionable romantic malady *le spleen*, his grave should have borne the epitaph designed for another romantic hero – the quotation from *Obermann* placed by Sainte-Beuve at the head of *Le Vie de Joseph Delorme*:

He met no striking misfortunes. But he found himself, when he entered life, on a long trail of disillusionment and disgust. There he remained, there he lived, there he grew old before his time, and there he died.

His wife survived him by ten years. In 1864 Herzen received a letter from Naples purporting to contain a spirit message from his dead wife Natalie, who exhorted him to abjure the cares of this world and to seek in religion purification from his sins. There was no signature; but he recognized the handwriting of Alexandra Engelson.

CHAPTER 6

First Years in London

WHEN in the late summer of 1852 Herzen first came to England, he believed, with the easy middle-aged cynicism of the early forties, that his life was over. An overwhelming tragedy had destroyed beyond repair the foundations of his personal happiness. His public activities had been emptied of all hope or meaning by the universal triumph of reaction. Nothing was left for him but to pass the residue of his years in inconspicuous and ignominious retirement, saving what he could, for the sake of his children, from the poor wreckage of his domestic life, and finding such expression for his political creed as was possible in the only European country where liberty was not altogether stifled. For nearly four years this mood endured. Then, almost without knowing it, he found his heartstrings responding once more to the familiar, intimate touch of passion and romance; and about the same time he entered on the most important phase of his public career. But it was during these painful and difficult first years in England – years in which he possessed neither domestic intimacies nor settled occupation – that he formed his most vivid impressions of the country in which he had pitched his tent.

Herzen never concerned himself to any extent with English affairs; and his caustic pen has not left for the benefit of posterity any systematic analysis of English life in the fifties of last century. The impressions which may be gleaned from his private letters are not at first sight particularly flattering.

Life here [he wrote to a Russian friend in 1855] is about as boring as that of worms in a cheese. There is not a spark of anything healthy, vigorous or hopeful. Victor Hugo described us admirably when he called the English 'un grand peuple – bête.' Conservatives and radicals are both rubbish – and mediocre rubbish at that. The *émigrés* are no better. Expect nothing of *them;* they are dead men burying their dead.

A week or two later he still more cursorily dismissed the English as 'the lowest race of mankind, *positively* stupid, and marvellously ill-bred'.

Yet this was not Herzen's constant mood or his considered judgement. 'Beyond all manner of doubt,' he wrote to his Swiss friend Karl Vogt in 1857, 'England, with all the follies of feudalism and toryism which are peculiar to it, is the only country to live in.' And a long passage in *My Past and Thoughts* in which he contrasts the qualities of English and French civilization is by no means altogether in favour of the latter.

The Frenchman is a complete contrast to the Englishman. The Englishman is a solitary creature, who likes to live in his own house, stubborn and defiant; the Frenchman is a creature of the herd, quarrelsome, but easily settling down to pasture. Hence two completely parallel lines of development with the Channel between. The Frenchman is constantly making declarations, interfering in everything, instructing everybody, teaching everybody everything. The Englishman waits, does not interfere at all in other people's affairs, and would be more ready to learn than to teach, only that he has no time – he must be off to his shop.

The two corner-stones of English life – individual liberty and inherited tradition – scarcely exist for the Frenchman. The coarseness of English manners maddens the Frenchman (and it is indeed disgusting, and poisons life in London); but he does not see behind it that rude strength with which this nation has defended its rights, that unbending obstinacy which will allow you, by flattering his passions, to do anything with an Englishman rather than make him a slave who takes pleasure in the gold braid on his livery, and delights in his chains if only they are covered with laurels.

The world of self-government and decentralization, an independent, capricious growth, seems so barbarous and incomprehensible to the Frenchman that, however long he lives in England, he never understands her political and civic life, her law and her judicial system. He is lost in the uncoordinated variety of English laws as in a dark forest; he altogether fails to notice the tall, majestic oaks which compose it, and how much charm, poetry and good sense may be found in this very variety. He hankers after a little code with nicely swept paths, with lopped trees and with policemen-gardeners in every alley.

It was a period when Englishmen were particularly insistent on their civic rights and liberties;* and these never ceased to excite Herzen's wonder.

The confidence [he continues] which even the poor man feels when

* J. S. Mill's famous treatise *On Liberty* was published in 1859.

he closes behind him the door of his dark, cold, damp hovel, changes the whole outlook of a man . . . Until I came to England the appearance of a police officer in a house where I was living always produced an indefinable disagreeable feeling, and I was at once morally on my guard against an enemy. In England a policeman at your door merely adds to your sense of security.

This liberty was sometimes carried to lengths which filled Herzen with stupefaction. No incident in English public life filled him with such amazement as the hostile agitation against the Prince Consort on the outbreak of the Crimean War. To the exile from the land of the Tsars it seemed incredible that public meetings should be held to demand the impeachment of the consort of the reigning sovereign, and that urchins could go about the street unmolested shouting for the Prince to be sent to the Tower.

But Herzen's impressions of England were, and remained, those of the disinterested spectator. They were the product of detached observation rather than intimate knowledge. The traditional attitude of the English towards the immigrant foreigner precluded any real contact between Herzen and the inhabitants of the island. His opinions excluded him from ordinary English society; for at this period in England, as another *émigré* remarks, 'agnosticism was scarcely compatible with the idea of a gentleman'. He made fleeting appearances from time to time in those select radical circles which patronized continental democracy and republicanism. He met one or two of the literary lions of the day, including George Henry Lewes and Thomas Carlyle, 'a man of immense talent, but extremely paradoxical'.* But these were public rather than private acquaintanceships; and there was during this period only one English family which admitted him to any degree of intimacy.

Herzen owed this one circle of English friends to Mazzini, whom he had met at Geneva in 1849. During the earlier years of his residence in England, Mazzini had been the victim of an intrigue which created an immense popular scandal. It was discovered that British postal officials had, at the instigation of the Austrian police, been tampering with Mazzini's correspondence.

* A characteristic letter of Carlyle to Herzen has been preserved in the Herzen archives and is reproduced in Appendix B (p. 326).

Among those who were prominent in the exposure of this affair was one William Ashurst, a solicitor and a radical, who had taken part in the campaign for the Reform Bill, and was reputed by his family to have inspired Rowland Hill with the never-to-be-forgotten idea of the penny post. Ashurst and his wife, who had three grown-up daughters, lived in a country house at Muswell Hill, a suburb so remote and inaccessible that their guests of an evening often had to walk four miles to 'The Angel' at Islington, before they could find a cab or an omnibus to convey them back to town. Mazzini became a constant visitor at this house; and his correspondence with the Ashurst family is a charming relic of his long residence in England.

The Ashurst girls were duly married, Matilda to Martin Biggs, a solicitor practising in Sevenoaks, Emilie to Sydney Hawkes, and Caroline to James Stansfeld, Hawkes and Stansfeld being partners in a brewery at Fulham. In 1850 Matilda Biggs visited Nice; and she brought with her a letter of introduction to Herzen from Mazzini. The acquaintanceship thus established was renewed when Herzen came to England. Matilda invited him to her home in Sevenoaks (it was his first glimpse of the English countryside), and through her he met the other members of this eccentric and gifted family. Of the women, Emilie Hawkes* seems to have been his favourite; but of their husbands he was most closely associated with Stansfeld. Stansfeld went into Parliament, where he was conspicuous for years as the defender of the right of asylum and of the cause of political refugees in England. In the sixties he became Junior Lord of the Admiralty in Palmerston's cabinet. But his ministerial career was brief. It transpired that he was in the habit of allowing his name and address to be used as a cover for letters sent to Mazzini by Italian republicans and revolutionaries. He was fiercely attacked in the House of Commons by Disraeli, who declared that the Junior Lord of the Admiralty was 'in corres-

* During Herzen's stay in England, Emilie divorced her husband and married an Italian named Ventura, a follower of Mazzini. In 1866 Ventura died, and Herzen wrote to Mazzini from Geneva a letter which throws some light on his friendship with the Ashursts. 'Poor Emilie!' he wrote. 'The recollections of my first years in London ('52 and '53) are so closely bound up with my own troubles, with Madame Ventura and with all your circle at that time that my heart bled when I read your words.' The letter is reproduced in *Mazzini's Letters to an English Family*.

pondence with the assassins of Europe'; and he only saved the government from serious embarrassment by his resignation.

But these and other English acquaintances did not at any time play a large role in Herzen's life. His constant associates during his first years in England were the multitude of political refugees who, since 1848, had flocked together from every corner of Europe to the one spot of European soil where they could still live and talk and conspire in peace. They formed themselves into more or less coherent national groups. Among the Italians, Mazzini was the recognized and unrivalled master. The Hungarians acknowledged the leadership of Kossuth, the Poles of Worcell. The French divided their allegiance between Louis Blanc and Ledru-Rollin, the protagonists of the revolution of 1848, the former the author of the famous *Histoire des Dix Ans*, the latter of a pamphet *De la Décadence de l'Angleterre*. The Germans, dispersed and disunited abroad as at home, had no accepted leader for their numerous colony of exiles. These five nationalities – Italian, Pole, Hungarian, French and German – formed the main body of refugees; and Herzen, who represented a country not hitherto associated with the democratic movement, was a welcome complement to the agglomeration. He was doubly welcome for the reason that, unlike nearly all the other refugees, he had a well-filled purse, and was not disinclined on occasion to loosen its strings for the benefit of his less fortunate fellows. The traditional hospitality of the Russian *grand seigneur* asserted itself even in foggy *bourgeois* London. Herzen kept open house, and any exile down on his luck knew that he could come, any evening, to drink his wine, to smoke his tobacco, and to talk, gaily or gravely as the mood served, till any hour of the night.

But although his friendships were almost exclusively political in character, Herzen's excursions into public life were rare events. His Polish associates were the first to draw him from his seclusion. He made his first public appearance at a meeting held at the Hanover Rooms, on 29 November 1853, to celebrate the anniversary of the Polish insurrection of 1830. Worcell presided; and speakers of several nationalities disserted on the sufferings of Poland and her coming resurrection. Herzen, a brilliant controversialist in private life, lacked platform experience. In introducing him to the audience, Worcell explained that 'in his own country the orator had never been allowed to speak in public', and asked permission for him to speak from a manuscript. This speech, read in French (for Herzen never learned to speak English with ease), ended with the slogan: 'An independent Poland and a free Russia'; and at the end of the oration Worcell, falling on Herzen's neck, 'forgave Russia in the name of Poland', while 1,500 people applauded this reconciliation of the sister Slav nations. Herzen would have been in the seventh heaven of delight if the demon of scepticism within him had not brought to his mind, at the moment of this triumph, a fragment of dialogue from the famous Russian satirical comedy *The Misfortune of Being Clever*:

'" – And what do you *do* at your club?'
'" – We shout, brother, we shout."'

Eighteen months later Herzen spoke at another public meeting, whose character, both representative and social, is made clear by the handbill announcing it:

Commemoration of The

GREAT REVOLUTIONARY MOVEMENT OF 1848
ALLIANCE OF ALL PEOPLES

An
international
soirée
followed by
A Public Meeting
will be held at
St. Martin's Hall,
Long Acre
on
Tuesday, February 27, 1855

The following distinguished representatives of European Democracy have been invited:

FRENCH: Louis Blanc, Victor Hugo, Barbès, Felix Pyat, Ledru-Rollin, Raspail, Eugène Sue, Pierre Leroux.
GERMAN: Kinkel, Marx,* Ruge, Schapper.

* Marx refused the invitation to attend. 'I will nowhere and at no time appear on the same platform as Herzen,' he wrote to Engels, 'since I am not of the opinion that "old Europe" can be re-juvenated by Russian blood.'

ITALIAN: Bianciani, Saffi, Mazzini.
HUNGARIAN: Teleki, Kossuth.
POLISH: Worcell, Zeno-Swientoslawski.
RUSSIAN: Herzen.
ENGLISH: W. Coningham, J. Finlen, Cooper, Mayne-Reid, J. Beal, Gerald Massey.

Ernest Jones, President.
Alfred Tallandier, French Sec.
Dombrovski, Polish Sec.
M. Bley, German Sec.
B. Chapman, English Sec.

Tea on Table at Five. Doors open for meeting at half-past
Seven, to commence at Eight.

Double Tickets, 2*s*. 6*d*.; Single ditto, 1*s*. 6*d*.; meeting ditto, 3*d*.
Tickets may be had at St. Martin's Hall.

Although the Crimean War was now in progress, Herzen was, as *The Times* reported, 'received with enthusiasm', and his speech was 'the most remarkable of all'. He spoke of the coming revolution, and of socialism as 'the young heir of the dying old régime'; and amidst the applause which greeted him as he sat down, a lady, variously described as English or Polish, presented him with a bouquet of flowers.

In the meanwhile, in February 1854, Herzen had assisted at another noteworthy occasion of a semi-public character, which was extensively reported both in the English and trans-Atlantic press. Mr Saunders, the American consul, gave a banquet to a dozen of the principal foreign refugees in London. Among Herzen's fellow-guests were Garibaldi (who was on a visit to London, and whom he now met for the first time), Mazzini (the real organizer of the banquet), Orsini (whose attempt, a few years later, to assassinate Napoleon III nearly brought about a rupture between England and France), Kossuth, Ledru-Rollin, Worcell and other refugee leaders. One Englishman, Sir Joshua Walmsley, M.P., graced the banquet in virtue of his well-known radical sympathies; and the party was completed by the American Ambassador James Buchanan, a future President of the United States.

The first business of the evening was to effect an introduction between Kossuth and Ledru-Rollin; for owing to the stubborn refusal of each to make a first call on the other, they had never been able to meet. The combined act of Mazzini and Buchanan brought them together with such perfect simultaneity that neither the haughty Hungarian aristocrat nor the touchy French *bourgeois* could be accused of having so far demeaned himself as to make the first advance. The company then sat down to dinner, the card which marked Herzen's place bearing the superscription 'the Russian Republican'; for he had become, in these days, an institution rather than a person. The presence of the Ambassador set a dignified tone. Like a true diplomat, he talked affably to the republican guests, 'just as he had talked affably to Orlov and Benckendorff in the Winter Palace when he was ambassador to Nicholas I'. But there were, to Herzen's surprise and disappointment, no speeches. Nobody should be able to say that an American Ambassador had been associated with a political demonstration.

The Ambassador retired early; and Kossuth's dignity did not permit of an Ambassador leaving before him. Their simultaneous departure was followed by a certain relaxation in the sobriety of the proceedings. Mr Saunders, wishing to drink the long-deferred toast of the 'world republic', departed to mix a bowl of 'American punch made of old Kentucky whisky'; and Mrs Saunders strummed the *Marseillaise*, in those days still a revolutionary and international anthem, on the guitar. Presently the punch arrived. Mr Saunders (to follow Herzen's narrative)

tasted it, was satisfied, and poured it out for us in large teacups. Suspecting nothing, I took a good gulp, and for the first minute gasped for breath. When I came to myself, I noticed Ledru-Rollin also about to take a gulp. I stopped him.

'If you value your life,' I said, 'go gently with this refreshment from Kentucky. I, yes, I, a Russian, have burned my palate, my throat, and my whole alimentary canal; and what will it be like for you? In Kentucky they must make their whisky of red pepper soaked in vitriol.'

The American smiled ironically, delighted at the weakness of the Europeans. An imitator of Mithridates* from my earliest years, I alone passed up an empty cup and asked for more. My chemical affinity with alcohol raised my prestige enormously in the eyes of the consul.

'Ah, yes!' he said. 'It is only in America and in Russia that people know how to drink.'

* Who protected himself against the risk of poisoning by taking poison in homoeopathic doses.

And there is another still more flattering resemblance, thought I. It is only in America and in Russia that they know how to flog bond-slaves to death.

So ended 'the *red* banquet given by the defender of *black* slavery'. Herzen did not disturb the harmony of the occasion by giving utterance to these barbed comparisons.

*

Meanwhile Herzen's domestic affairs settled themselves on an unexpected basis. He spent his first winter in London in a house in the neighbourhood of Regent's Park, rented from a sculptor of catholic tastes, who had adorned his drawing-room with busts of Queen Victoria and of Lola Montès, the famous courtesan. Here Herzen lived with his son Sasha and the Austrian General Haug, who had accompanied them to London. His daughters, Tata and Olga, had been left behind in Paris in the care of the Reichels. Herzen's letters to Maria Reichel are a fruitful source of information regarding these years of his life.

Herzen had come to England with no plans for the future. He spoke of staying a few weeks or a few months. In his most imaginative moments he never dreamed of an almost unbroken residence of more than twelve years. But as the winter passed and he began to settle down in this gloomy foreign city, he felt the need of re-establishing his family circle. The first anniversary of Natalie's death was approaching; and he could no longer bear separation from his daughters. He took a large house in Euston Square; and here in May 1853 the girls came over to join him, accompanied by their German nurse, Maria Fomm, who had been with them since their mother's death. Olga was now two and a half, and Tata eight. Sasha, who was going on for fourteen, already had five visiting tutors to teach him. It was time Tata had her first lessons; and Herzen engaged as her teacher a German lady named Malwida von Meysenbug.

Fraulein von Meysenbug was the daughter of a French father of Huguenot extraction and a German mother. Her father had settled in Cassel, where Malwida was born in 1816; and his German title was the reward of services rendered to Prince Wilhelm II of Hesse. The education of Malwida was purely German and Lutheran. It had a predominantly religious flavour. The growing child thought much of the other world; and her sickly constitution entitled her to contemplate, with becoming satisfaction, the prospect of her early admission to it. These youthful hopes were not fulfilled; for she lived to enter her eighty-seventh year. But although she soon shed the religious convictions of her adolescence, Malwida retained throughout life the passionate earnestness imparted by her upbringing. A light touch and a careless *joie de vivre* were qualities which she neither possessed herself nor admired in others.

She was romantic after her own manner. She lived, as she tells us in her *Memoirs*, in 'an imaginary world of sublime virtues, of horrible crimes and persecutions, and striking triumphs of good over evil'; her first adolescent *Schwärmerei* was, appropriately enough, for the Lutheran pastor who administered her first Communion. But her heart and her conduct were alike austere. She disliked, or disapproved of, the light-minded diversions of her contemporaries; and at the age of twenty-seven she had her one serious love-affair. She heard the twenty-one-year-old son of her revered pastor preach his first sermon, and fell in love with him on the spot. His name was Theodore Althaus. 'His face was pale,' she writes in her *Memoirs*, 'with sharp-cut noble features of the southern races. His long, thick black hair reached, after the manner of the students of the day, to his shoulders. His brow was the brow of thinkers and martyrs.' An intellectual friendship developed between them; and they discussed eagerly, by word of mouth and by correspondence, the problems of religion, ethics and politics. Young Theodore did not long remain faithful to the doctrines in which he had been reared. In 1846 he wrote a pamphlet under the ambitious title *The Future of Christianity*, in which he denied the divinity of Christ and advocated the foundation of a new church on a non-dogmatic basis; and his political opinions took on an equally uncompromising hue. Malwida's mind was more impressionable than her senses. Her innocence, but not her orthodoxy, survived her passionate intercourse with the young rebel. She quarrelled with her parents; and she shared and applauded – she may, in part, have inspired – Theodore's radical ideas.

She was not, however, destined to inspire a lasting passion. Her photographs suggest a strikingly handsome woman. But dignity of profile was nullified by a poor complexion and weak, obviously myopic eyes; and her contemporaries did not find her attractive. Herzen, a few years later, bluntly refers to her as 'an awful fright'. Soon Theodore moved to Leipzig and thence to Berlin, where he pursued his studies and became involved in the first stages of the revolution of 1848. Separation from Malwida tempered the warmth of his feelings for her; and after five years of ardent friendship, he showed signs of indifference which she could not ignore. Perhaps he had become too much absorbed in revolution. Perhaps he had reflected, at the age of twenty-six, that Malwida was six years his senior. She reproached him with neglect. He avoided an explanation as long as he could, and when at last she drove him into a corner, he frankly told her that 'if she had been more of a coquette, she would have played her cards differently and made a conquest of him'. He expiated his revolutionary activities by a term of imprisonment; and Malwida was forgiving enough to return afterwards to nurse him on a bed of sickness. He died early in 1852.

In the meanwhile Malwida had herself become suspect in the eyes of the Prussian police. While she was on a visit to Berlin, her papers were seized and she herself interrogated on her opinions and activities. Being, or imagining herself, in danger of arrest, she fled to Hamburg and embarked for London. Here she found Gottfried Kinkel, an old comrade of Althaus, and his wife Joanna, both refugees of the German revolution; and she settled near them, in the summer of 1852, in the genteel suburb of St John's Wood. Her experiences with the Berlin police had not abated her German patriotism; and when at the Duke of Wellington's funeral, which took place three months after her arrival in England, she heard the massed bands playing Beethoven's 'Funeral March', she reflected with satisfaction that 'the highest spiritual beauty still always comes from Germans'.

Of Kinkel and his wife, Herzen has left a pair of his most brilliant and characteristic portraits, immortal in their irony, penetration and malice:

Gottfried Kinkel was the leader of one of the forty times forty German sects in London. When I looked at him I always marvelled how so magnificent, so Jove-like a head had come to be planted on the shoulders of a German professor, and how a German professor had found his way, first on to a battlefield and then, wounded, into a Prussian prison. But perhaps the most remarkable thing of all was that all this, *plus* London, had not changed him in the least. A German professor he remained. Tall, with grey hair, and a greyish beard, his very appearance had in it a majestic quality and commanded respect. But he added to this a sort of official unction, something judicial or archi-episcopal, solemn, stilted and modestly self-satisfied. Different variations of this attribute may be found in fashionable preachers, ladies' doctors (particularly those who practise magnetism), advocates who devote themselves especially to the defence of morality, and the head waiters of aristocratic English hotels. In his youth Kinkel had studied theology; and even after he had freed himself from its influence, he remained a priest in his gestures. There is nothing surprising about this; even Lamennais, who cut so deep into the roots of Catholicism, kept to the end the appearance of an *abbé*. Kinkel's well-rounded and fluent speech, correct and free from anything extreme, sounded like a didactic discourse. He listened with studied condescension to others, and with sincere pleasure to himself.

Joanna Kinkel pursued her husband with remorseless admiration and equally remorseless jealousy, which served to render both of them ridiculous.

Kinkel always preserved his air of distinction, and she always preserved her admiration for him. They conversed with each other on the most everyday subjects in the style of society drama (the fashionable German *haute comédie*) or the didactic novel. 'Dearest Joanna,' he would say melodiously and distinctly, 'do be so good, my angel, as to pour me out another cup of this excellent tea.' 'I think it heavenly, my dearest Gottfried, that you should like it. Give me, my dearest, a few drops of cream.' And he would pour out the cream and gaze at her with affection, and she would gaze at him with gratitude.

Joanna mercilessly pursued her husband with unceasing, unsparing care. She gave him a revolver when it was foggy, and begged him to seek protection in special waistcoats against the wind, against evil tongues, against indigestible food and (secretly) against ladies' eyes, more dangerous than any wind or *pâté de foie gras*. In a word she poisoned his life with her barbed, unsparing jealousy and her incessant exhibitions of affection.

Joanna has another claim on the recollection of posterity. She has left a novel, *Hans Ibeles in London*, which was published in

Germany after her death and which, as the picture of the life of a foreign family in a mid-Victorian London suburb, merits the attention of every student of the period. Sometimes the humour is a trifle forced, as when the purveyor of a beetle-killer puts the Royal Arms on his business card and describes himself as 'Bug-Exterminator to H.M. the Queen and H.R.H. the Duchess of Kent'. Sometimes it is altogether unconscious, as in the following example of alleged English rudeness to the foreign invader:

A cabman, whom he [Ibeles] asked in quite correct English: 'Mister, will you be so good, to fare us upon the Queen's Street, by Mr Mutebell, in the house Nro. 3,' turned to one of his fellows and said: 'This gentleman speaks French, I cannot understand him.'

In general the novel is frankly autobiographical. Gottfried Kinkel appears in the character of the hero, the delicate, sensitive artist, an 'Endymion in middle life', whose one defect is a platonic weakness for the flattering attentions of the other sex; Joanna is the hero's noble, though faintly jealous, wife; and Malwida von Meysenbug is easily recognizable in the traits of the German governess, Meta Braun, who nourishes a hopeless passion for a fellow émigré. Unfortunately

she had never excited him or any other man to dream of her, because her spirit was wanting in any kind of charm which might so hold his fancy as to make him forget that she was not pretty.

Meta having failed to captivate the man of her heart, emigrates to Australia; and the hero and the perfect wife, after a last crisis of estrangement, are reconciled for ever on the concluding page. The upshot in real life was more tragic. A few years later Joanna Kinkel, in a mad fit of jealousy, committed suicide by throwing herself out of the window.

It was in the exalted and rarified atmosphere of the Kinkel household, not uncongenial to her own temperament, that Malwida first met Herzen in the winter of 1852–3. Before she left Germany, someone had presented her with a copy of Herzen's essays *From the Other Shore*; and she had been astonished to discover in the writings of this unknown Russian 'a reflexion of our lost ideal, our unfulfilled ambitions, our despair and our submission to fate'. The meeting confirmed her favourable impression. Herzen was at the time, as she records in her *Memoirs*, 'a thick-set powerful figure, with black hair and beard, rather broad Slavonic features, and remarkably brilliant eyes, which – more than any other eyes I have seen – reflected the living play of feelings within'. On Herzen's side the impression was equally agreeable. The acquaintance continued. Malwida was earning her living by giving lessons; and it was therefore natural that Herzen should apply to her when he decided to bring his daughters over to London.

Malwida was now in the late thirties; and the maternal instinct was the strongest of her unsatisfied passions. Her yearning affection went out to the motherless Herzen children. Tata, her pupil, was capricious and was already old enough to have a will and character of her own. But the helpless and winning Olga, who in grace and delicacy of feature resembled the mother she could not remember, stirred Malwida's deepest emotions. When lessons were suspended at the end of July, Malwida went to Broadstairs for a holiday. There she realized for the first time the place Olga had come to occupy in her life. She became almost hysterical with loneliness. She wrote to Herzen begging him to bring the children to Broadstairs and accusing him of selfishly clinging to the gaieties of London. But Sasha had a quinsy; Herzen was busy; and the children could not be sent alone. Herzen rebutted, with some asperity, the insinuation that Regent Street and Verrey's Café were the *summum bonum* of his existence. And he pointed out that the English sea, which he had seen at Folkestone, was 'far from being blue and beautiful, like the Mediterranean'.

When Malwida returned from Broadstairs her mind was made up. Herzen gave her a lead by complaining of the disorderly housekeeping of Maria Fomm, the German nurse. She wrote to him (even after they were living under the same roof they often communicated with each other by letter) offering to come and live in his house and take charge of the children. She added that, since the offer was made out of friendship and a sense of duty, she could accept no payment from him for her services, and would continue to give outside lessons in order to supply her needs.

The widower, with three young children on his hands and no taste or talent – as he frankly admitted – for the education of the young, accepted the offer with alacrity; and in November 1853 Malwida von Meysenbug entered the Herzen household. The strong hand of the reformer soon made itself felt. It was exercised first on Herzen himself. His almost daily receptions of political refugees were the first stone of offence. Malwida, whose sympathies were intensive rather than gregarious, lost no time in expressing her disapproval of this international swarm of parasites, who treated the house in Euston Square as a place of free entertainment, and disturbed the domestic peace until far on into the night.

I told him frankly [she records in her *Memoirs*] that I had come not only in order to guide his children, as far as lay in my power, in the right path, but also to preserve the father for the children and, with his help, to create the happy home life in which childhood can alone flourish, in which one can sow the blessed seed which will some day bring forth flower and fruit. With the extraordinary frankness in dealing with himself which was one of his characteristics, and with the courage with which he always confessed his own defects, he admitted that his weakness was his inability to create such conditions; and he gave me full powers to do so. I advised him to appoint two evenings in the week in which to receive his acquaintances, and to issue strict orders that during the day and on the other evenings the house should be left in peace. He found that one evening was enough, and took the necessary steps; and in this respect we soon had complete peace.

Her easy victory over Herzen encouraged Malwida to face the problem of Maria Fomm. The relations between the two women soon became impossible. The nurse had been regarded, before Malwida's arrival, as a member of the family and the unquestioned authority in everything that concerned the children; she was treated by Malwida as an upper servant. The dispute extended to the children. For while Olga clung to Malwida, Tata would sometimes, from sheer perversity, take the nurse's side and refuse obedience to the new governess. Malwida appealed to Herzen. Characteristically, he made more show of resistance on Maria's behalf than he had made on his own. But the result was inevitable. Early in the New Year Maria was paid off; and Malwida ruled alone.

A hero to worship was, throughout life, the most consistent need of Malwida's romantic nature. Her enthusiasm was more remarkable than her discernment. As a young woman she had adored the long-haired Theodore. In her riper years she prostrated herself in turn before the more rugged grandeurs of Wagner and Nietzsche. For some months Herzen filled this essential role in her life. She looked after his physical and spiritual welfare; she governed his household; and she studied Russian in order that she might translate his writings into her mother tongue. But he owed her another and subtler debt of gratitude. When Malwida came to take her place in Herzen's family, memories of Natalie and Herwegh still obsessed and embittered him. Presently his mind began to clear.

One thought has certainly occurred to you [he said once to Malwida]: The evil that a German has done in my life, that you are trying to make good.

And when Malwida assented, he added:

Well, and you have succeeded.

In the spring of 1854, she induced Herzen to move to a house at Richmond; and in the summer she even persuaded him that the English seaside was less contemptible than he had supposed. The whole family spent September at Ventnor.

The New Year of 1855 was celebrated in a particularly solemn fashion. The Herzen family had just moved into a large house at Twickenham. There was a monster Christmas-tree, and a large number of guests of all nationalities had been invited. As midnight drew near, Herzen produced a copy of the new Russian edition of his volume of essays *From the Other Shore* (hitherto published only in German) and, summoning Sasha, read to him aloud, amid the hushed attention of the guests, the dedicatory letter *To my Son Alexander* which has remained prefixed to all subsequent editions of the work. The concluding sentences of the letter are admirably expressive of Herzen's temperament, opinions and ambitions at this time:

We do not build, we destroy; we do not proclaim a new truth, we abolish an old lie. Contemporary man only builds the bridge; another, the yet unknown man of the future, will walk across it. You perhaps will see it. Do not remain on this shore. Better to perish with the revolution than to be saved in holy reaction.

The religion of revolution, of the great social transformation, is the only religion I bequeath to you. It is a religion without a paradise, without rewards, without consciousness of itself, without a conscience.

Go in your time to preach it to our people *at home*: there they once loved my voice and will perhaps remember me.

I give my blessing to your journey in the name of human reason, of individual liberty and of brotherly love!

When the reading was over, the boy burst into tears and threw himself into his father's arms. The guests were deeply moved, and thought of their native lands which most of them would never see again. One of them confided to Malwida the opinion that Herzen was 'something divine'. It was a clear frosty night, and they went out into Richmond Park to recover from the emotions of this solemn scene. Its influence on young Alexander was transient. Like other sons, he refused to bow the knee to his father's gods. He grew up not, like his father, in the heady atmosphere of the romantic thirties, but in the solid, prosperous fifties of Victorian England. Revolution meant nothing to him, and the land of his birth was no more than a name on a map. After a stormy youth, he settled down to a model life of *bourgeois* respectability as a professor of physiology. His last twenty-five years were spent at Lausanne, where he died in 1906. He never returned to Russia, and as time went on Russian was less and less heard in his house.

The Crimean War came and went. Tsar Nicholas I died and was succeeded by Tsar Alexander II. Herzen's public activities increased. In the Herzen household Malwida held undisputed sway; and he made a will charging her with the education of his daughters in the event of his death. His life, in the spring of 1856, had become more tranquil, regular and uneventful than at any previous stage of his career. Then, on 9 April, as the family sat at dinner, a cab heavily laden with trunks drew up at the house in Finchley Road where they were now living.* The occupants came to the door. Herzen recognized the voice of Ogarev, the oldest and most intimate friend of his youth, now married to Natalie Tuchkov, the passionate and charming 'Consuelo' of Herzen's dead wife. Natalie was with Ogarev in the cab. Herzen had not seen Natalie for seven years, or Ogarev for nearly ten. He fervently embraced them both, brought them in to be introduced to Malwida and the children, and gave orders that no other visitor was to be admitted to the house for forty-eight hours.

* A list of Herzen's successive residences in London is given in Appendix C (p. 328).

Three days before the coming of the Ogarevs, Herzen's wedding-ring had suddenly snapped 'without any reason' during the night. It was the eve of his forty-fourth birthday. He was not superstitious, and ironically suggested that some of his friends might try table-turning in order to ascertain the meaning of the portent.

CHAPTER 7

Poor Nick: 1

'HERZEN,' remarked one of his contemporaries, 'is the ever-active European, living an expansive life and assimilating ideas only in order to clarify, develop, and disseminate them. Ogarev is quietistic Asia, in whose soul slumber deep thoughts unclear even to himself.' The psychologist of a certain school might find male elements predominant in Herzen, and female elements in Ogarev. The Englishman, mindful of their literary collaboration, will perhaps think of Addison and Steele, who present somewhat the same alliance of solid worth with wayward charm. These comparisons and contrasts are suggestive, but far from exhaustive; for the characters of these life-long friends are too full and vivid to be contained in a formula. From the time of their first meeting in 1825 and the oath taken in boyhood on the Sparrow Hills, they remained inseparable companions until they were parted by arrest in the summer of 1834. Then, for more than twenty years, with the exception of a short period in Moscow, they rarely met. In 1856 their paths converged once more in London. The present chapter, which traces the road travelled by Ogarev during these twenty years, serves as a prelude to their renewed relationship.

*

Nicholas Platonovich Ogarev – known to his intimates as Nick – was the son of a rich landed proprietor in the government of Penza. He seems to have been a victim, from his earliest years, of the scourge of epilepsy; but it was not until middle life that his symptoms became sufficiently grave or frequent to alarm his friends. He was involved, like the other members of Herzen's circle, in the so-called conspiracy of Sokolovsky. But his role was less conspicuous than that of his friend; and while Herzen was banished to distant Vyatka, the authorities were content to send Ogarev to the government of Penza to live, 'under supervision', on his father's estate at Aksheno. He was then in his twenty-first year. Old Plato Ogarev was a man of orthodox opinions and exemplary life. He was shocked by the company his son had kept in Moscow. In order to distract the young man from the dangerous attractions of poetry and philosophy, he urged the rival charms of a serf-girl from his estate, and introduced him to the fashionable society of the provincial capital.

The poet and philosopher in Ogarev protested bitterly against paternal intolerance and tyranny. But the young man was none the less susceptible to his father's more mundane promptings in respect of female charm. He was heart and soul a Romantic. But romantic love was a function of the soul, and took no cognizance of the indulgences of the body. Poor Nick always confessed to a weak head for women.

At fifteen [he afterwards wrote to his bride] I dreamed of the pure and heavenly love which I am now experiencing. At sixteen, my passionate imagination impelled me to fall in love, and I met with a disillusionment which shattered my faith in love. At seventeen, I desired to possess a woman, and I satisfied my desire without love on either side – a shameful commercial transaction between an inexperienced youth and a public prostitute. This was my first step on the road to vice. Man is so made that, once he has known a woman, he must continue. They say it is a physical necessity. I do not believe that; I believe that a man of pure heart should avoid every physical connexion from which love is absent, even if it be to the detriment of his physical well-being. But then I easily fastened on to the other theory and abandoned myself to vice. Sometimes I was tormented by remorse, but generally I lulled my conscience to sleep.

While therefore young Ogarev did not abandon philosophy or poetry or music, and even asserted his political convictions by declaring that his valet was the best man in Penza, he found time, during these first months of his exile, for other diversions. There was a liaison with a serf-girl, to whom he dedicated, by way of remorseful compensation, one of his best poems. Then, triumphantly launched on Penza society, he fell in love successively with two of his cousins. One of these affairs of the heart might have ended seriously. But before he had committed himself, the would-be suitor developed idealistic scruples:

I often think: Can I have an individual passion not founded on self-abnegation and on the life of the universe? Am I really an egoist? . . . I ought not to abandon myself to love. My love is dedicated to a higher

138

universal Love, the foundation of which is not an egotistical feeling of enjoyment. I must sacrifice my present love on the altar of world feeling.

The incompatibility between individual love and universal Love was an inconvenient theory for a young man of warm temperament like Nick Ogarev. It survived long enough to disappoint the hopes of his fair cousin. But it could not withstand for many weeks the gentler promptings of his heart. Later in the same winter, on 11 February 1836, he attended a ball given by the Governor of Penza, an official of the old school named Panchulidzev, and found himself sitting out with a young lady named Maria Lvovna Roslavlev. Her father was a local landed proprietor, who had almost ruined himself by indulgence in his twin passions for hunting and drinking; and her uncle was no less a person than the Governor himself. In a quiet corner, secluded from the noisy gaiety of the ball, they began to talk, as befits idealists, 'of the kingdom of heaven and the coming world'.

Suddenly [wrote Ogarev afterwards] there broke from our lips the words: 'I love you.' This moment was recorded by the angels in heaven, and it joyfully re-echoed in the great world of the soul.

The approval of the angels was endorsed by the parents of the young people; and on 26 April they were married. It was just a year since Ogarev had arrived in Penza. He cannot be said to have wasted his first year of exile.

It must not be supposed that Ogarev's marriage represented a betrayal of his romantic idealism. A solution was found for the unresolved contradiction which had nipped in the bud his passion for his cousin. The new gospel of the triumphant reconciliation of individual love and universal Love was proclaimed in an impassioned letter which he wrote to his bride three days before his marriage:

I feel that God lives and speaks in me. Let us go whither His voice calls us. My soul is strong enough to love you; it surely will be strong enough to follow in the footsteps of Christ for the liberation of mankind. For to love you means to love everything that is good, to love God and His Universe; your soul is open to the good and able to embrace it, your soul is all love . . .

Our love, Maria, contains within it all the germ of the liberties of

139

mankind. Our love is self-abnegation and truth; it is the faith that is in our soul. The tale of our love will be told from age to age, and future generations will preserve our memory as a holy thing.

It was not for nothing that the angels in heaven had echoed Ogarev's declaration of his love for Maria. The romantic identification of love and religion and virtue had seldom found an expositor at once so naïve and so spiritual. From the first year of his married life there has survived the manuscript, in French, of a *Profession de Foi*, through which he endeavoured to initiate his bride into the innermost recesses of his spiritual life. The title recalls the *Profession de Foi d'un Vicaire Savoyard*; and the inspiration seems to have come mainly from Rousseau and from the German Romantics, Herder and Schilling. 'All my life,' wrote this bridegroom of twenty-one, 'has been spent in the quest of love.' His philosophy of life was a philosophy of love – a sort of erotic pantheism.

The love of mankind for one another, this brotherhood so pure and fair preached by Jesus, is the reflexion of the bond which unites us, of the world-soul which resides in the universe. The love of man is founded in the love of God.

He was bold enough to tackle a problem which some philosophers of love have denied and others ignored.

Why does love exist only between individuals of the opposite sex? . . . In the animal it is mere instinct and perhaps a first realization of free-will. Man is matter transforming itself into the ideal. Resuming in himself the whole material world, man comprises in himself the physical attraction of one sex for the other, but he idealizes it, he raises it into an attraction of idea for idea, of soul for soul. And love becomes the highest self-expression of man on earth; it includes the whole man – i.e. the union of the material with the intellectual world – and the whole universe. That is why love absorbs, since the whole of human life is in it; to love is to live. When I love, it is I, man, a résumé of the material world, who raise myself towards this Godhead – towards the world of intelligence. I love, and in this word I see disappear the gulf which separates me from God, for I feel my body united with the soul, matter with idea, and love becomes a hymn of the material world to the Godhead. Matter itself is ennobled in me; it is no longer an instinctive, blind, brute desire which I feel. No! I seek a word to describe this sensation and here it is: Exultation! The kiss in human love, says Herder, is a proof of the nobility of man.

Beside this burning faith, George Sand's most impassioned
vindications of the duty to love pale into cold, crude materialism.

It is more difficult to draw a convincing portrait of Maria
during the first months of her married life; for the colours must be
borrowed from the subsequent testimony of hostile witnesses. She
seems to have been a year or two older than Ogarev. She was not
a beauty. 'The wife of your friend is ugly,' she boldly declares in a
letter written to Herzen to announce her marriage. But she adds
that she is 'neither vain nor light-minded and loves virtue for its
own sake'; and she may have been as poor a judge of her physical
as of her moral qualities. In a letter of Natalie Herzen's she is described as 'not young and not pretty, but highly educated and
intelligent'. The other Natalie, Ogarev's second wife, remembered her as a 'piquant brunette, lively and quick-witted, who
was always in a hurry'. There is no reason to doubt that she married for love. Women were as easily infatuated with Ogarev as he
with them; and Maria was promptly swept off her feet by his
impetuous suit. No intelligent young woman could have failed to
appreciate the high-falutin idiom in which he wooed. For it was
the fashionable jargon of the day; and both wooer and wooed
were steeped in the heady sentimentality of German Romanticism.
But Maria's nature was sensual rather than romantic. She was
capable and practical and matter-of-fact. Her eager insistence on
her financial interests, which in later life shocked Herzen and his
friends, may well have been the product of her experience with a
dissolute, spendthrift father and a reckless husband.

The first two years of the marriage have no recorded history;
and Maria, whatever her private feelings, entered well enough into
the role assigned to her by her romantic husband. But in the
spring of 1838 the Ogarevs began to weary of Penza, and thought
how pleasant it would be to spend the summer months in the
Caucasus. As a political deportee, it was necessary for Ogarev to
petition the authorities for permission to leave his place of residence. He lent 5,000 roubles to Panchulidzev the Governor, his
wife's uncle, who promptly forwarded the petition to headquarters
with a recommendation which ensured its favourable reception.
The Ogarevs went to Pyatigorsk. There they met Prince Odoev-
sky, one of the survivors of the December conspiracy of 1825. The
conversations took a political turn; memories of the oath on the

Sparrow Hills were revived; and Ogarev, who had just been read-ing Thomas à Kempis, 'knelt for hours before the crucifix and prayed that he might receive the crown of martyrdom for Russian freedom'. Maria found other amusements more to her taste; and it is here that we first hear murmurings of her devotion to the pleasures of society rather than to cultivation of the higher life.

In the following spring, the Ogarevs journeyed to Vladimir to visit Herzen and his bride. It was the first time Ogarev had seen Natalie or Herzen Maria; and the initiation of the two young wives into the friendship which united their husbands was celebrated with full romantic ritual. A fragment of a letter from Herzen describes the scene:

We are infinitely happy, the four of us! What a woman Maria Lvovna is! She is above all praise. Nick is happy indeed to have found such a companion.

I had kept the crucifix which Nick had given me at our parting. We four sank on our knees before the Divine Martyr, prayed, and thanked Him for the happiness which He had vouchsafed to us after so many years of suffering and separation. We kissed His pierced feet, and kissed one another exclaiming: Christ is risen!

Long afterwards, Maria referred to the scene as 'artificial and childish'. But she played her part throughout the four days' visit sufficiently well to earn the approbation of Herzen who, after their departure, wrote to 'his dear sister and friend' an impassioned letter:

Do you remember the solemn moment when we prayed? At that moment was completed the mystery of Natalie's union with you and of yours with us. At that moment we four became one. Hosanna! Hosanna!

Maria, how incomparably great is your Nicholas! I am ready not merely to range myself at his side, but to bow myself down to his noble soul, and to his alone! You have woven your graceful life into his life-poem, a poem broad as ocean and sky, and together you have become more glorious still! I bless you! By the strength wherewith man can move mountains, I bless you!

And the letter ends with the greeting:

Salut, amitié, sympathie eternelle!

Not many weeks before this touching reunion, old Plato Ogarev had died; and his son became the master of three estates in different parts of Russia comprising a total (since estates were usually measured by the number of serfs settled on them) of 4,000 'souls'. The largest of these properties was not at Aksheno, in the government of Penza, where the family resided, but at Belo-omut in the neighbouring government of Ryazan, where 1,870 'souls' tilled the soil in servitude. Ogarev had no more taste for agriculture than for any other practical pursuit; and he had a soft heart and democratic convictions. The 'beast-like conditions' of serf life were an offence to both; and he resolved to make a beginning by liberating his serfs at Belo-omut and handing over the estate to them. On the way back from the visit to the Herzens at Vladimir, he went to Belo-omut to carry out his project.

But he went alone; for the plan had been received by the realistic Maria without sympathy.

Can it be [he wrote to her from Belo-omut in April] that you will say, No? Impossible! I must, I must carry this through. I feel that this will be one of my good actions. Not indeed exactly a perfect one, because in fact I am losing nothing.

The condition which, for Ogarev, deprived the transaction of half its merit perhaps pacified Maria. There was a purchase-price which was payable to Ogarev by the liberated peasants in ten annual instalments. Serfs were normally suspicious of the generosity of their masters; and there were tedious negotiations, 'in which,' writes Ogarev, 'I was misunderstood by the clever, and not understood at all by the fools'. At length the contract was completed and, after two years more of bureaucratic delay, received the endorsement of the Tsar. When in 1877 Ogarev died, the grateful community of Belo-omut 'in memory of the unforgettable benefits bestowed by him' decided to provide an annual mass on the anniversary of his death for the repose of his soul; and the mass continued to be said down to the early years of the twentieth century. A few months after the outbreak of the European War, the centenary of Ogarev's birth was celebrated at Belo-omut by the descendants of the serfs whom he had freed more than seventy years before.

The rift of feeling which had opened over this question between Maria and her husband was soon widened by other developments.

In the autumn of 1839 Ogarev, having lent a further 5,000 roubles to Panchulidzev, secured the removal of the ban of exile which had rested on him for five years, and was allowed to return to Moscow. The death of his father had made him a rich man; and Maria, whose ambitions had hitherto been confined to a provincial capital, now saw the opportunity of playing in Moscow the more brilliant role to which her connexions and her husband's wealth entitled her. It was a perfectly natural ambition; but it was equally natural that those who remained of Ogarev's old Moscow friends should expect to welcome him back to the pleasant bachelor life of philosophy, poetry and political palaver, of high thinking and hard drinking, which he had led in his student days, not so many years ago. It is probable that Ogarev, who had an amenable nature, could have accommodated himself in the long run either to high society or to Bohemia. But he could not choose. He loved, in his broad warm-hearted way, both his wife and his friends. He tried to satisfy them both, and failed to perceive how impossible it was to reconcile their divergent demands on him.

There was soon open warfare between the two camps. Nobody quarrelled with Ogarev. Both his wife and his friends loved him too well; for few people could help loving poor Nick. But they fought each other over his prostrate body; and he suffered infinitely more than the combatants. Herzen, passing through Moscow on his way from Vladimir to Petersburg, took a hand in the fray. He heard one side of the question, and completely forgot his enthusiastic letters of only nine months before.

Madame Og. [he wrote to Natalie] is worse than I thought her. She is a woman without a heart, without even a sense of how to behave. She is already being talked about. Poor, poor Ogarev! And the bandage has not yet fallen from his eyes.

Herzen had an open quarrel with Maria, thereby reducing his friend to agonized despair.

My soul is torn in two [wrote Ogarev to him at this time]. The strife between friendship and love has rent me asunder. On both sides it is equally wounding. ... It hurts, brother, there somewhere inside me. A flame consumes me; at one moment I weep, at another the hurt aches so that I cannot weep. In all my life I have never suffered so much. I beg you in the name of friendship to make a great sacrifice for me: when you come to see us, take Maria aside, hold out your hand and say that you ask her to forget the quarrel between you, that Nick's friend and Nick's wife cannot be enemies, and that you must unite in my name. See, Herzen, I am weeping even now. I am a child perhaps. But I beseech you, in the name of friendship, re-unite the sundered elements of my soul.

The 'great sacrifice' was made in response to Ogarev's appeal. The formal reconciliation and hand-shaking took place. It was Herzen who made the advance; and Ogarev could not help finding greater sincerity in 'friendship' than in 'love'. But the reunion was transient and unreal; and a few days later Herzen, not more than half mollified, was writing again to Natalie about his friend's wife:

If there is poetry in her, it is not exalted poetry – affectations, coquetries and no heart. I do not believe she ever loved him. She is deceiving him – or if she does love him, what sort of love is it? Their quarrel over me reached such a pitch that she proposed a separation. Well, better separation than humiliation!

The quarrel between his friend and his wife was not the only blow which Ogarev's patient heart had to bear. Among Maria's favourite diversions during these months was the society of a young man named Ivan Galakhov. Galakhov was a friend of Herzen and Ogarev. His estate in the government of Penza lay near to Aksheno, and it must have been there that he first met Maria. He came of an aristocratic family and had served in the Guards. But he soon retired from the service into that life of emotional self-indulgence and critical self-analysis which was typical of the young Russian Romantics of his generation. Between Galakhov and Maria Ogarev there was, during the winter of 1840–41, a sentimental flirtation which set the tongues of Moscow wagging; and Ogarev, with more common sense than can generally be attributed to him, decided that the one chance of saving his marriage lay in escape from this poisoned atmosphere. He proposed a journey abroad; and Maria, avid above all things of change, welcomed the plan. But once more the authorities intervened. There were difficulties about the passport; and it was not till May or June 1841 that Ogarev and his wife were able to leave

Russia. By this time, the situation was to all appearance hopelessly compromised; and Galakhov followed in their wake to Karlsbad and Ems. It would perhaps be unfair to place on him any large measure of responsibility for the shipwreck of the marriage. Maria had tired of her husband; or perhaps she had tired, not so much of Ogarev, as of the idea of fidelity. She wanted a lover; and in the emotional and attentive Galakhov she seemed to have found a promising candidate for the honour.

The sequel proved that her perspicacity had been at fault on this occasion. Galakhov hovered round her in sentimental irresolution, now staying in the same town as the Ogarevs, now wandering aimlessly in the neighbourhood. His letters to Maria during these brief absences throw a curious light on his state of mind.

My dear, sweet, charming Maria [he wrote in July] how sad I am away from you! I think separation from you has never so tormented me. I embrace your knees. You have expressed for me so much devotion, affection, intimacy that this luxury has become one of my necessities – and yet I am compelled to give it up. But why go away? Why not remain together? Well, because there is contradiction in all things, and I cannot bear it any longer day by day without moving either in one direction or in the other.

Maria would gladly have assisted him to move in the direction of her own desires. But Galakhov, like a true Romantic, was more interested in the analysis of his own feelings than in the objective reality of Maria's feelings for him. In August he sought the seclusion of the minor British islet of Heligoland, and spent nine days there in a vain endeavour to resolve the hidden contradictions of his heart. Every day he wrote long and impassioned letters to Maria at Karlsbad. Maria had at any rate been frank with him. She had told him that she would rather take than give; that she disliked the words 'for ever'; that she could love no man long; and that she was incapable of imparting to her lover happiness, or at any rate repose. At Heligoland, Galakhov brooded on all these things and summed up the situation with the 'graceful melancholy' which had struck Herzen as the most conspicuous feature of his character.

When you love [he wrote to Maria] you are capable of every sort of madness, just like a man. But notwithstanding the masculine traits in your character you are more woman than any other woman. You are self-willed to the highest degree; it is no use reasoning with you. A man must force you to love him.

Maria was willing enough to be forced. But she could not endure any longer this unending, unfruitful analysis of her own character and of her lover's emotions; and when Galakhov reached Lübeck on the steamer which brought him back from his island retreat, he found awaiting him an indignant letter from Maria. It has not been preserved, but he quotes copiously from it in his answer.

For three years [she wrote] you have been making love to me. You have done everything to win my attention and to excite my inclination for you; and when at last you have succeeded, you halt in a state of uncertainty. You won my love. Why did you not take me? This is not how passion behaves. No, if you really loved me, you would stop philosophizing, you would not be held back by hesitations of principle. And what question can there be? Passion itself has rights of its own.

This letter impelled Galakhov to yet another analysis of Maria's state of mind; and at Lübeck, on the same night (18–19 August 1841), he sat down and indited a twelve-page reply.

To give yourself to a man [he wrote] is, you say, precisely as com-promising as to pour out a glass of champagne. You are right; it is just as natural – if only the consequences were the same. I desire you, you are mine, and that is the end of it. But in practice you refuse to assimi-late the possession of your body to the swallowing of a glass of cham-pagne. You reject that as a humiliating vulgarity; you demand as a condition sympathy, friendship, established relations. Excellent! I accept the condition. But then you must part with your husband, with his wealth and with his name; you are no longer entitled to them – that is as clear as the day.

Galakhov knew well whither this dialectic must lead; for Maria was not inclined to dispense with her husband's name and still less with his money. The letter concluded with what were virtually words of farewell; and instead of going to Karlsbad, Galakhov returned to Russia. But he continued to write to the lady whose embraces he had shunned; and at one moment he regretted, in a characteristic but scarcely gallant phrase, that 'he had not drunk the cup to the bottom'. In the last letter of all, written more than a year after the breach, he once more sums up Maria's character in a tone of lofty reprobation:

You have no moral or intellectual centre of gravity; yet at the same time your nature is not sufficiently passive to follow traditional principles quietly and submissively.

There is no evidence that these ineffectual lovers ever met again. Galakhov spent most of his remaining years in Paris; and there, in 1847, he married an Englishwoman, a Miss Eliza Bowen, Herzen being one of the witnesses of the marriage. Two years later he died of consumption.

The tragedy of Maria and Galakhov was a tragedy of imperfect accommodation. Maria, for all the boldness of her speech, had been born too late to accept in her own person the 'champagne' theory of love. She could not, after the manner of the eighteenth century, regard the commerce of the sexes as an exhilarating and stimulating pastime which engaged nobody to any superfluous display of feeling. Maria believed, with George Sand, that 'passion has rights of its own'; and these rights included the right to surround itself with a halo of idealization. There was nothing in this which need have shocked Galakhov. But typical Romantic though he was in his capacity for introspection, he retained enough of the traditional respect for marriage to shrink, in the last resort, from the seduction of a woman who was still the wife of his friend; and his constitutional incapacity to decide made him helpless in the face of the old-fashioned dilemma between love and loyalty. But these conditions were unlikely to recur. There were men in the world whose temperaments were less exacting and less unaccountable; and Maria rapidly recovered – perhaps more rapidly than Galakhov himself – from the humiliations of this abortive love affair. In the autumn of 1841, when Galakhov had returned to Russia, the Ogarevs went on to Rome. Maria spent the winter there; and poor Nick returned alone to Moscow.

It was clear that the marriage had reached the breaking point. Early in June 1842 Ogarev visited the Herzens in Novgorod. He had decided to return to Europe for a final discussion with Maria.

He means to have a separation from her [writes Herzen in his Diary]. God grant it! But will he have strength enough? By cunning and pretence she may still remain master of his gentle, honest nature.

148

The meeting between husband and wife took place at Mainz. It lasted for some days and gave Ogarev a permanent aversion for the pleasant city on the Main. He had appeared at the first interview trying to summon up courage to ask for a separation. He might have spared himself the agony of deciding. Maria forestalled him with the same demand, and made it clear that she intended to maintain it. She demanded a separation, a cash payment to meet her immediate needs, and the promise of an annual allowance; and she was willing, on these terms, to replace love by friendship.

It all came as a sad shock to poor Ogarev, who had never believed in the separation he had come to propose. He granted everything that was asked of him. He gave her a bond for 300,000 roubles, secured on his estates and bearing interest at six per cent, which would bring her in an income of 18,000 roubles; and Maria returned in triumph to Rome. For some time Ogarev drifted, thoroughly wretched, from place to place in Germany, writing letters to Maria which, for fervent devotion, scarcely yield to those of his courtship. They certainly are among the strangest letters ever written by a man to a wife from whom he had just obtained a separation. Presently he could bear it no longer and, as winter drew on, went to join Maria in Rome.

There he discovered – if he had not guessed it already – the cause of Maria's insistence. A flat in Rome was being shared at this time by a Russian poet named Maikov, whose correct verses still grace the anthologies, and a Russian artist named Vorobiev, whose even slenderer title to fame is the part played by him in the final disruption of Ogarev's first marriage. Maria was now living more or less openly with Vorobiev. Ogarev chivalrously assured her that his presence served to protect her reputation; but she seemed too indifferent either to welcome or resent it. So long as he behaved, he could stay or go as he pleased. He spent the winter in this humiliating position and returned to Germany.

You have the strongest character [wrote Herzen to him at this time] of anyone I know. You have an iron force – of weakness . . . The most painful facts dissolve into a sort of gentle humour, and between the most melancholy lines you read the hidden meaning which gives no cause for grief. Beneath your tears there is a child's smile, beneath your smile a child's tear. You have a broad comprehension of everything that is

149

human, and a dull incomprehension of everything that is particular to Ogarev.

It is doubtful whether Herzen ever understood, either now or later, the keenness of the pain which was sometimes concealed beneath Ogarev's ingenuous smiles and tears.

For more than a year Ogarev disappears from view. He was in Germany; he sought consolation in wine and women; and he continued to correspond with his wife. We know nothing more. Then in August 1844 Maria suddenly joined him in Berlin. She was pregnant; and it seemed convenient, from every point of view, that the child should be recognized as his. He had no objection. It would bring back a certain interest to his life. And he records the sequel in a letter to Moscow, the tone of which hovers between the cynical and the tragic.

My intention of becoming a father has been shattered. The child was born prematurely – dead. Its pitiful face I cannot forget. It happened eight days ago. My wife is well.

Three months later Maria returned to her lover; and this time Ogarev had the premonition – and perhaps the desire – that it would be their last meeting. On the eve of her departure he wrote a poem under the Byronic motto:

> So farewell! And if for ever,
> Then for ever fare thee well!

Its concluding couplets ran as follows:

The book is closed – our story is read to the last page; but my lips shall not reproach thee.

Farewell! Perhaps we may yet sometimes look back on life with a smile; and in perfect peace we shall name each other's names at our last hour.

More than thirty years later Ogarev lay on his deathbed in Greenwich. But if we may interpret a dying man's visions, it was not the image of Maria Lvovna which haunted his last moments.

*

Ogarev did not return to Russia till the following spring. He stayed for six months in Moscow. Then he went to his estate at

Aksheno, and spent two years there as a model landlord. In a poem of the period he enumerates his three ideals:

> that the village should flourish and prosper;
> that the children should be taught their letters;
> and that the peasants should be good without the whip.

And among his papers dating from this time has been found a detailed scheme, which was never carried out, of an *École Polytechnique Populaire*. It was a prosaic interlude in his stormy life – a period of recuperation from the emotions and excesses of his sojourn in Europe. But even here he was not without the consolations of human intercourse. Among his nearest neighbours was Alexis Tuchkov, whom we have met, together with his two daughters Elena and Natalie, as travelling-companions of the Herzens in France and Italy. The Tuchkov estate bore the name of Yakhontovo; and Ogarev was a frequent visitor there, particularly on festive occasions. Fifty years later, when Natalie wrote her *Memoirs*, she still remembered the skilful and original manner in which poor Nick honoured a toast, holding in his left hand a goblet of champagne and in his right a plate, which he would break at the critical moment, with one sharp tap, across his curly head.

So much of poor Nick's biography is necessarily set in a minor key that we arrive with relief at a passage of pure comedy. In the late summer of 1848, he invited to Aksheno the Countess Salias de Tournemir with her two children and a governess. The lady, who belonged to an ancient Russian family and had been married to a French count, was in her thirty-fourth year, and had not yet embarked on the literary career which was to make her famous as a journalist and writer of fiction.*

The invitation was decently explained by the fact of a distant

* Probably nobody has read her once popular novels since the writer in the last pre-war edition of the standard Russian encyclopedia, who reports on them as follows: 'The heroes of her stories and novels are men of the *grand monde*, without occupation, without will-power, and without intellectual ambitions of any kind; the attitude of the author to them is unsympathetic. Her sympathetic characters are her heroines, who typify virtue beguiled and innocent suffering. Love in the novels of Madame de Salias constitutes the only object for which the beams and scaffolding of the story are constructed.' The lady evidently drew her heroines from herself. May we assume that Ogarev sat as a model for some of her idle, weak-willed heroes?

relationship between them. Ogarev's present interest in the Countess was, however, of a sentimental kind; and the acceptance of the invitation showed that the interest was reciprocated. But before the frail beauty had time to surrender – before she even arrived at Aksheno – the situation had changed by an altogether unforeseen diversion. In the autumn of 1848 the Tuchkov family had returned home from their travels in Italy and France.

Ogarev seems, even before their foreign tour, to have taken a paternal interest in the almost grown-up daughters of his neighbour. But he did not discriminate between them; and his first letter after their return is addressed in polite French to 'Mesdemoiselles Helène et Natalie', and concludes decorously with what he calls his 'shakehands' to the girls and to their papa. But nine months abroad had worked marvellous changes in these two provincial young ladies; and Natalie in particular, who was now nineteen, had developed with startling rapidity under the romantic stimulus of Natalie Herzen's infatuation and George Sand's novels. Innocently and imperceptibly, a particular friendship sprang up between Ogarev and Natalie. His subsequent letters to Yakhontovo, not less decorous than their predecessors but significantly warmer in tone, are addressed to Natalie alone.

Ironically enough, it was the Countess herself who, unwillingly and unwittingly, set the match to these two inflammable hearts. At the end of November she and Ogarev were on a visit to Yakhontovo. Her feminine intuition probed Natalie's fluttering heart; and in an ill-judged moment she remarked derisively to Ogarev that 'the younger Tuchkov girl had fallen in love with him'. Ogarev signally failed to perceive that such an emotion was a subject either for ridicule or for contempt. He began to watch Natalie with reinforced interest and admiration; and having convinced himself of the perspicacity of Madame de Salias's observation, he was surprised to discover that his own jaded but ever gentle heart was beginning to flutter back.

The series of letters written by Ogarev to Natalie between the beginning of December 1848 and 9 January 1849 make delightful reading. There are twelve of them in all. Some of them took two or three days to write, and the collection would fill a small volume. When we consider that this period of less than six weeks was punctuated by a flying visit of Natalie to Aksheno and a four days'

visit of Ogarev to Yakhontovo, we may well believe his remark
that writing to Natalie had become his chief, if not his exclusive,
occupation. The poetry of his nascent love for Natalie alternates
charmingly in the letters with the comedy of his embarrassment
at the continued presence of the now unwanted Countess.

By way of complicating the situation, Madame de Salias had
seen fit to fall ill at Aksheno. Her malady seems to have combined
the symptoms of a feverish chill and of an attack of nerves brought
on by the realization of Ogarev's growing coldness. The ordinary
drugs did not help, and Ogarev resorted to heroic remedies.

On the night of the 5th to the 6th [he writes to Natalie] in sheer
despair, I suggested to Madame S. a supper and plenty of champagne.
It is bad for her general condition, but I thought perhaps it would
restore her nerves. Well, it succeeded! She is better, though the improve-
ment is only (I fancy) apparent. I was very drunk and extremely gay
(though the gaiety, too, was only apparent). At any rate, the result is
that Madame S. is calmer, though I am rather afraid of fever; and for
me, for the moment, that means a respite from the struggle.

But the effects of this original treatment were short-lived. The
letter continues on the morning of the 7th:

Madame S. is worse this morning. Not an attack of nerves, but
exhaustion, shivering, fever, perspiration and difficulty in breathing.
Listen: if this lasts, I shall not be able to leave – if only out of consideration for my duty as a host. And how can you come here? Today there
are 28 degrees of frost!

There is a further bulletin the same evening:

Madame S. has been very bad, i.e. an attack of nerves and violent pains
in the chest. I am dreadfully sorry for her, and yet at the very bottom
of my heart I feel irritated with her. You can easily imagine my state
of mind. Don't be angry, and don't repeat: 'Tu l'as voulu, Georges
Dandin.'

These reports on the health of the Countess interrupt the prattle
of this romantic lover of thirty-five, still scarcely conscious of his
love.

You regret last year [he writes in the same letter], the year, as you
call it, of happy care-free youth. For my part I am selfish enough not
to regret last year. I like last year, but I do not regret it, for I like this

year better. Is it because you are now no longer a child and therefore, since I am old, there is more equality between us? I don't know. I think it is rather because, cured by age of imaginary affections, I press more closely to my heart those affections which have a real foundation . . .

I am in a strange state just now. My body is sick to the point of exhaustion and fatigue. But my heart and mind are as calm as if I were completely happy. I feel my heart and mind so full of something – of energy, kindness, tenderness. Yes, dear friend! I feel that, old as I am, I am still full of life, and that I shall always have the strength to bear our troubles – yours with interest and my own with indifference.

On 19 December Natalie came to Aksheno for a few hours; and when she left, Ogarev found that she had become 'more and more indispensable to him'. His letters continue to harp on this note:

To be or not to be, said Hamlet. My 'to be' is to see you; and my 'not to be' is to know that I shall never see you again. Pardon! I am afraid of vexing you . . . I will not believe in so sad a future. I want you to live, and I want to live; and if I can contribute but the tiniest mite to the comfort of your life, I shall be content. I shall at any rate be able to help your studies with the little knowledge I possess. Little indeed, dear friend. I have lived much in feeling and in thought; but I have always been an alchemist. My science is made of dreams. As for my heart, it dreams no longer. My attachment to you is a reality . . .

No, I must stop writing to-day. I am too much inclined to tenderness. I have passed a dreadful day. Madame S. has been ill and unhappy and I have had to use all my strength to restrain myself; for, though I am really sorry for her, I can scarcely overcome the concentrated bitterness which is now my constant feeling for her. It is a torture which you happily do not know. I had to do everything to console her. I lied. She has the knack of putting me up against a wall, where I must either tell the truth which would annihilate her or lie. What am I to do? I preferred to be humane, despite all my desire to annihilate her on the spot . . .

I love you too much. I am inclined to tear up this letter, I am afraid of vexing you. Whatever you say, I am older than you. May yours be the happiness! I shall be content if I see you happy, or if I die at your side on the barricades.

Ogarev and his guests were once more invited to Yakhontovo for Christmas and the New Year. But when 24 December came Ogarev in his turn was ill. Madame de Salias went alone with the children, and her defaulting cavalier followed three days later. There are no records of the visit, and on 1 January they all returned to Aksheno. No sooner had they arrived – an hour after midnight – than Ogarev sat down to write to his Natalie.

On the journey I slept, sang and played with Marie [Madame de Salias's elder child] as if I were the jolliest person in the world; but I scarcely spoke to Madame. She seems to be altogether refraining from discussion and cross-examination. But that will come again presently. I don't feel in the least sad. Whether it is the prospect of seeing you again for a long time, or some inexplicable sense of happiness at the bottom of my heart, I don't know; but I feel that life is becoming rich and beautiful as it has never been before . . . I have recovered the light-heartedness of my early years, when all evil seemed transient and all happiness stable. I have faith in the present and the future, like a man who is just beginning to live. In what does my faith consist? What do I expect? No! Today I want to shut my eyes to these questions.

In the next letter Ogarev abandons the stiff and polite French, which had hitherto served the undeclared lovers for their correspondence, and turns, with a sigh of relief, to the more familiar and intimate Russian.

Do you know that since I returned here I have been doing nothing but write to you, play the piano and sleep? In the evening I report for duty.

The 'duty' was of course to amuse the Countess, whose departure was still unaccountably and maddeningly deferred. She was embroidering a bedspread for Ogarev as a parting gift, and he watched in angry impatience the leisurely progress of the work. Music was his only relief.

This evening [he wrote late on 4 January] I was furious, probably because, instead of going away to write to you, I stayed with Madame S., and had an argument in which I felt that I was being unkind, but could not stop myself. I took a sort of delight in playing the part of a brutal, downright man, an out-and-out egoist. That was wicked of me! I know that I am not brutal, but kindly by nature. But a malicious egoism made me want to hurt. How disgusting of me! I would never confess it to anyone but you. Then I sat down at the piano, and thought of you and music (let them in future be inseparable) and my mind flew away into another world, I did not begin to play, but rested my arms on the piano and closed my eyes; and all at once I could see

155

spring and a wood. I recollected an idea which has long been revolving in my mind. A lyric poem. Its subject is this. I am going at dawn into the wood. Everything gradually begins to stir. The sun, leaves, the dew-covered flowers, the birds, the insects. I walk on through this awakening world. What sights and sounds! Slowly mid-day draws on; it is stifling. I rest in the shade. Through the trees you can see the blue sky, in which sight is drowned. All around the sounds, the little voices, which you can only hear in a forest. Then storm! Storm in the forest – you don't know what that is like! And then stillness, the evening sun and the evening fragrance. Last of all, I come out of the wood into the moonlit night. My journey is over.

These musings at the keyboard were succeeded by a curious scene, which is related (after an interval of twenty hours) in a further instalment of the same letter.

I was busy the whole night with Marie, putting on leeches (she had croup, but is better now), and towards morning I felt hungry. I ordered something to eat, and jokingly suggested champagne. Madame Salias insisted on having something to drink. I tried to dissuade her, but did not hold out. My character is weak enough in general, and in that par-ticular respect – well, you know. I agreed, and we drank up two bottles of champagne. Of course, she was drunk and I was not. I was merely bored and disgusted. At ten o'clock, not without difficulty, I got her to bed, went to bed myself and slept till evening.

His share of the two bottles, though insufficient to intoxicate, at least gave him the courage to hint to his companion that her impending departure was to be a 'separation for ever'. But he might have spared his pains; for in the evening the wily Countess assured him that she had been too drunk to remember a word of the conversation.

It is in this same letter, the longest of the series, that Ogarev first canvasses the possibility of divorcing Maria and marrying Natalie. Natalie prided herself too much on her advanced opinions to consider these formalities important. But a few days later Ogarev returned to the subject:

You laugh at the idea of *a wedding*. My dear, you are quite wrong. In itself it is indifferent, but it will save us from general persecution; it has no other significance. We understand realities too well for anything to embarrass us. You know that I should not assert any rights to your person. You would still be perfectly free, but you would have a *friend* at your side. For me, I need nothing more. Probably I shall never fall in love again. If I did, I should merely tell you. And you can love anyone you please. I love you so, that your happiness is dearer to me than anything. I should still be happy, for your friendship is my inalienable possession. *Ergo*, we should be completely free.

The words deserve to be remembered in the light of the subsequent history of this 'free' marriage.

The last letter of all was written on 9 January. Madame de Salias was to have left on that day, but had been prevented by a sore throat. Ogarev was once more in despair. He would wait a day or two longer. Then, if the Countess did not take her departure, he would come to Yakhontovo and refuse to return to Aksheno until she had really gone. The story of Madame de Salias's final exit from Aksheno was unfortunately never written; and the next document in the collection is a joint letter from Ogarev and Natalie announcing to the Herzens in Paris their love and their happiness.

Old Alexis Tuchkov, who was 'advanced enough in his talk, but very different when it came to acts', was not pleased to learn that his nineteen-year-old younger daughter had fallen in love with a married man of thirty-five, even though the man was one of his best friends. But he took the news more calmly than might have been feared. He only asked that, before deciding to dispense with marriage, Ogarev should endeavour to arrange for a divorce from his first wife. He even accompanied the young people to Petersburg to consult lawyers; and the Herzens were asked to approach Maria, who was now in Paris with Vorobiev. In nineteenth-century Russia, divorce by consent was a relatively simple matter; divorce, where one party objected, a virtual impossibility. Unfortunately Maria, living happily enough in adultery, had no desire to marry her lover; and she desired still less to oblige her husband. She greeted Herzen's efforts at mediation with unstinted abuse of himself and of all concerned; and an attempt to employ the Herweghs as negotiators met with no better reception. 'With all due respect to Madame Natalie,' she wrote to Herwegh, 'I think her such a little fool, that short of killing me, you will get nothing out of me.' And in her bold aggressive hand she scrawled across the back of the letter: 'And this is for all Ogarev's friends.'

There was nothing to be done. Herzen vented his spleen by describing Maria, in a letter to Ogarev, as a 'Messalina of the gutter'; and on a hot summer day of 1849 Ogarev and Natalie went off unblessed by the priest, to spend a radiant but illicit honeymoon in the Crimea. A few days before Natalie left the family roof at Yakhontovo, her sister, Elena, married a friend of Ogarev and Herzen named Satin.

It is at this point that the reader must be introduced to a bewildering series of financial transactions which, in their ultimate result, reduced Ogarev from the status of a wealthy landowner to that of a beggar and a parasite. The refusal of Maria to consent to a divorce had filled the Tuchkov family with pardonable resentment; and the effects of their exasperation must be traced in Ogarev's subsequent proceedings. It must have been at their instigation (for he himself was neither sufficiently resolute nor sufficiently vindictive) that he decided, by way of reprisal, to stop the payment of Maria's annuity, thereby defaulting on the bond which he had given her in 1841, and which was secured on the whole of his landed possessions. The step was a hazardous one; for there was no doubt that Maria, who had never shown any inclination to moderate her financial appetites, would take legal action to enforce her claim. But the ingenious and implacable Tuchkovs were ready with an answer to this threat. In order to defeat Maria's pretensions, Ogarev was induced to transfer to Elena's bridegroom, Satin, the whole of his Aksheno estate, the purchase price being payable by Satin, out of the revenues of the estate, in ten annual instalments. This somewhat disingenuous transaction proved fatal to Ogarev's financial welfare; for Satin, through ill-will or insolvency, defaulted on his obligation, and only a few insignificant and belated payments were ever made by him. But for the moment the device served its purpose. When Maria brought and won her action against her husband, she found no property on which distraint could be made except a small estate of Ogarev's called Uruchia in the government of Orel; and this, his sole remaining possession, was sold for her benefit by order of the court.

Of the three estates which Ogarev had inherited on the death of his father twelve years before, nothing now remained to him. He had ceded Belo-omut to his liberated serfs, and the payments due to him from that source were approaching their end; he had lost Uruchia, sold to satisfy Maria's legal claim; and he had transferred Aksheno, his old home, to Natalie's brother-in-law. He remained, for the rest of his days, a dependant on the bounty of his oldest friend. Some provision must be made for the future; and about the time of his elopement with Natalie he borrowed 45,000 roubles from Herzen, and purchased a paper-factory in the government of Simbirsk.

A curious interlude followed. It will be recollected that Ogarev's wife was a niece of Panchulidzev, the governor of Penza. Panchulidzev's vanity suffered from the public slight placed on his *protégée* by Ogarev's desertion of her; and it is difficult to say whether his next proceedings were prompted by official zeal or by personal spite. The European revolutions of 1848 had terrified Nicholas I of Russia. Suspicion, espionage and mass arrests were the order of the day. Early in 1849, about the time when Ogarev was becoming intimate at Yakhontovo, Panchulidzev reported to Petersburg that Tuchkov had, since his return from Paris, been 'wearing a beard and expressing in the presence of young people free-thinking and anti-religious ideas'. The secret police, instructed to make inquiries, discovered that Ogarev was engaged in writing 'works of a revolutionary character'; and finally, in September, just after Ogarev's elopement with Natalie, the Chief of Police in Petersburg received a moving appeal from Maria's drunken and decrepit father, Roslaslev. It merits quotation as a specimen of contemporary manners:

YOUR EXCELLENCY,

Your Excellency's well-known uprightness gives me the courage to solicit Your Excellency's protection. The facts are these. My daughter, married to N. P. Ogarev of the government of Penza, has been abroad for two [*sic*] years on account of illness. Meanwhile Ogarev, having become friendly with Tuchkov, a landowner of the government of Penz, joined, under Tuchkov's influence, the sect of communists. I have become convinced of this not only by report, but by the actions of Tuchkov, Ogarev and his friend Satin. The two latter, who were fellow-students at the University, had previously been suspects and were for a long while under supervision. Ogarev left his wife owing her a substantial sum of money which was secured by a mortgage, and which he would of course have paid if he had not joined the sect of communists under the influence of Tuchkov, the chief leader of the sect.

This is how it all happened. Tuchkov handed over his elder daughter to Ogarev, just as unfortunate women are handed over to men in brothels. Ogarev, having taken his pleasure of her, decided – I do not know why – to pass her on to his friend Satin, this time in legal marriage, giving Satin as her dowry his ancestral estate of 400 souls. Continuing his former habits, he next received from Tuchkov his other daughter. Thus these gentlemen communists worked hard to plunder the unfortunate Ogarev and succeeded, sending him off to enjoy himself with the young lady in the Crimea. From these actions I am clearly convinced that there was a settled plan to get him out of the country and to leave his legal wife, my daughter, without payment. Be gracious, Your Excellency, protect the innocent. I am an old man and have no other joy in life except my daughter. Give order that Ogarev shall remain in Russia and shall pay my daughter; give her the possibility to exist and to return to her country.

It took the authorities some five months to digest this remarkable document. Then, in February 1850, they acted on it. Tuchkov, Ogarev and Satin were arrested and haled to Petersburg; and there, in solitary confinement, each was required to answer a questionnaire based on Roslaslev's letter and Panchulidzev's original indictment. Nothing was spared to them. The beard grown by Tuchkov in Paris, the 'free-thinking and anti-religious ideas', the 'sect of communists', the strange relations between Ogarev and the Tuchkov sisters, were all included in this indictment, which savoured not so much of the misplaced ingenuity of secret agents as of the malicious gossip of the tea-table. It was even alleged against Tuchkov that he had, 'in order to court popularity, invited his foreman, a simple peasant, to sit down in his presence'. The prospects looked black. Immediately on his arrest Ogarev had smuggled away a letter to Herzen in Paris bidding him farewell 'for long years'. But the ways of the Russian police were incalculable; and on this occasion clemency prevailed. The denials of all three men were found to tally in every particular; the existence of the 'sect of communists' remained unproven; and in April all three were set provisionally at liberty. In the following December they were included in the general amnesty on the occasion of the twenty-fifth anniversary of the accession of Nicholas. Ogarev took the only revenge in his power on the man whom he believed to be the culprit. He wrote an ostentatiously polite letter to Panchulidzev, asking him to repay 'without interest' the 5,000 roubles he had lent him 'on the occasion of his visit to the Caucasus', and the further 5,000 roubles lent before he obtained permission to return to Moscow. The reply of the Governor is not extant; but ten years later Panchulidzev was removed from his post for abuses committed during his governorship. He had then been Governor of Penza for twenty-eight years. The central authorities cannot be accused of having acted with undue precipitancy.

But Ogarev and Natalie had to bear, as they wrote to the Herzens, not only the 'hatred of enemies' but the 'slander of friends'. Even the few survivors of the Moscow set adopted an attitude of conventional disapproval. Tuchkov accepted the inevitable with a heavy heart, such independent spirit as he possessed having been broken by the fright of his arrest; and Elena and Satin, from the vantage point of respectable wedlock, looked askance at the irregularity of the position. It was regular enough in nineteenth-century Russia for a married man to have mistresses, or a married woman lovers. But for a man and an unmarried girl of the land-owing aristocracy to live openly together, in defiance of divine law and human custom, was worse than immoral; it was politically unorthodox. Only the Herzens stuck fast to their romantic principles and applauded the lovers from afar; and the blow was all the greater when the news of Natalie Herzen's death, and hints from Herzen of the torment of her last months of life reached them from Nice.

In the meanwile Ogarev settled down at the paper-factory in the unexpected role of a businessman; and here he and Natalie passed, in retirement and quasi-connubial bliss, the years from 1850 to 1855. Life at the factory was uneventful. Ogarev found the work uncongenial, but showed more application to it than might have been expected. Natalie rapidly exhausted the pleasing novelties of housekeeping. She tried self-education, and found herself a dull pupil. She tried her hand at fiction, and sent one of her stories to the popular journal *Notes of the Fatherland*; but the editor returned it with the comment – surely written with his tongue in his cheek – that a tale about the mistress of a married man was unfit for insertion in his respectable columns. She tried gardening, and found more satisfaction than she had anticipated in the sheer physical labour of digging. She was not unhappy, and

she was devoted to Ogarev. But the routine of her daily life, lonely
and childless, and lived in the unconfessed self-consciousness of a
false social position, provided no adequate outlet for her faculties
or for her emotions.

Herzen, established in London since the autumn of 1852, constantly urged them to join him there; and Natalie, at any rate,
was eagerly anxious to escape from Russia. Practical difficulties
and sheer inertia still chained them to the spot. But as time went
on, the impulse grew stronger and the obstacles, one by one, fell
away. In the spring of 1853 Maria Ogarev died in Paris. In her
last years Vorobiev had been replaced by a Frenchman, to whom
she left the scanty remnants of her fortune. The news did not
reach Ogarev and Natalie until nearly six months after the event.
In the salad days of their love they had spoken of marriage with
derision as 'a superfluous and unnecessary common-place'. But
they now made haste to regularize their status. One barrier to the
grant of a passport was thus removed.

Nearly two more years elapsed. Then in 1855 providence, in the
form of an outbreak of fire, destroyed the paper-factory, and left
the Ogarevs without any resources, any occupation, or any in-
ducement to remain. They spent the winter at Petersburg. It was
not a particularly successful time. Ogarev, returning after many
years to congenial society, enjoyed himself in his own way; and his
way was to drink too much in the festive company of his friends.
Alcohol increased the frequency and the virulence of his epileptic
fits, and Natalie became for the first time seriously alarmed for
his health. Nor did she fit well into the new surroundings. The
years of social ostracism had made her morbidly sensitive.
The first symptoms of the hysteria of later years began to appear.
She felt herself, probably without reason, ignored and despised. She
was sure that Turgenev, who years ago had dedicated a story to
her, now hated her. Tolstoy, when invited by Ogarev to their
lodgings, failed to appear; and she took his absence as a personal
slight to herself. The only one of her husband's literary friends with
whom, curiously enough, she was completely at home was the
rather simple-minded Ostrovsky, the popular author of *bourgeois*
comedies.

It was always a troublesome business for one who had been a
political suspect to obtain permission to leave Russia; and

Ogarev, who was no longer in a position to dispense munificent
loans to susceptible officials, had to invoke the patronage of a
cousin who happened to be a general. At last the passport was
granted. The final preparations were made; and in March 1856
the Ogarevs set forth on their journey. Their first stop was at
Berlin. Ogarev had known the city in his days of wandering,
heart-ache and debauchery. Since then nearly ten years had
elapsed, and there had been a revolution. But he could detect
little alteration in the aspect of the Prussian capital. The only
good result of the revolution, he declared, was that smoking was
now permitted in the street. The only other changes were those of
fashion.

There are still few Englishmen in Berlin [he wrote to his father-in-
law]. But the Germans have learned to wear the Highland cloak instead
of an overcoat. It is rather comical to meet a fine gentleman walking
about in a shawl! Ladies on the other hand wear great-coats like a
man's. Well, it's all a matter of habit.

From Berlin Ogarev and Natalie went straight on, through
Brussels and Ostend, to London. Natalie returned to Russia when
life had used and broken her, twenty years later; her husband had
stood on Russian soil for the last time.

CHAPTER 8

The Recurrent Triangle

THE coming of the Ogarevs broke, like a tempestuous sea, into the calm unruffled pools of Herzen's daily existence.

The first storm was one of those episodes which nobody foresees but which, once they have happened, are recognized by everyone to have been inevitable. Natalie Herzen long ago had bequeathed the care of her children, in the event of her death, to her dear Consuelo; and as she lay on her death-bed the name of the other Natalie was the last that crossed her lips. Four years had passed since that day; but it was natural that Natalie Ogarev should now, in virtue of that trust, expect to assume the role of foster-mother to Herzen's motherless children. It was equally natural that Malwida von Meysenbug, who had devoted herself to her new responsibilities with the concentrated passion of her whole being, should resent the faintest hint of an authority over the children which might claim to supersede hers.

The two childless women, both sexually unsatisfied and both possessed by an almost hysterical yearning for children, were predestined rivals. They instinctively recognized each other as such from the outset; though it must be said, in justice to Natalie, that it was Malwida who first provoked, and gave expression to, their mutual enmity. For Malwida it was no mere question of personal jealousies; professional, even national, principles were at stake. She had the traditional German faith in pedagogic theories, and believed herself particularly fitted, by patient study, for the rearing of children. It was at once apparent that Natalie, on the other hand, was equally innocent of theory and of practice, and that a week of her haphazard indulgence might spoil the results of six months' good German discipline. In particular, the eager, disorderly generosity of the Slav temperament shocked Fräulein von Meysenbug's ascetic precision. Malwida had already had trouble in convincing Herzen that 'useless gifts and toys merely blunt children's taste for good and useful things, and encourage the spirit of destructiveness which is already strong enough in the young'. Herzen had ended by accepting her ban on these demoralizing knick-knacks. But the trouble began again in an exaggerated form with Natalie, who confessed that she 'could not pass one of those lovely London toy-shops without wanting to buy everything in the windows and bring it home to the children'. Remonstrances had no effect; and Malwida appealed in despair to the children's father.

The appeal embarrassed Herzen. The single-minded devotion of Fräulein von Meysenbug inspired in him the most sincere and respectable emotions of gratitude and friendship. But his feelings for the Ogarevs were of a different calibre. Their arrival in London had been a romantic reunion of hearts long severed by an unkind fate; and, for the first time since his own Natalie's death, they had brought into his domestic circle the breath of his native land. Loyalty to his dead wife made him desire to respect her wish that the upbringing of her children should be entrusted to her dearest friend. It rejoiced his heart to hear Natalie Ogarev tell them tales of the Russia they would never see, and talk to them in the Russian language which Tata had half forgotten and Olga had never known. Herzen soon perceived that Malwida frowned to find Russian come into its own again as the language of the house, and to hear her charges addressed in an alien tongue which she could not understand. He was uneasy and indecisive. He suggested to Malwida that she should have a friendly discussion with Natalie. Malwida rejected the proposal as useless. He did not want a break; but if she forced a break on him, it was clear whom he would choose to sacrifice.

The consciousness of her impotence filled Malwida with bitterness. She had the courage to prefer a surgical operation to a long, dull pain. One day, seven weeks after the heavily laden cab had drawn up at the house in Finchley Road, she took the frightened children's hands in hers, exhorted them to remember that solemn moment whose significance they would one day understand, and bade the nurse conduct them to Madame Ogarev. Then she walked out of the house, carrying with her her few portable possessions. Nobody saw her go save an Italian servant, who offered consolation by telling her that her departure boded no good to those left behind. Next day, Herzen sent Sasha and Ogarev to Malwida to convey to her the assurance of his undying esteem and gratitude. But in a letter to Maria Reichel he expressed himself more bluntly:

Ah! these Germans, particularly Germans of the female sex, and particularly those who are afflicted with the virgin innocence of old maids!

The summer passed quietly. Ogarev himself, after the convivial winter in Petersburg, had reached England in a deplorable state of health. In the past twenty years epilepsy, sexual indulgence and chronic alcoholism had taken toll of his constitution. The doctor whom Herzen called in would not answer for his life, and prescribed a régime whose principal features were rest and complete abstinence from alcohol. Such stern discipline was seldom prescribed, and more seldom observed, in Russia. It made a strong impression on Ogarev, and in the peaceful surroundings of Finchley Road his condition began to improve steadily. When Malwida departed, the Ogarevs, who had hitherto been installed in lodgings close by, became permanent guests in Herzen's house.

The house had, however, one important drawback. It was semi-detached; and when, on Sundays, Herzen's friends assembled to make merry and play the piano and sing Russian songs in chorus, vigorous taps were heard from the other side of the wall, summoning them to observe the amenities of the English sabbath. This was too much for Herzen. He liked frequent changes of residence and he soon found a new abode in a more rural neighbourhood, sheltered from the sabbatarian English world by a large garden. Early in September, the whole family moved to Laurel House (more usually called, after its owner, 'Mr Tinkler's') High Street, Putney.

It was now more than four years since Herzen at Nice held his dying wife in his arms and swore vengeance. Time had assuaged his wrath and mellowed his sorrow. The castigation of the seducer had receded into the limbo of things which, having proved unattainable, are seen to be unimportant; and Herzen had confined himself, since his arrival in England, to the pleasanter duty of canonizing the victim. He liked to speak of his late wife as one who had suffered many things, and who had borne her sufferings with saintly devotion and fortitude. And to whom could the story of her trials and her vindication be more fittingly or more frequently told than to her dearest friend, the other Natalie? The soul of Herzen and the soul of Natalie Ogarev held communion over the grave of the martyred saint. Mingling their tears, they shared the happiness of many hallowed memories; and from these reverential celebrations Ogarev, who had scarcely known Natalie Herzen, was perforce excluded.

The incendiary properties of shared emotion – even when the emotion has a quasi-religious character – are notorious; and a disinterested spectator, if one had been present, might have had little difficulty in foreseeing the *dénouement*. Herzen would put his arm round Natalie and jestingly ask Ogarev's permission to kiss her. It was perhaps equally dangerous to grant, or to withhold, this agreeable licence; and Ogarev was not the man to refuse it. He rejoiced that Herzen's affection for Natalie was forging a new link between himself and his life-long comrade; and he was relieved to find that there was no repetition of the strained relations which had grown up between his friend and his first wife. Even Herzen did not recoil from this second experiment in the romantic ideal of triangular friendship; for circumstances alter cases, and experience seldom teaches in matters of the heart.

But they were not left for more than a few weeks to inhabit in primitive innocence this romantic paradise. One day – it seems to have been even before their migration from Finchley Road to Putney – they were talking together; and Herzen, sitting on the floor at Natalie's feet, took her hand. Natalie experienced once more the 'magnetic feeling' of which she had been conscious when her husband's friend first embraced her. The contact sent the blood hotly coursing through her body; and meeting Ogarev's eye, she saw that he was gazing at them with tragic understanding. From this scene, which she records two years later in a letter to her sister, Natalie seems to date both her own and her husband's knowledge of her physical passion for Herzen. Only Herzen himself, simple-minded as ever in his personal relationships, did not understand the quality of the feelings which had been kindled between them. Herzen at forty-five was set and middle-aged. He had lived through many tragedies, and chose to look on himself as an old man who has done with life. The sprightly Natalie, thirsting for joys and passions yet untasted, was seventeen years his junior; and she might without incongruity have passed for his daughter.

He concealed his feelings for her, even from himself, under the harmless mask of paternal tenderness; and if it had depended on him alone the mask might never have been torn off. This is not the story of an experienced man of the world who seduces a guileless and impressionable young wife from the path of conjugal fidelity. Seduction there was; but Herzen was the victim, not the seducer.

In Natalie's infatuation for Herzen there was a large, perhaps a preponderant, element of animal heat. The history of her marriage to Ogarev cannot be written in detail; for the material does not exist. But there are clear indications of its failure to satisfy the physical side of Natalie's nature. It would not be fair to say that experience had belied the romantic promise of their wooing. Ogarev was, and remained to the end, a romantic figure. The sentimental schoolgirl, who had fallen in love with him at Aksheno, still survived in the maturer Natalie; and the appeal of Ogarev to her softer feelings was as irresistible as ever. He touched her heart in a way no other man ever could. But Natalie was not all heart. She had brought to Ogarev the fresh and vigorous desires of unspoiled youth. His love for her, as she wrote afterwards, was the 'last flicker' of a spent and jaded organism. The first years in the country had passed tolerably well; but the last winter in Petersburg had sapped Ogarev's remaining strength and broken his health. Natalie became more and more bitterly conscious of the inequality of her marriage.

> I gave myself up to him [she wrote to her sister Elena], I loved him, and he was almost the only link which bound me to life. But in secret I knew well that life could have given me something more, and that it was not that which I had wanted.

She had sacrificed herself and her youth to Ogarev; and the consciousness of her sacrifice bred an ever-increasing indulgence in the poisonous emotion of self-pity. Her unsatisfied longings gradually crystallized themselves into a passionate desire for children. The sexual appetites of Ogarev had not abated with advancing age. 'I am dissolute through and through,' he confessed to Herzen about this time; 'and I have to work hard to restrain the animal side of my passions.' But early indulgence had left him incapable of having children. The knowledge of his sterility had come to Natalie at an early stage of their life together before marriage. She describes the revelation in another letter written several years later to her sister:

I remember what alarm there was at the mere idea that I might become pregnant. Everybody feared it; but *he* – yes, it was then that he dealt me that terrible blow, like a child that knows not what it does. I understood; but I loved him, and my desires were unchanged, I only thought that I could be a mother and everything to *him*. It was indescribably painful; but love for the child that was not, and a sort of pride, forced me to keep silence and even to pretend the opposite.

For the moment there must have been, blended with other emotions, a sense of relief. But when Maria's death enabled them at last to marry, the denial of her maternal instincts turned to unmitigated tragedy. Her childlessness weighed on her 'like the heavy hand of the Commander in *Don Juan*'. She brooded on it; and it became at once the cause and symbol of her unrest, the focal point of her thwarted passions. Once they reached England, she could not help contrasting the weak, lovable, pathetic Ogarev with the normal, virile and masterful Herzen – *l'homme moyen sensuel*, who had steered an even course between the extremes of debauchery and asceticism. Circumstances compelled her to live under the same roof, and in closest intimacy, with her husband's friend; and her senses quickly betrayed her.

The crisis came not long after the removal to Putney in September 1856. Even Herzen began to notice that Natalie's friendship for him was 'of a more passionate character than he could have wished'. In the wooing which followed the traditional roles of the sexes were reversed. Herzen, alarmed by the symptoms which he had detected, feigned a coldness which he by no means felt. He began to avoid Natalie, and tried to put the brake on the headlong course of their intimacy. Natalie insisted. She did not understand, or pretended not to understand, his motive in avoiding her. She was hurt, deeply hurt, and protested bitterly that she had done nothing to deserve the indifference of a friend. Herzen's affection for Natalie was sincere; and he was a man of flesh and blood. He reassured her, and consoled her. In the process of consolation fatal words were spoken and irrevocable confessions made. Herzen and Natalie were declared lovers.

The sequel is narrated by Natalie herself in her Diary:

When I saw that Herzen, vanquished by my passionate love, had fallen in love with me, I at once rushed to Ogarev. I understood his pain; it seemed to me that in his place I should never have been able to bear it. All at once the past floated before my eyes in such clear and bright colours, that I was terrified and could not take a step further until I knew how Ogarev regarded it. To take it as he took it, with such infinite broadness of understanding, would have been beyond the power of any – yes, I boldly say, of any other man. He took it with a kind of simplicity which is peculiar to his tender and tolerant nature. I understood everything, and I began to love him still more. He seemed somehow nearer to me than before. I sought his helping hand to enable me to vanquish my passionate attachment to Herzen. I sometimes think he would have liked to do it. But he did not give me his hand; he did not want me to make any sacrifice. Often during these days I felt that he was in pain, and every time the sight of his pain tore from my breast a cry of agony, a prayer for help inspired by the heavy consciousness of my own impotence.

She might have found salvation in flight and even suggested that she should return to Russia; but, continues the Diary,

Ogarev was against my departure. He could have saved me; but he did not wish to cause me pain even for a moment, and did not wish me to make a sacrifice for him.

Only Ogarev, the resigned and agonized spectator of these events, has left no record of his emotions. He did not reproach Natalie. It was in his nature to reproach himself rather than others; and perhaps he felt that a marriage such as theirs gave him no right to judge her. Seven years later, when her unhallowed love had reached its climax of tragedy, he was to address to Natalie a haunting poem in which he begged her forgiveness for the wrong he had done her:

> Forgive me! I am to blame.
> 'Twas I who spoiled your tender age,
> I tore asunder the sacred ties,
> Idly inflamed your mind,
> And fanned, wittingly or unwittingly,
> The spirit of irrational self-will.
> I spread in your soul
> The restlessness of petty intolerance,

The barrenness of scepticism,
And the unbridled abandon of the passions.
Forgive me! I bow before you
A sinner's head . . .
But I was weak, I was in love;
I was not your elder brother, but your slave.

Now he bowed his head in silence – a silence which wrung Natalie's heart, and plagued her conscience, more than any words could have done. He did indeed gently remonstrate with Herzen. But, more faithful to his principles than Herzen himself had once been, he confined his remonstrance to one particular. He reproached Herzen, not with having stolen his wife's affections, but with having said nothing to him about it. Marriage was free, and love was irresistible; but the claims of friendship demanded open confession. It was not the act, but the lack of frankness accompanying it, which constituted the offence against the romantic canon. The reproach seems to have been conveyed by letter; at any rate Herzen chose that medium for his answer. It must have been a difficult answer to write, though Herzen was happily insensitive to the parallel – which inevitably suggests itself to the reader – between his own position now and that of Herwegh six years before.

I had long wanted, my dear friend, to take counsel with you, and kept silent because I shrank from destroying the harmony and quietness of your life, and because I wished to spare both you and Natalie. To say what you said to me is ridiculous. Am I capable of dealing you a blow, of being insincere, when I am always sincere with everyone and when my own wounds are still unhealed? It is my desire to finish my life with you, and I believe we shall finish it together hand in hand.

I noticed that N.'s friendship for me was of a more passionate character than I could have wished. I love her with all my heart, deeply and warmly, but this is not passion. For me, she and you are the same. You are both my family and – with the children – are all that I have. At first (it was after we came to Putney) I tried to keep aloof. She did not understand, and was so hurt that I naturally hastened to reassure her. Then, too, I could not, as one who had long been cut off from any warm feminine affection, fail to be touched by her sisterly devotion. You desired it yourself; and in my pure-hearted intimacy with your wife I saw a new pledge of our triple union. When I saw once more that she was being carried away by passion, I thought it was all the result of her ardent character and of her inability to control herself . . .

The thought that this would pain you gave me no rest and tormented me as much as your illness did at first.

Whatever barriers I tried to erect, *you both* broke through them. I deserved your confidence. I stand before you fearless and blameless, friend of my youth; but one step further – and a new abyss opens at our feet.

I want to keep you for myself, and myself for you. But for this you must give me your hand and your counsel, and – above all – your unquestioning confidence.

A friend, a brother could not be nearer than I am to Natalie; and I will employ all my love for you both to preserve this bond. There is no power, no passion on earth which can part you from me. That N. loves me very much, is right and proper; that her love has assumed a certain character is not my fault. But, my friend, to eliminate this can only be achieved by great gentleness.

The uncertainty of our chronology leaves it doubtful how long the two lovers struggled with their passion. The declaration of love is recorded in a letter from Natalie to her sister of 27 November 1856, six months after the Ogarevs' arrival in England. It is probable, though not quite clear, that when this letter was written she was not yet Herzen's mistress. But when we reach our next dated source, the Diary kept by Natalie from June to August 1857, the liaison is already of some weeks', or perhaps some months', standing. The letter from Herzen to Ogarev must fall somewhere between the declaration of love and the consummation of the liaison.

The union with Herzen gave Natalie transient satisfaction. For a few moments she seemed to have found in him the 'equal' love which she had missed in her marriage with Ogarev. For a brief space she sunned herself in the 'bright thought' of being to both of them a 'loving, devoted sister'; and Ogarev dreamed of 'the union of three persons in one love'. Most women might have found Herzen a satisfactory lover. But Natalie had not the gift for happiness. Immoderate and impulsive in her passions, she was no less impulsive and immoderate in her remorse. Their love, once it had been consummated, seemed to her a 'monstrosity'. Already in August 1857 she could write in her Diary that she 'had taken an important step in her life without due reflexion and had paid dearly for it'. Morbidly eager for self-humiliation, she looked back on their wooing, and told herself that Herzen's love for her had been mere sensual excitement, kindled by provocation on her side. She had jealous, tormenting dreams, in which she saw him fondling other women. His love, even if sincere, was for him 'of secondary importance or less'; it was not 'the deep, pure love which gives such profound faith in mankind'. Natalie was still a Romantic; Herzen, after the manner of disabused Romantics, had become a cynic. She was conscious of 'a chilly blast blowing from him'. In such an atmosphere romantic love could never flower; and she too took refuge in cynicism.

> To dream at our time of life [she wrote bitterly] of some impossible beautiful, poetical, harmonious life is inadmissible. I was mistaken. *He* enjoys it in his own fashion; and what if I fail to sympathize and do not appreciate *his* view of life? Get out of the way – it is high time! Personal relationships mean so little to him and so much to me. I love him, but I know that I cannot be satisfied with what he gives me.

The worst of all was when other emotions, which had seemed almost dead, revived in her breast, and proved to her that Ogarev's hold on her heart was far stronger than she had imagined in her moments of sensual intoxication. 'By her sleepless nights, by her unceasing, silent, secret tears' she knew now that Ogarev was 'no less dear to her than before'. She began to make involuntary comparisons between the two men and the state of her feelings for them, and these comparisons were not at all to Herzen's advantage.

> Ogarev is in pain; he cannot conceal that from me. Today he was strangely irritable and curt with me and this hurt me more than any of Herzen's outbursts. Herzen, even when he is not in the right, is always consoled by the consciousness of his own rectitude; Ogarev, who really is in the right, makes no fuss about it. I am afraid, my legs give way under me, and the arm which I used to press so closely to mine abandons me. Instead there is this new arm, full of energy and of cold criticism of my defects. I cannot lean on it. I feel in it little love; there is friendship, and there is a sort of condescension which is more bitter to the heart than the worst insult.

Ogarev now often absented himself without explanation for hours at a time, and came back the worse for drink. Natalie began to feel that she had poisoned his life. 'His worst enemy could not have hurt him more.' And her belated pangs of conscience in regard to her husband discharged themselves in bitterness on the head of her lover. 'I only wish,' she wrote once to Herzen, 'that *he* could look on me with *your* indifference.'

On this tumultuous sea of uncoordinated emotions Natalie drifted and tossed for many months. She no longer felt any firm ground beneath her feet; and she ceased to be able to respect herself. Her character became capricious and uneven. Herzen was irritable and overbearing; and the tragedy of guilty love was supplemented by the vulgar comedy of petty domestic quarrels. Ogarev, who took no part in these scenes, perhaps suffered from them most. He has left us a 'sketch for a comedy' under the title *Bedlam; or A Day of Our Life*, which, by an anticipated use of the medium of Chekhov, depicts in vivid colours the heartrending futility of daily existence at Laurel House, Putney.* In the long run Natalie was honest enough to blame nobody but herself; and the consciousness of her guilt became the key-note of her misery. She would gladly have died; but the thought of being buried in the English style, 'solemnly and coldly, in Highgate Cemetery', acted as a deterrent. Like many who speak much of death, Natalie was destined for a long and tormented life. Another stage in her career was approaching. Early in 1858 she found herself pregnant.

A discovery which, in other conditions, would have meant the fulfilment of Natalie's most sacred ambition, filled her and Herzen with nothing but consternation. It would introduce an element of open scandal into their relationship; it would complicate the position of Ogarev; and it would forge a new and permanent link between them at a moment when their passion had almost reached breaking-point. It gave Natalie food for much bitter reflexion. Her sins, and the circumstances of her life, had turned to gall the sweetest and purest of human delights. Russian peasant women, she remembered, always went to confession before child-bearing; and a letter which she wrote in August to her sister served her for the same purpose.

Death has overtaken me in London in the guise of a revival – a fictitious, imaginary revival – of youth. I am not the same person, Elena dear, whom you used to press so tenderly to your heart and call your sister; she no longer exists. The person who left you all out of love for Ogarev is dead. It is a good thing you did not come to London. It

* This curious and revealing document should be read in Appendix D (p. 329).

would have hurt me to see you. With you silence would be a lie, a crime; and it is uncanny for a misshapen skeleton to look at living beings and to feel that nobody notices that he is a skeleton. And all this at the moment when a new creature is making its appearance in the world, a creature which once upon a time might have been ardently desired; but now strength, energy, light, will-power, repose are lacking. How am I to greet my child? With the same bitter tears with which I greeted its first movement in my wcmb?

It was in such conditions that Ogarev realized, in the queer phrase which he had used in Berlin fourteen years before, his 'intention of becoming a father'. A girl was born on 4 September 1858. She was duly registered as Ogarev's child. Her full name was Elizaveta Nikolaevna – the second name being the patronymic from Nicholas; and she came to be called Liza. On 6 September Herzen informed his son (who, for decency's sake, had been hurried off to Switzerland a few weeks before the event) that mother and child were both doing well.

The lull which followed the birth of Liza was brief. A move from Putney to Fulham produced no change in the moral atmosphere; and the same conditions of daily friction soon prevailed again in all their former virulence. Readers of *Bedlam; or A Day of Our Life* will have divined that Ogarev did not hold Herzen blameless. He respected Herzen. But his sensitive heart was filled with deep pity for Natalie; and pity finds excuses more readily than respect. He sums up the situation in a long letter, remarkable for its understanding, which he wrote to Herzen in the summer of 1859:

You are both cruel. That is why it is difficult to set your relations in a higher key. If I succeed in raising her, you ruin everything by your cruelty. If I raise you, it is she who is inexorable. All the same, it is you who, by your upbringing, should be better able to master the human heart. You are conscious of your strength in dealing with human problems in general; but you do not care a damn for particular individuals. She suffers from a defect of character which only a mother's care could heal. I shall do all I can. But if I fail, if instead of helping, you continue to display your rational-egotistical malice (just as she displays her irrational-egotistical malice) then – then, I ask only one thing. Keep me as a faithful employee of the printing-press, but let me live by myself . . . Perhaps this is cruelty on my part. But you have both deserved it.

175

And he concludes with a diagnosis which, by its insistence on the love-hate complex, recalls the psychological probings of the earlier Romantics and anticipates the still profounder analyses of Dostoevsky:

She loves you passionately, and therefore jealously; and there are no bounds to her passionate jealousy or to her (*sui generis*) hatred. There love, passion and hate are so fused into one monstrous discord that it takes a fine ear to distinguish the notes.

From this torment there was no escape, so long as continuous contact inflamed the sore. Like the Engelsons years before, Herzen and Natalie were drawn and held irresistibly and fatally together by the twin emotions of love and hatred, now reinforced by common love, jealous on both sides, of their child. It was worse perhaps for her than for him; for his work still occupied the major part of Herzen's life and thought. Natalie had no such escape from herself; but at the worst moments she took refuge in the idea of a return to Russia and her family – the one sheet anchor of safety in a storm-tossed world. In the summer of 1859 she actually obtained her passport. But she lacked the courage to act on the decision, and in a few months it was too late. Ogarev disobeyed a formal summons of the Russian Government to return to his native country. The sentence of excommunication was pronounced; and the ban extended, as a matter of course, to his wife. The frontiers of Russia were closed against her.

The veto made it seem to Natalie all the more essential that she should be re-united, if only for a short time, with her beloved sister. If she could not go to Elena, Elena must come to her. In the spring of 1860, Elena and her husband applied for a passport for foreign travel. The passport was granted, but by a characteristically spiteful precaution was made valid for all countries except England. It was well known that most European countries were still closed to Herzen; and the Russian authorities calculated that, by imposing this restriction, they would prevent a meeting between Herzen and Satin. The calculation was correct. But the limitation on Herzen's movements did not extend to Natalie; and she was able to spend the summer of 1860 with Elena and Satin in Germany and Belgium. She was accompanied by Liza and an English nurse and by Tata Herzen.

The journey provided a respite from domestic broils; but it brought to a head the problem of Olga. Perhaps Olga was difficult and obstinate. Perhaps Malwida had already spoiled her before she came into Natalie's hands. At any rate, Natalie had never succeeded in winning the affections of Herzen's second daughter. Her treatment of the child was brusque and irritable; and since the birth of Liza the last remnants of tenderness had disappeared. When Natalie went abroad, the nine-year-old girl could neither be sent with her nor left uncared for at home. The faithful Malwida was still in the background; and she took Olga to live with her in the house of some German friends where she lodged. It was, as Herzen realized too late, the first step towards permanent separation; and it was a step which, once taken, could not be retraced. Olga could not be brought back; it would be unthinkable once more to substitute Natalie's capricious harshness for Malwida's patient and jealous care. Before Natalie returned from the Continent, Malwida asked and obtained permission to take Olga with her to Paris for the winter. The child never returned, except as an occasional visitor, to her father's house. Herzen had to thank Natalie for the loss of one of his children; and a fresh element of mutual reproach was added to the growing bitterness of their relations.

Natalie came back to England on Christmas Eve 1860. She had exchanged angry and despairing letters with Herzen while she was abroad. But seven months of separation had done their work. Sores had had time to heal, and insults to be forgotten; and for the moment there was something like a reconciliation. It was sealed by a resumption of physical relations; and within a few weeks Natalie was pregnant again. The summer – a summer of relative tranquillity punctuated by violent storms of irritation – was spent at Torquay; and in November twins were born. They were registered by the Registrar of St Mary, Paddington (Herzen now lived at Orsett House, Westbourne Terrace, just behind Trinity Church) as the children of 'Nicholas Ogareff, editor of *The Bell* Russian newspaper' and 'Natalie Ogareff, formerly Tuchkoff'; and their names were recorded as Alexis and Helen respectively. When they first began to lisp intelligibly they called themselves 'Lola-Boy' and 'Lola-Girl'; and these names clung to them throughout their short life and in the memory of their parents.

The care of three small children occupied and exhausted Natalie, physically and emotionally, for the next two years; and there was a partial respite in the warfare of mingled love and hate. It was the period of Herzen's most feverish political activity and of the last gleam of happiness which either he or Natalie were to know.

Meanwhile Ogarev had found a new source of consolation and of interest in life. About the time of the birth of Natalie's first child he had met, in the course of his now frequent pilgrimages to the public houses of central London, a prostitute who frequented these establishments in search of customers. Her charge for a visit was half a sovereign and Ogarev went with her to her room. He liked the girl, and the visit was several times repeated. He asked her about herself. Her name was Mary Sutherland. She was getting on for thirty – the same age as Natalie; and she had a boy of five called Henry, who was boarded out with friends while she earned the wherewithal to support him. Ogarev inquired the extent of her needs. She explained that she could with care make both ends meet on thirty shillings, or three visitors per week; and he promised, visit or no visit, to guarantee her this sum.

Some days later, Ogarev once more met Mary on the streets. There had hitherto been no bargain, not even any suggestion, that she should change her mode of life. He said nothing. But she could see how this chance encounter pained him, and she understood for the first time that he had conceived a passionate, sentimental desire to reform her. New vistas opened before her mind. She calculated that if she could abandon her profession and take the boy to live with her, thirty shillings a week would be more than ample for her requirements. She assured him eagerly that she would never go on the streets again; and when he tormented himself with doubts she suggested that if she moved away from the prostitutes' quarter to some remoter spot where he could visit her, her temptation and his anxieties would both be removed. The Ogarevs and Herzen were still living in Putney; and some time during the autumn of 1858 Mary Sutherland was conveniently installed in lodgings at Mortlake.

But the complete story of poor Nick's last and happiest love belongs to a subsequent chapter.

CHAPTER 9

The Great Quinquennium

I T is a curious circumstance that a man who, at the age of thirty-five, a minor and insignificant man of letters, had left Russia for ever, should have become ten years later the most powerful figure in the Russian political world. It was an age when journalism as a political force was unknown in Russia, and unimportant even in the rest of Europe; and the story of *The Bell* newspaper is a unique episode, not only in Herzen's life, but in modern history.

You can work on men [wrote Herzen in *My Past and Thoughts*] only by dreaming their dreams more clearly than they can dream them themselves, not by demonstrating their ideas to them as geometrical theorems are demonstrated.

For the space of about five years, Herzen, living in London, dreamed, in visions of unprecedented clearness and splendour, the aspirations of enlightened, liberal Russian opinion, both inside and outside Russia. In tones of fervent missionary zeal and in a pungent literary style, he proclaimed aloud the hopes which Russia scarcely dared to confess even to herself. The conjuncture soon passed; and the vision faded. But the memory remained in history. These five years from 1857 to 1862 were the most fruitful and important of Herzen's life.

It was the ingenious and eccentric Engelson who had first suggested to Herzen the issue of a regular journal in London.

You should publish a review [he wrote in October 1852] in three languages – English, French and German. It should come out at first twice monthly, then every week, and should be similar in size and price to the *Sunday Times*. The English section, with its sale in England and America, would cover the (certain) losses on the French and German sections. In order to get money in England for such a tri-lingual review, you would have to guarantee its success; and its success, i.e. a big sale in the English-speaking countries, can only be secured by getting good names as contributors. . . . You understand in what sense they would agree to work. They would preach on the Continent the theory of Free Trade, of universal peace, of the union of peoples on the basis of Free Trade and a brotherly distribution of commerce. Wars and robberies would, of course, find no support from your contributors. But the idea of colonization would be strongly advocated, and in general their aim would be to make the Continent love England. On the other side of the Ocean, slavery would be denounced, but the occupation of the whole of America by the United States warmly approved.

Herzen, who possessed an abundance of the common sense which was so conspicuously absent in Engelson's character, discarded this fantastic project without discussion; and the genesis of *The Bell* must be traced to quite other sources. Not many months after his arrival in London, Herzen was invited to contribute to the needs of a Polish printing-press conducted by the Polish refugees. He responded to the appeal; and the idea suggested itself to him of setting up on his own account a Russian press. The founts were purchased second-hand in Paris; and in the spring of 1853, the Free Russian Press was installed on the premises of the Polish press at Regent Square. It was afterwards transferred to premises of its own, first in Judd Street, and later at Thornhill Place, Caledonian Road. But it retained the Polish associations of its origin in the person of one Ciernecki, a faithful employee who continued throughout its career to be its technical manager. Another Pole named Tchorzewski, a gentleman of loftier social pretensions, but no less dependent on Herzen's bounty,* kept a bookshop in Soho, where the publications of the Free Russian Press were exposed for sale, and where a circulating library of French novels and other foreign works was available to subscribers at the rate of twopence a volume or sixpence a week.

The output of the Press was at first confined to occasional pamphlets on Russian political subjects written by Herzen himself. Herzen took an almost childlike delight in the new toy.

When a bookseller in Berners Street [he relates in the volume issued to celebrate the tenth anniversary of the Press] sent round for ten

* Natalie Ogarev in her *Memoirs* describes Tchorzewski as possessing 'the exterior of a gentleman'. He was fair with a thick ruddy beard and 'affectionate eyes, particularly when they were looking at a member of the fair sex'. He liked to act as *cicerone* to rich Russian visitors to London. He was too proud to accept payment in this capacity; but he relied on his clients to entertain him sumptuously in return for his services.

shillings worth of copies of *Baptised Property* [a pamphlet on serfdom], I took that for success, gave the boy a shilling tip, and with *bourgeois* delight put away in a special place the first half sovereign earned by the Russian Press.

His pride was not without excuse. It was the first time an independent Russian press had ever existed; and the bare notion of being able to print in Russian these slashing attacks on the Russian Tsar and all his works seemed incredibly audacious and exhilarating. The Tsarist authorities could themselves scarcely believe their eyes. Some hundreds of copies of these early pamphlets found their surreptitious way over the Russian frontier, and were passed from hand to hand in wonder and admiration by the bold spirits of the rising generation. Some of them Herzen himself, in a spirit of bravado, sent through the post to important Tsarist officials. There is evidence in the official archives of the anxiety which these proceedings excited in Petersburg.

The success (political though not, of course, financial) of these fugitive publications at length suggested to Herzen the creation of a periodical which would pursue the same objects in a more regular manner. The immediate impetus was given by two unconnected but almost simultaneous events. In March 1855, the death of Nicholas I brought to an end, after thirty years, the most tyrannical and oppressive reign in the history of nineteenth-century Russia; and less than a month later, the British Chancellor of the Exchequer, introducing his annual budget in the House of Commons, announced the abolition of the Stamp Duty on newspapers and other periodical publications.

The encouragement given by the latter measure to the production of newsprint (more than a hundred new journals of every kind were founded in England during the next few months) make it an incomparably more significant event in history than the demise of a Russian autocrat; but the change in the occupancy of the Russian throne loomed larger in contemporary opinion. When Herzen in his Thames-side villa at Twickenham read in *The Times* the dignified head-line 'Death of the Emperor of Russia', he felt that life had suddenly acquired a new meaning. He summoned a group of village boys, whom he found at his garden gate, to rejoice with him at the removal of his enemy and theirs (it was the middle of the Crimean War); and having distributed a judicious largesse of small silver coins he sent them' away shouting in sympathetic enthusiasm 'Hurrah! Hurrah! Impernickel is dead!' In the evening, a host of Russian and Polish refugees assembled in his house to celebrate the event. The air was buoyant with excitement and optimism. The new autocrat of Russia, Alexander II, was pledged to break with the traditions of his father, to end the scandal of the Crimean War and to introduce liberal reforms. It seemed a propitious moment to launch the new journal. Preparations were pressed forward; and at the beginning of August the first number of *The Polar Star* came from the press. The title was that of a short-lived journal published more than thirty years ago by the heroes of the 'Decembrist' rebellion, whose savage repression had been the first act of the reign of Nicholas I. A vignette of the five Decembrists who had suffered on the gallows adorned the cover of the new *Polar Star*, and underneath was a quotation from Pushkin: 'Hail, Reason!' The tyrant who had executed the Decembrists was dead. Reason reigned in his stead; and Herzen, the spiritual offspring of the Decembrists, was there to speak in the name of reason.

The Polar Star was a rare and intermittent constellation. A single number appeared in 1855, and two in 1856. Occasional issues continued to appear in the following years. But the success of *The Polar Star* and the arrival of Ogarev inspired Herzen with a more ambitious design. *The Polar Star*, a solid journal with literary pretensions selling at eight shillings a number, could never have a wide circulation. Something more popular was needed; and he decided to found, with Ogarev and himself as joint editors, a new paper entitled *The Bell*, which was published monthly, or later on twice a month, at the price of sixpence. It began its career on 1 July 1857, and was issued regularly for exactly ten years. During this decade, two hundred and forty-five numbers appeared, the first hundred and ninety-six (down to April 1875) being published in London, the remainder in Geneva. In 1868 *The Bell* experienced a transient revival, being published no longer in Russian but in French, with an occasional Russian supplement. In 1870, after Herzen's death, the terrorist Nechaev appropriated the name and issued six further numbers. Thereafter, the voice of *The Bell* was silent for ever.

*

The beginning of Herzen's career as a journalist offers a suitable vantage-point for a review of the curious development which took place in his ideas between the years 1849 and 1855. When Herzen left Russia at the beginning of 1847, his eyes were turned towards the west. He believed, with all the intensity of his romantic faith, in salvation from the west; and salvation could only come through revolution. The failures of 1848 and 1849 rapidly and bitterly disillusioned him. It was difficult, after this humiliating fiasco, to believe in the saving virtue either of revolution or of western civilization. Proletariat and *bourgeoisie* were alike discredited. The western proletariat had proved itself cowardly, inefficient and ill-organized; and in the savageries of the western *bourgeoisie*, which had risen to defend its privileges and its money-bags, Herzen saw something quite as repulsive as the worst misdeeds of an aristocracy by right of birth. The Romantic and the revolutionary combined in him to vent their spleen on a common enemy – the despised *bourgeois*. Hatred of the *bourgeoisie* became his strongest feeling – all the stronger for being irrational and instinctive. The *bourgeois* quality of French and English life represented everything that was most antipathetic to the spacious tastes of the Russian gentleman.

The finite, limited personality of the westerner [to quote once more from *My Past and Thoughts*] which impresses us at first sight by its specialization, finally astonishes us only by its onesidedness. The westerner is always satisfied with himself; his self-satisfaction is an insult. He never forgets the personal aspects of a question. His position is generally a cramped one, and his outlook is adapted to his petty surroundings.

Bourgeois revolutionaries of the calibre of Ledru-Rollin are regarded by Herzen with frank contempt – the contempt of the gentleman for the shopkeeper or the clerk; and there is an element of coldness even in his respect for Mazzini. It is significant that the exiles who excite most unstinting admiration are the gentle Polish aristocrat Worcell and the unabashed Italian *condottiere* Orsini.

Herzen's growing distaste for Europe was conditioned and inflamed by a revived longing for his own land. He had left it in a mood of disgust, of thankfulness to escape from a polluted air which poisoned his spiritual existence. But a man does not throw off so easily the traditions and prejudices of his birth. 'I never felt more clearly than now,' he wrote to his Russian friends in July 1851, 'how Russian I am'. And in one of his first writings to be published abroad he speaks, in almost mystical language, of that 'inborn force' which 'through, and in spite of, all external accidents, has kept safe the Russian people and conserved the unshakeable faith which it has in itself'. By a familiar psychological process, absence increased his capacity and his inclination to idealize that which he had lost.

> Our village scenes have not been driven from my memory [he wrote in 1853 in *Baptised Property*] by the view of Sorrento, or by the Roman Campagna, or by the frowning Alps, or by the richly tilled farms of England. Our unending meadows, covered with even verdure, have a tranquillizing beauty of their own. In our spreading landscapes there is something peaceful, trusting, open, defenceless, gently sad . . .

When *The Bell* began to appear, a whole decade separated him from the personal experience of Russian realities. The Russian peasant, the Russian intelligentsia, even the Russian autocracy, were wrapped in a haze of sentimental retrospect; and there were many moments when their broad incalculable diversity seemed to him better than the narrow, crushing uniformity of western civilization. Pain and terror reigned, it was true, in Russia as in Europe. But in Russia they were 'the birth-pangs of the future', in Europe merely 'the death-pangs of the past'.

It is seldom recognized how often a man's political convictions reflect his intimate personal experience; and it is odd to remark how closely Herzen's denigration of the west and idealization of Russia are related to the drama of his private life. Herzen had left Nice in 1852 maddened by a frenzy of hatred for Herwegh and of devotion to the memory of Natalie; and he recovered his sanity only when, after his establishment in England, he succeeded in sublimating these feelings in the sphere of political activity. The explanation may sound fanciful to those who have not studied the sources; but these leave no doubt of its accuracy. Herzen yielded to a common human impulse when he sought to impart to his own sufferings a universal, transcendental significance. 'Two Russian natures at grips with western rottenness' is his summing-up, twelve months after his arrival in London, of the inner meaning of his domestic tragedy. 'Faith in Russia saved me,' he wrote in 1858 in the preface to a new edition of *Letters from France and Italy*, 'when I was on the verge of moral ruin.' And the 'moral ruin' which threatened him was not merely, and not primarily, the disillusionment of the abortive revolutions of 1848–9, but the collapse of his whole spiritual being which had followed the revelation of Herwegh's baseness. In pronouncing the eternal damnation of Europe, he slaked at last his thirst for vengeance on Herwegh; and in his cult of Russia he venerated the memory of the martyred but immaculate Natalie.

But Herzen was not altogether a blind sentimentalist; and he would never have been possessed by these dreams of a purified and regenerate Russia if there had not been facts to justify the splendid vision. The facts may, to the objective historian, appear jejune and commonplace; but in the eyes of contemporaries, they had a vital and peculiar significance. In 1856, Russia had lost a European war; and the first important act of Alexander II was to sign a humiliating peace. A vanquished nation normally, it appears, finds consolation in attributing defeat to the short-comings of its own organization rather than to the prowess of its enemies. At the end of the Crimean War a universal cry went up throughout Russia that the system of government must be changed. The system of Nicholas I had been an unmitigated autocracy; and any change must, therefore, be in the direction of liberty. Alexander II had the wit to perceive that his only chance of keeping his throne was to appear as the champion of reform; and about the time of the Peace of Paris he significantly told the landowners of Moscow that 'it was better to begin the abolition of serfdom from above than wait for it to begin itself from below.' The Tsar was on the side of reform; the end of serfdom was in sight; and there was no limit to the hopes and expectations of the reformers.

Of this mood of triumphant optimism Herzen reaped the full harvest. In *The Bell* he put forward the three slogans which constituted his minimum programme – the liberation of the serfs, the abolition of corporal punishment, and the abolition of the censorship of the printed word; and for the moment nobody felt this programme to be beyond the limit of sober prevision. By this fortunate and unique concurrence of events, *The Bell* succeeded in pleasing nearly everybody. It pleased the survivors of Herzen's own generation – the Russian radicals of the forties. It pleased the new liberals whose taste for change had been begotten on the Crimean battle-fields. It pleased, by its vague idealization of the Russian people, the rising generation of Moscow Slavophils, whose zeal for everything Russian and hatred of the Petersburg bureaucracy still fitted comfortably into the framework of the prevailing enthusiasm for reform. It did not altogether displease Alexander himself, whose liberal instincts, though feeble, were sincere. For it availed itself of the tactful and convenient fiction that the Tsar was personally responsible for the virtues, but not for the vices, of his subordinates; and its vigorous attacks on the latter might help him to overrule the small recalcitrant clique of official reactionaries. *The Bell* remained in theory a forbidden publication. But it was freely smuggled into Russia, and found its way even into the Imperial household. It was usually printed in a first edition of 2,500 copies; but most of the earlier numbers ran into a second edition. It was a stupendous circulation for a journal produced and circulated by two exiles in a country where not one man in ten thousand had the faintest understanding of the subjects which it treated or of the language in which it was issued.

Opposition, of course, soon raised its head, and from both wings. There were, almost from the outset, those who thought that Herzen did not go far or fast enough and others who thought that the pace was already too hot to be safe. In the autumn of 1858, Herzen received from Chicherin, a member of his old Moscow circle of friends, a long and detailed indictment in which he was accused of light-heartedly fomenting a spirit of criticism and discontent, of exciting popular unrest, and of undermining the foundations of the Russian state. Herzen printed this indictment, with his own reply to it, in *The Bell*; and the incident, having made a passing sensation, was forgotten. Then, just a year later, Herzen received a similar complaint from the opposite camp. The rising young radical journalist, Chernyshevsky, writing under the pseudonym of 'A Russian', reproached him with falling away from the revolutionary radicalism of his youth and warned him that 'Russia had been ruined for a hundred years past by believing in the good intentions of her Tsars'. This article, too, was published in *The Bell*. In these days, criticism was still scarce enough to be inspiring, and merely served to emphasize the strength of the position which Herzen had acquired in Russian political life.

Herzen thoroughly enjoyed his unique reputation. A pilgrimage to his house in Putney, or Fulham, or Westbourne Terrace, became a regular part of the programme of every Russian visitor to London. For a Russian tourist to leave London without having seen Herzen was as unthinkable as to go to Paris and fail to visit the Louvre. Officials, businessmen, and professors – a few of them old friends, but for the most part persons unknown to him – maintained a constant stream of visitors, especially in the summer months. Following the practice established by the good Malwida, Herzen set apart Sunday for the reception of these extraneous guests. He welcomed them with the traditional Russian hospitality; and on Sundays there were rarely less than ten or twelve strangers at his table. Once there descended on them – nobody quite knew whence or how – an authentic Russian peasant in Russian costume. He was received with unbounded enthusiasm, almost with veneration; and young Sasha, now eighteen, was deputed to show him the sights of London. But Herzen's feelings cooled when the pair failed to re-appear until eleven o'clock the next morning, and proved quite unable to give any coherent account of the sights which had detained them.

But perhaps the oddest of all Herzen's visitors during these years was a scion of one of the oldest Russian noble families. In the spring of 1860 Herzen received an illiterate letter in Russian from a small hotel in the Haymarket. It was an appeal for assistance from five servants of Prince Yury Golitsin, who found themselves stranded, penniless and ignorant of the English language, in London. They had come direct from Petersburg by sea, while their master, travelling via Constantinople, had not yet arrived. Herzen with his customary open-handedness guaranteed their hotel bill pending the arrival of the Prince.

Ten days or more later a smart brougham drawn by two greys drew up at the door of Park House, Fulham; and there stepped from it a tall, sturdy, bewhiskered dandy of about thirty-five, 'looking like an Assyrian bull-god'. Prince Yury Golitsin was a noteworthy figure, even among the Russian aristocrats of his day. He had had an irregular upbringing, his mother being dead and his father indifferent to his fate. He had married young and quarrelled with his wife; and his principal claim to notoriety was his taste for giving public concerts with an orchestra of serf musicians trained and conducted by himself.* He had met Herzen on a previous journey abroad, and since then he had sent him occasional items of Russian news (usually discreditable to the authorities) for insertion in *The Bell*.

This last activity of the Prince soon attracted the unfavourable notice of the Russian police, who invited him to take up his residence in the small provincial town of Kozlov and not to leave the district until further notice. Golitsin found this restraint on his liberty too irksome to be borne. He dispatched five of his servants to London by way of Petersburg, and decided himself to travel secretly to the same destination, alone and by a devious route. On the way, his impedimenta unexpectedly increased. In Voronezh, he eloped with a young lady who was visiting the city with her mother on a religious pilgrimage. In Galatz he found a new lackey of remarkable linguistic qualifications. In Alexandria he bought a crocodile. He reached London without further adventure save with the English customs officials, who insisted on a payment of fifteen shillings for the crocodile. It seemed to Prince Golitsin odd that a country which admitted, freely and without question, any and every variety of the human species, should stand on so much ceremony with a harmless reptile.

The Prince took the largest house he could find in Porchester Terrace, and insisted that a carriage and pair should, after the Russian fashion, be on duty day and night at the door in case he should at any moment need them. The ready cash at his disposal did not exceed a few hundred pounds; and, in view of the manner of his departure from Russia, he could not hope to draw on his resources in that country. For a time it was easy for so perfect an exponent of the grand manner to live on credit. But presently difficulties began; and the young lady from Voronezh aggravated them by presenting him with a son. The financial stringency became humiliating. The servants were dismissed; and the Prince was even known to ride in an omnibus.

---

* It was Prince Golitsin's father who ordered from Beethoven three quartets (now known as op. 127, 130 and 132) and failed to pay for them when delivered. The son may be presumed to have acquired by inheritance both his musical taste and a certain *insouciance* in financial affairs.

But the most rigorous economies could not suffice to fill the void created by a non-existent income. The Prince made a creditable effort to turn his musical talents to commercial uses. He published several pieces of popular dance music. There were 'Herzen Valses' and an 'Ogareff Quadrille'; and the latter ran into a second edition, decorated on the outside with a coloured print of the Kremlin. There was a 'Courier Gallop' with a highly-coloured Russian *troika* galloping furiously across the cover, and a 'Kozlov Polka' with a representation of a large Russian village, evidently intended for Kozlov and bitterly labelled 'Exile Town'. But the royalties received from Messrs Chappell and Messrs Boosey on these excellent compositions can scarcely have sufficed to maintain even the most modest establishment. The Prince gave a series of orchestral concerts at the St James's Hall, Piccadilly, which were a brilliant success. But even these did not remedy his financial plight; for he spent the proceeds on a magnificent banquet for the performers. Finally the inevitable happened; and at a concert in Cremorne Gardens he appeared at the conductor's stand in the company of a policeman, who escorted him back to the debtor's prison when the performance was over. It was the last and greatest of Golitsin's eccentricities that he never appealed to Herzen for money. Herzen had warned him, on his first arrival, that life in London was expensive. The Prince had ignored the warning; and pride would not allow him to confess to his mentor how apposite the warning had been.

But Golitsin was still in his glory when the event occurred which was the culminating point of Herzen's public career. On 3 March 1861 (or 19 February according to the old calendar) the emancipation of the serfs was proclaimed in Russia. The principal objective for which *The Polar Star* and *The Bell* had struggled was thus attained at a single stroke. Alexander II had nobly justified the hopes which they had rested on him. Herzen was filled with joy and pride; and when, after some delay, the text of the proclamation reached London, he determined to hold a 'monster *fête*' at Orsett House to celebrate this cardinal event in the history of his country. The following notice appeared in *The Bell* for 1 April:

The Free Russian Press in London and the editors of *The Bell* will celebrate on the evening of April 10th at Orsett House, Westbourne

Terrace, the beginning of the emancipation of the serfs. *Every Russian of whatever party who sympathizes with the great cause will receive a fraternal welcome.*

Selected Russian guests were invited to a dinner on the same day; and ladies and distinguished foreigners, such as Mazzini and Louis Blanc, were also bidden to the evening reception. Tata Herzen, who was now sixteen and took lessons in drawing, designed the decorations. Above the portico floated two coloured flags bearing the inscriptions embroidered by Natalie Ogarev and by Tata herself, 'Freedom of the Russian Peasant' and 'Free Russian Press'; and the outside of the house was illuminated by seven thousand gas jets. There was an orchestra from eight to eleven o'clock, the cost of which Herzen estimated at four pounds; and its programme of music included, besides the *Marseillaise*, a *pot-pourri* of Russian popular airs composed for the occasion by Prince Golitsin and entitled *The Emancipation Fantasia*. The house was crammed to the doors; and in the street outside the crowd of curious spectators was so great that special police were called in to control it.

But across this triumphant day there fell, in dramatic fashion, the first shadow of the decline and fall. Herzen had nourished the secret intention of drinking at the dinner to the health of the Tsar – a gesture of reconciliation which would, he felt, make a sensation throughout the Russian world. A few minutes before the guests arrived, tragic news was brought in. A riot had broken out in Warsaw, and the Russian troops were firing on the Polish mob.

The crime was too recent [wrote Herzen afterwards]. The wounds had not yet closed. The dead were not yet cold. The name of the Tsar died on our lips.

He renounced the intended gesture; and the only two toasts drunk were 'the emancipated Russian people' and 'the independence of Poland'. An atmosphere of gloom descended on the festival; and though, in the evening, champagne and music momentarily dissipated the clouds, the occasion remained in Herzen's memory as an embarrassing blend of jollification and mourning. The day had been planned to celebrate the first great triumph of *The Bell*. In fact, it sowed the first seed of its decay.

In *The Bell* of 1 May, three weeks after the festival, the place of honour was occupied by *Mater Dolorosa*, an article in which Herzen denounced Alexander II for the Warsaw massacres.

Only forty days! [were the bitter concluding words].

Why did not *this man* die on the day when the liberation manifesto was published to the Russian people?

On the day when this article appeared, a Russian visitor – so runs the story told by Natalie Ogarev in her *Memoirs* – came to Herzen. 'Today,' he said solemnly, 'you have buried *The Bell*, and you will never raise it again from the dead. It is buried.' The story is not true. For Natalie is rash enough to name the visitor; and he did not reach London till August or September. But Natalie's dramatic sense was not altogether at fault. The publication of this article marks an epoch in Herzen's career. It was not only his first open attack on Alexander II in person; it was the first stage in a series of events which, culminating in the great Polish insurrection of 1863, brought about the downfall of *The Bell*.

CHAPTER 10

Bakunin; or the Slippery Path

In the autumn of 1861, some six months after the emancipation of the serfs, Herzen received a letter from San Francisco. His old friend Michael Bakunin, fresh from eight years in Austrian and Russian prisons and four years in Siberia, wrote from that port to announce that he had made his escape through Japan, and was travelling round the world, as fast as ships could carry him, to London. Herzen sent to New York, at his pressing request, a sum of money sufficient to enable him to complete his journey, and inserted in *The Bell* the following notice:

Michael Alexandrovich Bakunin is in San Francisco. He is free! Bakunin travelled from Siberia via Japan and is on the way to England. We joyfully bring this to the knowledge of all his friends.

In private – if, once more, we may believe Natalie Ogarev – Herzen's delight was tempered by apprehension. He had not seen Bakunin for fourteen years; but he had retained a vivid impression of his personality. 'I confess,' he exclaimed, 'that I dread Bakunin's coming. He will probably ruin our work.' The exclamation can scarcely be regarded as historical. Natalie, when she wrote her *Memoirs* in her old age, liked to attribute these sage premonitions to the heroes of her youth.

It was one evening between Christmas and the New Year when Bakunin, who had disembarked at Liverpool from the trans-Atlantic packet and come straight down to London, burst into Orsett House just as Herzen and Ogarev were sitting down to supper. Natalie, weak from recent child-bearing (the twins were five weeks old), lay on a couch in an adjoining room. 'What! do you get oysters here?' was Bakunin's first question. Then, going in to Natalie, he exclaimed: 'It is bad to be lying down. Get well! we must work, not lie down.' Presently Kelsiev, a close friend at this time of Herzen and Ogarev, appeared on the scene and was presented to the new arrival. It is he who relates the following conversation, which is perhaps an apt dramatization rather than

192

an accurate record. Bakunin was inquiring about the course of
political events.

'Only in Poland there are some demonstrations,' said Herzen; 'but
perhaps the Poles will come to their senses and understand that a rising
is out of the question when the Tsar has just freed the serfs. Clouds are
gathering, but we must hope that they will disperse.'
'And in Italy?'
'All quiet.'
'And in Austria?'
'All quiet.'
'And in Turkey?'
'All quiet everywhere, and nothing in prospect.'
'Then what are we to do?' said Bakunin in amazement. 'Must we
go to Persia or India to stir things up? It's enough to drive one mad; I
cannot sit and do nothing.'

The clash of temperaments and opinions was latent from the
outset; and Herzen at least soon had the wit to divine it. Physically, Bakunin had aged and coarsened, almost beyond recognition.
A giant in stature, he had swelled enormously in bulk, and now
weighed twenty stone. He had lost all his teeth; and he allowed
his thick, curly hair and beard to grow in luxuriant neglect. Only
the clear, flashing eyes and shaggy eyebrows recalled the handsome young dandy of thirty-five whom Herzen had last seen in
Paris. But mentally Bakunin had scarcely changed. The feverish
energy of the forties seemed to burn within him unabated; and –
more incongruous and disconcerting still – his opinions were those
of twenty years ago. He had come back into the world like a ghost
of the past. He was like a man awakened from a long trance, who
tries to take up life again at the point where he laid it down, and
expects to find everything around him in the same position as at
the moment when he lost consciousness. Bakunin had not, like
Herzen, witnessed the collapse of the revolution and the final
ignominious extinction of political liberty all over the Continent
of Europe; and he inquired helplessly for news of a struggle which
had ceased ten years ago. He raved about pan-Slav federation;
and he was told that the Slavonic Congress of Prague, at which he
had played a leading role, was an historical curiosity of the distant
past. He denounced the tyranny of Alexander II, from whose
clutches he had so hardly escaped, in the same terms in which men

had been wont to rail against Nicholas I; and he was bewildered to learn that this same Alexander was the Tsar-Liberator, the patron of progress and reform, the star of hope of a regenerated Russia. Time had stood still for Bakunin for twelve years, while the world, turning on its axis, had revolutionized the thoughts and opinions of his former associates.

There were other and more personal grounds of incompatibility. Herzen had been born of a German mother, and had now spent fifteen years in western Europe. He had derived from one or other of these advantages a *bourgeois* taste for orderliness which was shared by few Russians and which was altogether anathema to Bakunin; and he has left us, in *My Past and Thoughts*, a mordant sketch of this stage in the career of the great revolutionary:

Bakunin recovered in our midst from nine years of silence and solitude. He argued, preached, gave orders, shouted, decided, arranged, organized, exhorted, the whole day, the whole night, the whole twenty-four hours on end. In the brief moments which remained, he would throw himself down at his desk, sweep a small space clear of tobacco ash, and begin to write five, ten, fifteen letters to Semipalatinsk and Arad, to Belgrade and Constantinople, to Bessarabia, Moldavia and White Russia. In the middle of a letter he would throw down his pen in order to refute some reactionary Dalmatian; then, without finishing his speech, he would seize his pen and go on writing. This of course was all the easier as he was writing and talking on the same subject. His activity, his leisure, his appetite, like all his other characteristics – even his gigantic size and continual sweat – were of superhuman proportions; and he himself remained, as of old, a giant with leonine head and tousled mane.

At fifty he was still the same wandering student, the same homeless Bohemian of the Rue de Bourgogne, caring nothing for the morrow, despising money, scattering it on all sides when he had it, borrowing indiscriminately right and left when he had none, with the same simplicity with which children take from their parents and never think of repayment, with the same simplicity with which he himself was prepared to give to anyone his last penny, reserving for himself only what was necessary for cigarettes and tea. He was never embarrassed by this mode of life; he was born to be the great wanderer, the great outcast. If anyone had asked him what he thought about the rights of property, he might have replied as Lalande replied to Napoleon about God: 'Sire, in the course of my career I have never found the slightest need to believe in Him.'

194

The only member of the Herzen household who regarded the newcomer's behaviour with unmixed appreciation and approval was the three-year-old Liza. Child understood child; and 'big Liza' soon became Bakunin's nickname at Orsett House.

Bakunin found lodgings first in Grove Road, St John's Wood, and then, still nearer to his friends, in Paddington Green. For a while the first transports of reunion masked personal and political divergences. Sincere hatred of oppression, and an equally sincere, though undiscriminating, enthusiasm for that vague entity 'the Russian people' sufficed to cement the alliance. The liberation of the Slav peoples was a cause to which Herzen still paid lip-service, even though he sometimes laughed at the unpronounceable names of the Czech, Serb and Dalmatian patriots whom Bakunin took under his wing. Not long after his arrival Bakunin wrote a manifesto *To My Russian, Polish and Slav Friends* which was issued as a special supplement to *The Bell*. It was a reiteration of his old policy of the disruption of the Austrian Empire and the creation of a free Slavonic federation. 'My last word, if not my last deed', he had written in the letter from San Francisco, 'will be the disruption of the Austrian Empire'; and he still remained faithful to his programme. It had sounded well enough in 1848 when Austria was, to all appearance, on the verge of collapse. But in 1862, when the young Emperor Francis Joseph was solidly and comfortably installed in the seat of authority, all this rhetoric seemed sadly obsolete and misplaced. Herzen allowed the chill blast of common sense to blow on it; and the continuation of the manifesto (for it had been intended as a first instalment) never appeared. Save for two short and unimportant items, the fragment *To My Russian, Polish and Slav Friends* remained Bakunin's last, as well as his first, contribution to *The Bell*.

The dream of a revolutionary triumvirate slowly faded.

I have not lost a jot of the faith with which I came to London [wrote Bakunin in May to his two associates] or of the firm intention to become, at all costs, a third in your alliance – that is the one condition in which union is possible. Otherwise, we will be associates and if you like, friends, but completely independent and not responsible for one another.

Herzen chose the latter alternative; and Bakunin's next political essay *The People's Cause* – a vigorous attempt to place on the Tsar the responsibility for the coming revolution – was published independently in pamphlet form. But the parting was not without bitterness. Bakunin's temper was no more controllable than his actions; and he accused Herzen of being 'haughty, contemptuous and lazy'. Herzen wrote a barbed retort in which he seems to have suggested (the letter has not survived) that Bakunin would be well advised to transfer his residence and his activities to Paris. Here is Bakunin's apology, in a letter of 17 July 1862:

> My fault, Herzen. I beg of you, don't be angry. Through my inveterate clumsiness I let slip a bitter word when there was no bitter feeling in my heart. But suppose it had fallen to *your* lot to receive all the notes you have written to me? You would long ago have wished me not in Paris, but in Calcutta. But joking apart, you must know, Herzen, that my respect for you has no bounds, and that I sincerely love you. I will add that, without any *arrière pensée* and with entire conviction, I place you higher than myself in every respect, in abilities and knowledge, and that for me in every question your opinion carries immense weight. So why should you want to banish me to Paris, even if we had had a chance difference of secondary importance?

From the practical standpoint, Herzen was perfectly right. It was impossible to work with Bakunin. But human sympathy is a little on the side of 'big Liza'. Bakunin's outbursts of temper were like the evanescent anger of an affectionate child. Herzen's resentment was stored up in his heart until it found an outlet in some venomed shaft which poisoned and rankled.

The rift between Herzen and Bakunin was significant of a turning-point in Russian, and even in European, political thought. In the political sphere, the Romantics had been, for the most part, content to identify themselves with democracy. Under democracy, according to the well-known though questionable theory propounded by Rousseau, the governing and the governed form one and the same entity; and democracy is therefore the only form of government compatible with the liberty and dignity of the individual. Herzen, who never saw democracy at work till after he left Russia, had embraced the democratic theory with all the candid ardour of susceptible youth. His first experiences in Europe drove him rapidly from romantic faith to romantic disillusionment. He despaired, somewhat too readily, of democratic Europe.

But after the accession of Alexander II, he acquired, as we have seen, a new-born faith in democratic Russia; and this faith expressed itself, through the great quinquennium of his political activity, in a mood of radiant optimism. Even when the optimism waned, the faith remained intact. In the last years of his life Herzen experienced the bitterness of the prophet proclaiming in the wilderness a cause which was more and more emphatically rejected by his own countrymen. But even in these years, confirmed sceptic though he had become, he never for a moment doubted the validity of the democratic principle as a solution of the political problem. It was not the principle which had played him false; it was the will of mankind to apply it.

The story of Bakunin is different, but equally characteristic. He was not merely, like Herzen, a Romantic by conviction; he was a Romantic by temperament. The optimism and the faith in human nature, which were inherent in the romantic creed, were sometimes sorely at variance with Herzen's subconscious predilections; but for Bakunin they were of the marrow of his bones. Bakunin believed as passionately as Rousseau in the innocence of untrammelled, unperverted human nature; and, possessing a more original and more daring mind than Herzen, he drew his own conclusions from the romantic premises. He saw mankind everywhere oppressed by the claims of autocracy; and he could work heart and soul with Herzen so long as the task before them was to encourage mankind to throw off these chains. But when he came to England at the end of 1861 and found his former friend deeply committed to the cause of Russian democracy, the ways of the two men parted for ever. Bakunin stood far nearer than Herzen to his own countrymen; and he shared to the full the instinctive Russian distrust of democracy. He saw no logical reason, on the romantic hypothesis, to prefer the chains of democracy to the chains of autocracy. If human nature merely requires the enjoyment of its native freedom to achieve perfection, it follows that the constraint imposed by states and governments is in itself noxious, irrespective of the form of the state or the composition of the government. The true believer could only advocate a return to nature, and the destruction of all governmental units or institutions resting on force; and anarchism, which was the ultimate goal of Bakunin's political thought, was merely the logical outcome – or the logical *reductio ad absurdum* – of the romantic doctrine. When that goal was reached, a stage in the history of human thought had been completed. Human ingenuity could travel no further along that road. It only remained for Marx to initiate a new departure in political theory, and to overthrow, in the person of Bakunin, the last and most consistent exponent of political Romanticism.

But this event took place ten years after the date at which we have now arrived; and for the moment the issue in Russia lay between the modified autocracy of Alexander II, the constitutional democracy of Herzen, and the revolutionary anarchism of Bakunin. The twelve months which followed the emancipation of the serfs were a time of sifting in Russian political thought. The emancipation was, so far as imperial decree could make it, an accomplished fact; and the Russian intelligentsia, which had united to welcome it, now began to divide into two opposing groups. Some thought that the cause of reform, having achieved this well-advertised success, could safely rest on its laurels for another generation. Others, whose democratic appetites had been whetted but not satisfied, felt that autocracy was on the run and that now if ever was the time to demand far-reaching concessions. The former drifted slowly but surely into union with the conservatives; the latter became declared revolutionaries. In the summer of 1861, a secret society – the first of the new reign – sprang up under the title *The Great Russian*. It lasted only a few months, and did nothing but print and circulate a few inflammatory proclamations. But it was a straw which showed the direction of the wind; and it prompted a hitherto somnolent government to measures of vigilance and repression.

It now merely required some striking event to bring this situation to a head; and the requirement was soon met. In May 1862 extensive and destructive fires broke out in Petersburg, ravaging the poorer quarters of the town where the houses were almost exclusively of wood. It has never been definitely ascertained whether these fires were, as the police alleged the work of revolutionaries; or, as the revolutionaries themselves contended, the work of *agents provocateurs* employed by the police; or merely the result of a tragic series of accidents. But public indignation was aroused. The belief in arson was general. The authorities took strong repressive measures against radicals and 'nihilists'. The latter, branded as incendiaries, steeled their hearts and determined in future to stick at nothing; and liberal opinion, taking fright, sought refuge in the conservative fold. The split in the intelligentsia, which had declared itself almost immediately after emancipation, was intensified; and from the summer of 1862 onwards there was open and implacable warfare between the two parties. The parties thus aligned remained in existence, under varying guises but without essential change, until the revolution of 1905.

This re-grouping of parties had its immediate reaction on Herzen and *The Bell*. During the past twelve months *The Bell* had given to the new radical movement a hesitating and half-hearted support. Herzen, following the natural bent of his character, remained sceptically noncommittal. But Ogarev was more susceptible to the seduction of new and daring designs; and in September 1861, while Herzen and the family were at Torquay, he rashly inserted in *The Bell* a vigorous revolutionary manifesto by one of the young radicals, named Nicholas Serno-Solovievich. Herzen mildly reproached Ogarev with his excess of zeal; and in the next number there appeared a leading article which, by damning Serno-Solovievich with faint praise, contrived to dissociate *The Bell* from the more extreme of his opinions. But the disavowal made, as frequently happens, less impression than the original indiscretion. Despite himself, Herzen had, in the eyes of the world, taken an important step on the road to revolution; and in the turmoil which followed the Petersburg fires he reaped the full fruits of an equivocal position. The conservatives and timid liberals, in their anti-nihilist frenzy, fell upon Herzen as the true begetter of nihilism; and the wilder organs of reaction did not scruple to accuse him of direct complicity in arson. The story gained credence; and a girl student fresh from Russia visited him at Orsett House to inquire, in the name of his former liberal supporters, whether he had really helped to set fire to the capital. Meanwhile the revolutionaries on their side denounced him as a false friend, who had betrayed the revolution by dallying with the unclean powers of Tsarism, and who even now had the simplicity to believe in the possibility of progress by constitutional means. Herzen was caught between two fires. The decline in the popularity of *The Bell* was shown not only by a diminishing circulation, but by a falling-off in the number of correspondents who surreptitiously sent news of events in Russia. For the first time there was a difficulty not merely in selling, but in filling, the paper. Herzen, with a sinking heart, read the danger signals from the right and left. He had identified himself with constitutional liberalism; and there was no future, in the Russia of the sixties, for the constitutional liberal. He suffered the common fate of the moderate man in times of crisis. 'The liberal party,' he wrote to a correspondent in August 1862, 'will be ground out of existence between the two wheels.'

But while Herzen hesitated gloomily at the parting of the ways, and Ogarev moved timidly and haltingly towards the extremist camp, there was neither gloom nor timidity nor hesitation in the mind of Bakunin. His character and his career ranged him beyond question with the revolutionaries. His optimism was unquenchable. In Herzen's words, he 'always mistook the second month of pregnancy for the ninth'.

There is no doubt [he had written in May to Garibaldi] that Russia is striding rapidly towards revolution. When will it break out? That is the question. Perhaps in 1863, perhaps a few years later. We are making all possible exertions to hasten it and to unite it with the movements of all live peoples in Europe.

Herzen regarded with his customary scepticism both the prospects of revolution and the policy of 'hastening' it; and he disliked his friend's methods even more than his policy. Bakunin was not merely a believer in revolution as a means to an end. He was an artist in conspiracy and intrigue, and loved them for their own sake. He revelled in all the paraphernalia of mystification. He was soon writing letters to be smuggled into Russia in which Herzen is referred to as 'private gentleman', his son Alexander as 'junior', and Ogarev as 'the poet' – disguises which, one would think, could scarcely puzzle the most simple-minded police officer. Presently he sends a more elaborate code, in which Herzen becomes 'Baron Tiesenhausen', Ogarev 'Kosterov', a prison 'a café', a Turk 'a shoemaker', and so forth. But Bakunin was incapable of caution or reserve; and his ingenuity proved more dangerous to the revolutionaries than to the government. These incriminating letters fell into the hands of agents of the Russian

Government; and several of his correspondents paid for his indiscretion by transportation and hard labour.*

In the meanwhile events in Russia had stung the revolutionaries to fresh subterranean activity. The place of the defunct *Great Russian* was taken by a new secret society calling itself *Land and Liberty*. By the autumn of 1862, a Central Russian National Committee had been formed in Petersburg; and in January one of the principals, Sleptsov by name, journeyed to London for a conference with Herzen and Ogarev. The new name seemed to have been specially devised to appeal to Herzen; for *Land and Liberty* was a slogan which had frequently graced the columns of *The Bell*. Herzen received Sleptsov with guarded approval; but Ogarev eagerly consulted Mazzini, that past master in revolutionary intrigue, on the organization of secret societies. Bakunin, who scented revolution from afar, could not be kept away from the discussions. He felt himself in his native element. He threw himself with all his unbounded might and energy into the work of the new society, and drew after him the faltering but not unwilling Ogarev. Herzen followed, with a bad grace and a heavy heart. It is difficult to see what else he could have done – unless he could bring himself to retire altogether from the political arena. The cause of constitutional reform was dead. He was in the position of a man to whom one road only is open, and that a road which leads to almost certain destruction. On the last day of February 1863 (by the old style, 16 February) *Land and Liberty* began to distribute surreptitiously in Russia the first number of its political broadsheet *Freedom*; and in *The Bell* of 1 March there appeared the following notice:

We learn from a reliable source that groups in the capital and the provinces have united with one another and with committees of officers to form a single society.

This society has taken the name of LAND AND LIBERTY.

In the strength of this name it will conquer!

LAND AND LIBERTY! The words have a familiar sound to us. With them we first appeared in the dark night of Nicholas' reign; with them

---

* More than twenty letters written by Bakunin during this summer found their way into the hands of the Russian secret police and are preserved in the Russian official archives. The letter to Garibaldi quoted above was intercepted by the Austrian police, who obligingly sent a copy to their *confrères* in Petersburg.

we greeted the early dawn of the coming day. LAND AND LIBERTY was the theme of our every article. LAND AND LIBERTY was blazoned on our banner here abroad, and on every sheet which issued from our London press . . .

We greet you, brothers on the common path! Eagerly we shall follow your every step, tremblingly await your tidings, lovingly pass them on; and our love will be the unsullied love of men who rejoice to witness the growth of what they have striven for all their life.

With your holy banner you are destined to serve the cause of the Russian people.

It is in the nature of things inevitable that few documents of an outlawed secret society should have survived; and it is difficult to reconstruct in detail the developments of the next few weeks. Two draft constitutions of the society are extant in Ogarev's handwriting with corrections by Herzen. One of them provides that 'the Council of the Society is established abroad and is attached to *The Bell*', the other that 'the chief Council of the Society *Land and Liberty* consists of the editorial board of *The Bell*, from which all instructions issue'. It would seem that at one moment Herzen hoped, by taking the control into his own hands, to mitigate the dangers which he had foreseen. This scheme did not materialize; but there is in existence an 'instruction to foreign agents of *Land and Liberty*' written on the printed notepaper of the Central Russian National Committee and dated 17 April 1863, in which Herzen is named as 'the chief representative of the Society *Land and Liberty* abroad'.

Scarcely, however, had the organization of the society been completed than misfortunes began to befall it. Sleptsov, instead of returning to the post of danger in Petersburg, had a nervous breakdown and retired to Switzerland. Utin, another member of the Central Committee, took fright and fled from Russia. Another number of *Freedom* appeared in July to scandalize the police; and two other proclamations were issued and distributed. But the backbone had already gone out of the enterprise; and during the winter of 1863–4 it went rapidly through the successive stages of dissolution, leaving scarcely a trace behind. Herzen was left to feel that his gloomiest premonitions had been fulfilled, and to lament that he had nailed the colours of *The Bell* to so tottering a mast.

In the chapter devoted in *My Past and Thoughts* to his relations with Bakunin, Herzen pauses to ask himself a 'melancholy question'.

How and whence [he exclaims] did I acquire this habit of yielding with a grumble, of combining docility with protest and revolt? On the one hand, the conviction that I ought to act in such a way; on the other, willingness to act quite otherwise. This immaturity, this inconsistency, this indecision, have done me in the course of my life an infinity of harm, and have deprived me even of the feeble consolation of knowing that my mistakes were involuntary and unconscious. I have made my blunders despite myself; every disadvantage of the course I adopted was patent before my eyes . . .

How many misfortunes, how many disasters less there would have been in my life if I had had the strength, on all important occasions, to obey myself. I have been accused of being easily carried away. It is true I have sometimes been carried away; but that is not the important point. Even when I yielded to my impressionability, I always paused; and thought, reflexion, consideration nearly always gained the upper hand – in theory, though not in practice. Herein lies the whole difficulty of the problem – why I have always allowed myself to be led *nolens volens*. The cause of my easy compliance is a false shame, and sometimes perhaps the promptings of my better nature – friendship, love, indulgence. But why did I allow all that to vanquish logic?

Herzen was not thinking of Bakunin alone. The 'friendship' was for Bakunin. But the 'love' was for Ogarev; and the 'indulgence' perhaps – since his personal life was never far from Herzen's thoughts – for Natalie, who had offered him a fatal love which his better judgement would have refused.

But long before the final collapse of *Land and Liberty*, its affairs had been overshadowed by the great Polish insurrection of 1863, which forms the background of the next chapter.

CHAPTER II

Poland; or the Cruise of the Ward Jackson

THE final suppression of the kingdom of Poland in 1831 removed the Polish question from the field of practical politics for almost exactly a quarter of a century. Tranquillity reigned in Poland under the régime of blood and iron which was Nicholas I's ideal of good government; and the Polish cause was represented by a handful of discredited and disconsolate exiles in London, Paris and Brussels. The accession of Alexander II in 1855 inaugurated a new era. Half-forgotten hopes and ambitions revived. The more enlightened of the new Tsar's advisers began to toy with the idea of 'administrative autonomy' for the oppressed province. The ferment of Polish nationalism was once more at work.

The situation was complicated by the existence of two opposing factions in the Polish camp. The Polish exiles abroad had long ago split into aristocratic and democratic factions. Two parallel organizations now sprang up in Warsaw: the Committee of the *Shliakhta* or Gentry, and the Central National or Popular Committee. The former hoped for a 'liberation' which would leave the landed nobility political masters of the new Poland; the National Committee sought freedom not only from the alien Russian yoke, but from the not less galling tyranny of the Polish *Shliakhta*. This division of aims and interests was accompanied by an equally fundamental divergence of policy. The Polish gentry tended towards cooperation, where such cooperation was possible, with the Russian authorities. The Polish democrats found their natural allies among the Russian radicals and revolutionaries.

It was inevitable in these circumstances that the Russian Government should seek to play off Polish aristocrats against Polish democrats. But there were peculiar difficulties in the way of this policy. The ancestral estates of many of the leading Polish nobles dated back to the spacious days when Poland sprawled comfortably across eastern Europe from the Baltic to the Black Sea, and embraced large stretches of Lithuania, White Russia and

204

the Ukraine, where Polish landowners ruled over an indigenous population of serfs. The 'free' Poland of which the Polish *Shliakhta* dreamed included these tracts of non-Polish territory. The Poland recognized by Russia as a possible field for the grant of 'administrative autonomy' was the so-called 'Congress' Poland, whose eastern frontier conformed too closely to ethnographical limits to satisfy Polish aspirations. The territorial appetites of the Polish gentry made cooperation between the Russian Government and the Committee of the *Shliakhta* always precarious. Between the National Committee and the Russian revolutionaries the bond was closer; for both sides subordinated the territorial to the social question, and were prepared to solve the former, at any rate on paper, by a vague reference to the will of the populations concerned. But even among the Polish democrats there were many who did not refrain, when the opportunity offered, from putting forward the same extravagant pretensions as the nobility to territorial aggrandizement.

The latest phase of the Polish question had begun in the summer of 1862. In that year Alexander, in pursuance of his policy of conciliation, sent his brother, the Grand Duke Constantine, to Warsaw as Regent of Poland; and a compliant Polish aristocrat, Marquis Wielopolski, was nominated civil governor of the country. The National Committee replied to these gestures by attempted assassination. A Polish tailor shot at the Grand Duke, and two printers at Wielopolski; and it became clear that the Polish democrats preferred the realities of social revolution to a more or less fictitious autonomy administered, under Russian supervision, by the Polish nobility. These attempts, and the inevitable reaction in the other camp, made open conflict certain. Throughout the autumn the National Committee was busy with preparations for the coming struggle. It sent a continuous stream of secret emissaries to western Europe to woo sympathy and support in that quarter, and to Russia to conclude an effective alliance with the Russian revolutionaries.

Information of these events soon reached London, and produced on Herzen and Bakunin the impressions consonant with the contrasted temperaments of the two men. Both were deeply committed by conviction and tradition to the cause of Polish independence; but the issue had hitherto remained purely academic.

The tidings that the Polish National Committee was about to appeal to the arbitrament of force were received by Herzen with misgiving and alarm, by Bakunin with unalloyed enthusiasm. The old war-horse scented the familiar atmosphere of plot and counter-plot, of intrigue, invective and guerrilla warfare. He enjoyed once more the delicious sensation of work to be done which was worthy of his superhuman endowment of energy and courage. The Polish question had never been far from Bakunin's heart; and in the summer and autumn of 1862 he felt like a man whose dearest hopes are suddenly and unexpectedly on the point of being fulfilled.

In the latter part of September there arrived in London three Poles named Hiller, Padlewski and Milowicz. They were bearers of a letter from the National Committee at Warsaw to the editors of *The Bell*, appealing for assistance from the Russian democrats for the Polish cause. They came first to Bakunin, who brought them to Herzen. A delicate discussion ensued. Herzen agreed to print the appeal in *The Bell* with a reply of suitable warmth. But he demanded in return that his visitors should, in the name of the National Committee, formally renounce those territorial preten-sions which were so fatal a bar to Russian-Polish cooperation. While the discussion proceeded, Bakunin sat restive and impa-tient; and when the Poles had gone he rounded angrily on Herzen for his coldness and pettiness in driving a bargain with friends whom he should have embraced at sight. The visitors agreed to Herzen's terms; and a phrase was inserted in the appeal to safe-guard 'the right of the peasants to the land which they cultivate and every people to dispose of its own fate'. The letter was pub-lished in *The Bell* of 1 October and Herzen's reply in the following number. Meanwhile Herzen, who could no more help his sceptic-ism than Bakunin his uncalculating ardour, shook his head and suspected that concessions made so lightly on paper would be found to mean nothing in practice. His hesitations became a byword among his friends; and a remote cousin, who was a pro-fessional photographer in Paris, made by combining two plates, a freak photograph of Herzen remonstrating with Herzen for his attitude on the Polish question.

The same issue of *The Bell* which published the reply to the National Committee also contained an appeal to the Russian officers serving in Poland not to participate in military operations against Polish insurgents. Some of the officers, with extraordinary courage and independence, sent to Herzen a signed manifesto of sympathy with the Poles; and one of them, Potebnya by name, visited London in November. In the meanwhile Polish emissaries had been sent to Petersburg, and had obtained from the organizers of *Land and Liberty* a promise to engineer revolutionary movements in Russia simultaneously with the Polish outbreak.

In all these plots and negotiations Bakunin displayed his unfailing energy and optimism. He was passionately convinced that, once the insurrection began, the Russian army in Poland would go over in a body to the insurgents and that the revolution would be carried on to Russian soil. He revelled in the usual paraphernalia of pseudonyms, cryptograms and false addresses; and he carried on an enraptured correspondence with a sympathizer in Paris who turned out to be a secret agent of the Russian police. A combination of Bakunin's enthusiasm and Herzen's experience might have achieved something; but each went his own way, and instead of combination there was petty friction and mutual mistrust.

The insurrection so elaborately planned was mismanaged from the outset; or rather, perhaps, the outbreak when it came was too spontaneous for deep-laid plans to be carried into effect. For some years past, conscription for the Russian army had not been applied in Poland; but the Russian authorities, knowing what was in the wind, hit on the well-worn device of forestalling the revolt by forcibly recruiting the rank and file of its supporters. A selective levy, confined to the urban proletariat, was ordered on 15 January 1863; and the recruiting officers set to work forthwith. The hand of the National Committee was forced by these measures; and after a week of hasty preparation, the insurrection began with a simultaneous attack on all Russian garrisons in the night of 22–23 January. The Russians afterwards alleged that the National Committee had failed to warn the Committee of Russian Officers, and that declared sympathizers with the Polish cause had been attacked indiscriminately with the rest. If this was not true, it was at any rate believed; and the latent enmity between Pole and Russian which only enthusiasts like Bakunin could ignore, came at once to the surface. Polish hopes were disappointed. Not a

Russian officer or man went over to the insurgents; and in Russia itself all remained quiet. But desperate guerrilla warfare went on all over Poland; and tense excitement gripped Europe. There had been nothing like it for fifteen years – since the failures of 1848 and 1849. 'This much is certain,' Marx wrote eagerly to Engels in February 1863, 'that the Era of Revolution is now once more fairly opened.'

The Polish outbreak made it impossible for Bakunin to remain in London. It was well enough for Herzen, the man of letters, to sit quietly at home, celebrating in *The Bell* the initial successes of the insurgents, denouncing the brutalities of the Russian authorities, appealing to the Russian troops not to fire on their Polish brothers and, in private, expressing the gloomy conviction that things would come to a bad end. Bakunin, the man of action, the stormy petrel of revolution, must be on the spot. Poland was ablaze; and he must be there to fan and spread the flames. There was for the moment no very obvious way of reaching Poland; and he did what seemed the next best thing. In February he took ship for Sweden.

Scarcely had he started, when an opportunity occurred which he would have embraced with open arms. The outbreak of the Polish insurrection had inspired the younger Polish *émigrés*, most of whom lived in France, with the laudable ambition to play an active role. Some were content to smuggle themselves into Poland through Germany. Others, rejecting this pedestrian plan, evolved the grand project of organizing a descent by sea on the Baltic coast. They collected for the purpose the substantial sum of 700,000 francs, most of which was subscribed by a wealthy Pole named Branicki. Nearly two hundred men were recruited. The majority were Poles; but there was among them a sprinkling of Frenchmen, Italians, Hungarians and Southern Slavs. The commander of the expedition was a certain Colonel Lapinski, a Polish freebooter who had fought against the Russians in the Causasus. His second was a Jew named Stephen Poles, *alias* Tugendgold, whom Herzen suspected, apparently without cause, of being a Russian spy; and one Demontowicz accompanied the expedition as 'civil commissioner' representing the 'revolutionary government' which had been set up in Warsaw. Among its members was Ladislas Mickiewicz, the son of the great Polish poet. On 14

February, the little army proceeded from Paris to London to await embarkation for the Baltic.

This was the initial mistake. For the ample supply of guns, rifles and ammunition, which had been ordered from the firm of Whitworth, was not yet ready for shipment; and nobody had considered the problem of transport. The legionaries spent some of their enforced leisure drilling in the neighbourhood of Woolwich, where their exertions soon excited curiosity and secured the publicity which they least desired. *The Globe* published an article on 'The Polish Legion'; and by the time the ship had been chartered and was ready to load, the expedition had ceased to be a secret not only to the readers of *The Globe*, but to the Russian Government. On 19 March Baron Brunnov, the Russian Ambassador at the Court of St James's, informed Lord Russell that the steamer *Gipsy Queen* of Hartlepool was expected in the Thames to take on board arms, ammunition and two hundred Poles bound for the Baltic; and he hinted that the ship, being destined for warlike operations against a friendly Power, might properly be detained by Her Majesty's Government. The information was accurate in every detail save one. The ship chartered by the legionaries was not the *Gipsy Queen*. It bore the less romantic name of *Ward Jackson*; it was commanded by Captain Robert Weatherley; and on 20 March it arrived at Gravesend and began to load. Next day the customs authorities, prompted by Lord Russell, came on board, discovered that part of the cargo described on the ship's manifest as 'hardware' consisted, in fact, of arms and ammunition and, pending investigations, refused the ship clearance papers. In the meanwhile, two customs officers remained on board.

The bold Captain Weatherley and the organizers of the expedition were, however, men to make light of such obstacles. The legionaries were instructed to assemble at Fenchurch Street station at 10 p.m. on 21 March and a special train was ordered. The professional sceptic, Herzen, who relates the whole story with more than a grain of malice, declares that some of the legionaries mistook the hour and arrived at the station at 10 a.m. The error was singularly inopportune. For our heroes had, from motives of secrecy or economy, omitted to discharge their financial obligations; and the delay exposed them to the shrill pursuit of a small army of landladies and other interested females. Herzen however names Hull as the port of departure and makes other blunders; and we are perhaps entitled to treat this part of his narrative as picturesque fiction. In any event, the special train moved off at 10 p.m. amid the sympathetic cheers of a multitude of spectators; and about an hour earlier the *Ward Jackson*, minus clearance papers, but having on board two protesting customs officers, weighed anchor at Gravesend and slipped down the river.

This section of the journey, at any rate, was a masterpiece of organization. Ship and train reached Southend simultaneously soon after midnight. The customs officers were put on shore; the warriors were taken on board; and the *Ward Jackson* proceeded on her piratical way. When next day the Russian Ambassador presented another note, the Foreign Office somewhat naïvely replied that 'the sudden departure of the *Ward Jackson* from the river renders unavailing any further steps on Your Excellency's part to procure information in corroboration of the suspicions which you entertained and communicated to me of the destination of that vessel, or on the part of Her Majesty's Government to prevent her from engaging in any enterprise contrary to Law'. Baron Brunnov had to rest content with the cold consolation of this well-rounded official phraseology.

In the meanwhile Bakunin, somewhat to his surprise, found himself lionized in Stockholm as the famous victim and enemy of the Russian Government. His friends in London had reason to distrust his discretion; and until the *Ward Jackson* had sailed they carefully refrained from informing him of the expedition. But he was a force which could not be ignored; and he was an invaluable asset in any enterprise requiring dash and courage. The expedition once safely dispatched, telegrams were sent to him both by Herzen and by the London agent of the Polish National Committee; and he was invited to join the *Ward Jackson* three days hence in Helsingborg, her first port of call. Bakunin set out at once from Stockholm. But there was no railway to Helsingborg; and when he reached it, the *Ward Jackson* had already been lying in the roads for twenty-four hours. The captain and the leaders of the expedition had installed themselves in the local hotel to await the important new recruit; and the little town buzzed with excitement.

The arrival of Bakunin was the signal for a council of war, in the course of which Captain Weatherley seems to have realized, for the first time, the uncommercial risks of the enterprise for which he had been engaged. The gallant captain had been willing enough to exhibit his daring at the expense of customs officers of his own nationality; but he had no desire to try conclusions with an unknown quantity in the shape of a Russian cruiser. His apprehensions were increased on learning that, owing to the exceptionally mild season, the ice had already broken in front of Reval, the Russian naval port; and they were not removed by the assurance of one of his passengers that they had plenty of powder on board and intended to blow up the ship rather than submit to capture. A violent gale sprang up the same afternoon to reinforce the captain's scruples; and for two days more the *Ward Jackson* lay storm-bound in the Helsingborg roads. On the third day the weather abated. The captain's hesitations were overcome; and they set sail, with Bakunin on board, ostensibly for the island of Gotland on the Swedish shore of the Baltic.

Captain Weatherley had however other designs. Alone with a handful of seamen in the midst of this gang of hot-headed foreign desperadoes, he preferred guile to open resistance. On arrival off Copenhagen, he declared that he must put into port to take in fresh water, four days' stay at Helsingborg not having sufficed for this purpose; and he promised that the operation would not occupy more than two hours. Having brought the ship safely in, he went straight ashore and paid a visit to Sir Augustus Paget, the British Minister. The nature of the interview is not recorded. But Captain Weatherley did not return to the *Ward Jackson* that night, and announced next day that he would not sail in her again so long as there was a single Pole on board. The rest of the crew thereupon also deserted, leaving on board only the legionaries, the chief engineer and a Danish pilot. Bakunin himself hurried to the British Legation. Sir Augustus Paget received him with complete cordiality. He agreed that Captain Weatherley had behaved like a rascal, but refused to believe that he was in Russian pay. He expressed polite sympathy, and regretted that he could not compel the captain and the crew to sail. He could only refer the legionaries to the Copenhagen agents of the owners of the *Ward Jackson*; and he remarked that, by a curious chance, these same agents were suppliers to the Russian fleet, and were at the moment preparing to coal a Russian cruiser which was expected in the port. Bakunin was charmed with the interview, and found Sir Augustus 'a perfect gentleman'. The agents were obliging, and agreed to supply a Danish crew to take the *Ward Jackson* to Malmo, the nearest Swedish port, which was only two hours distant. There the legionaries would have once more to shift for themselves. The offer was accepted *faute de mieux*; and on the afternoon of 30 March, nine days after the departure from the Thames, the expedition came to rest in Malmo. The adventurers were hospitably received and accommodated in the town. The Swedish authorities seized the ship and removed the explosive part of the cargo.

The inglorious conclusion of the cruise of the *Ward Jackson* did not, however, end the adventures of Colonel Lapinski and his legionaries. For two months they remained idle in Malmo, their numbers steadily diminishing and their spirits falling as the news from Poland grew less and less hopeful. Early in June, more arms and ammunition were obtained, and a Danish sailing-vessel named *Emilia* was chartered for a last desperate attempt. This time more serious precautions were taken against publicity. It was announced that the remaining legionaries were returning to England. They were in fact taken to Copenhagen and embarked on a ship bound for London; and it was only in the Sound that the transfer to the *Emilia* took place. The manœuvre was undetected by the Russian scouts, and the *Emilia* sailed unsuspected into the Baltic.

At the north-eastern extremity of the Prussian coast stretches a long narrow spit of land enclosing a sheet of water known as the Kurische Haff. The plan was to land in boats on the spit, to carry them across it, and then row over the Haff to the mainland. From this point a march of two or three hours across Prussian territory, where they hoped to elude observation, would bring them to the Lithuanian border. The scheme was hare-brained enough; but it met with disaster at an unexpectedly early stage. The boats had been purchased in Hamburg; but it had occurred to nobody to ascertain whether they were seaworthy. When the *Emilia*, under cover of night, reached the projected spot, the first of the boats was lowered and thirty-two of the adventurers, Poles and Frenchmen, entered it. No sooner had they pushed off than the boat began to fill with water and sank like a stone. In the darkness and confusion only eight rescues were effected; the other twenty-four occupants of the boat were not seen again. The numerical and moral resources of the party were so severely sapped by this loss that the whole expedition was, by common consent, abandoned. The rank and file of the legionaries returned to Sweden, and thence to England, where they were lodged at Woolwich pending disbandment. The leaders remained in Sweden, and engaged in mutual recriminations with one another and with Bakunin on the causes of the disaster. The last pathetic document of the expedition is a letter written from Woolwich by one of the survivors, who describes himself as 'literally starving' on a pittance of one and threepence a day, and begs his friends to find him an opportunity of 'dying worthily for Poland instead of dying here of want'.

Bakunin, who had taken no part in the last forlorn hope on board the *Emilia*, spent the summer of 1863 in Stockholm. His reputation was somewhat tarnished by his share in an expedition which had ended not merely ignominiously, but ridiculously. The great Polish rebellion was being surely and slowly crushed, in default of foreign support, by the overwhelming weight of the Russian armies. But Bakunin's energies were in no wise impaired; he could not remain idle. Poland being a lost cause, his thoughts turned once more to his native country. He corresponded surreptitiously with what was left of the National Committee of *Land and Liberty* in Petersburg; he intrigued in Finland in the hope of stirring up a new revolt against the Russian Government; and he smuggled (or so he boasted) seven thousand copies of various revolutionary proclamations into Russia. In the midst of his other activities, he found time to complete the ruin of his relations with Herzen by a violent quarrel with Herzen's son.

Young Alexander, now twenty-five, had recently enjoyed to the full the youthful prerogative of giving his father grounds for anxiety. Sent to Switzerland five years before to complete his education, he had fallen in love with a German-Swiss girl, a relative of Herzen's friend Karl Vogt; and there was an informal engagement. Herzen regarded the match with disfavour, and was relieved when Alexander went off on a scientific expedition to Iceland. Absence and reflexion did their work; and on his return the engagement was broken off. But worse was to follow. Alexander

213

came back to England; and there he seduced a respectable girl of the working classes named Charlotte Hudson, who bore him a child.

Herzen had long wished to initiate his son into the political arena; and there was now an additional reason for getting him out of the country. In May 1863, with Bakunin's full approval, he sent him to Stockholm. It is not clear what functions Herzen expected the young man to perform; but he certainly did not anticipate the sequel. Young Alexander, who had hitherto shown neither inclination nor aptitude for politics, gave Bakunin to understand that he was, in virtue of his father's position, the accredited representative of *Land and Liberty* in Sweden. Bakunin replied that he already occupied that position and would brook no interference. The two stood their ground and quarrelled. Alexander seems to have been unusually vain and foolish, even for his age; and Bakunin was an irresponsible child. They spent the next few weeks in Stockholm slandering each other to their common friends. At length Herzen recalled his son. Officially, he blamed both equally for this absurd and undignified *contretemps*. But paternal indulgence naturally led to a further exacerbation of his feelings for Bakunin.

Events now moved rapidly towards the final rupture. After Alexander's departure Bakunin reigned alone in Stockholm. In August, at a public banquet, he proclaimed himself the representative of *Land and Liberty*, and delivered a grandiloquent speech in its honour. Naïvely tactful (for his audience was, politically, a mixed one), he described it as 'a patriotic society on a broad basis – conservative, liberal and democratic at the same time'. It embraced, he declared, all classes of the Russian people – 'generals and officers *en masse*, higher and lower officials, landowners, merchants, priests and sons of priests, peasants and millions of dissenting Old Believers'. It was organizing its own finances, its own administration, its own police; and soon it would have its own army. Finally, it had concluded 'a formal alliance' with the Polish National Committee, which had now become the provisional revolutionary government of Poland. Bakunin stretched out a hand of welcome, in the name of *Land and Liberty*, to all 'Swedish patriots'.

It is not known what impression the speech made on its Swedish auditors; but Herzen in London was furious. He did not much care about the indiscretion; for he had long lost the little faith he had once had in *Land and Liberty*. But his exact mind could not tolerate a man who lived so little as Bakunin in the realms of hard fact, who took his most fantastic dreams and proclaimed them to the world as realities. It mattered nothing that Bakunin had made himself ridiculous by his absurd boastfulness; it mattered little that he had made *Land and Liberty* ridiculous; but it mattered a great deal that he had exposed to ridicule those who, like Herzen and Ogarev, had publicly associated themselves with him and with it. Herzen threatened formally to disavow Bakunin in the pages of *The Bell* and was dissuaded with some difficulty from this course by the more tolerant Ogarev.

The autumn revealed the damage that had been done to *The Bell* by its association with the Polish venture. The Polish insurrection had aroused all the chauvinistic instincts latent in Russian society. The official press fanned the traditional Russian hatred of Poland; and Herzen and his friends were denounced no longer as reformers, but as enemies of their country. The friend of Poland could only be the foe of Russia. In the eyes of the average Russian, *The Bell* became the organ not of enlightenment, but of treason; and its circulation, which had thriven for many years under police persecution, now sank, under the influence of war hysteria, to insignificant dimensions. To complete its discomfiture, a Pole named Petkiewicz, who was probably in the pay of the Russian Government, published in Brussels an 'open letter' in which he accused 'Herzen and Co.' and 'the London triumvirate' of having lured Poland to rebellion by promises of help from a powerful and widespread revolutionary organization, which had turned out to be nothing but a myth. The 'open letter' was widely quoted in the Moscow press. The tiny grain of truth in the accusation, and the attempt to identify Herzen and Ogarev with Bakunin's worst excesses, drove Herzen to frenzy. Ogarev dissuaded him once more from a public quarrel; but in December he wrote an article in *The Bell* in which, quoting the accusation against 'Herzen and Co.', he pointedly remarked:

Whom he includes in this 'company' we do not know. The editors of *The Bell* are not a whole company, there are only two of them: Herzen and Ogarev.

Everybody understood that this meant the formal renunciation of Bakunin; but it did no good to *The Bell*. Herzen did not escape the penalties of the former alliance, and was merely jeered at by the official press for his belated attempt to jettison an indiscreet associate.

In October, Bakunin at last left Sweden and returned to London. Herzen was absent abroad, and the inevitable meeting between the two men was postponed. It took place at the beginning of December in Paris. Financial transactions, in which Bakunin displayed his usual disorderly indifference to questions of debit and credit, had raised Herzen's anger to boiling-point and he met his former friend in a mood of feverish irritation:

I shall see Bakunin [he wrote to Ogarev on the eve of the meeting] though I find the prospect terribly distasteful; for I dislike falsehood. This is my present to you, Ogarev.

But the encounter went off better than might have been expected. Herzen was too modest or too ashamed to refer to his financial grievances, and too weary or too hopeless to reproach Bakunin once more for his share of responsibility in the decline of *The Bell*. Bakunin, relieved perhaps at not being reminded of inconvenient monetary obligations, seemed 'whole-heartedly anxious for peace and determined to do nothing to make a scandal'. They parted with a cordiality which was a little forced on both sides. Herzen, still brooding on his suffering and his wrongs, returned to London. Bakunin, who seldom had time for retrospect or regret, turned his face resolutely southwards and continued his journey to Italy. There he spent the next four years, during which he did not once cross Herzen's path. Their subsequent meetings were few and insignificant. But Bakunin will reappear in a strange episode which followed Herzen's death.

The pen-portrait of Bakunin in *My Past and Thoughts* has been cited in a previous chapter. It is fair to quote here Bakunin's summing-up of Herzen, less brilliant in colour, less pungent in criticism, but equally apt:

Herzen has presented, and continues to sustain, the Russian cause magnificently before the public of Europe. But in matters of domestic policy he is an inveterate sceptic, and his influence on them is not merely not encouraging, but demoralizing. He is, first and foremost, a writer of genius; and he combines all the brilliant qualities with the defects of his profession. When liberty has been established in Russia, or when it begins to be established, he will be, beyond question, a powerful journalist, perhaps an orator, a statesman, even an administrator. But he decidedly has not in him the stuff of which revolutionary leaders are made.

CHAPTER 12

Herzen's Last Years

IT is said that only the young or the sick – sick in body or soul –
keep diaries. Herzen's Diary falls into two periods. In the days of
his youth he confided to it the sorrows of his exile and the story of
his wooing of the first Natalie. After his marriage, it was laid aside
for more than twenty years. Then, in the sixties, it was opened
once more, mainly to receive, on anniversaries or other appropriate occasions, gloomy reflections on the sufferings and calamities
of the intervening years. In the New Year of 1864 he made the
following entries:

> Since 1851 I have never entered a new year with such a feeling of
> horror; I see no hope of any bright point either in my personal, or in
> my public, affairs. . . .
> Even life-long ties are giving way. We are humiliating ourselves in
> each other's eyes. Is it old age? The laurels are fading; there remain
> only old faces trying to look young.
> No harmony in domestic life. The task is growing more difficult, the
> egoisms more obstinate – and it will all fall on the rising generation.
> Everywhere around, gloom, horror and blood.

The year 1864 justified the presentiment. It saw *The Bell* pursue
its rapid decline into impotence and insignificance; and it was a
year of unrelieved domestic misery culminating in overwhelming
tragedy.

The birth of the twins had finally dissipated Herzen's dream
of seeing all his children united under the same roof. In the
summer of 1862, Malwida declared her intention, for reasons of
health, of transferring her residence from Paris to Italy, and
proposed to take Olga with her. Experience had shown that Olga
could not live with Natalie: and to separate her now from Malwida was unthinkable. Herzen perforce agreed to Malwida's
proposal and, with a heavy heart, made another. Tata's position
at home was becoming ever more difficult. The gloomy nerve-
ridden atmosphere of Natalie's house had nothing to offer an
eighteen-year-old girl. In such surroundings work was impossible;

218

and Tata had professed a desire to develop her talent as an artist. In justice to both families, whom he loved equally, Herzen knew that they must live apart. When Malwida departed for Italy at the beginning of December, he sent Tata with them. The separation was bitter to the unhappy father, and none the less bitter because the cause of it had been of his own making. The only consolation he could offer himself as he saw them off at the station was that Tata's education had been virtually completed under his care, and that she had not grown up, as Olga was growing up, ignorant of her mother tongue.

The summer of 1864 saw the whole family, including Malwida, re-united for the last time on English soil. They spent it together at Bournemouth, a small watering-place conveniently accessible by omnibus from the nearest railway station at Christchurch. Here Natalie's frenzy of self-pity and self-assertion reached a new high-water-mark; and she broke such bounds of discretion as had hitherto restrained her. Hitherto Natalie had scrupulously respected the secret chamber of Herzen's heart – the Holy of Holies where he worshipped the memory of his dead wife. Hitherto she had taken, or appeared to take, her full share in the cult. She had her own niche in the shrine as the friend to whom the dying mother had bequeathed the care of her children; and the cult even served to sanctify her liaison with Herzen. Natalie often found consolation in the thought that there above, somewhere in another world (in which, in her less emotional moments, she did not believe), Natalie the first was looking down and blessing the union between the man who had been her husband and the woman who had been her dearest friend. It was peculiarly characteristic of the later Romantics to assume the approval of another world for their illicit love affairs. 'I am sure,' exclaimed Emma Bovary to her first lover Rodolphe, 'that our mothers together there in heaven are blessing our love'.

But the cult was, after all, too artificial to wear well. Natalie did not really deceive herself. She knew that her namesake and friend, whose human qualities she understood far better than Herzen had ever done, was no more qualified than most mortals for the pedestal and the halo of a goddess; and she was galled by the consciousness that, in Herzen's heart and thoughts, the dead wife counted, and would always count, for more than the living mistress. She was aggrieved, just as she had been aggrieved in Petersburg when Ogarev's friends obviously thought more of him than of her. There was no immediate provocation. But one evening at Bournemouth, when Herzen was reading aloud to Tata the chapters from *My Past and Thoughts* which told the story of his wife's tragedy – the chapters which were only to see the light fifty years after his death – something suddenly snapped. Natalie broke into the story with wounding and derisive words. A scene of wild recrimination followed. Taunts were exchanged which could not be lightly forgotten. A whole month passed without a reconciliation; and Herzen found it difficult even to maintain 'outward decency' for the sake of the children. He told Natalie that she would 'cover them all with shame'. She laughed harshly and retorted that 'if she had the money, she would show them a thing or two'. She threatened to take her children away to Russia, and talked of sending a petition to the Tsar. Herzen replied, in writing, that if she did so, he would publish to the whole world the secret (which she had hitherto concealed even from her mother) of the children's parentage. Neither threat was perhaps to be taken seriously. Both Herzen and Natalie had reached a point at which the desire to wound had swallowed up every other emotion.

But if Natalie had, at this time, no serious intention of returning to Russia, she shared the common illusion of the hysterical that she would be better off anywhere rather than where she was. Life in England had become intolerable. Many family councils, stormy and bitter, were held during this summer at Bournemouth; and there it was decided that Herzen should, after twelve years' residence, abandon his English domicile and transfer his family and belongings to Switzerland. There were public, as well as domestic, reasons for the change. The circulation of *The Bell* which, in the day of its prosperity, had fluctuated between two and three thousand, had now sunk to a paltry five hundred. It was visibly dying; and removal to Geneva, where of late years many refugees had congregated, seemed to offer the last desperate hope of reviving its prestige.

Geneva possessed, in Herzen's eyes, another advantage over London. It was nearer to Italy, which seemed likely to become the permanent residence of his older children, including his son Alexander, who had just taken a post as lecturer in physiology in

Florence. Of Tata's future it was still difficult to speak. Her migration had not been an unmixed success. Olga was the unique passion of Malwida's heart. Malwida was too one-sided, too concentrated to hold the balance even between the sisters; and when they quarrelled, Tata was always in the wrong. On this, or any other question, it was impossible to argue with Malwida. Her conviction of her own rightness was overwhelming. Herzen began to find her almost as hysterical as Natalie. 'They take it in turns,' he wrote to his son from Bournemouth, 'to go off their heads; and Tata, who is less childish than either of them, calms them down.' Some other provision would have, sooner or later, to be made for Tata; and this seemed on the whole easier in Geneva than in London.

The case of Ogarev presented special difficulties. His inveterate drinking habits, the growing frequency of his epileptic fits, and the general collapse of his health seemed to render a change of scene urgently desirable. But Ogarev's lethargy resisted all movement; and Mary Sutherland had become a necessary adjunct to his life. One by one, his objections were overruled, and he agreed to the move provided he was allowed to take Mary with him. Another difficulty of a somewhat similar character then presented itself. The family had hitherto supported Charlotte Hudson and her child in London. Young Alexander might have been content to forget his youthful indiscretion. But Herzen would not abandon a child in whose veins some drops of his own blood flowed; and Charlotte Hudson refused an invitation to surrender her son. In the end, therefore, Charlotte and the boy, whose name was Alexander but who came to be known by the sobriquet of Toots, were both included in the Geneva caravan.*

The main issues being thus settled, a protracted debate ensued on the date of departure. It ended in a compromise. The impatient Natalie would leave England with her three children in November. The reluctant Ogarev would remain until the following

* Herzen's attitude to Toots was not free from the inconsistencies bred of an embarrassing situation. He would not give the boy up to his mother. But he was furious when his son gave him his own name of Alexander and, subsequently, when Mary Sutherland tried to make a respectable woman of Charlotte by calling her 'Mrs Herzen'. The boy grew up under the name of 'Alexander Herzen', and settled in Italy, where he died on 1 January 1933.

spring. Herzen, having deposited Natalie and the children somewhere in France for the winter, would go on to Geneva to make
arrangements for the installation there of the family and the
printing-press. He would then return to England to supervise the
departure of Ogarev, Tchorzewski, Ciernecki and the printing-
press, and the other camp followers.

The programme was carried out. But its execution was interrupted in the early stages by a brutal and heartrending tragedy.
No sooner had Herzen and Natalie arrived in Paris with the three
children than a diphtheria epidemic visited the city. Both the
twins, who had just passed their third birthday, succumbed to the
disease; and on 3 December the girl died. In this moment of
tragedy, the responsibility for every decision rested exclusively on
Herzen. As the little coffin was borne away to Montmartre, where
it was to wait eventual transportation to the family vault at Nice,
he reflected how much it would have amused the dead child to
play with the magnificent silver tassels on the pall. Then, after
eight days, the boy followed his sister. Ogarev hastened over from
London. But he was obviously in no state to travel alone, and he
increased rather than relieved Herzen's cares. Herzen and Natalie
had few acquaintances in Paris; and by a strange coincidence the
only one who proffered comfort and assistance was Madame de
Salias, whose unwanted presence had embarrassed and enlivened
the courtship of Ogarev and Natalie fifteen years before.

This double grief swept away from Herzen's heart all the bitterness and resentment of the last months; but it almost deprived
Natalie of her sanity. She reflected that she, and she alone, had
insisted on immediate departure when the others would have been
content to winter in England. She remembered that it was she
who had insisted on a halt in Paris instead of travelling straight
through to the South. By her obstinacy, twice repeated, she had
aimed the fatal stroke at the heads of her children; and she
denounced herself, to any who cared to listen, as their murderess.
Occasionally her mind would wander back from the tragedy of
their death to the tragedy of their birth. An unexpected streak of
puritan theology revealed itself in her, and she saw in the death
of the twins a retribution for her own guilt. The guilt was not hers
alone. At such moments she hated Herzen, the partner of her sin,
as much as she hated herself. For weeks after the tragedy she never

undressed, and snatched a few hours' sleep on a chair or couch as she wandered aimlessly from room to room. For twenty years or more she kept a notebook in which she religiously recorded the dreams in which her dead children appeared to her.

It was essential to remove Liza from the infected city. Four days after the second death, Herzen and Natalie travelled with her to Montpellier. She caught cold on the journey. But no infection developed; and after two or three days of sickening anxiety she recovered rapidly. After Christmas, Herzen left Liza and her mother in Montpellier and went on to Geneva. There he found, without much difficulty, through a Russian friend, a spacious country house surrounded by a well-wooded garden on one of the high roads leading out of the town. It bore the imposing name of Château de la Boissière. It contained more than thirty rooms, and had once been occupied by an authentic Grand Duchess, the divorced wife of a younger son of the mad Tsar, Paul I. In spite of these distinctive features, the rent was only 5,000 francs a year. In London foreigners were expected to pay more than natives, and Herzen's furnished houses had never cost him less than six guineas a week. The magnificent Château de la Boissière represented therefore a considerable economy in his budget.

When the arrangements in Geneva were complete, Herzen returned to Montpellier and eventually to London. His last few weeks in England were spent in Ogarev's lodgings at Richmond. The few necessary farewells were spoken, the few remaining preparations made for the final departure. The last number of *The Bell* in England would appear on 1 April. Then Ogarev, Ciernecki and the rest of the party would strike camp and move by easy stages to Geneva. Herzen in the meanwhile would transport the two little coffins from Paris to Nice, would pick up Natalie and Liza at Cannes, and would reach the Château de la Boissière in time to welcome the travellers from London.

On the evening of 15 March 1865, Herzen embarked at Dover on the Calais packet and left English shores for ever. In the course of twelve and a half years he had struck no roots in the country. He had found there a haven of refuge, but not the arms of friendship. The English had been toleration itself. They were too busy with their own affairs to interest themselves in his. They did not mind what the foreigner thought of them; and they made it clear that they seldom thought anything at all of the foreigner. The stranger was received everywhere with courtesy, but with fundamental indifference. There had been nothing to warm the expansive sides of Herzen's nature. As he took his leave, his impressions were perhaps unduly clouded by the personal sorrows of the first and the last years of his stay in England. His mind naturally dwelt on the circumstances of his arrival and of his departure, and forgot the joyous moments that lay between. But as he looked back afterwards on these years of his life, there was not much that was specifically English whose loss he mourned – not much except Colman's mustard, English pickles and 'mushroom ketchup'. Only the two Poles had some regrets for the land of their adoption. The gallant Tchorzewski, marooned in grim Geneva, sometimes missed 'les belles vues de Haymarket' – the fashionable prostitutes' quarters; and Ciernecki and his wife, who had lived for five years on the premises of the printing-press in Caledonian Road, 'still dreamed of the open skies of King's Cross, and the broad horizons of Tottenham Court Road'.

The great reunion at the Château de la Boissière took place in the middle of April. Ciernecki and the printing-press were safely installed in one part of Geneva, and Mary and Charlotte with their offspring in another. But Herzen soon experienced the force of the Horatian maxim about those who hasten across the sea. Ogarev continued to drink; and Natalie found Geneva as intolerable a place to live in as London or Bournemouth. The restless misery of the past year proved to be as compatible with the Swiss as with the English climate. Even the magnificent Château failed to fulfil expectations; and Herzen discovered that 'comfort had been sacrificed for the sake of reception rooms'. Recriminations were soon resumed.

I cannot make out [wrote Herzen to Ogarev on 5 June] what she wants me to do. What does she want? How can she go to Russia? What does she want to 'announce' about her separation from you? And to whom? These are all the old chronic misunderstandings. Where does she want to begin? Tata knows, Sasha knows. She doesn't mean to announce it to the police? And to go to Russia for the winter! Even you cannot find a solution, but think over the answer. I shall end by saying: 'Do what you think best. Two are dead; take the third on your own responsibility.'

Before the summer was over, Natalie had had violent quarrels
with Tata, with Olga and, of course, with Malwida von Meysenbug. She even talked of returning to England, whence she had so
precipitately fled. In September she carried off Liza with her to
Montreux at the other end of the lake.

Liza was now seven; and neither her mother nor her English
governess, Miss Turner, was an ideal companion for this high-
spirited and highly-strung child.

> Natalie has lost her remaining capacities [wrote Herzen to his son
> at this time] for bringing up a child. When Liza is naughty, she weeps,
> talks of death, etc. Miss Turner is a little fool, but good-natured, i.e.
> she is not a fool, but an Englishwoman – by English standards that is
> not so stupid.

It was time Liza should begin to receive a more regular education;
and the search for a school became the constant theme of Natalie's
uneasy Odyssey. No school ever pleased her; and when she
wished particularly to annoy Herzen she would talk blandly of
starting a school of her own. The winter at Montreux was followed
by a few weeks at Lausanne. Next autumn they tried Nice. The
graves of her dead children drew and riveted Natalie to the little
town by the sea, so full of tragic memories for the house of Herzen;
and at Nice they remained for two years. The atmosphere of the
mausoleum, irresistible to the mother, may have been less con-
ducive to the normal growth of her surviving daughter; but here,
in a school kept by an American woman, Liza seems to have had
the only consecutive education that ever fell to her lot. Then there
was a fruitless search for a school in Alsace, followed by experi-
ments, in the last year of Herzen's life, at Brussels, Florence and
Paris. The unhappy Herzen, throughout this period, divided his
time between Natalie and Geneva; and the years were an unending series of taunts, tears and threats. Here is an extract from one
of Herzen's letters to Natalie written in 1866, which does not
differ in substance from a dozen others:

> After yesterday I came away feeling as if I had passed through a
> serious illness. You dared to propose that I should not see Liza for
> several years! You could do that after all that has happened, knowing
> that she is necessary to me! That I will never permit – first let me go
> mad or die. You think that I am afraid of the judgement of society

because I don't want the crowd to drag us and our names in the mud. You are wrong. I will make your friends near and far judges of this attempt to ravish from me, by your unrestrained caprice, the child whom I have been trying to save by my boundless love. This crime I will never allow you to commit. I will demand as judges your sister, your father. I will find people who will come specially from Russia.

It is odd to meet again, in these pathetic ravings of the distracted old man, the notion of the 'court of honour' which he had once tried to invoke for the confusion of Herwegh.

Between such storms of rage and weeping there were flashes of reconciliation and the making of new resolves for the future. Such moments were, on Natalie's side, accompanied, and perhaps dictated, by a revived ardour for sexual intercourse. It was the only certain way of pleasing Natalie; and Herzen would have pleased her more if he had exhibited less philosophical detachment.

> Only intimate relations [he wrote to Ogarev] can put her right for the time. Yes, but it is an awful remedy. You can take my word for the fact; I have studied it and am sure.

Made today, such a diagnosis might be merely the facile expression of a fashionable theory. Made in 1867 by one who had never dabbled in problems of morbid psychology, it carries conviction. Too passionate to maintain her stability unless her sexual appetites were fully and freely satisfied, too romantic to divorce this satisfaction from the ties of sentiment, too honest, or too ignorant of her own needs, to form new ties for the purpose of satisfying her physical lusts – Natalie Ogarev is a figure more familiar to us in modern literature than in that of the age to which she belonged. Nor had misfortune abated by one jot her yearning for children and ever more children. Twice or thrice during the period under review she imagined herself pregnant; and the expectation of a child, which would have driven some women in her plight hysterical, completely restored, for the few weeks while it lasted, Natalie's equanimity and amiability. With the discovery of her mistake, chaos came again over her darkened mind.

*

The flight of Natalie and Liza to Montreux shattered Herzen's last hopes of a united family life at the Château de la Boissière. Malwida and Olga had returned to Italy. Only Tata and Ogarev were left. Ogarev's condition grew worse and worse. He had several fits at times when nobody was near to tend him; and twice he fell with a lighted candle in his hand. Once, apparently when on his way to visit Natalie and Liza at Montreux, he collapsed by the roadside, and was taken in a semi-conscious state to the police station at Vevey. The police attributed his condition, perhaps correctly, not to epilepsy but to alcohol; and he was rescued with some difficulty by his friends. Obviously he required constant watching, and could no longer be safely left to himself. But here Ogarev's lethargic obstinacy raised an insuperable barrier. He would not hear of anything in the nature of a nurse or an attendant. If he must be looked after, he would be looked after by Mary and no one else. There could be no question of Mary's coming to live at the Château. On this Herzen, for the sake of family propriety, imposed an absolute veto. Ogarev must therefore go to Mary. A cottage was found in the pleasant suburb of Lancy; and here, in the spring of 1866, the former owner of four thousand serfs was installed in the company of Mary and Henry Sutherland, and Charlotte Hudson and Toots.

When Ogarev had gone, the Château stood more clearly than ever revealed as an expensive folly. Herzen and Tata moved across to a small flat on the Quai Mont-Blanc, the new residential quarter on the opposite bank of the lake. A year later there was another move to the Boulevard Plainpalais in the centre of the town. Herzen, constantly on the move, had lost all need or taste for a settled home. Since the glorious days of Orsett House, he had never lived under the same roof for more than a few months at a time. He became in fact what in spirit he had been since the great trek from Moscow in January 1847 – a wanderer on the face of the earth.

Nor did the transfer of the printing-press to Switzerland assist Herzen's political fortunes. In England, *The Bell* had incurred the undying antagonism of the timid Russian liberals who preferred patriotism to freedom. It had lost its circulation in Russia; but it had still retained, for what it was worth, its prestige among the little colony of political refugees in London. In Geneva even this backing was forfeited. The Russian exiles in Switzerland were numerous; but they were men of a new generation and of another school of thought. Even at the moment when he was renting the Château de la Boissière, Herzen had had his misgivings.

The last two days [he wrote to Ogarev on 2 January 1865] I have perceived that, despite the *palazzo* which Kasatkin has found for me, Geneva is impossible, or at any rate almost impossible, owing to these busybodies and intriguers. Perhaps they are well-meaning people, but their self-importance blackens the landscape.

Herzen stifled his apprehensions; but they were more than justified by the event. From the first moment there was open enmity, bitter and mutual, between Herzen and the Russians in Geneva.

Its causes were deep, but not, except to Herzen himself, obscure. Herzen belonged to the Russian generation of the forties. For all his enlightenment, he retained in a large measure the traditions and habits of the Russian aristocrat. Romanticism was his religion, liberalism his political faith, and constitutional democracy his ideal for Russia. The generation of the sixties had grown up in a Russia which Herzen never knew. In London, he had had a first brush with Chernyshevsky and, later, with the champions of *Land and Liberty*. But the nihilists *en masse* were a new and strange phenomenon to him when he came to Geneva. These young men were materialists by religion, and revolutionaries by precept and by practice. Their opinions were clear-cut and decisive. For Russia, the first step towards reform was to bring down with a crash the whole existing system; the second step it was premature to discuss. They were in all things aggressive. The forties seemed to them an almost antediluvian epoch; and Herzen's political writings inspired them with the contempt felt by a healthy schoolboy for the fairy-tales of his childhood. The first Geneva issue of *The Bell* contained an open letter from Herzen to the Tsar on the recent death of the latter's eldest son. It exhorted Alexander to mend his ways, and was in substance a thinly veiled denunciation. Herzen put his best work into it, and thought it a good piece of fighting journalism. When the young radicals clamoured against it, it merely showed him how captious and how dishonest the young radicals were. He could not understand that its every word was an offence to men who believed that the only legitimate instrument to use when dealing with autocrats was not the pen, but the revolver or the bomb.

Political differences may be bitter; but they lack that peculiar degree of personal exasperation which arises when questions of cash are at stake. Herzen in London had always been ready to put his hand in his pocket for the sake of needy refugees. His generosity did not come to a standstill when he crossed the Channel. But in Geneva the claims on his charity were far more numerous than in London; and his resources had of late been severely strained. His three elder children all continued to depend on his support; and now they were no longer collected under the family roof, the expected subsidies were larger. Natalie and Liza were now a separate establishment to be maintained. The printing-press, which once nearly paid for itself, had become a heavy financial burden. Even his income was not intact; for among his investments were bonds of some of the southern states of the American Union. The ever increasing demands of the Russians in Geneva ended by getting on his nerves. 'I gave and gave, and then I got tired of giving', he told a visitor during his first year at Geneva. 'I am no Croesus.'

The Russians of Geneva, unprepared as they were to accept Herzen as their political oracle, might have been willing to use him as their banker. But when they discovered that he was not an inexhaustible source of revenue, they turned on him with all the asperity of humiliated independence. Murmurs began to circulate about the strange principles of this millionaire-revolutionary. Had he not sold his land and his serfs for a good price when he left Russia? Was he not the friend of Rothschild? Did he not own a house in the fashionable quarter of Paris, and bonds of most of the capitalist governments of Europe and America? Had he not received from wealthy sympathizers large funds to be devoted to furthering the revolutionary cause? Yet here he was in Geneva, living like a royal personage in a luxurious mansion, publishing a journal which had never been revolutionary and which had long ceased to be read, and refusing all aid to his poorer and humbler brethren who were actively working for revolution. Such rumours went the round of the Russian colony in Geneva, and magnified themselves as they went. Feeling ran high; and jeers and insults were flung at Herzen in the streets by excited compatriots.

The ablest and most energetic of Herzen's radical opponents was a young man named Alexander Serno-Solovievich. He was a younger brother of the Nicholas Serno-Solovievich whose article in support of *The Great Russian* had been so rashly published by Ogarev in *The Bell*. Nicholas returned to Russia, was arrested by the police, and died while serving his sentence in Siberia. The arrest of his brother worked on the nerves of the impressionable Alexander. By this time he too had left Russia. He visited London, where he was amiably received by Herzen, and eventually settled down in Geneva. He found a home there in a *pension* kept by a Russian lady, a Madame Shelgunov.

Madame Shelgunov was a noteworthy figure. Her husband was a young radical publicist. He held fashionably advanced views on the relations of the sexes and the obligations resulting from marriage; and his wife had, with his consent and approval, taken as her lover a friend and colleague of his, one Mikhailov. Unfortunately, the attentions of the Russian police robbed her, at one fell swoop, of husband and lover. Both spent some months in prison, and were then transported to Siberia. The doubly-bereaved wife and mistress followed them thither; and there was a brief and ecstatic reunion. But Madame Shelgunov soon discovered that her health required a prolonged residence in some more clement zone. She emigrated to Geneva and, with her customary enterprise, established a modest *pension* for Russian exiles. About the time Alexander Serno-Solovievich arrived, she was ready for a fresh adorer; and Alexander filled the role with distinction. He was an ardent and excitable lover. His nerves had never quite recovered from the sentence and death of his brother; and Madame Shelgunov was secretly rather afraid of him. But fear added spice to passion. He was exciting as well as excitable. Moreover his radical principles were unimpeachable; and the lady, though fickle in regard to individuals, was always faithful to her convictions.

In time, Madame Shelgunov began to tire of this unrestful lover. She was now pregnant by him; and when the child was born, she quietly sent it away to her husband in Siberia, to be brought up with the boy whom she had (in the more orthodox sense of the term) presented to him some years before. Some lovers might have been relieved at this practical and expeditious method of dealing with an encumbrance. But Alexander was made of more passionate stuff. Having discovered what had happened, he stormed and raved about the sacred rights of paternity and threatened to kill his mistress. But he had already lost his hold over her. Madame Shelgunov was now bored as well as frightened. Resourceful as ever, she persuaded the local authorities that Alexander was in a mental state which rendered it inadvisable to leave him at large. He was accordingly removed to an asylum; and his mistress, having thus successfully disposed both of her infant and of her lover, was ready once more to face the radical society of Geneva.

These events occurred not long before the arrival of Herzen at the Château de la Boissière; and Natalie relates how, as they were all sitting one evening at the Château, Alexander Serno-Solovietich burst, dishevelled and wild-eyed, into the family circle. He had just escaped from the lunatic asylum; and after falling on his knees and begging Herzen's pardon for all the insults he had heaped on him, he retailed at length the story of his grievances against his late mistress. This tale, like others which embellish Natalie's *Memoirs*, is not strictly accurate. For Alexander, safely immured in the Geneva lunatic asylum, had not yet had an opportunity of insulting Herzen, and did not do so till some time after the latter had left the Château de la Boissière. It is probable that his exit from the asylum was less dramatic than Natalie pretends. At any rate, he was not required by the local authorities to return to it; and he spent the next four years in Geneva in political activities which were terminated only by his death, at the age of thirty-one, in the year 1869.

It was in the summer of 1866 that the warfare between Herzen and the radicals entered on its decisive phase. In April, about the time when Herzen was moving from the Château to the Quai Mont-Blanc, a young student named Karakozov fired at Alexander II in Petersburg. It was the first attempt to use assassination as a political weapon, and led to a new deepening of opinion for and against 'nihilism'. *The Bell*, true to its principles, refused to approve the attempt, and referred to its author with contemptuous anonymity as 'some fanatic'. The radicals, who made Karakozov their hero, raged furiously against Herzen. Herzen aggravated the offence by publishing yet another 'open letter' to the Tsar. The sniping went on. Then in December he wrote a long article, which ran through several numbers of *The Bell*, under the ironical title *Order Triumphs*. Its earlier sections were merely a repetition of the oft-told tale of Herzen's views on European and Russian politics, and made no particular stir. But the sting was in its tail, in which Herzen set out to define his relations to the radicals. Paying a handsome tribute to the radical leader Cherny-shevsky, who had been sent to Siberia in 1864, he boldly declared that there had never been any antagonism between the movement headed by Chernyshevsky in Russia and the movement abroad represented by Ogarev and himself. 'We served as the mutual complement of one another.' In this way Herzen held out the olive-branch to the radicals; and the implication was latent that those who attacked him now were no true disciples of Cherny-shevsky.

This passage lashed the Geneva radicals, and in particular Serno-Solovievich, to a frenzy of indignation. They had no journal at their disposal. But funds were somehow collected to enable a public reply to be made. It took the form of an open letter to Herzen, signed by Serno-Solovievich, and privately printed at Vevey in the spring of 1867, under the title *Our Domestic Affairs*. It was not often that Serno-Solovievich enjoyed the luxury of print; and he unloaded himself of all the stored-up eloquence which had hitherto found its only outlet in stuffy *pensions* and over-heated *cafés*.

I have long since ceased [he wrote] to read, or at any rate to be interested in, your sheet. Hackneyed, long familiar sounds; rhetorical phrases and appeals, ancient variations on an ancient theme; witticisms, sometimes fairly clever, but more often flat; commonplaces about 'Land and Liberty' – all this has become too tedious, too boring, too repulsive . . .

Yes, the young generation has understood you. Having understood you, it has turned away from you in disgust; and you still dream that you are its guide, that you are 'a power and a force in the Russian state', that you are a leader and representative of youth. You our leader? Ha! Ha! Ha! The young generation has long outstripped you by a whole head in its understanding of facts and events. Failing to perceive that you have been left behind, you flap your enfeebled wings with all your might; and then, when you see that people are only laughing at you, you go off in a rage and reproach the younger generation with ingratitude to their teacher, to the founder of their school, the first high-priest of Russian socialism! You are a poet, a painter, an artist, a story-teller, a novelist – anything you please, but *not* a political leader and still less a political thinker, the founder of a school and a doctrine . . .

So you were the complement of Chernyshevsky! You marched shoulder to shoulder with Chernyshevsky! Such an idea I never expected even from you, and I have studied you closely . . . You the complement of Chernyshevsky! No, Mr Herzen. It is too late now to take refuge behind Chernyshevsky! *Troppo tarde*, the opportunity has passed. Between you and Chernyshevsky there was not, and could not be, anything in common. You are two opposite elements which cannot exist side by side or near one another. You are the representatives of two hostile natures, which do not complement, but exterminate each other – so completely do you differ in everything, not only in your philosophy of life, but in your attitude to yourself and to other people, not only in general questions, but in the minutest details of your private life . . .

Conceit is your great misfortune, it completely blinds you . . . Come down to earth; forget that you are a great man; remember that the medals with your effigy were struck not by a grateful posterity, but by yourself out of your bloodstained wealth. Look more closely at what is going on around you, and you will then perhaps understand that dry leaves and paper snakes interest nobody . . . that you, Mr Herzen, are a dead man.

Herzen read this crude butchery in a mood approaching despair. In subtlety of argument he could have shown himself more than a match for any Serno-Solovievich. He could perhaps have given him points in a mere vulgar slanging-match; for, a year later, he referred to his radical enemies as 'this syphilis of our revolutionary lusts'. But no invective and no subtlety could refute – indeed, they would rather reinforce – the brutal fact which the pamphlet had so relentlessly driven home. Herzen had lost the confidence of the rising generation. He might still be right in his own eyes; but he was no longer in the van of a great movement. His strategy might be perfect; but the rank and file would not fight under his leadership. He was a general without an army. He bowed his head to the blow. He was an old man, and very tired. 'The brochure of S.-S.', he wrote to Natalie, 'is so disgusting that we do not care to send it to you.'

For many months now he had longed to be free of the useless

burden of *The Bell*. Ogarev still wrote; but he could no longer be relied on – if he ever could be relied on – to take his share in the hack-work of editorship. The mechanical production of the paper was still, of course, in Ciernecki's capable hands. But the sole responsibility rested on Herzen; and with his now constant journeyings and failing health he could not support the load. A brilliant idea suggested itself. On 1 July, *The Bell* would celebrate its tenth birthday. Let the celebration take the form of a six months' holiday. Had he been a younger man, Herzen would have found some resounding answer to the impudence of Serno-Solovievich. Now the dignified reply was silence. *The Bell* had rung steadily for a whole decade, without faltering or changing its note. It had earned a respite.

In his heart Herzen knew that this was the end. He was only fifty-six; but the disappointments of his public, and still more of his personal, life had broken him down before his time. The first stages of diabetes made their appearance, and he was a martyr to eczema. Talk about doctors and cures begin to loom large in his correspondence. *The Bell* resumed publication on 1 January 1868. It was now published in French in order to appeal to an international, instead of a purely Russian, audience; and there was an occasional Russian supplement to remind people of what it had once been. But the enterprise was doomed to failure. 'Do the French want to know the truth about anything,' wrote Turgenev, 'let alone about Russia?' The twigs were damp, and the fire would not kindle.

> We have gone astray [Herzen wrote gloomily to Ogarev when the first number appeared]. It is clear that nobody wants either the French or the Russian *Bell*. In such conditions I cannot work.

He adds that the radicals regard them as 'restless old men who have lost their wits'; and the tone suggests that he is more than half inclined to agree with the definition. *The Bell* struggled on in French throughout the year 1868, and collapsed from inanition.

*

It was during this summer of 1868 that Herzen, feeling perhaps that it was for the last time, once more gathered around him all the scattered members of his fold. He rented for a month the magnificent Château of Prangins, which rises in its well-wooded grounds above the Lake of Geneva, not far from Nyon; and here in the middle of August the party began to assemble. First Herzen himself arrived with Natalie and Liza and Tata. Then Ogarev was fetched from Geneva, immobile as ever and reluctant to escape, even for a few short weeks, from Mary's jealous care. Then came Olga and Malwida, who had been staying in Germany; and finally Alexander with his young bride Teresina, whom he had married a fortnight before in Florence. The reunion lasted until the middle of September. At peace with himself and the world, the old man presided over his tribe with the dignity of the patriarch and the munificence of the *grand seigneur*, and recaptured, for a few short weeks, the sense of that broad and spacious life which knows no vulgar everyday cares of politics or of money, that life of the Russian gentleman which instinctively remained, even in his most revolutionary moments, his ideal of personal well-being.

But as he looked round the table, there were many clouds before his eyes, and many dark thoughts assailed him. Of the tragedy of Natalie there was nothing to say which had not been said a thousand times in the last ten years. It was better not to think any more about that (for that way madness lay), and to pray secretly that nothing would happen to mar the short-lived summer peace of Prangins. Far deeper were Herzen's feelings as he watched his oldest – his only real – friend, the comrade both of the aspirations of his youth and of the triumphs of his middle years. Both Herzen and Ogarev had been badly battered in the struggle of life. But while the former sought a passing refuge in a comfortable country house on the shore of a Swiss lake, Ogarev had retired for ever into a rococo castle in Spain of his own devising, peopled in part with the gracious forms of a romantic past, and in part with the illiterate, coarse-grained progeny of an English slum. Ogarev had become an enigma. The incongruity of past and present did not concern him; he lived equally and indifferently in both. He did not belong any more to this world; and when he sat, silent and abstracted, among his fellow-men, you could not be sure whether his brain was bemused with the fragrance of poetry or with the fumes of alcohol. Herzen was a man of flesh and blood; and material conditions, using the term broadly, were nine-tenths of life to him. He could not live, like

235

Ogarev, unspotted by surrounding squalor, in a world of dis-embodied wraiths.

Of his children, whom he loved so dearly, Herzen could look with almost unclouded gratitude and confidence on Tata and Liza. Tata, now in her twenty-fourth year, had become the companion and confidant of his declining years. She had not developed any remarkable capacities; and in this respect his fond paternal ambition had perhaps been disappointed. But he felt that, even if he were to die now, he could trust her sterling qualities of head and heart. She was a Russian, and she was his daughter; and he could pay her no greater compliment. Nor had he any fears for Liza. At ten, she was already the most precociously intelligent of all his children, and perhaps the most like him. Her irregular education seemed to have quickened, rather than impeded, the development of her mother wit. She was, naturally enough, rather spoilt, rather too self-conscious and self-assertive; but these things would pass. He had for her the old man's indulgence for his youngest child. He was content with her. She would make a figure in the world; and though she had no legal right to his name, she would bring honour upon it.

He passed to his only son. It was more than twelve years since that New Year's Eve in Richmond when he had solemnly dedicated young Alexander to the cause of Russia and the revolution. The promise had not been fulfilled. Alexander could not be induced to take more than a polite interest in the fatherland he had last seen in his eighth year; and, by a common reaction of youth against its environment, he would hear nothing of politics and revolution. Herzen, grieved at the defection, thought his son weak and irresolute. He was susceptible to female charm – his father had been the same before him; and he had not managed his affairs well. First there had been the broken engagement with the Swiss girl; then the open scandal of Charlotte Hudson and Toots; and now, suddenly and unreflectingly, he had plunged into a hasty marriage with an Italian girl of lowly origin.

It had been a strange romance. Tata, during her stay in Florence, zealously pursued her studies in drawing and painting. One day she and her brother had watched a bevy of working-girls troop out of a neighbouring factory. One of them, a striking brunette of sixteen, attracted their attention; and Alexander carelessly remarked that there before their eyes was a beauty more worth painting than the elderly housemaid whom Tata was wont to use as her model. The suggestion bore fruit. The girl was approached; and after long negotiations (for her parents were reputable workpeople and looked on the invitation with suspicion) it was agreed that she should, for a suitable fee, sit to Tata for her portrait.* The model, whose name was Teresina Felici, proved to be not only beautiful but intelligent. Brother and sister continued their interest in her after the sittings were over. Alexander was impressionable, and Tata kindness itself; and between them they arranged that Teresina should be given the vestiges of an education. She was a ready learner. Her beauty ripened, and Alexander's interest ripened with it. Two years after the first meeting, he spoke of marriage; and despite Herzen's bitter opposition, the betrothal took place. In response to his father's entreaties, Alexander promised to wait a year. But nature was too strong; and the marriage was hurried through, without his father's consent, at the beginning of August 1868.

The girl was an undoubted beauty. But she was, Herzen complained, 'plebeian through and through, cold and calculating . . . and worships money out of regard for her former poverty'. She had 'neither birth nor breeding nor education'; and she spoke no language but her own. The worst of it all was that Alexander was perfectly content. He would spend the rest of his days teaching Italian or Swiss students, living in cramped comfort with his *bourgeois* Italian wife and begetting a host of *bourgeois* Italian children. Herzen himself, at Alexander's age, had already made a romantic marriage, had served one sentence of exile for his opinions and was qualifying for another. He was already a figure in the world. Young Alexander – he reflected with more than a shade of contempt – was not the man his father had been.

But the darkest cloud of all crossed Herzen's face as he watched the delicate features and graceful figure of Olga, now approaching her eighteenth birthday. When nearly ten years ago Natalie's temper had driven Olga from home, and he had let Malwida take her first to Paris and then to Italy, had he stopped to think that he was losing his second daughter for good? Had it occurred to

* The portrait of Teresina painted on this occasion is still in the possession of Mlle Herzen.

him that there, in a strange land and among strange people, she would form a new circle of interests and relationships, and that now, when she stood on the verge of womanhood, her father's speech and thoughts would be utterly foreign to her? But this was what had happened. There were rumours already of a suitor in the shape of a young French *savant* named Monod. Herzen, who had met him, thought him 'a capable, honest conservative'. But what a fall for a daughter of Herzen to think of marrying a typical member of the hide-bound French *bourgeoisie*! In any case, whether that came to anything or not, Olga was lost to him. He had sincerely thanked Malwida, all these years, for saving his daughter from Natalie's ungovernable character; and she had separated Olga irrevocably from him.

He looked at Malwida, as she sat among them, with the old mixture of respect which he could not refuse, and of dislike which he could scarcely conceal. She was as sure of herself as ever, just as single-minded, just as *unscrupulous* in the pursuit of any aim which she recognized as good. She had developed (it had not required much development) into a prim, self-important old maid, who talked much of her ailments and of the climates in which she could, or could not, live. Flannel had become her religion; and she preached flannel as the cure for all the ills of the flesh. If a man had swallowed arsenic, Herzen jested, she would tell you that he could be saved by wearing flannel. In her devotion to Olga, the years had made her still more concentrated, more possessive, more suspicious. Lynx-eyed, she watched every attempt at a *rapprochement* between Olga and the other members of the family as a threat to her own peace of mind. Things passed off not too badly at Prangins. But when, six months later, in a last effort to recover – or at any rate to know – his child, Herzen invited Olga to visit him for a month alone, the answer was a firm refusal. 'It would not be fair to Malwida.' The rebuff cut the father to the heart. Olga had passed completely under the domination of Malwida's iron will. He wrote to his son of Malwida's 'criminal egoism disguised under a veil of idealism'. At last he spoke bitter words even of his daughter:

Olga in reality loves nobody; but she is devoted to Meysenbug like a child to a nurse who spoils it, defends it and conceals its faults.

*

They had all conspired, out of respect and affection for Herzen, to make the reunion at Prangins a success. But they were all relieved when, in the middle of September, it came to an end. Malwida had been counting the days till she could remove her ward from the dangerous and uncongenial atmosphere of Russian disorder. Alexander, conscious of the hard core of disapproval beneath his father's civil reception of himself and his bride, had no desire to prolong the ordeal. Ogarev slept badly at Prangins; and every few days he received from Geneva lovingly impatient epistles in Mary Sutherland's sprawling hand. Between Herzen himself and Natalie there was a threatened recrudescence of the eternal debate about Liza's education. The appropriate farewells were exchanged; and they all packed up and dispersed – for the last time. Herzen, warned by his doctors of the seriousness of his disease, went off for a six weeks' cure to Vichy. Before Christmas, Natalie and Tata both caught small-pox – a calamity which relieved for a few weeks the usual moral tension. Herzen had then before him only one more year of weary wandering.

The last months of his life were startled, and his end perhaps hastened, by a narrowly averted tragedy. In the autumn of 1869 he was in Paris with Natalie and Liza. Tata was at Florence with Alexander and his wife and Olga and Malwida. Tata had in the last few weeks been receiving the attentions of an Italian named Penizi. His impetuous wooing pleased; but his character inspired mistrust. Tata hesitated. Herzen was by no means anxious for his favourite child to marry an Italian, and wrote cautionary letters from Paris begging her to postpone a decision until she was more sure of the state of her heart. Scenting opposition, the ardent Penizi pressed his suit. He demanded an immediate answer. Tata put him off. Then one day he produced a pistol, became melodramatic, and valiantly announced his intention of blowing his brains out. Tata remained irresolute; but instead of carrying out his threat, Penizi adopted the less drastic alternative of going round the town and spreading various slanders at Tata's expense. In fact, his conduct bore a superficial resemblance to Herwegh's behaviour to the first Natalie; and the story groups itself neatly round an epigram, variously attributed to Herzen or to Tata herself, that 'she had found her Herwegh'.

The reader may be inclined to agree with Herzen's comment

239

that nothing would have happened if there had been a sensible woman on the spot. But Tata had nobody to consult except the weak and amiable Alexander, the young and irresponsible Teresina, and the prim, unsympathetic Malwida. Her temperament was impressionable. She was not used to meeting young men who threatened themselves with pistols. She had a serious nervous breakdown, in which she imagined men lying in wait in darkened rooms to murder themselves or her. A telegram was sent to Herzen which terrified him by referring to 'mental derangement'. He packed in a few hours and rushed southwards with Natalie and Liza. Leaving them at Genoa, he posted on to Florence. Things there were not quite so bad as he had been led to fear. The delusions engendered by the shock were already passing; and the principal symptoms were physical exhaustion and extreme nervousness. He nursed his child with a mother's tenderness and anxiety; and in a fortnight he brought her safely away from the associations of Florence, travelling back by easy stages to Paris. Natalie and Liza came with them. Olga and Malwida followed a few days later. They had business of their own in Paris, not unconnected with a young French *savant* named Monod.

It thus happened that, when Herzen, a few weeks later, was overtaken in Paris by his fatal illness, he was surrounded by three of his four surviving children. On 14 January 1870, he complained of a pain in the chest and side; and on the next day the doctor diagnosed inflammation of the lungs. For several days his condition was serious, but not desperate. On 19 January he seemed to rally and dictated a characteristic telegram to Tchorzewski at Geneva:

Great danger past. Disgusted with the doctors here as everywhere. Will try to write tomorrow.

The same evening delirium came on, and in the early morning of 21 January he died. Tata, Natalie and Liza, Olga, Malwida and Monod were there at the end.

Herzen had outlived his political importance. Few people in Paris knew him; and his death made no sensation. Only the police, irascible and nervous (for Pierre Bonaparte, the Emperor's disreputable cousin, had just shot a radical journalist, and the funeral had almost become a riot), suspected the possibility of a demonstration, and insisted that the *cortège* should leave for Père-Lachaise an hour before the advertised time. Only a handful of friends followed the coffin. In February the body was removed to the family vault at Nice; and two years later an unfortunate life-size statue in bronze was erected over it. There Herzen, stern and frock-coated, still looks out from his lofty pedestal over the blue Mediterranean.

CHAPTER 13

A Voltairean among the Romantics

ACROSS the pages of Herzen's life in the sixties, there flits the figure of another Russian political exile: Prince Peter Dolgorukov. Between the destinies of Herzen and Dolgorukov there is, at first sight, the closest analogy. Both were members of the Russian aristocratic, land-owning caste. Both had, of their own accord, abandoned their native country to seek that freedom of thought and speech which were withheld from them on Russian soil. Both were proscribed by the Russian Government; and both devoted their lives to attacking the Russian Government through the medium of the public press. But here the resemblance ceases. In character and tradition the two men present a fundamental contrast. In years Dolgorukov was younger than Herzen; but in spirit he belonged to an earlier generation. Dolgorukov was a true scion of one of the great Russian families which had ruled Russia under the successors of Peter the Great; and it was accident of personal idiosyncrasy which made him a rebel instead of a minister. Among the other refugees abroad he never felt himself completely at ease; and the sense of incongruity was generally mutual. He shared their political opinions; but their most intimate feelings were alien and antipathetic to him. Dolgorukov was an eighteenth-century rationalist, Herzen and Ogarev nineteenth-century idealists. If Herzen was a sceptic, he was so by reaction from disappointed hopes. Dolgorukov was a sceptic by tradition and life-long conviction. He was a Voltairean among the Romantics.

Peter Dolgorukov was born at the end of 1816 and became an orphan in the first year of his life. He was brought up by his grandmother; and at a suitable age he entered, as his aristocratic lineage demanded, the Imperial Corps of Pages. He seemed destined like his grandfather, father and uncles, for a brilliant military career. But in his fifteenth year some offence, the nature of which is not recorded, led to his degradation, and eventually to his dismissal from the corps. This early misfortune embittered his whole subsequent career. The blot on his scutcheon ruined his chances of distinction in any branch of the imperial service. He obtained, by influence, a minor post in the newly-created Ministry of Public Instruction; but its humble rank made it seem, in the eyes of the ambitious young man, less a favour than a disgrace. Nor was he well received in Petersburg society. His appearance was unprepossessing and he had a slight limp. He tried to compensate these disadvantages by the skilful use of a caustic tongue; and his mastery of this weapon still further diminished his popularity.

He had his friends, however, among the fashionable young men about town. He was patronized among others by the Netherlands Minister, Baron Heeckeren, an elderly *roué* who found compensation for his own failing powers in abetting the intrigues and adventures of the rising generation. He probably participated in many malicious pranks. But here too ill luck dogged him; for one of these pranks has branded his name for ever in the pages of history. Young Dolgorukov knew the manners and customs of the society in which he moved; and when in the autumn of 1836, being then not yet twenty, he penned an anonymous lampoon at the expense of Alexander Pushkin, he must have been alive to the possibility of a tragic *dénouement*. Men of that time took the lives of others, and risked their own, for far less galling insults. But he could not, for all his wit and malice, foresee that his victim would be celebrated by posterity as the greatest of Russian poets, and that, nearly a hundred years later, biographers, literary historians, and handwriting experts would still be labouring to unravel the minutest threads of this tragic skein and to establish his guilt.

The fatal document, which was circulated simultaneously to Pushkin and to several of his friends, ran in its original French text as follows:

Les Grand-Croix, Commandeurs et Chevaliers du Sérénissime Ordre des Cocus, réunis en Grand Chapitre sous la présidence du vénérable Grand-Maître de l'Ordre, Son Excellence D. L. Narychkine, ont nommé à l'unanimité Mr Alexandre Pouchkine coadjuteur du Grand-Maître de l'Ordre des Cocus et Historiographe de l'Ordre.

Le secrétaire perpétuel:

C-te J. Borch

243

The implications were brutally obvious. Dmitri Naryshkin had for many years occupied a conspicuous position at the court of Alexander I, where his wife queened it as favourite royal mistress; and Count Joseph Borch was another nobleman whose wife had furthered his career by the generous, but discriminating, distribution of her favours. Natalie Pushkin rivalled these noted beauties in charm and, some said, in frailty; and there were even rumours that she had kindled the amorous susceptibilities of Nicholas I. Her husband might well seem to be marked out for high promotion in the Serene Order of Cuckolds.

No conclusive proof of Natalie's infidelity has ever been forthcoming; and Pushkin may have been speaking the truth when he tried to shield her reputation. But it is certain that both she and her sister were, during the autumn and winter of 1836, amorously inclined to a handsome young Frenchman named Georges Dantès. The young man had recently been adopted by Baron Heeckeren as his son and, adding the Baron's surname to his own, called himself Dantès-Heeckeren. When Pushkin received the Diploma of the Order of Cuckolds, he immediately suspected the hand of Baron Heeckeren. He knew that his wife's name had been compromised by her friendship, however innocent, with Dantès. He saw in the whole affair a contemptible plot against his honour by father and adopted son; and he challenged the younger man to a duel.

The duel took place, after several futile attempts at reconciliation, in February 1837. Pushkin was mortally wounded. Dantès fled the country. The Tsar demanded the recall of the Netherlands Minister and refused to receive him before his departure. And there, despite elaborate investigations by the police, the affair ended. Although nobody doubted that the lampoon had originated in the circle of Baron Heeckeren, its precise authorship remained uncertain. Suspicion was divided between the Baron himself, a certain Prince Gagarin and Prince Peter Dolgorukov. But the excitement soon waned; and it was only twenty-five years later that a writer named Ammosov, in a pamphlet on *The Last Days of Pushkin*, first definitely cited Dolgorukov as the author of the lampoon. Dolgorukov, who was in London at the time, issued an indignant denial, which was published by *The Bell*, and by other Russian journals. Once more, interest died down for lack of evidence; and the issue remained unsettled till 1927. In that year two original copies of the ninety-year-old lampoon, together with specimens of the handwriting of Heeckeren, Gagarin and Dolgorukov, were submitted to a handwriting expert of the Criminal Investigation Department in Leningrad. The expert pronounced unhesitatingly that the lampoon was written, in a disguised hand, by Dolgorukov.

Not long after the duel and death of Pushkin, Dolgorukov abandoned all pretence of an official career and went to Paris. The study of genealogies had become his hobby; and in the past history of the great Russian families he found an ample field of interest for his malicious and inquiring spirit. In January 1843 he published in Paris, under the pen-name of 'Count Almagro', a pamphlet entitled *Notice sur les familles de la Russie*. It was a livelier work than its title suggests; for Dolgorukov depicted the ancestors and ancestresses of most of his friends as blood-stained and inhuman monsters whose most venial pastimes were treason and regicide. The authorities soon discovered the identity of 'Count Almagro'; and Dolgorukov found himself invited by Kiselev, the Russian Ambassador in Paris, to return to Russia. Somewhat surprisingly, he declared himself ready to comply with the summons 'so soon as he had had time to consult his doctor and repair his carriage'. But no sooner had he set foot on Russian soil than he was arrested and, after examination, exiled for twelve months to Vyatka, where Herzen had so recently served a longer sentence of banishment for a less glaring indiscretion.

For some years Dolgorukov remained quiescent. He appeared to have learnt his lesson, and occupied himself with the preparation of a monumental *Collection of Russian Genealogies*, which was free from the scandalous matter of the Paris pamphlet. In 1848 came the interlude of an unhappy marriage. Like most of the young men who had frequented Baron Heeckeren, Dolgorukov preferred homosexual pleasures; and the sole satisfaction which he sought in wedlock was that of cynically and brutally ill-treating his wife. She bore him one child – a son, and then left him for ever. The *Collection of Russian Genealogies* was finished and published in four volumes between 1855 and 1857, and was received with some applause. But this comparatively respectable achievement did not long suffice to nourish Dolgorukov's pride of authorship. It

245

merely whetted his appetite for some more garish success. He remembered the gay days of Count Almagro. He reflected that he was now past forty, and that his consuming ambition to make his mark in the world was still unsatisfied. In 1859 he left Russia for good; and, after a brief interlude in Italy, where he interviewed Cavour at Turin and fought a duel at Florence, he settled once more in Paris. He realized his estates, and succeeded in transferring abroad a capital sum of nearly a quarter of a million roubles.

The remaining nine years of Dolgorukov's life were spent in self-imposed exile; and it is these years which give him his place in the present gallery of portraits. It may be that the success of Herzen and *The Bell* had excited Dolgorukov's jealous ambition before he left Russia. In any case the example of Herzen became, for the next few years, his main source of inspiration. In April 1860 he brought out in Paris, this time under his own name, a book entitled *La Vérité sur la Russie*. Abandoning the light personal gossip of 'Count Almagro', he subjects to a damaging review the history and institutions of his country, and puts forward elaborate proposals for reform in every branch of the administration. He refers to Alexander II in terms of exaggerated and hypocritical politeness. But previous Tsars fare less well at his hands. He quotes with approval Napoleon's dictum that Alexander I was 'as false as a Greek of the Byzantine Empire'; and the thirty years' reign of Nicholas I is described as 'a thirty years' war against civilization and good sense'. Even of existing institutions none save the person of the Tsar are spared.

> The Russian Government at the moment [he writes in conclusion] is exactly like a vessel rocking on the ocean at the mercy of the elements and without any direction. The captain is animated by the best intentions; but the boatswains and the pilots are incredibly stupid. Between them and the passengers there is an unconquerable mental aversion and incessant strife. The captain cannot make up his mind to replace them by capable men. He prefers to wait for the boatswains and pilots to die, and for the capable men to reach a state of tranquil old age, before entrusting to the latter the management of the ship; and in the meantime the vessel may run on a reef. . . .

In *La Vérité sur la Russie* Dolgorukov is careful, while expressing personal esteem for Herzen, to separate himself from Herzen's opinions. Herzen is a socialist; he, Dolgorukov, is a constitutional monarchist. But notwithstanding this difference of opinion, his weapons have, clearly enough, been borrowed from Herzen's armoury. His scheme of reforms includes such favourite ideas of Herzen's as the liberation of the serfs with land, the abolition of corporal punishment and the suppression of the censorship. He sent a copy of his book to Herzen, and during the summer of 1860 came over to London to visit him.

A number of letters of this and the following year beginning 'Honoured Prince!' testify to Herzen's satisfaction with this new and distinguished recruit to the cause. 'Dolgorukov's book,' he wrote to a friend, 'is fairly good. Many anecdotes about the galley-slaves whom we in Russia call ministers.' In public he spoke of it more warmly. He greeted the book in the pages of *The Bell*, and sought to smooth away the apparent differences of principle between Dolgorukov and himself by explaining that there were doubtless circumstances which rendered necessary such 'transitional forms' as constitutional monarchy. His only complaint was that Dolgorukov had half concealed the identity of some of his victims by using initials instead of their full names.

In the autumn of the same year Dolgorukov founded a Russian journal entitled *The Future*, which was printed in Leipzig and published in Paris. The imitation of *The Bell* was flagrant but flattering. He gracefully explained to Herzen that he was playing *ut-minor* to the latter's *ut-major* – 'which leads me to conclude,' writes Herzen to Turgenev, reminding us that he lived in the golden age of the pun, 'that *The Future* is the *frère uterin* of *The Bell*'. *The Future* came to an untimely end in a few months, the Russian authorities having (if we may believe Dolgorukov) applied 'golden measures of persuasion' to the printer. It was succeeded by *The Just Man* published at Brussels, first in Russian and then in French (under the title *Le Véridique*); and this in turn gave place to *The News-Sheet*, which continued its precarious existence till 1864. None of these publications, though they acquired a certain notoriety for their revelations of the private lives of prominent Russians, past and present, ever enjoyed the moral authority of *The Bell*. Prince Dolgorukov was a man of parts. He possessed in abundance that species of talent which readily mistakes itself for genius. But he rivalled Herzen neither as a thinker nor as a stylist; and above all he lacked the essential quality of inspiring confidence in his own sincerity. There is no valid ground for regarding his opinions as insincere. But when his conduct is analysed, personal spleen and personal ambition always appear to the discerning eye as the principal ingredients of his character.

In the meanwhile Dolgorukov's career as a publicist was punctuated, and nearly arrested, by an episode from which it required all his skill and self-assurance to extricate himself. The origins of the affair went back to 1856, when he was engaged, in Russia, on the last volume of his *Collection of Russian Genealogies*. Among the families whose genealogy was to appear in this volume was that of Prince Vorontsov. Like many Russian noble families, the Vorontsovs purported to trace back their lineage to Rurik and the Varangians. But the mists of antiquity had gathered round its earlier course; and it was open to the cynical to pretend that the contemporary Vorontsovs represent a mere seventeenth-century revival, unauthorized by any continuity of blood, of an ancient name. In 1856 Prince Dolgorukov wrote to Prince Michael Vorontsov asking him to supply documents which might throw light on the 'dark places' of the family tree. The letter was couched in terms of exaggerated courtesy; but in the same envelope was found an unsigned note in a disguised handwriting in the following terms:

His Excellency Prince Vorontsov possesses a sure means of procuring that the genealogy shall be printed in the Russian Book of Genealogies in the form which suits him. This means is to pay to Prince Dolgorukov 50,000 silver roubles; then everything will be arranged according to his desire. But there is no time to be lost.

What Prince Vorontsov thought when he received this missive is not on record. He wrote a formal and polite reply to Prince Dolgorukov's letter, and added the following postscript:

To my great astonishment I found in your letter an unsigned note in a hand which does not appear to resemble yours. I send you a copy of it. You will perhaps succeed in discovering who has had the audacity to place such a note in a letter sealed by you with your seal. I have considered it necessary to keep the original with the letter with which you have honoured me. But when we meet I am ready to hand you the note in case, as may happen, you desire to use it for the purpose of discovering the writer.

Prince Dolgorukov expressed astonishment at the extraordinary 'note in an unknown hand' which had found its way into an envelope sealed with his own seal; but he showed no desire to pursue the investigation. In the course of the year Prince Michael Vorontsov died; and the incident seemed to have ended for ever.

Dolgorukov was not however so easily rid of the affair. Prince Vorontsov had talked; and when in April 1860 Dolgorukov published in Paris *La Vérité sur la Russie*, a reviewer in a news-sheet called *Le Courrier du Dimanche* took the opportunity to relate the whole story of the demand for 50,000 roubles, stating roundly that the note was the work of Dolgorukov and suppressing only the name of the person to whom it was sent. It was impossible to remain silent under this public accusation; and Dolgorukov wrote a reply which the *Courrier de Dimanche* inserted in its next issue. He disclaimed all knowledge of the note, hinted that it was a fabrication of Prince Vorontsov, and alleged that, though he had demanded the production of the original, it had never been forthcoming. The last statement was flagrantly incorrect. Vorontsov had offered to produce the note, and Dolgorukov had tactfully ignored the offer. But the other party to the transaction, being dead, could not contradict him; and it seemed once more that the scandal had been suitably interred.

The new allegation against Prince Vorontsov was, however, too much for his eldest son, who had succeeded to the title. Prince Simon Vorontsov brought an action against Dolgorukov in the civil court of the Department of the Seine for defamation of his dead father's character. He asked the court to pronounce that Dolgorukov was the writer of the anonymous demand for 50,000 roubles, to compel Dolgorukov to publish the verdict at his own expense in certain journals, and to award the costs of the action to the plaintiff. A duel between two Russian princes, each impeaching the other's honour and veracity before a French court, was a spectacle which excited some interest in the Paris of the Second Empire. The trial dragged on from December 1860 into January 1861. The original of the anonymous missive was produced. A handwriting expert was invoked; and he pronounced it to be in Dolgorukov's hand. In virtue of this pronouncement, the court found for the plaintiff, and satisfied him on all three points.

A less resourceful character than Dolgorukov might have

succumbed to this crushing blow. Dolgorukov used it to enhance his prestige by the acquisition of a martyr's halo. He proclaimed, promptly and vociferously, that the whole affair was a political plot; that the police of Alexander II had conspired with the police of Napoleon III to punish him for the subversive opinions expressed in his book; and that, where political interests were at stake, proceedings in a French court were notoriously a travesty of justice. The verdict might even be explained away on grounds of personal influence. Everybody knew that the Duc de Morny, half-brother to the Emperor, held all the strings of the administration of justice in his hands. The Duc de Morny was married to a Troubetskoy; and there was a natural alliance between the ancient and princely house of Troubetskoy and the ancient and princely house of Vorontsov. These pleas were ingenious and plausible; and Herzen, among others, was taken in. Burning with righteous indignation at the victimization of a political exile, he wrote in *The Bell* in language of unusual violence:

> Rarely has a court given a verdict in such complete disregard of positive proofs, except of course in the country where judges are selected from the rabble of Russian aristocrats living in Russia.

Unfortunately, the Soviet handwriting expert who re-examined the document in 1927, and who can scarcely be suspected of complicity with the police of Alexander II or of Napoleon III, had no hesitation in endorsing the verdict of the French court. He, too, found that the anonymous demand for 50,000 roubles, like the anonymous diploma of the Serene Order of Cuckolds, came from the pen of Prince Peter Dolgorukov.

There were indeed some, even at this time, who were not impressed by Dolgorukov's protestations of innocence. Turgenev, as a resident in Paris, perhaps knew more of the affair than Herzen. He lived in a state of lofty detachment from political issues, floated easily between the two camps, and by no means shared Herzen's firm conviction that, in a difference of opinion between a Russian political exile and a French court of law, the latter was necessarily wrong. He showed on this occasion an unusual power of discrimination, and wrote to Herzen as follows:

> You will be well advised if in the future you refrain from touching the affair with your little finger. Dolgorukov – between ourselves – is

morally a dead man, and not altogether without reason. You have done everything you could in *The Bell*. It was necessary to support him for the sake of a principle; but now leave him to his fate. He will try now to creep right down your throat; but spew him out. Needless to say, this doesn't oblige you to support the Vorontsovs. Pose as a Jupiter who stands high above all these quarrels.

But Herzen was in no mood to listen to the remonstrances of common sense. He had got it into his head that Dolgorukov was a man, if not of his own stamp, at any rate in his own position, and that it would be treason and cowardice to desert him in the hour of his need. Another opportunity occurred in the following year of demonstrating his loyalty. When Ammosov published his pamphlet accusing Dolgorukov of the authorship of the lampoon on Pushkin, Dolgorukov issued, in his own *News-Sheet*, an indignant denial of any complicity in the affair. Herzen once more accepted the *démenti* without question, and reprinted it in *The Bell*.

But notwithstanding these services, it is clear that Herzen's attachment to Dolgorukov was political rather than personal, and that relations between the two were most cordial when they did not meet. In 1863 Dolgorukov settled for a short time in London; and friction was constant. Dolgorukov had retained far more than Herzen of the essential prejudices of the Russian aristocrat; and the superior and overbearing manner which made him unpopular as a youth in Petersburg was not softened by age and exile. His temper provoked some embarrassing incidents. One of the pleasantest of these is related by Natalie Ogarev in her *Memoirs*. 'It should be remembered,' she explains, 'that the English consider stale bread more healthy, and prefer it to fresh bread, it being easier to cut stale bread into the thin slices which they smear with butter and eat in great quantities at afternoon tea.' Prince Dolgorukov was ignorant of this strange national taste; and when, at a country hotel, he found stale bread on his plate he pitched it incontinently out of the window. The waiter was equal to the occasion. He approached Tchorzewski, who accompanied the Prince, and inquired sympathetically whether his friend was often subject to these attacks. Tchorzewski had difficulty in acquitting the Prince of the suspicion of insanity by explaining that he was a 'very cross gentleman'.

Sometimes the offence was more serious. One Sunday, after

dinner at Herzen's house at Teddington, Dolgorukov broke into violent abuse of Poland in the presence of several Poles who were sitting at the table. Herzen lost his temper and shouted that no attacks on martyred Poland should be heard in his house. Dolgorukov snatched his hat and stick and rushed away without saying goodbye to anyone; and relations were broken off for ten days. Such incidents were apparently not infrequent. Another quarrel of comic character illustrates the quality of Dolgorukov's temper in his declining years. He overheard Herzen's French cook, Jules, grumbling that he gave more trouble in the house than all Herzen's other guests put together. Whipping out a knife which he always carried, Dolgorukov began to abuse and threaten the cook. The cook threw himself incontinently on the Prince. The scuffle became alarming. The combatants were separated by Herzen and a friend; and Dolgorukov raged that he would not set foot again in the house till Jules was dismissed. The sequel crowns the story. Finding that Herzen had no intention of losing his cook, Dolgorukov invited Jules to his house; and a reconciliation was effected over a bottle of champagne.

The quarrel with Jules took place after both Herzen and Dolgorukov had migrated to Geneva; and here in 1867 Dolgorukov published the first volume of his so-called *Memoirs*. No book has ever borne a more misleading title. It consists of a systematic *exposé* of the activities of the principal Russian families in the first half of the eighteenth century – a monotonous and nauseating record of filth, blood and torture. Herzen in *The Bell* welcomed it with an enthusiasm which the modern reader will hardly share; but even he would have liked something more distinctly compromising to the contemporary rulers of Russia.

We have seen the great-grandfathers of our Petersburg and Moscow matadors [he concludes the review]. Let us now have a look at their grandfathers; and we could sincerely beg the author before long to acquaint us with their fathers.

The first volume of the *Memoirs* represents the last event in Dolgorukov's curiously barren and stultified career. In the summer of 1868 he lay dying, a prey to dropsy, at Berne. His only son, a youth of eighteen, had come from Russia to visit him. But the unhappy man had never believed in human virtue; and he had certainly no reason to expect filial affection. The conviction grew on him, as he lay there helpless, that his son had been sent by the Russian Government to obtain possession of his papers – those compromising notes for further volumes of the *Memoirs* which would come dangerously near to his own times. His failing mind turned to the one friend of whose sincerity and honour (though he had often quarrelled with him) he could feel no doubt, the one friend who still, perhaps, retained some vestige of faith in him. He sent for Herzen to make him his executor and the inheritor of his papers.

Herzen, who happened to be at Lucerne, responded to the appeal. He travelled to Berne; and on the way he met George Henry Lewes and Mary Ann Evans, whose company revived his drooping spirits. He had not yet guessed the horror which awaited him at the bedside of the dying Prince. 'No tragic writer,' he afterwards told Turgenev, 'has ever invented anything more terrible. Some day perhaps I will describe that death-bed.' He has left no literary record of it. *My Past and Thoughts* never reached the later sixties. But the disjointed phrases of a letter which he wrote to Ogarev while still under the immediate impression of the event sketch for us the stark outlines of the scene.

Dolgorukov is very bad [he wrote on 11 July, five weeks before the end] but his strong constitution holds out like a fortress. They have drained the water from his legs and it is flowing continuously. His face has completely fallen in and become somehow more dignified. He speaks disconnectedly and his eyes are dim. He does not know how near death is, but he fears it. Above all, a terrible struggle is going on within him. He was immeasurably glad to see me, but not demonstratively – he kept pressing my hand and thanking me. In the whole world he trusts only me and my substitute Tchorzewski. In the morning he sent for Tchorzewski and Vogt and declared that his son had poisoned him in the night, and had poured some yellow liquid out of a bottle. (Better not repeat this to anyone.) Then, after various fearful accusations, he sent Vogt to tell his son to return at once to Russia, and promised that he would spare him and hush the matter up. Vogt, himself terrified, gave the message. The son, of course, flared up. Then Dolgorukov called him and begged his pardon. When I came in, he sent everyone away and, putting both hands on me and raising himself up, he stared at me with bewildered eyes. 'Herzen, Herzen, for God's sake, tell me – I trust nobody but you, respect nobody but you – is all this madness and delirium?' 'You can see for yourself that it is madness. Nothing has happened to you.' 'Yes, yes, evidently, it was delirium. What do you think about it? Delirium?' (And this ten times over.) Then suddenly, letting fall his eyes he repeated twice: 'No, but from now on, for God's sake, watch what they are doing to me.'

Herzen could do no more; and two days later, after another wild scene between Dolgorukov and his son, he escaped from the nightmare. On 17 August a lingering end crowned at last this ill-starred existence. Until the approach of death unnerved him, Dolgorukov had always been too good a rationalist to believe in, or to feel the need of, human affection; and his convictions had never been more than the instrument of his ambition. He died unlamented. In the obituary notice which appeared in *The Bell*, perfunctory expressions of regret are hastily followed by the triumphant assurance that his papers were 'in safe hands', and would one day contribute to the discomfiture of the minions of Tsardom.

At the last moment Herzen had declined the role of literary executor. The papers passed into the 'safe hands' of Tchorzewski; and the strange story of their fate belongs to a later chapter.

CHAPTER 14

The 'Affaire Nechaev'; *or the First Terrorist*

In any history of revolution the masterful figure of Sergi Nechaev must find a place. Nechaev was one of those who, by the sheer force of a dominant personality, impose themselves on their contemporaries and on posterity. In a meteoric career, which ended at the age of thirty-five, he achieved literally nothing. He had few followers; and these few deserve the name of dupes rather than of disciples. The conspiracy which bore his name, and for which many of them suffered imprisonment and transportation, was not even a fiasco; it was a mare's nest. Nechaev believed in the overthrow of the existing order, not because he had, like Herzen, a romantic faith in democracy or, like Bakunin, a still more romantic faith in human nature. He believed in revolution as a tenet valid and sufficient in itself; and he believed in nothing else. His originality and his historical importance lie in the unconditional quality of his belief, and in the manner in which he translated it into practice. He did not merely proclaim, he acted on, the hypothesis that morality does not exist, and that in the interests of revolution (of which he himself was the sole judge) every crime in the calendar, from murder to petty larceny, was legitimate and laudable. Even this might not have been so utterly disconcerting. But Nechaev carried logic further still. He applied these principles with equal alacrity to his enemies and to his so-called friends. He deceived everyone he met, and when he was no longer able to deceive, his power was gone. His audacity was unbounded; and he carried personal courage to the extreme limit of foolhardiness. He is an unparalleled and bewildering combination of fanatic, swashbuckler and cad.

Sergei Nechaev was the son of a Russian village priest – a despised, ignorant and frequently immoral class of the population. He had – for one of his origin – a distinguished scholastic career, which served mainly to kindle his inordinate ambition. His enemies afterwards called him 'illiterate' or 'half-literate'; but we must assume that these terms of abuse were directed against his manners or his morals rather than against his education in the narrower sense of the word. He was probably destined for his father's vocation; and at the age of twenty-one, which he reached in 1868, he was a teacher of divinity in a school at Petersburg. Student circles in the Petersburg of the sixties seethed with revolutionary ideas; and young Nechaev proved particularly susceptible to them. He soon became the leading spirit in a little group of students whose ambition it was to promote a revolution in Russia. It is not proved that they had any organization or indulged in anything more dangerous than youthful conspirative talk. But the attentive authorities were well aware of their doings. Before long Nechaev and his comrades were hauled before the police and rigorously interrogated; and Nechaev was placed under 'police observation'.

The ingenious and enterprising young man, sensing danger or bored with the humdrum career of a schoolmaster, decided to disappear and – what was more – to make a reputation for himself by his disappearance. He sent to his comrades a note telling them that he had been arrested and was being conveyed to 'an unknown fortress'. The note purported to have been thrown by him from the window of a police van and forwarded by an anonymous student who had chanced to pick it up. There was nothing wildly improbable in the story; and his student companions had no difficulty in believing it. By the time they had organized a mass meeting to demand his release, Nechaev was well on his way south. In March 1869 he slipped across the frontier with a false passport, and made his way to Switzerland, the spiritual home of the martyrs of revolution.

It was no mere coincidence that the first person whom Nechaev approached on his arrival in Geneva was the veteran Bakunin. In the camp of the extremists Bakunin was now at the height of his reputation. His immense revolutionary prestige attracted the young man, who hoped one day to share it, but who had nothing at present to his credit but energy, belief in himself, and a fertile imagination. Like all Bakunin's visitors, Nechaev was impressed by the gigantic form and magnetic personality of the old warrior; and he resolved to impress in turn. He explained that he had just escaped from the Peter-and-Paul fortress, where he had been imprisoned as a ringleader of the students' revolutionary movement. He had come to Switzerland as delegate of a Russian Revolutionary Committee, which had its headquarters in Petersburg and which was laying a train of revolution throughout the country.

Bakunin had never before met anyone whose talent for bluff surpassed his own. Above all, he had never met anyone who possessed his own singular taste for inventing political societies of which he was the commander-in-chief, and of which the rank and file scarcely existed outside his own imagination. But by a fortunate, though illogical, dispensation of providence those who delight to hoodwink others are themselves, as a rule, most easily hoodwinked. Scepticism had no place in Bakunin's temperament; and he believed implicitly everything Nechaev told him. The young man shared Bakunin's own gift of compelling the admiration and confidence of new acquaintances; and Bakunin was infatuated at first sight, as others had so often been so infatuated with him. He soon began to call Nechaev by the tender nickname of 'Boy' (for Bakunin had retained a few words of English from his year's stay in London). The most affectionate relations were established; and Bakunin expressed the utmost eagerness to share the labours and the laurels of the Russian Revolutionary Committee. A queer story afterwards circulated among the Russian *émigrés* in Switzerland that Bakunin had given Nechaev a paper promising him implicit obedience 'even to the point of forging bank-notes', and had signed it, in token of complete submission, with a woman's name 'Matrena'. This declaration is alleged to have been found among Nechaev's papers after his arrest and destroyed; but the story is too lightly attested to warrant credence. If any document bearing such a signature existed, 'Matrena' was probably a code-name (a form of mystification in which Bakunin delighted) not invested with the sinister significance which rumour attached to it.

The circulation of the story, true or false, is a sufficient indication of Nechaev's ascendancy over the old revolutionary. The infatuation must be explained in part by Bakunin's circumstances. He had quarrelled with Herzen; and the weak and amiable Ogarev, slowly drinking himself into insensibility, no longer counted as a warrior in the revolutionary cause. In any case, both of them had lost effective touch with Russia. The arrival of

Nechaev brought to Bakunin a breath of his native land. He would never see it again. But it still, in the midst of his international preoccupations, sometimes haunted his dreams; and here was a chance of working for the cause of revolution in the country which was still nearest to his heart. No other land could appeal to him in this way. The sentimental side of his nature, which seemed to have died with his memories of home and childhood long years ago, revived and re-opened for this dangerous and seductive Russian 'Boy'.

The new enthusiasm aroused him from the lethargy which, in these later years, was apt to creep over him. When Herzen came to Geneva in May – it was the last meeting between the old friends – he found that Bakunin 'had much improved in health, had lost fifty pounds of fat by dieting, but was consuming enormous quantities of meat and wine'. He was working like a locomotive, but a locomotive 'which has got too much steam up and has run off the rails'. During the spring and summer a dozen or more proclamations and pamphlets were printed in Geneva for distribution in Russia by Nechaev. They bore titles like *To the Students of the University*; *To Our Young Brothers in Russia*; or *The Catechism of a Revolutionary*; and some of them were signed with Nechaev's name. Most of them were written by Bakunin, some perhaps by Nechaev himself, and one or two by Ogarev. A single number of a new journal was published under the title *The People's Justice*; for such was the name which Nechaev gave to his imaginary organization.

Bakunin did not, however, content himself with this purely literary collaboration. Whether the declaration signed 'Matrena' ever existed or not, there is no doubt about the authenticity of another document which is in itself sufficiently remarkable. It is dated 12 May 1869 and runs as follows:

The bearer of this is one of the accredited representatives of the Russian section of the World Revolutionary Alliance. No. 2771.

It is signed 'Michael Bakunin', and the seal affixed to it bears the words 'European Revolutionary Alliance, Central Committee'. It is odd, though characteristic, that Bakunin made no effort to introduce his new *protégé* into his 'Secret Alliance', a secret society of a nebulous character through which he had hitherto sought to promote the cause of revolution in Europe. He did not, so far as we know, even inform him of its existence. He could not resist the temptation of inventing, on the spur of the moment, an entirely new World or European Revolutionary Alliance which was never heard of again; and he gave the certificate a number which implied, for those who chose to be impressed, that this unheard-of organization had at least 2,770 other agents performing its behests in various corners of Europe. Thus did Nechaev, the self-styled representative of a non-existent Russian Revolutionary Committee, receive from Bakunin authority to act in Russia as the representative of a non-existent European Revolutionary Alliance. It was a delicious situation which can have few parallels either in comedy or in history; the interesting point, on which evidence fails us, is whether both were equally deceived.

But there was a solid element of reality about another aspect of the association between these two magnificent charlatans. Both needed money; and both lacked the inclination, though not the ability, to earn it by everyday methods. It was several years since Bakunin had first talked of writing his memoirs; and about this time he received a tempting offer for them from Buloz, the famous editor of the *Revue des deux Mondes*. But so long as he could borrow, Bakunin's pride forbade him to resort to the vulgar expedient of working for his daily bread. The arrival of Nechaev provided an excellent opportunity for raising money by more congenial means. Every good revolutionary would certainly contribute to the cause which Nechaev had come to represent; and, pending the outbreak of the revolution, those who were preparing it might regard themselves as legitimately entitled to live on the funds provided by these hypothetical donors.

There was moreover something still more solid in prospect. In 1858 a rich and eccentric Russian land-owner named Bakhmetiev was converted to communism and, with the consistent fanaticism of the Russian idealist, went off to found a model community on an island somewhere in the Pacific. On his way, he visited Herzen and Ogarev in London; and finding that he had more money about him than seemed necessary for the realization of his project, he left with them the sum of £800 for revolutionary propaganda in Russia. Having performed this charitable act, Bakhmetiev vanished into the Pacific and was heard of no more; and his very existence might have seemed a fairy-tale but for the entry, in the books of a London bank, of a credit of £800 standing in the joint names of Herzen and Ogarev. These two, with their habitual scrupulousness and caution, had been content to use the interest on this sum for the purpose of their propaganda; and in 1869 the capital of the 'Bakhmetiev fund' was still intact. What could be more appropriate, asked Bakunin, than to spend this fund, of whose existence he had probably learned from Ogarev, on the revolutionary enterprise sponsored by 'Boy' and himself?

The life-long scepticism of Herzen had been intensified by old age. He had seen Nechaev at Geneva and thoroughly disliked him. He had no confidence in Bakunin; and he would not hear of the plan. But the feeble and demoralized Ogarev, living in Geneva, was no match for the constant pressure of Bakunin and Nechaev; and at their instance he continued to pester Herzen with letters in support of their proposal. Herzen, weary and infirm as he now was, cared too little to resist these importunities indefinitely; and at the end of July he agreed that Ogarev should dispose as he pleased of one half of the fund. He pleaded none the less that the money would be better spent in establishing a revolutionary printing-press in Geneva, and added – rather tartly – that such an enterprise might even provide Bakunin with a securer livelihood than Nechaev's Russian adventure. The appeal was unheeded. The sum of 10,000 francs (£400) passed into the hands of Bakunin and thence, presumably somewhat diminished, into those of Nechaev.

The visit of Nechaev to Switzerland had indeed succeeded beyond all reasonable expectation. He had obtained a mandate signed by the famous revolutionary Bakunin in the name of a European Revolutionary Alliance, which (whatever his personal opinion of its value) would serve to impress his student coadjutors in Russia; and now he had secured, for his untrammelled personal use, a substantial sum in ready cash. Possessed of these valuable accessories and armed with bundles of tracts and proclamations, he returned to Russia at the end of August. The winter was to be spent in organization; and he assured Bakunin that the projected revolution would begin without fail on 19 February 1870, the ninth anniversary of the liberation of the serfs.

It says little for the skill or vigilance of the Russian police that

Nechaev, with this record and with these intentions, was able to enter Russia, to spend three months there, to commit a notorious crime and to return in no particular haste, unscathed and unmolested, to Switzerland. But this is what happened. Nechaev set up his headquarters at Moscow. The name of Bakunin was still one to conjure with in revolutionary circles; and Nechaev, as representative of the mythical European Alliance, demanded implicit obedience from all his followers. His ideas of organizing a revolution were elementary in character. They seem to have been confined to the formation of groups of five, each of which constituted a secret revolutionary committee. The functions of these groups were ill-defined, but they had one singular and characteristic feature. No group had any contact with, or was even known to, any other group; all depended absolutely on the directing and coordinating will of Nechaev.

The elaborate investigations subsequently made by the police failed to discover any concrete plan of revolution prepared by this remarkable organization. It partook almost exclusively of the element of bluff and make-believe, which formed so important a part of the revolutionary activities of both Bakunin and Nechaev. But one achievement for which it was responsible was real enough. In Moscow a student named Ivanov, who belonged to one of the famous groups of five, showed an inclination to neglect the first and most peremptory obligation incumbent on members of the society – unquestioning obedience to Nechaev's commands. Nechaev saw the importance of quelling incipient mutiny by a dramatic *coup*. He feared, or pretended to fear, that Ivanov would denounce them; and he persuaded the other members of the group to join him in murdering the prospective traitor. He would thus achieve two objectives. He would remove a rebel, and he would bind the others to himself by complicity in a common crime. Nechaev differed from his comrades by his perfect readiness to practise in cold blood the ruthlessness of which they only talked. The murder was Nechaev's work. The other four members of the group were present. But they were seized with a last minute panic which almost ruined the whole plan; and their inglorious role was confined to acquiescence rather than assistance.

The murder of Ivanov, on which Dostoevsky based the plot of his novel *The Devils*, took place on 21 November 1869. Four days later the victim's body was found in a pond. The details of the crime quickly became known and created an enormous sensation. Nechaev, genuinely surprised at the magnitude of the disturbance, perceived that he could no longer count on the lethargy of the police, and made preparations for flight. He left Russia about the middle of December; and at the beginning of January 1870 he reappeared in Switzerland.

A change had occurred meanwhile in Bakunin's mode of life. His domestic circumstances were peculiar. He had married, in the years of his exile in Siberia, Antonia Kwiatkowski, the daughter of a Polish merchant in the city of Tomsk. She was twenty-five years younger than her husband, pretty, empty-headed, self-indulgent, and devoid of any spark of that fierce energy and revolutionary enthusiasm which animated her husband. It was an odd marriage for her to make, and can perhaps only be explained by the lack of other suitors in the dull society of a little Siberian town. On his side the marriage was odder still. For women had never appeared, at any period of his life, to interest or attract Bakunin; and all the evidence goes to show that this giant of superhuman energy was sexually impotent. His wife followed him to Europe after his escape, joined him in Sweden, and travelled with him to France and Italy. In Naples she fell in love with an Italian lawyer named Gambuzzi, a socialist and a political adherent of Bakunin; and she became his mistress. In 1867 the Bakunins moved from Italy to Geneva; and there, soon after their arrival, Antonia gave birth to a son.

In the spring of 1869, about the time of Nechaev's first visit to Geneva, Antonia set out for Naples with the child on a visit to her lover. Before long she wrote that she was again pregnant, and would return to her husband later in the year. Bakunin was not in any way shocked. He neither demanded nor expected fidelity; and he was full of affectionate feelings for his foolish, amiable wife and for her offspring. But he had been stung into sensitiveness by the Geneva gossip which had followed the birth of the first child. He had now few ties which held him to Geneva; and he decided to go into retirement for the winter, informing only a few intimates of his whereabouts. The choice fell on the Italian corner of Switzerland; and early in November he established himself in the little lake town of Locarno. It was 'like the kingdom of heaven', he wrote to Ogarev, 'after the dry and stuffily prosaic atmosphere of Geneva'. It was also twice as cheap. In December Antonia, now eight months gone with child, came from Italy to join him.

When therefore in January 1870 Nechaev came back to Geneva, he found Bakunin no longer there. He obtained the address from Ogarev and, early in February, made a pilgrimage to Locarno. He found his friend and accomplice engaged on the unexpected task of translating Marx's masterpiece *Das Kapital* into Russian. For Bakunin was now once more a pauper; his wife had just presented him with a daughter; and he had received a commission from a Russian publisher to translate *Das Kapital* for a price of 1,200 roubles (£120), of which 300 roubles had been paid in advance. Bakunin was already thoroughly tired of Marx's contorted periods; and it did not take Nechaev long to convince him that uncongenial hack-work of this kind was unworthy of a genius which should be employed in the more direct promotion of revolution. The 300 roubles received and already spent seemed at first to constitute an obstacle; but Nechaev undertook to deal with that aspect of the matter. How far Bakunin interested himself in Nechaev's ways and means of liberating him from his contract is not known. But they consisted in writing a peremptory letter to the publisher, who was requested, in the name of the secret committee of *The People's Justice*, to leave Bakunin in peace, and threatened with the unpleasant consequences which would ensue in the event of noncompliance with this order. The fate of Ivanov may have suggested to the publisher, a Russian Jew named Polyakov, that the threat was not altogether an empty one.*

The removal of this obligation relieved Bakunin of an uncongenial occupation. But it also deprived him of the prospect of obtaining a further 900 roubles from the same source, and it did not solve the problem of existence; for neither he nor Nechaev could live on the non-existent resources of an imaginary committee. They bethought themselves once more of the Bakhmetiev fund. Herzen had just died in Paris; and Ogarev, as the surviving depositor of the fund, was presumably entitled to dispose of the

* This incident figures in the charges which Marx brought against Bakunin in 1872, and which led to the expulsion of Bakunin from the International.

remaining half of it. The idea was too opportune for its execution to be delayed for a moment. Bakunin urgently begged Ogarev to claim it from the executors of Herzen's estate.

> This is not only your right [he wrote on 22 February], it is your sacred duty; and to this sacred duty all feeling of personal delicacy must give way. In this affair you must act with Roman sternness, you must be a Brutus.

Bakunin did not content himself with letters. On reflexion, the issue seemed too vital. He borrowed 80 francs from the son of his landlady to pay his fare, and in the middle of March, came up to Geneva (whither Nechaev had preceded him) to be on the scene of action.

Ogarev did not fear to be a Brutus or decline the Roman role assigned to him. He wrote to young Alexander Herzen who, with the alacrity of one anxious to wash his hands of a tiresome subject, recognized the obligation, and came to Geneva in person to pay over the money. The occasion was formal. There were present – besides young Herzen and Ogareg – Bakunin, Nechaev, Natalie Ogarev, Tata Herzen and two or three other Russians. The sum of 10,000 francs, representing the second moiety of the fund, was handed by young Herzen to Ogarev (who gave him a receipt), by Ogarev to Bakunin, and by Bakunin to Nechaev. Nechaev gave no receipt, leaving his friends to rely on his 'revolutionary honour'; and when a few weeks later, Ogarev asked for one, he replied curtly that it was not the habit of his committee to give receipts.

This noteworthy event did not long remain secret. Gossip was rife in revolutionary circles in Switzerland, and spread to London, where Karl Marx eagerly snapped up so savoury a trifle.

> Among other things [he wrote to Engels on 24 March] there is the interesting fact that Bakunin, who had hitherto raged furiously against Herzen, began, immediately after the latter's death, to sound a paean of praise. He has now achieved his purpose: the propaganda funds, about 25,000 francs a year, which the wealthy Herzen received from Russia (from his party there), have now been transferred to Bakunin. This sort of 'inheritance' Bakunin seems to like, despite his prejudice against inheritance in general.

Marx, always anxious to believe the worst of his adversaries, swallowed whole this curious farrago of fact and fiction; and in a letter to Kugelmann a few weeks later he boldly asserts that Herzen had been in receipt of an annual subsidy of 25,000 francs from the 'pan-Slav, pseudo-socialist party in Russia'. But it was in the long run more important to discredit the living Bakunin than the dead Herzen; and two years later Marx was still assiduously circulating the report that Bakunin was living on subsidies received from Russia. At length in 1872 Bakunin took the matter in hand. He induced Ogarev to sign a paper declaring that 'Bakunin was not present when the money was handed over to Nechaev by me [i.e. Ogarev] in the presence of Natalie Herzen.' But Ogarev was, by the end of 1872, too weak in body and mind for his signature to carry much conviction. In matters of fact, Bakunin was both unscrupulous and imaginative; and his presence on the occasion in question is attested by a disinterested witness in the person of young Alexander Herzen. His role in the affair is clear. He was the prime instigator of the transfer, and the channel through which the money passed. But the sole beneficiary was Nechaev.

The Bakhmetiev fund was not the only nest-egg on which Bakunin and Nechaev, during their conference at Locarno, had cast covetous eyes; for the financial needs of the revolution were a bottomless abyss. The next episode in this unedifying story centres round the person and the possessions of Herzen's eldest daughter. Tata's first thought when her father died was for Ogarev, who had borne the blow in lonely seclusion at Geneva. She hastened to Geneva to visit him; and this kindly impulse had far-reaching results.

Tata Herzen, like her brother and sister, had acquired from her father a comfortable little fortune. Unlike them, she had also inherited from him a sincere though ill-defined enthusiasm for revolution. It had already occurred to Nechaev that both her enthusiasm and her fortune might suitably be pressed into the service of the revolutionary cause; and her arrival in Geneva provided a splendid opportunity. Tata was by nature romantic and impressionable; and she had just recovered from the unfortunate affair with the Italian Penizi. It was a moment when she would be particularly susceptible to new attractions and a new object in life. Ogarev served once more as the willing, though unconscious, tool of Nechaev. In the absence of that enterprising young man (who was with Bakunin at Locarno), he fired Tata's excited imagination with talk of imminent revolution in Russia, of the close cooperation between exiles abroad and revolutionaries at home which Nechaev had come to establish, and of the proposed revival, which Nechaev had skilfully mooted, of *The Bell*. In the meanwhile, in default of other occupation, she endeavoured to introduce some measure of order into the chaos of Ogarev's papers, and tried to believe that she was engaged on work of revolutionary importance. She returned to Natalie in Paris, and firmly announced her intention of settling in Geneva.

The announcement was a signal for a pitched battle. Young Alexander, who had succeeded to the dignity of the head of the house of Herzen, protested against his sister's project and alleged her health as an objection. Bakunin, primed by Nechaev, had no more scruples about Tata's fortune than about the Bakhmetiev fund; and fearing that Ogarev might weaken, he appealed to him with his usual impassioned vehemence.

You must, and you alone can [runs his letter of 22 February] save your eldest girl.* Whether she will be able and anxious in the future to work for the Russian cause we shall see later. You will not, of course, do violence to her opinions and her desires in the name of abstract patriotism and in defiance of her health and happiness – that would not be in your character. But *I* think and *you* think, that she will find in the Russian cause a new life; *they* think the opposite. The future will show who is right and who is wrong. But first you must save her. *Because, Ogarev, I have no doubt whatever that if she remains with them she will go off her head.* You must free her from *their unconscious but instinctive* egoism, which they conceal *from themselves* under a mask of golden reason and everyday *bourgeois* common sense. Is poor dear Tata to have no other outlet in her life but to become nursemaid to Alexander's children, or 'mother's help' to Natalie, or companion to that really insane Germano-Wagnerian Pomeranian Virgin,† with the consolation of being allowed to paint nice little pictures *ins Blaue hinein?* . . .

* i.e. Tata. The family affairs of Herzen and Ogarev were sufficiently con-fused; and Bakunin writes as if not only Liza but all Herzen's daughters were nominally the children of Ogarev.

† i.e. Malwida von Meysenbug. She had met Wagner in Paris in 1860, and was at this time a fervent devotee. 'Pomeranian' seems to be an unprompted flight of Bakunin's imagination.

You must insist that Tata should come to you; and in order to prevent them from refusing *on the pretext that you are* exalté *or insane or have lost your wits,* you must pretend to be the most rational of beings. Write to them not a flaming patriotic letter, but a well-reasoned one with a dash of scepticism. For them scepticism is common sense; and it was in this common sense that our dear Herzen died.

It might perhaps have been retorted, if anyone more critically minded than Ogarev had read this letter, that the 'unconscious but instinctive egoism' was not a monopoly of one side.

Tata's resolution proved unshakeable; and Alexander appealed to Natalie not to let her go to Switzerland alone. Towards the end of February Natalie, Tata and Liza travelled together from Paris to Geneva, and took rooms in a small *pension* not far from Ogarev. Alexander wrote to Natalie in terms of evident relief:

I thank you from my heart for your letter. It rather alarmed me for poor Tata, and I have been very worried about her. But I confess that her last letter reassured me. She is no longer sick; but she has been carried away. She says that all this is in order to discover what is going on, that if she finds that she does not agree with their aims or methods, or that she can do nothing, she will give it up and come to me. All we can do is constantly to keep before her the unfavourable sides of the whole business and, when she is convinced, then get her away.

But scarcely had Natalie and Tata settled down in Geneva when a new scandal occurred. A collection of Herzen's posthumous works was being prepared for publication. During the last year of his life Herzen had written a series of *Letters to an Old Comrade.* The 'old comrade' was Bakunin; and the 'letters' were a reasoned but vigorous attack on his whole policy, which was not inaptly characterized as 'blind stumbling after the Unknown God of Destruction'. Bakunin and Nechaev somehow learned at Locarno that these letters were destined for inclusion in the first volume of the posthumous works. It seemed important, in view of their designs both on the Bakhmetiev fund and on Tata's inheritance, that they should be able to pose as the spiritual heirs of Herzen; and from this point of view, publication of the letters would be singularly inopportune. They decided to prevent it. They first tried peaceful persuasion through the intermediary of Ogarev.

But it soon became clear that more drastic steps were necessary; and Nechaev bethought himself of the method so successfully employed in dealing with the Russian publisher of *Das Kapital*. On 7 March a communication was sent to young Alexander bearing the imprint of the 'Bureau of Foreign Agents of the Russian Revolutionary Society *The People's Justice*'. It summoned the 'family of Herzen' to desist from the publication of these letters, and added that, if this warning were disregarded, *The People's Justice* would be compelled to resort to 'less delicate' measures. But the threat proved an empty one. Nechaev had misjudged his man; and the only emotion excited by the ultimatum was indignation. The *Letters to an Old Comrade* duly appeared; and no member of the Herzen family suffered from the avenging hand of *The People's Justice*.

These events made Alexander all the more anxious to rescue his sister from the ill-omened influence under which she had fallen. But it was for the time being impossible to move her. In the middle of March Bakunin, hot-foot in pursuit of the Bakhmetiev fund, arrived in Geneva, and for the first time introduced Tata to Nechaev himself. Nechaev counted on his personal magnetism to achieve the object of his ambition; and pressure was at once brought to bear on her to place her services and her fortune at his disposal. Bakunin and Ogarev, the former active and insistent, the latter passive and compliant, both lent themselves to this disagreeable game. 'A young and pretty woman can always be useful,' remarked Bakunin, when Tata asked how she could serve the cause; and he went on to suggest that there were rich men, young and old, whose heads might be turned in the interests of the revolution. A few months later, when he had broken with Nechaev, Bakunin wrote of him in terms of unusual candour:

If you introduce him to your friend, his first aim will be to sow dissension, scandal and intrigue between you and make you quarrel. If your friend has a wife or daughter, he will do his best to seduce her and get her with child, in order to snatch her from the power of conventional morality and involve her, despite herself, in a revolutionary protest against society.

The indictment comes oddly from so stout a protestant against the existing social order; and it comes more oddly still from one who, three months earlier, had done his utmost to convert the daughter of an old friend into Nechaev's tool.

It was not Bakunin's fault if Tata Herzen escaped unhurt from the snare he had helped to spread for her. The first task on which Nechaev employed her was the innocent and unadventurous one of addressing envelopes; and from this he proceeded to the suggestion that she should draw the designs for forging banknotes. A more immediate issue, however, was his project of reviving *The Bell* as a propaganda organ for his ideas; and for this purpose he needed both Tata's money and the name of Herzen. But Nechaev knew nothing of restraint or tact; and he lacked experience in dealing with young ladies who had received a sheltered education and imbibed conventional notions of morals and behaviour. The girl, at first dazzled and fascinated, became frightened. Natalie Ogarev, behaving for once with good sense, reminded her of her father's antipathy to Nechaev; her brother was frankly hostile to the whole affair; and after a struggle Tata refused her name to the new publication. Nechaev, raging against the obstinacy of this 'bread-and-butter miss', had to fall back on Ogarev; and the first number of a new series of *The Bell* opened on 2 April 1870 with the following preface:

To the New Management of ' The Bell'.

I transfer to you this new edition of *The Bell* with the firm conviction that you will accept it with wholehearted devotion to the cause of Russian Freedom. You will not betray the standard borne aloft by Herzen, whereby every free-thinking man could declare his thoughts and opinions, without prejudice, of course, to the main purpose of the liberation of Russia. In this conviction we can never have cause for disagreement, and I shall remain to the end of my life your devoted collaborator.

N. OGAREV

The Bell in its new form was a complete fiasco, and ceased to appear after the first six numbers. Its brief career was presumably financed from the Bakhmetiev fund.

With the short-lived resurrection of *The Bell* Nechaev reached the summit of his prestige and success. There was no decisive event to mark the beginning of the decline; but from this point, for some intangible reason, everything began to go badly for him.

A Russian named Lopatin, whose revolutionary credentials were unimpeachable, arrived in Geneva. He was the only man who had seen Nechaev at work both in Russia and Switzerland; and he made the most of his knowledge. He told Tata Herzen, and anyone else who cared to listen, the true story of the murder of Ivanov. He explained that the scars on Nechaev's fingers were the death-marks of the victim who, in his agony, had bitten the murderer's hand to the bone.* He assured his audience that Nechaev had never been in a Russian prison, and that the alleged escape from Peter-and-Paul, of which he still boasted, was a fabrication second in audacity only to that of the Russian Revolutionary Committee and its vast organization, which had no existence outside Nechaev's creative brain. Not everybody believed Lopatin. But the doubts were damaging to Nechaev's credit. Moreover, Russian diplomacy and the Russian secret service had become active in the chase; and even the Swiss authorities were convinced that Nechaev was a dangerous character. In May, a young Russian *émigré* named Serebrennikov was mistaken by the police for Nechaev, and kept under arrest for some days until his identity could be established. Nechaev himself remained concealed in Geneva or in the surrounding country, moving on rapidly from place to place and never leaving an address. Once Tata was sent by Ogarev on a secret mission to Nechaev at the little mountain village of Le Locle in the Jura. Once Natalie and Tata had him in hiding for a week in their house. But the spell was broken; and they now made no secret of their impatience to be rid of an embarrassing guest.

The end came in a violent quarrel with Bakunin. It is odd that none of our abundant sources for the Nechaev affair gives any coherent account of the rupture; and the field is therefore open to speculative reconstruction. Friendly biographers of Bakunin speak of his inability to tolerate any longer Nechaev's singular imperviousness to moral considerations. More detached observers recall the proverb about thieves falling out. The explanation of the quarrel is probably both financial and psychological. Already in February Bakunin had, in his own words, 'overcome false shame',

* It is curious to note that in Dostoevsky's novel *The Devils*, which follows closely the story of Ivanov's murder by Nechaev, the murderer's finger is bitten not by his victim, but by the suicide-maniac Kirillov.

and presented to Nechaev 'the conditions on which he could give himself up entirely to the cause'. He even named his terms in plain figures – figures which throw an interesting side-light on the cost of living in Switzerland at this period: 150 francs a month if he remained at Locarno, and 250 francs a month if he were required to come to Geneva. But Nechaev, in the spring of 1870, was no longer the friendless wanderer who had appeared in Switzerland the year before. He had climbed on Bakunin's shoulders to a position of some eminence in revolutionary circles and, thanks to the Bakhmetiev fund, of material independence. In brief, he no longer needed Bakunin. He had fathomed the veteran's vanity and his helplessness in practical things; and he saw that he had nothing more to hope or fear from him. It was certainly not worth while to pay for his support; and gratitude was a quality not recognized by Nechaev. Bakunin was not invited to participate in the new issue of *The Bell*; and when he wrote a letter criticizing the ambiguity of its programme, it was printed with an editorial reply which referred to 'men of petty self-esteem who hold aloof from active work on the pretext of disagreement on this or that point of detail'. Bakunin felt bitterly the young man's contemptuous neglect. His pride was made to pay dearly for his infatuation. He was himself by nature sufficiently imperious, and was seldom overburdened with scruples; but he had met more than his match in this imperious and unscrupulous 'Boy'.

On 14 June Bakunin wrote to Ogarev from Locarno that 'a rupture with Boy seems inevitable'; and it took place when he came to Geneva in the following month. Nechaev, who still hovered between the roles of reckless fanatic and piratical adventurer, felt that the game was up. He did not care. He had squeezed these Russian fools dry; Switzerland had become too hot even for him. He decided to transfer his activities to the broader arena of London. He carried off with him a bundle of compromising documents belonging to Bakunin, Ogarev and others, stolen – or so Bakunin alleged – in case a favourable opportunity should occur of blackmailing their owners. Bakunin spent the next few days writing letters of warning to political associates in various countries to whom he had formerly commended 'Boy' as the apple of his eye.

The story of Nechaev may be rapidly concluded. In London he founded a new Russian periodical *The Commune*, which lived to publish two numbers. The first of these contained an attack on Herzen, and an open letter to Ogarev and Bakunin, in which Nechaev made bold to claim from them 'the balance of the Bakhmetiev fund'. The sum in question amounted to 1,410 francs 50 centimes, which apparently represented interest outstanding at the time the fund was wound up and which had remained in Ogarev's hands; but as part of it, at any rate, had already been 'lent' by Ogarev to Bakunin, it was presumably not available. Of Nechaev's stay in London not a trace remains. Two years later he was rash enough to return to Switzerland. He settled in Zürich under a false name and passport. But his presence was betrayed by a Pole named Adolf Stempkowski, a sign-painter who, from having been a Polish patriot in the insurrection of 1863, had become a Russian secret agent. The Russian Government succeeded in convincing the Federal Government that the murder of Ivanov was a common, not a political, crime; and the Swiss authorities, instead of harbouring Nechaev as a political refugee, decided to extradite him as a criminal. Bakunin relates that, hearing of Nechaev's danger and bearing no malice for the past, he sent a messenger to Zürich to warn him. Nechaev shrugged his shoulders, remarked that 'the Bakuninists were trying to drive him from Zürich', and remained in his fool's paradise until, a few days later, the police came to arrest him. This rather dubious anecdote enables Bakunin to close with a sort of moral victory for himself the pathetic chapter of his relations with Nechaev.

Nechaev stood his trial at Petersburg in a mood of unbending defiance. He protested vociferously against being arraigned as a common criminal and not as a political offender, and he was dragged away shouting from the court. The sentence was twenty years' penal servitude, and should normally have been served in Siberia. But the authorities preferred to keep this dangerous young man more closely under their eye, and clapped him into the fortress of Peter-and-Paul. There is a legend that he contrived, through a complacent sentry, to communicate with his friends outside the prison, and that, when asked by the latter whether they should concentrate their efforts on liberating him or on assassinating the Tsar, he emphatically urged them to ignore his fate and to work day and night for the murder of the oppressor. Nechaev failed to perform the exploit, which he had once boastingly attributed to himself, of escape from those grim walls. But he had the satisfaction of learning, in the ninth year of his captivity, that the murder of Alexander II had been successfully accomplished. Not long after, he died of scurvy in the thirty-fifth year of his age.

CHAPTER 15

The 'Affaire Postnikov'; *or the Eternal Spy*

AT the end of the sixties of last century the most important and successful agent of the foreign section of the Russian secret police was one Karl Arved Roman. He was of Lettish stock, and of comparatively humble origin. He chose a military career. His distinguished services in the Crimean War gained him rapid promotion, and he rose to the rank of colonel. But he had other qualities besides military prowess; and early in the sixties he was appointed to the famous Third Division of the Imperial Chancery, the headquarters of the secret police. In 1869, in which year he attained the age of forty, he retired on a pension, and went abroad 'for the sake of his health'. He chose Switzerland as his place of residence; and there he continued to place his valuable services at the disposal of the Third Division.

His first success abroad was one of those simple strokes which are the mark of genius. A year had elapsed since the death of Prince Dolgorukov at Berne. The preservation of his papers in the 'safe hands' of Tchorzewski, which Herzen had announced with triumph in *The Bell*, caused corresponding apprehensions in Petersburg. Dolgorukov had boasted much of the revelations he would one day make; and nobody knew what damaging secrets these famous papers might contain. But for months nothing was heard of them. Tchorzewski lacked the energy and the funds necessary for their publication. He had done nothing to justify the trust reposed in him by the dying Prince when, by a heaven-sent chance, there appeared on the scene a retired Russian colonel named Postnikov, a declared sympathizer with the revolutionaries, who was prepared not only to undertake the publication of the Dolgorukov papers, but to pay a round sum in cash for the privilege. The sum was, according to one account, 7,000 roubles. Tchorzewski snapped up the bait and, with the full encouragement of Herzen and Ogarev, handed over the documents. The money which paid for them came from the coffers of the Third Division; and the retired colonel Postnikov was no other than

274

Karl Arved Roman. The compromising papers were soon lodged safely in Petersburg.

This successful *coup* was carried out in October 1869, not more than two months after Roman's arrival in Switzerland. He soon found himself employed on another piece of work. During the winter of 1869–70 he received instructions to discover, without giving alarm to the object of his quest, the whereabouts of the notorious Princess Obolensky. Zoe Obolensky deserves a place of her own in any catalogue of unconventional nineteenth-century Russian aristocrats. She was a daughter of the ancient Russian house of Sumarokov, and she married into the scarcely less ancient Russian house of Obolensky. Her husband, Prince Obolensky, was a faithful servant of the Tsar, and had filled without discredit the office of Civil Governor of Moscow. But for some time past the behaviour of the Princess had excited unfavourable comment. It was not so much that she exhibited a marked distaste for her husband's society, and preferred to live, with her children, almost continuously abroad. Such domestic mishaps were not sufficiently rare to justify a first-rate scandal. But there was in Zoe's misconduct an air of conviction and bravado which distinguished her from the ordinary category of errant wives. The trouble was not confined to her actions. Improper behaviour in a Russian aristocrat constituted at first a failure in tact. Improper opinions were an unpardonable crime; and the Princess Obolensky's opinions, though vague, were decidedly and ostentatiously radical in complexion.

The scandal became notorious about the year 1865, when the Princess and her children were resident in Italy. She rented a palace in Naples, and her establishment consisted of a small army of tutors, governesses and servants, and a private physician whom she brought with her from Russia. The city of Naples had long been famous for its skill and persistence in the conduct of subterranean revolutionary intrigue. It was now five years since the march of Garibaldi and the Thousand had achieved the 'liberation' of Naples and its incorporation in the newly-made kingdom of Italy; but these events had not been allowed to interfere with the venerable tradition of political discontent. The impetuous liberators had promised the advent of a golden age. But the Neapolitans were not slow to discover that the current alloy still contained a generous admixture of baser metal; and voices were even heard to whisper that King Victor Emmanuel, reigning in Turin or Florence, was no better than a reincarnation of their own King Bomba of blessed memory, whose tottering throne had so hardly survived the revolution of 1848. Round this local nucleus of potential conspirators there gathered a motley array of national and international revolutionaries; and for all such the Princess Obolensky, with the open-handed hospitality of the Russian aristocrat, kept open house. In the summer, when life in the city became impossible, she engaged half of the largest hotel on the island of Ischia, and continued to entertain her guests, with the same lavish hand, amid cooling breezes from the Mediterranean. The Princess was one of those who found no incompatibility between high living and democratic thinking.

Among the disciples of revolution who basked in the luxury of Zoe Obolensky's hospitality were two Slavs: Bakunin, who had come to settle in Naples with his wife, and a Pole named Mročkowski. Bakunin had set to work in Naples to build, from such material as lay ready to his hand, an International Brotherhood of Revolution. Its policy made up in emphasis what it lacked in precision; and its organization was even vaguer than its policy. The nucleus of the Brotherhood was formed by a handful of Italian journalists and lawyers, and its international character seems to have been limited to the presence in it of Bakunin himself until, by a happy stroke, he enrolled among its members the Princess Obolensky. The advantages of the arrangement were mutual. The Princess was gratified by the feeling that she was now an authentic conspirator; and Bakunin enjoyed a greater profusion of creature comforts than he had ever known since he first set out from Russia on his wanderings twenty-five years before.

But in the long run, Mročkowski had more to offer the unconventional Princess than had Bakunin. It was customary in the nineteenth century for moral and political orthodoxy to go together; and the Princess would have felt herself inconsistent if she had not thrown both overboard simultaneously. The enterprising and dexterous Pole so far insinuated himself into her favour as to become her lover; and Zoe, in that spirit of bravado which so much aggravated her offences in the eyes of her family, made no attempt to conceal the fact. Mročkowski also joined the

International Brotherhood; and there is even a record of a journey undertaken by him to France and Belgium to woo new adherents to the cause.

The Neapolitan idyll lasted two years; and in 1867 Princess Obolensky and her lover moved to Switzerland and took a house on the outskirts of Vevey. By a strange coincidence, or because he did not wish to lose sight of so munificent a patroness, Bakunin abandoned Italy about the same time and settled down at Geneva at the other end of the lake. But either the revenues of the Princess, or her enthusiasm for Bakunin, were on the wane; and from the date of his arrival in Switzerland Bakunin resumed the life of penury and occasional benefactions which was characteristic of his later years. Even the lovers seem to have relapsed into an obscure existence which contrasts unexpectedly with the ostentatious grandeur of Naples; and little had been heard of them for two years when, about the end of 1869, Roman received orders to report on the whereabouts of the wandering Princess, who had culpably neglected to inform either her husband or the appropriate Russian consul of her address.

The motive of these instructions was soon revealed. Prince Obolensky, incited thereto by his father-in-law Count Sumarokov, had displayed a sudden interest in the fate of his children, who had been exposed for some five years to the contamination of their mother's opinions and manner of life. The two noblemen applied to the Russian Government for assistance in recovering the children; and the Russian Government applied in turn to the Swiss Federal Government. Roman had no difficulty in locating the Princess and her unconventional household; and at the beginning of 1870 Prince Obolensky travelled himself to Switzerland to superintend the rescue of his offspring. A member of the Swiss Federal Council awaited the Prince at the Vevey railway-station; and accompanied by a party of gendarmes they drove to the villa of the unsuspecting Princess. Mročkowski does not seem to have been present; at any rate he plays no part in the scene. The Princess was pushed away by gendarmes while, amid her shrieks, the abduction of the children was safely effected. Zoe never saw her children again. She and her lover went to Mentone where, her sources of revenue having dried up, Mročkowski earned his living as a photographer. Roman's mission had once more been crowned with success; and Bakunin, who feared that Nechaev might share the fate of Princess Obolensky's children, indicted a fierce denunciation of the Swiss authorities under the title *The Bears of Berne and the Bear of St Petersburg*.

But a more important piece of work now awaited the trusty and successful agent of the Third Division. The murder of Ivanov and Nechaev's flight to Switzerland had roused the police from the singular lethargy with which they had regarded the audacious young man's earlier adventures; and Roman was entrusted with the task of discovering the whereabouts of Nechaev. This was an altogether different matter from shadowing Princess Obolensky. Nechaev, unlike the Princess, guessed that there would be a hue and cry after him and was well on his guard. Roman saw only one hope of running to earth this important quarry: to worm himself into the confidence of those who might be expected to know Nechaev's secrets. The circle of Herzen, Ogarev and Tchorzewski was a useful starting-point; and since he made his bow in that circle as the retired colonel Postnikov, the prospective editor of Dolgorukov's papers, he must at all costs maintain the role. He must get on with the business he professed to have begun. He proposed to his masters in Petersburg nothing less than that he should, in fact, publish the Dolgorukov papers, omitting such passages as might be too distasteful to the authorities. He need not, he pointed out, be in any particular hurry; Tchorzewski had already wasted a whole year. And once the work was published he could, if necessary, buy up the whole edition from the printer and thus ensure that no copies got into circulation. But publish he must; and above all he must have the original papers back from Petersburg in order that Ogarev and Tchorzewski (Herzen had just died in Paris) might from time to time see them in his possession. Otherwise suspicion would certainly be aroused. Publication would cost the Third Division 4,000 francs, plus 3,000 francs for his personal expenses for six months. The sum was considerable; but the bait was the chance of tracking down Nechaev to his secret lair.

The Third Division, whose organization was still primitive, had few agents of the calibre of Roman; and above all they had no idea how to find Nechaev. Roman's plan shocked them. But he conclusively proved that there was no alternative; and at last, in

278

reluctant admiration of his enterprise and ingenuity, they consented. Roman, who circulated in the name of Postnikov between Paris, Brussels and Geneva, received back Dolgorukov's papers, or such of them as the authorities thought not too unfit to print. He elaborately discussed with Tchorzewski and Ciernecki the order and manner of their publication; and he employed an old *émigré* named Mechnikov, who had fought under Garibaldi, to translate them from Russian into French.

Having thus established for himself an unimpeachable 'cover', Roman-Postnikov set about the work of extracting from his new friends a clue to Nechaev's whereabouts. He made Tchorzewski royally drunk at the public expense and, having conveyed him home in a semi-conscious condition, took the opportunity of ransacking his flat. But neither Tchorzewski's papers nor his conversation betrayed the precious secret; and Roman was forced to conclude, correctly enough, that he did not know it. During the early months of 1870 he became a bosom friend of Ogarev and was soon calling him by the affectionate diminutive used by his intimates, Aga. But he described Ogarev in his reports as a man 'who has drunk himself into oblivion'; and no coherent information was forthcoming from this quarter. He met Natalie Ogarev, whom he calls 'Madame Herzen'; but he obtained nothing from her but a portrait of 'her late husband'. Roman was clever. But Nechaev had taken his precautions. He seldom stayed long in one place, and never gave his address to his best friends.

These negative results were a sad disappointment both to Roman and to his employers. The latter were exacting and suspicious task-masters; and Roman saw the prospect of his mission, and even his career, ending in disgrace. But at the critical moment a new line of country opened before him. In the middle of April 1870 he was introduced by Ogarev to Bakunin, who had arrived in Geneva from Locarno. A few weeks earlier, Roman in one of his reports had linked Bakunin with Ogarev as 'men whose career is finished,' and had given, admittedly at secondhand, the following description of Bakunin:

Bakunin has not long to live. He is in an advanced state of dropsy, and it has gone to his brain. He has become, they say, like a wild beast in consequence (on the top of everything else) of his ungovernable temper and his inability to satisfy his sexual appetites.

After the meeting, we hear no more from Roman of Bakunin's physical or mental decay. The agent is only too anxious to justify himself in the eyes of his masters by insisting on the value of his new acquaintance. There was no doubt that Bakunin was at this time in close alliance with Nechaev; and there were even rumours that Nechaev was staying with him at Geneva in the same house. Roman made haste to verify this report by calling on Bakunin the very day after the introduction had been effected. He found Bakunin in a *pension* on the outskirts of the town. He stayed long enough to convince himself that Nechaev was not on the premises, and that Bakunin was not expecting him in the near future. More than that, at a first visit, the most skilful spy could scarcely be expected to discover; and unfortunately, before Roman had time to improve the acquaintance, Bakunin returned to Locarno.

Roman had a strong motive, in his reports to Petersburg, for exaggerating Bakunin's importance; for he wished to provide a justification for his own continued employment. But there is no doubt that he, like so many others, had fallen under the spell of the shaggy, toothless veteran. Bakunin was clearly the most impressive personality among the Russian revolutionaries in Switzerland. He was not only the most probable source of information about Nechaev; he deserved, from the point of view of an agent of the Russian Government, close attention for his own sake. Roman urged this view on the authorities in Petersburg with all the eloquence and ingenuity at his command.

But the impression had not been made exclusively on one side. Bakunin did not forget the ingratiating manners and the ingenuous revolutionary enthusiasm of the visitor; and when he came to Geneva once more in July, he hastened to call on 'the gallant colonel'. It was the moment of the quarrel with Nechaev. By Nechaev's defection, Bakunin had lost his sole direct contact with his native land. Postnikov seemed admirably qualified to fill the void. Though so ardent a revolutionary, he was – he explained – not yet compromised at home, and could travel freely to and from Russia. It seemed a heaven-sent opportunity. Bakunin told him that he and Ogarev desired to start a new monthly journal to take the place of *The Bell*. All they needed was someone who could go to Russia and bring them back authentic news of revolutionary doings there. The retired colonel Postnikov was the very man to undertake such a mission; and the more he hesitated, the more Bakunin and Ogarev insisted. The friendly argument produced a close intimacy; and after a week Bakunin had few secrets from his new ally. If he did not divulge Nechaev's hiding-place, it was only because he did not know it himself. But about the proposed journey to Russia, Postnikov still hesitated; and nothing had been decided when Bakunin again returned to Locarno at the end of the month.

The cause of the hesitation was simple. Postnikov was willing. But Roman had to telegraph to Petersburg for permission and for funds. It was, he did not fail to point out, an excellent opportunity for him to make a verbal report to his superiors and obtain fresh instructions. The necessary authority was at length received, and Ogarev telegraphed to Bakunin at Locarno the glad news of Postnikov's impending departure. Before leaving, Postnikov dined with his dear friend Ogarev to celebrate the latter's birthday and made him a present – once more, no doubt, at the public expense – of a pipe.

Besides the collection of information, another delicate mission had been entrusted by Bakunin to the agent of the Third Division. Bakunin had left Russia thirty years before, in 1840, and had revisited it only as a prisoner. His father and mother were now long since dead. But he had never received his share (or what he considered to be his share) of the family property; and letters to his brothers and sisters had either been ignored – perhaps they had never reached their destination – or had met with purely evasive answers. Bakunin now not only charged Roman with a further letter, but begged him to visit his old home at Premukhino in the province of Tver and make a personal appeal to the family, bearing witness to the straitened circumstances in which their unfortunate brother was compelled to live. Roman faithfully executed these commissions. He personally delivered the letter (after a copy had been deposited in the archives of the Third Division) at Premukhino; and he brought back seventy roubles for Bakunin. The pettiness of the sum suggests an act of charity rather than the recognition of a claim. Roman, on his return to Geneva, handed over the money to Ogarev for transmission to Bakunin, and methodically took a receipt, which he forwarded with his next report to the authorities at Petersburg.

Roman reached Geneva in the first days of September, in the midst of the excitement caused by the *débâcle* of Sedan, the proclamation of the Third French Republic and the imminent investment of Paris by the Prussians. The startling events of the past few weeks had resounded even in peaceful Locarno. The outbreak of war between the French and Prussian Governments seemed, to those who were the declared enemies of all governments, a heaven-sent opportunity; and Bakunin looked eagerly round for signs of the coming revolution. He penned a highly inflammatory pamphlet in the form of imaginary *Letters to a Frenchman*. Its aim was, as he explained in a letter to Ogarev, to prove that 'if social revolution does not ensue in France from the present war, socialism will be dead for many years throughout Europe'.

Bakunin did not pretend to maintain, as between the warring powers, the impartiality which his principles might have seemed to demand. A hatred of things Teutonic flows in the veins of every Slav; and Bakunin, in addition to this common heritage, had dabbled in the teachings of the Slavophils who believed that Peter the German was the source of all that was evil in modern Russia. His feelings for France were of a different hue, but no less highly coloured. The French Revolution had, beyond all manner of dispute, given birth to modern socialism; and the only socialist theories of which Bakunin had any understanding were made in France. France was the pioneer and the champion of the new enlightenment. If therefore he rejoiced at the downfall of Napoleon III, Bakunin was inexpressibly shocked at the prospect of seeing France overrun by Prussian troops and the French people brought under the hated Teuton yoke. He called loudly for a popular upheaval in France which would not only repel the invader but light the train of revolution throughout Europe.

It was on Lyons that Bakunin's gaze was mainly fastened. Lyons was one of the principal industrial towns of France. It was the nearest of them all to the Swiss border, and, most important of all, it was an active group of his political friends and disciples, the most important of whom was one Albert Richard. The moment was critical. Public opinion in Lyons hesitated, not between Empire and Republic (for after Sedan Napoleon had scarcely a friend left in France), but between the Republic of Gambetta and a new revolution. Bakunin's friends hoisted the red flag and summoned their master to the scene. The veteran decided 'to shift my old bones to Lyons and there play, perhaps, my last role'.

It thus happened that when, on 9 September, Postnikov set out from Geneva to Locarno to report in person on his Russian visit, Bakunin was already on his way from Locarno to Geneva and Lyons. There was a dramatic meeting in the streets of Lucerne, where Postnikov was waiting for the Locarno stage-coach (the Gotthard had not yet been pierced, and there was no railway to Italian Switzerland) in which Bakunin had just arrived. Bakunin, hastily dropping his two portmanteaux, threw himself into Postnikov's arms and embraced him three times on the cheek; and it was in these strange surroundings that he received, from an agent of the Russian secret service, his first greetings after many years' silence from his brothers and sisters. Postnikov had nothing to do but to retrace his steps. He travelled with Bakunin as far as Berne. The funds of the Third Division provided him with a first-class railway ticket. His less affluent companion travelled second; and it was perhaps this inequality which suggested to Bakunin the suitability of the occasion for obtaining a loan. He asked for 250 roubles. In a burst of candour he added that he could not, 'as an honest man', promise repayment on a definite date, but that he would return the money at the first opportunity. Postnikov hedged. He was not sure whether this was the kind of item which the Third Division would pass in his accounts. But Bakunin, as they paced the platform together at a wayside station before returning to their several compartments, insisted; and there was nothing for it but to comply. Postnikov had not so large a sum on his person in cash. But he promised to hand it to Ogarev, to be forwarded to Bakunin, as soon as he reached Geneva.

The two travellers parted at Berne. Roman returned to his headquarters at Geneva. Bakunin went on to Neuchâtel to arrange with his friend Guillaume the printer for the publication of *Letters to a Frenchman*. They met again in Geneva a few days later on the eve of Bakunin's departure for Lyons; and Bakunin urged the 'gallant colonel' to accompany him. In the course of the conversation he let fall the exciting information that Nechaev was in Lyons. Roman reported in haste to Petersburg and asked for authority to pursue his quarry on French soil.

Bakunin left Geneva on the evening of 14 September with two comrades, a Russian and a Pole, and reached Lyons on the following day.

The confusion in Lyons was complete. On the fall of Napoleon III a republic had been proclaimed, and a 'Committee of Public Safety' had installed itself in the Hotel de Ville. Its title was high-sounding and breathed the traditional spirit of revolution. Its political aims were uncertain; and it was by no means clear what it was trying to 'save'. Some spoke of saving the revolution; others wanted to form a 'sacred union' of all parties to save France from Bismarck. The first act of the Committee was to send three delegates, of whom Albert Richard was one, to Paris to negotiate with the new republican government of Gambetta, its relations to which were quite undefined. Finally, on the day of Bakunin's arrival in Lyons, municipal elections were held; and the short-lived and rather ridiculous Committee of Public Safety abdicated in favour of the new municipal council.

Bakunin, a giant among pygmies, soon took the situation in hand. His first thought was to form, as usual, a revolutionary committee. In the absence of Richard, he lodged with a tailor named Palix; and Palix's flat became the headquarters of an improvised revolutionary organization which called itself, with singular inappropriateness, the 'Committee for the Saving of France'. Bakunin was now once more in his element; it was the first time since the glorious days of 1848 that he had tasted the intoxicating joys of revolution.

My head is in a whirl [he wrote to Ogarev]; so much to be done. There is no real revolution here yet, but there will be. Everything is being done and prepared for the real revolution. I'm out for all or nothing, and I hope for an early triumph.

He went about addressing meetings of working-men. His ready eloquence met everywhere with brilliant success. Resolutions were passed demanding the abolition of officers and the substitution of commanders elected by the men; the release of soldiers imprisoned for political offences; the levying of contributions from the rich; and the publication of a list of 'spies and *provocateurs*'. For the moment Bakunin was the most popular man in Lyons. 'On the first day of a revolution', someone had said of him in

Paris in 1848, 'he is a perfect treasure; on the second day, he ought to be shot'.

Encouraged by this initial success, the 'Federated Committees for the Saving of France' (for the single committee had already increased and multiplied in Bakunin's brain) drafted a proclamation, which was placarded in the streets of Lyons on 26 September. It bore some twenty signatures, including those of Bakunin, Palix and Richard; but its style clearly betrays the hand of Bakunin. Here is the text of this characteristic document:

French Republic

REVOLUTIONARY FEDERATION OF COMMUNES

The disastrous situation of the country, the impotence of the authorities, and the indifference of the privileged classes have brought the French nation to the brink of an abyss.

If the people organized for revolution fail to act at once, the future is lost, the Revolution is lost, all is lost. Inspired by the immensity of the danger and considering that desperate action by the people cannot be delayed a moment longer, the delegates of the Federated Committees for the Saving of France, having met in session at the Central Committee, propose to adopt forthwith the following resolutions:

1. The administrative and governmental machine of the State, having become impotent, is abolished.

The French people resumes full possession of its destinies.

2. All criminal and civil courts are suspended and replaced by the justice of the people.

3. Payment of taxes and mortgages is suspended. The taxes are replaced by the contributions of the federated communers, levied from the rich classes in proportion to the needs of the security of France.

4. The State, having ceased to exist, cannot intervene in the payment of private debts.

5. All existing municipal organizations are suppressed, and are replaced in all the federated communes by Committees for the Saving of France, which will exercise full powers under the immediate supervision of the people.

6. Each Committee in the chief town of a Department will send two delegates to the Revolutionary Convention for the Saving of France.

7. This Convention will meet immediately at the Hôtel de Ville of Lyons, being the second city of France and in the best position to provide energetically for the defence of the country. This Convention, supported by the whole people, will save France.

TO ARMS ! ! ! ! ! !

It appears from the record which Richard has left of these events that the French members of the Committee for the Saving of France shared neither the faith nor the optimism of their Russian colleague and leader. They were secretly unconvinced of the efficacy of Bakunin's methods of saving France; and they were still more sceptical of the popularity of these methods with the French proletariat. His tempestuous energy had dragged them with him into signing the proclamation; but the hare-brained attempt to translate this programme into action was forced on them only by unforeseen circumstances when they had gone too far to draw back. The defunct Committee of Public Safety had, in a moment of enthusiasm, nationalized the factories and turned them into National Workshops; and the municipal council, which inherited this blessing from the Committee, found the experiment a drain on its limited resources. It chose this inauspicious moment to reduce wages in the National Workshops from three francs to two and a half francs a day. Such an action was well calculated to arouse indignation even in breasts which had no abstract interest in revolution. The Committee for Saving France met to consider the situation. Bakunin wished to improve the occasion by a general call to arms of the working class. It was true that their proclamation had ended with the words 'To Arms ! ! !' But that was a piece of rhetoric which committed nobody; and Bakunin was alone in wishing to proceed from words to action. He was outvoted; and the Committee merely decided to organize a peaceful demonstration.

On the next day, in response to the appeal of the Committee, a crowd some thousands strong collected at mid-day in front of the Hôtel de Ville. Delegates of the workmen entered the building to demand the restoration of their three francs a day; but the municipal councillors had prudently provided themselves with other engagements, and were not on the premises. When this was discovered, the infuriated crowd broke into the Hôtel de Ville, the members of the Committee after them. Nobody quite knew what to do next. There had only been time for the delivery of a few speeches when a detachment of the National Guard appeared. They cleared the crowd from the building, arrested Bakunin and one or two others, and re-established order.

But the bloodless battle of 28 September passed through as many varying phases as a real engagement. An hour later the crowd had broken in once more, disarmed the feeble detachment of the National Guard and released Bakunin. The Committee found itself, somewhat to its own surprise, once more master of the situation. It resolved not to let slip another opportunity, and sat down to deliberate on the formation of a provisional government. Bakunin, never at a loss, advised the arrest of the Mayor and the leading *bourgeois* citizens. But it was not clear by what force these arrests were to be carried out; and nobody else had any suggestions at all. Presently companies of the National Guard began to converge on the square. The members of the Committee, looking from their windows, saw themselves surrounded no longer by enthusiastic supporters but by the *Chassepot* rifles of the Guard; and when dusk came on, they slipped away in ignominious concealment from the Hôtel de Ville. By nightfall, the municipal councillors were reinstated, none the worse for their flight. The next day Bakunin, having borrowed his fare from Palix, left Lyons stealthily by train for Marseilles. In his later accounts of the tragicomedy of Lyons, he freely attributes the failure to the 'treachery' and 'cowardice' of other members of the Committee, including Richard, of whom he never spoke with respect again; and the Frenchmen retorted by abuse of this domineering Russian who had taken it on himself to teach them, the heirs of the greatest revolution in history, how revolutions are made.

In the midst of the commotion of the 28th, another personage had arrived in Lyons – the retired colonel Postnikov. A few days earlier he had received a letter from Bakunin begging him to borrow 500 roubles from Tchorzewski for the needs of the revolution. 'Either we shall die,' Bakunin had written, 'or we shall repay the money very soon'; for despite his theoretical views on private property, he clung firmly to the conviction that a successful revolution was a lucrative proposition for its promoters. The letter had been followed by a telegram in which Antonie begged her sister Julie to 'come at once to Lyons and bring views of Switzerland'. In this naïve cypher, 'Antonie' meant Bakunin 'and sister, Julie' Postnikov; and the views of Switzerland were the newly-printed *Letters to a Frenchman*. The 500 roubles were not to be had; but Postnikov duly arrived in Lyons carrying 300 copies of the famous pamphlet. He failed, however, to find his friend that day, and on the next heard that he had already fled. As for Nechaev, the other object of his search, there was no trace of him. Either he had never been in Lyons at all (the more probable hypothesis) or he had left it before the outbreak. Roman-Postnikov returned crestfallen to Geneva, and explained in an apologetic strain to his employers.

He had reason to anticipate their displeasure at this fruitless journey. They curtly ordered him to return to Lyons and continue the search for Nechaev, in whom they were far more interested than in the infirm and discredited Bakunin. Reaction had triumphed meanwhile in Lyons. The authorities were in a nervous state; and somebody had just fired at the Mayor. The police followed Postnikov's proceedings with interest, and came to the sage conclusion that he was an accomplice of Bakunin. He was arrested, and released only on condition that he left the city within twenty-four hours. 'For nine years I have served,' he wrote feelingly in his report, 'and nobody has ever insulted me. And now I have lived to bear the insults of these low, vulgar Frenchmen.'

On returning to Geneva in the latter part of October, Postnikov found two letters which had been written to him by Bakunin from Marseilles. The first begged him to contribute whatever he could afford to the 'common cause'. The second enclosed a letter which he was to forward, 'observing the greatest precautions', to Bakunin's brothers; and though it has not been preserved, we may safely assume that it, too, contained an appeal for money. The letter was duly forwarded by Roman to his employers, who posted it to its destination. The incident tickled the chief of the Third Division, who annotated Roman's report with a chuckle:

The old revolutionary does not imagine that the Third Division carries its tenderness for him so far that it actually sticks stamps on his letters to his brothers.

Bakunin spent three weeks in strict concealment at Marseilles. He lived, in the absence of contributions to the 'common cause', mainly by selling his few possessions. Then the position became too dangerous. The local members of the International raised enough money for his journey home and secured the complicity of a friendly captain. He shaved his beard, cut his shaggy mane and donned a pair of blue spectacles; and in this disguise he was smuggled on board a ship leaving for Genoa. It was his last sight of France. By the end of October he was back in Locarno.

The last stage in this charming friendship between the apostle of revolution and the agent of the Third Division was now approaching. Police-spies are not always melodramatic villains; and it is odd to trace in Roman's reports the growth of a real affection for his unsuspecting quarry. He had come to regard the helpless and toothless old revolutionary as his own peculiar charge; and again and again, in face of the insistence of his chiefs on the importance of finding Nechaev, he returns to the necessity for 'thoroughgoing observation of Bakunin'. Back in Locarno, Bakunin soon wrote that his resources were once more exhausted. His family was threatened by a refusal of the shopkeepers to supply any longer on credit even the simplest needs of daily life. He had so far lost faith in his star that he did not even promise repayment of the loan which he begged. But he would give a receipt and the 'gallant colonel' could collect the money, next time he visited Russia, from Bakunin's share in the family estate. It was not in Postnikov's heart to refuse; and the 300 roubles which he sent, though they appeared in the accounts of the Third Division, were clearly a matter of sentiment rather than of business.

But the separation was near. In January Roman, who had just published a first instalment of the Dolgorukov papers (cautiously limited to the times of Catherine the Great), and who had now frankly confessed his inability to throw any further light on the whereabouts of Nechaev, was finally recalled to Petersburg. In Geneva he paid a farewell visit to Ogarev, who shed maudlin tears over his past life, spent in vain labour for an ideal which was farther than ever from realization. The farewell meeting with Bakunin took place in Berne. The old man's health had been sapped by the failure at Lyons and by the hardships of his flight.

He breathed heavily, complained of swellings and pains in his legs, and ate and drank little. But his spirit was unbroken; and he still talked gaily of the break-up of the Austrian Empire – his dream for thirty years – and of the general European war which would make propaganda possible in Russia itself. War, he felt, was imminent; and he begged particularly that Postnikov would, on his arrival in Russia, study ways and means of propaganda on the Volga and in the Urals, which he considered the most promising fields for this missionary enterprise. He invited Postnikov to visit his brothers at Premukhino; and finally, he asked for a last loan of sixty francs. The two men embraced and parted, Postnikov knowing, and Bakunin perhaps suspecting, that they would meet no more. Bakunin wept like a child.

The departure from Switzerland ended for ever the brief but remarkable career of the retired Russian colonel Postnikov. Nor had Karl Arved Roman long to live; for he died within a year of his return to Petersburg. Neither Bakunin nor Ogarev ever discovered the identity or the vocation of the secret agent of the Third Division whom they had entertained unawares.

CHAPTER 16

Poor Nick: II

WHEN in 1858 Nick Ogarev, at the age of forty-five, fell in love with Mary Sutherland, he embarked for the last time as an adventurer on the sea of romance. It did not seem a brilliant start. His wooing of his first wife in Penza, and of Natalie Tuchkov at Aksheno, had been hedged about with all the pure fragrance of celestial love. His courtship of Mary Sutherland began with a sordid, commonplace solicitation in a drab London public-house. By a whim of destiny, the end of all these ventures belied the promises of the beginning. Ogarev's romantic ideals, disappointed and shattered by Maria and by Natalie, were triumphantly vindicated in the person of the English prostitute. His last years were passed, unexpectedly and incredibly, in the atmosphere of secure tranquillity which comes from domestic harmony and from a consciousness of faith justified. It is by far the most romantic chapter in Ogarev's romantic life.

There was in Ogarev's behaviour more continuity than may at first sight appear. In fact, all that he did, when he established Mary Sutherland at Mortlake, was to exchange one romantic ideal for another. The dream of 'the union of three persons in one love', which had followed the discovery of his wife's infatuation for Herzen, faded rapidly away; and he substituted for it that other favourite dream of the nineteenth-century Romantics – the regeneration by love of a fallen woman. It was not his first pursuit of the fleeting vision of the purified prostitute. In 1847, in the interval between his final desertion by Maria and the affair with Madame de Salias, he visited the famous fair of Nizhny Novgorod and indulged, according to one of his letters of the period, in a 'drunken debauch'. He brought back with him from the fair a prostitute whom he tried to educate and who 'behaved so well that he would never have expected it of her'. The experiment was evidently short-lived, and its end is not on record. But we have here, even before his marriage with Natalie, the germ of the feeling which, ten years later, was to flower into his romantic infatuation for Mary Sutherland.

Ogarev had never enjoyed happiness in love. And if his earlier, and far more promising, dreams of happiness had proved to be no more than vain and embittering illusions, what guarantee had he that this new dream would not crumble to dust when he tried to handle and grasp it? It was a question which even the incurably romantic Ogarev could not help putting to himself. He clung desperately to this last straw of faith. But he had serious and tormenting qualms of doubt. He doubted the reality and depth of Mary's affection for him and – worse still – he doubted, in face of the evidence of his own heart, the reality and depth of his feelings for Mary. In a letter to the cool and dispassionate Herzen he discounted his happiness with the assumed indifference of a man of the world.

That I at my age should be loved by an uncultivated creature – simple-minded to all appearance, though perhaps, God knows, cunning enough – is of course impossible. There may be on her side 'friendship for a good fellow' [Ogarev uses the English words]; and on my side it is, I suppose, a case of an old man's passion. See what a nice position! I cannot give myself up to it without *arrière-pensée*; and this *arrière-pensée* – a doubt of the reality of the feeling on either side – represents the tragic element in my life. But at the same time a cheerful and gentle mood prevails more often than any other. It would all be a ridiculous joke if painful scepticism at one moment were not balanced at others by the consciousness of a strange happiness; and our actual relationship is getting on to a serious footing . . . Meanwhile she, as an *enfant du peuple*, remains uneducated and childish, though she is far from stupid and is sometimes quite remarkable in the way she understands serious things. Whether she is cunning, I cannot tell. There is something gentle in her behaviour which does my heart good – that is the truth; and if she is being cunning in order to live comfortably on thirty shillings a week and have her boy with her, I gladly pardon her for that; it is too natural. The result is that I am afraid and grieved and glad, and that Unreason triumphs.

This letter was followed by a conversation, and the conversation by a further letter in which Ogarev once more expressed himself to his friend with a sceptical detachment which he was certainly far from feeling:

What is my motive? The possibility of giving a decent education to a being who is capable of being educated, a being whose peculiarities (arising from lack of training) are not too angular, in which I feel the need of an altogether naïve devotion. I may be mistaken, yes! But I am old enough and strong enough to be able to go away without hurting myself in the least. I shall save the boy, for the boy (without partiality) has remarkable talent and a kindly nature. But of course I look for something more, namely that

> On my sad declining years
> Love shall cast a parting ray.

. . . Well, suppose I am wrong, i.e. mistaken! Then I shall save the boy. I am incapable, no doubt owing to my age, of a helpless infatuation. Besides, I can feel my influence working, and I know it is good. If I fail it will not kill me. But to attempt to raise (pardon the silly word) a fallen woman and a child is worth taking some trouble. Such opportunities don't occur every day. If I fail, so much the worse, it won't kill me. And if I am not mistaken? The mere chance of success is worth the risk of being mistaken . . .

If it is a mistake, I shall not cry over it, and I shall save the boy – that's decided.

By a miracle in a thousand, it was not a mistake. For six years Mary Sutherland lived at Mortlake with her son and Ogarev visited her, loving her and providing for her financial needs and superintending her education and that of the boy. More than thirty letters written by him to her during this period survive.* They are remarkably uniform in tone and character. Most of them are undated, but this must be one of the earliest:

Dear Mary, I cannot tell you how pleased I am with your new lodgings. They seem altogether well adapted to a quiet and happy life. I thought about many things last night. Since I have been drinking only water, I feel myself so clear in everything I do – and your lodgings are so comfortable. Now we must try seriously to learn and study – both you and the boy; now I can be an energetic teacher. Let us fix certain days in the week and begin to work. You ask me why? Because, my dear, everything that is capable of broadening the understanding and

* It need hardly be said that these letters, as well as Mary's letters to Ogarev which will be quoted later, were written in English. Unfortunately they are available only in a Russian translation which can scarcely preserve the savour of the original where one of the writers was a foreigner and the other illiterate.

the mind will give you more interest in life – interest of the most honourable kind – and will make it easier for you to bring up the boy. I am so full of this idea that I shall do my best to teach you everything that I can explain to you of what I know and think. We must perfect our understanding; that is the only way to a peaceful and honourable life, and the only way to attain a happy old age without regret or remorse. Let us begin to work seriously next week. I love you so, my Mary, and the boy too. I want you both to become the best creatures in this world, with which I am far from enchanted. I bless and kiss you, my child.

Good night.

Another letter a few days later, the most ardent of the whole collection, continues this queer blend of love-making and grammar:

I cannot express how glad, how happy I was, my child, my Mary, to read your letter. And is it really true that you love me so much? Is it really true that I, an old man, can be loved so much, can be so happy? Oh, you are surely jesting with me; if it were a jest, I should go mad. No, I have real confidence in you, and am as happy as a youth who loves for the first time in his life. Let me kiss you a thousand times, my Mary, let me kiss you to death. I am so happy that I begin to fear death – a thing which never happened to me before. I want to live. I am so full of life, so young, that sometimes I am ashamed of the feeling; it is so contrary to my age and even to my character. But I know one thing – that I forget all my sufferings in your kiss, and that I would live and die with your kiss.

Of course, there are a lot of mistakes in your letters, Mary, but there is something else in them – the true language of the heart; and it is this which delights me. I can only write these few lines to-day; I have no time for more. But to-morrow I will write you your first grammar lesson and explain to you the construction of *verse*. You will see that the lesson will not be so dull as you perhaps think. At any rate I will try to make it interesting for you.

Good night, my Mary.

The fundamental humility of Ogarev's character keeps these letters entirely free from the tinge, which few in his position could have avoided, of patronage and superiority. There are others in which he speaks of Mary, without any suggestion of affection or mock modesty, as his moral counsellor and guardian. Here is a characteristic note:

My dear, dear, dear and a thousand times dear Mary. Thank you for your kind letter, thank you for your warnings against my drinking. All those who have loved me have told me the same thing, and you – you must save me from this vice which disgraces me. If I have really helped you in your life, you must save me. And I will tell you how. But how I have neglected your writing! And all on account of my drunkenness. We must take counsel together about everything, my Mary. I kiss you from my whole heart. You shall be my good angel.

There is another letter of self-reproach on a different score:

How could it happen that I was afraid of the presence of the Prince and his wife,* and did not take my place beside you as would have been natural? Was I afraid of gossip – perhaps not on my own account? Was I afraid that you yourself would be embarrassed if I came up to you? Or am I simply a coward in the face of public opinion, in a matter on which, by my most inward conviction, I hold that opinion in contempt? This idea gives me no peace and makes me despise myself. And what if, instead of embarrassment at my coming up to you, you had felt only *chagrin* at my disappearing without having taken you by the hand? What if I insulted you simply because I did not think properly about my behaviour and fell under the influence of my own cowardice? Perhaps you will laugh over this letter, my dear, but I assure you there is no worse feeling than contempt for oneself.

In spite of his passionate devotion to Mary and of his romantic belief in the equality of man, Ogarev was bound to submit to certain social prejudices. He never sought to impose Mary on Herzen or on his family; and so long as they remained in England, Mary continued to live alone with her son in lodgings where he visited her. Chance helped him to solve one of the problems inherent in such unestablished unions by providing Mary with an occupation for her long lonely hours. In her lodgings at Mortlake she found a woman living, with the eight survivors of her ten children, in a basement kitchen, where there was seldom anything to cook and where a single bed provided the only sleeping accommodation the family possessed. The woman's husband was in prison for fraud. She was, according to Ogarev's report to Herzen, 'really an educated woman, though with a slight tinge of religiosity, brought on by her sufferings'. She had been a

* There is no clue to the identity of the Prince, unless it was Prince Golitsin; in which case the 'wife' must have been the young lady from Voronezh.

governess before her marriage, knew French, and liked to show verses she had written in happier days. Now she worked as a seamstress, and the older children made toys to sell in an unavailing effort to provide the family with enough to eat. The bustling, good-natured Mary shared food and clothing with them, helped with the work, and received in return lessons in English grammar. Ogarev contributed a pound for their support, and begged another pound for them from Herzen. The innumerable children were heaven-sent playmates for Henry, and Ogarev heartily approved; for though they went barefoot and were underfed, manners cost nothing and they had been nicely brought up. Their mother had stared want too long in the face to be embarrassed by the social standing of her benefactress, or to inquire into the sources of the charity bestowed on her.

Generally speaking Ogarev is too much absorbed in the cares of love and education for his letters to throw much light on the English life of the period. But there is an occasional lapse into *faits divers* of this order, culled from the contemporary press:

Two young girls in Chelsea have died of hunger; they were so thin that there was no flesh on their bones and their skin was of a greenish colour. A man was hanged who had cut his throat, but who had been brought back to life. They hanged him for suicide. The doctor had warned them that it was impossible to hang him as the throat would burst open and he would breathe through the aperture. They did not listen to his advice and hanged their man.* The wound in the neck immediately opened and the man came to life again although he was hanged. It took time to convoke the aldermen [*sic*] to decide the question what was to be done. At length the aldermen assembled and bound up the neck below the wound *until he died*. Oh my Mary, what a crazy society and what a stupid civilization.

The following comes from another letter:

You can read in the paper the discussion in Parliament on the increase in the number of child murders. Somebody proposed to open an institution to which women and girls could hand over their children, so that the birth and education of the children would cost them nothing. In my country such institutions exist. But the majority in Parliament rejected the proposal as *immoral*. You will understand once more why Robert Owen had no success in this country.

* It will be recollected that the execution referred to must have taken place in public. Executions in England were public until 1868.

Throughout the greater part of this period Ogarev was living, no longer under the same roof with Natalie and Herzen, but alone in lodgings. He had continued to endure the 'Bedlam' of Putney until the house was given up in November 1858; and he once more lived with Herzen at Alpha Road, Regent's Park, during Natalie's absence on the Continent in 1860. Soon after Natalie's return, the cup of his suffering overflowed, and he fled to a furnished room in Richmond, whence he could more easily take refuge in Mary's arms at Mortlake. But Ogarev was as incapable as Herzen of remaining long in the same spot; and his irregular and intemperate habits led to trouble with landladies. We hear of him in Sydenham, in Putney, in Wimbledon, and finally again in Richmond. The assurance given to Mary in the first flush of enthusiasm that he was 'drinking only water' was forgotten. The clearness of vision which he had ascribed to the uses of this beverage proved, in the long run, less delectable than the blinding intoxication of alcohol. Solitude removed the last social and conventional restraints on self-indulgence; and these years of loneliness in London lodgings, tempered by sentimental pilgrimages to Mortlake, mark a decisive step in the decay of Ogarev's health and faculties. At the age of fifty, which he reached in the last year of this rake's progress through the London suburbs, he was already an old man.

It was in April 1865 that Ogarev, accompanied by Mary and shepherded by Ciernecki, made the difficult passage from London to Geneva. The first year in Geneva was spent by him at the Château de la Boissière in conditions which have been described in an earlier chapter; and Mary continued, as in London, to live apart. Then in the spring of 1866 came the move to the suburb of Lancy, where they installed themselves for the first time under the same roof. Ogarev's habits were abated, but not cured, by the establishment of this quasi-marital relationship. In February 1868 he once more fell in the street and broke his ankle. He never fully recovered the use of his leg, and for the rest of his days moved uneasily on crutches or on a stick. Shortly after the accident he and Mary removed to a little house in the quaintly named Rue des Petits Philosophes. 'It is good for the road to have a great one,' wrote Herzen to Tata, 'and not bad for Ogarev to be so modest.' The house was surrounded by a flower-garden, and its southern wall was covered by a vine; and in these idyllic conditions Ogarev lived a life of 'mineral immobility tempered by the vicinity of a tavern to the right and a tavern to the left'.

From this time onward Mary, as his nurse and attendant, became a physical as well as a moral necessity of Ogarev's existence. He could not stir without her; and except for his brief visit to Prangins in the summer of the same year, they never again allowed themselves to be parted. All Mary's earlier letters have disappeared; but chance preserved, in the archives of the Herzen family, a set of five which she wrote to him during his stay at Prangins. The half illiterate Mary is, as one might expect, almost completely inarticulate on paper. Her letters might pass for classics of the commonplace; but they reveal the depth of her solicitude for Ogarev as well as the limitations of her mind. They are completely uniform and monotonous; and almost any extract would serve as a fair sample of the little collection:

Lord, how time flies! I got your letter on Friday and was so pleased; I had begun to think that something had happened. And now how are you? I was so glad to find your socks, I will send them by Mr T[chorzewski]. Probably Mr T will call tomorrow, but I do not know for certain. Now I will say good night, my darling, I am so tired, I will finish tomorrow. One little kiss.

I am better, but tomorrow I must go about my bandage. The one they have made for me doesn't fit. They must stretch the old one, and I must get them to make another exactly like the old one. Today I have had a busy day full of various trifles. I expect Mr T is still at Berne. Today it is Sunday, just seven o'clock in the evening, I expect you are all just having supper. My monthlies have not yet come on. I am glad you have breakfast in your own room. I haven't taken the iron yet as I have been taking magnesia, my stomach was in a very bad state. How is Toots? Give him a kiss from me. If Mr T comes, I will send him some of his things, but I expect they will not keep him long, they said two days.

No, I am not drinking much beer now. It is just nine o'clock. I had supper with Henry. He has not been out, he has been working all day. He sends you greetings. I am so glad you are keeping well all this time. Your room must be very nice with a view on to the lake. I am very glad Olga has a good voice. The story of the ladies and the jam made me laugh. I should like to know your dreams. I have never once dreamed about you. I shall post this letter this evening, last thing, so that you may get it tomorrow.

Good-bye, my dear, I kiss you very tenderly.

The surviving fragments of correspondence between Ogarev and Mary cannot supply a complete or coherent picture of this queer relationship; but no doubt can remain of the sincerity of their mutual devotion. The letters nowhere contain a word of reproach, of irritation, of disaccord, of anything but the most perfect harmony and confidence. 'She never insulted me,' wrote Ogarev in his last year, 'always treated me with respect and with gratitude for Henry's education, looked after me in my illness, and struggled with me against my drinking habits, though she never dared to interfere with them.' There is indeed a constant temptation, when writing of Mary Sutherland, to follow Ogarev's own example and to substitute for the living woman the romantic lay-figure of the prostitute purified by love. It becomes difficult to re-capture the living personality of the woman who once walked the London streets and solicited in the public-houses of the West End.

Such unpleasant traits as we find in our material about Mary Sutherland come for the most part from the bitterly hostile pen of Natalie Ogarev. It is she who tells the story of the dreadful end of Charlotte Hudson, young Alexander Herzen's former mistress. It happened in 1867, when Charlotte, abandoned and forgotten by her lover, was living with her boy Toots under the same roof with Ogarev, Mary and Henry at Lancy. This is how Natalie Ogarev relates the tragic event in her *Memoirs*:

When she [Charlotte] came from England with little Toots, they put her in Ogarev's house; but Mary soon became jealous of the affection which Charlotte inspired in Ogarev and in her own son Henry. Charlotte loved Ogarev as a father; and when she heard from Ogarev reproaches which she did not understand she realized that Mary had been blackening her character to Ogarev. On the last day she wept bitterly, asked Mary for vodka, and was given it. In the evening she disappeared; and this gave the virtuous Mary a chance to spread the story that Charlotte had left the child in her care and run off with a new lover. But the Rhône punished Mary and avenged her unhappy victim. Four years later it released from a sandbank and brought to the surface Charlotte's body. The police recollected the disappearance of an English girl from Lancy, and invited Mary to inspect the remains of her victim; there was still a boot on one foot and a bunch of keys in a pocket. Mary recognized the keys and the remains. Did not her heart shudder at her wicked slanders?

It requires the concentrated vindictiveness peculiar to Natalie Ogarev to find the main motive of Charlotte Hudson's suicide not in the heartless desertion of her lover, but in the petty persecution of her compatriot.* But the story possesses certain elements of verisimilitude. Mary Sutherland found herself isolated in a foreign country in the company of another Englishwoman who was younger and more attractive than herself, and who, though probably of similar social origins, had been content with a single lover and had maintained herself on a higher place of self-respect. It was unlikely that relations between the two women and their children would be smooth or easy. Jealousy was an emotion which Mary, with all her limitations, thoroughly understood; and if Charlotte showed, voluntarily or involuntarily, any signs of finding favour with the mild and impressionable Ogarev, Mary's jealousy must have been virulent and unsparing. When Charlotte disappeared, Mary was probably relieved that there was now no one to contest with her the possession of Ogarev's affections; and she may well have felt a glow of self-conscious virtue in the belief that Charlotte was now no better than she had once been herself. Such at any rate is a conjectural reconstruction, on the hint supplied by Natalie, of Mary's state of mind at the time of Charlotte's tragic end.

Another episode, also recorded by Natalie, shows more pleasingly and more convincingly how Mary Sutherland could, on occasion, return to the traditions of her origin and class. It was in 1870, when the Swiss authorities were still hesitating whether to arrest and surrender Nechaev to the Russian Government as a common criminal, or to accord him the right of asylum as a political refugee. The colony of Russian exiles assembled one evening in a Geneva café to discuss their attitude. Were they to dissociate themselves from Nechaev as a malefactor, or to declare themselves 'solid' with him and petition the Swiss Government on his behalf? Natalie Ogarev, who attended the meeting with Tata Herzen, found herself sitting, by accident or design, beside her husband. The debates were heated and loquacious. Ogarev was,

---

* When Charlotte Hudson's body was recovered in 1870 Ogarev wrote his last poem; and his diagnosis of the tragedy is at once kinder and simpler:

> Her brain gave way – so difficult was her life;
> And love and home-sickness drowned her.

as frequently happened, not entirely sober; and he took no part
in the proceedings except to murmur inaudibly from time to time:
'Take pity on him! Petition for him!'

At midnight, when the meeting was about to break up in
confusion, Mary Sutherland burst into the café. Her steps were
unsteady; but Natalie Ogarev, unused to the righteous emotion of
the woman who retrieves her man at closing-time from the public-
house, was perhaps uncharitable in supposing her to be drunk.
Mary could not be expected to understand why a bevy of exiled
Russians had assembled by night in a café to discuss their 'solidarity' with Nechaev; why Ogarev should have once more succumbed to the twin temptations of politics and alcohol; and,
above all, why he should be sitting, in fuddled amity, side by side
with the wife who had shamelessly and heartlessly deserted him
twelve years or more ago. These things were not provided for in
Mary's philosophy. She reacted in a perfectly normal way. She
elbowed her way roughly through the crowd until she reached
Ogarev's side and, raising her fists, began to abuse Natalie in
good cockney. Natalie looked round for help, protesting in mock
alarm that 'she did not know how to fight'; and Nechaev and
some other Russians quietly removed Mary from the café.
Nechaev, who had seen much of Ogarev's *ménage* in recent weeks,
expressed the judicious opinion that Ogarev would 'get it' when
he arrived home.

The death of Herzen at the beginning of 1870 was an irretriev-
able blow to his life-long friend. So long as Herzen lived, the
movement which he had created remained, at any rate in outward
semblance, intact; and in this movement Ogarev occupied an
honoured and uncontested place. But when Herzen died, the
whole organization dissolved in dust, like a body in which life has
long been extinct. Ogarev's revolutionary career was ended. He
served for a few months as a tool in the hands of Bakunin and
Nechaev, who threw him aside when they discovered that his
pliancy was mere weakness. The family was scattered; and there
was no motive other than lethargy and habit to bind Ogarev to
Geneva.

The final impulse to change the manner and place of his abode
seems to have come from a quarrel with Natalie. Ogarev had a
gentle, wistful love for the daughter who bore his name; and as

long as Natalie, wandering restlessly between France, Switzerland and Italy, sometimes brought Liza to see him, he would probably have been content to remain. But eventually – it was in or about 1873 – the inevitable happened. An open and irremediable clash occurred between the disdainful, vindictive Natalie and the jealous, susceptible Mary Sutherland. It is recorded by Ogarev in words of characteristic mildness and humility:

Natalie came lately to my house to abuse Mary, saying that everyone marvelled how a man like myself could have linked himself with a woman from a pot-house, and that the Russians in Geneva had ceased to visit me on that account. All I can say is that those who were really my friends have not ceased to come. As for false friends, their not visiting me was a cause for rejoicing and certainly not for *chagrin*. Besides, Natalie might have regarded me as a pot-house man rather than Mary as a pot-house woman. She might have remembered my drunkenness at the time when I was studying chemistry at Yakhontovo and used to drink neat spirit out of the test-tubes. . . .

I translated Natalie's insults to Mary, who at once asked her to go away. Since that time I have not seen Natalie, and have of course no desire to see her. I wrote a letter to explain how mean and cruel her last visit had been. She never answered this letter, and only wrote to me another abusive letter to which I refused to reply. In that way I designed to sever all relations between us, and seem to have succeeded – to my complete satisfaction.

Remembering her treatment of Olga Herzen (now Olga Monod) I cannot regard Natalie as an upright and good-hearted woman. I am only sorry for poor Liza; but there is nothing to be done, you cannot help. Natalie's influence will spoil any life. The defects of her character, i.e. malice, envy and self-love, are more cruel and more inescapable than our sinful but guileless vices.

Such was the epitaph of the bright romance which had begun a quarter of a century before, to the discomfiture of Madame de Salias, in that gay exchange of visits and letters between Aksheno and Yakhontovo.

Next year the decision was taken. Save for Tata Herzen, who came to see him from time to time, Ogarev was now utterly cut off from his Russian friends and his old associations. Twenty years of life abroad had left him, stranded and abandoned, in the faithful and jealous arms of his English mistress and nurse. It was natural that the future should rest with Mary, and it was natural that she, who had preserved all her insularity and could never master foreign speech or ways, should take him back to her own country. In September 1874, having sold all their furniture except a dining-table, they embarked at Genoa on a ship bound for Newcastle-on-Tyne. Thence they travelled south and settled in a small house in a mean street of Greenwich. The choice must have been Mary's; it may have been her native place.

The story of poor Nick is now almost at an end. He lived on for nearly three years, in a room surrounded by the relics of his dead friends. A bust of Granovsky stood prominently on a bracket in the corner. On the walls hung photographs of Herzen, Belinsky and Stankevich and a large oil painting of himself as a young man; and there was a frame which contained, side by side, portraits of Herzen, Bakunin and himself surmounted by the proud legend 'Champions of Liberty'. Of the comrades of his own generation only Bakunin still lived on; and it was a rare event when – it happened in November 1874 – a letter reached Greenwich from the old veteran, now settled with his wife's family in the little lake town of Lugano.

Most important of all [wrote Bakunin] write to me how and with whom you are living, whom you meet and with whom you spend your time. I fear that the English society of your wife (without the blessings of the Church), to whom I send greetings, cannot be particularly interesting for you, and that in London, more than ever and more than anywhere, you will feel lonely; and at our age such a feeling is hard to bear. There is one consolation – the nearness of death.

But Bakunin, though broken in health, still kept the eager restless spirit of youth; and the mood of resignation did not last more than a few moments. He ends the letter with an appeal to his old friend to read John Stuart Mill's *Autobiography*, on which (together with the works of Schopenhauer) he had recently been engaged.

Have you read the *Autobiography?* If not, read it without fail. An extraordinarily interesting and instructive work. Write to me what you are reading, and recommend to me anything worth while. We have done enough teaching, brother. In old age it is time to learn again. That is more cheerful.

But it was seldom that any voice now reached Ogarev from the busy, turbulent world of which he had once formed a part. His retirement was complete; and there were none of those who had once loved him to notice how his faculties were failing. 'I cannot ride in any kind of carriage,' he wrote to his sister in Russia, 'it makes my head go round. I only go for walks in Greenwich with my lame leg, but I can walk quite comfortably.' His mind was gradually returning to childhood. He talked often and incoherently of his own country and the days of his youth. When a rare Russian visitor came to Greenwich, through 'a yellow fog thick with the odour of coal-dust, sulphur and salt fish', to pay her respects to the old revolutionary, he asked her whether Russian gendarmes still carried halberds – an accoutrement which they had already discarded before he reached manhood. Mary Sutherland, 'small, dark-haired, less angular and less self-satisfied than most Englishwomen', bustled helpfully behind the tea-pot, and explained that this was not one of Nick's best days. But when the visitor said goodbye to the frail figure in a blue jacket under the gas-jet in the hall, she felt that she had before her only the empty husk of what had once been a man. Poor Nick was only sixty-two. But disease and indulgence had exhausted his vitality; and he faded slowly and painlessly away.

When, at the beginning of June 1877, it became certain that his end was near, Mary telegraphed for Tata Herzen. She came, escorted by Gabriel Monod, Olga's husband. Poor Nick was now only intermittently conscious. He recognized Tata, and spoke to her in English, the language of his old age. He lay for several days in a state of coma interrupted by moments of dim consciousness. In his last incoherent murmurings, barely heard by the listening Tata, he reverted to his native tongue. They related not to Mary Sutherland or to Natalie Tuckhov or to Maria Roslaslev – the only women who had held more than a passing sway over his gentle heart – but to Herzen, the unique friend, who for good and evil had dominated his whole life. Then on the afternoon of 12 June he stopped breathing.

Tata did not stay for the funeral. The sole link had snapped which had made it possible for her to support the company of Mary Sutherland; and there were fleas in her bed. She chose a site for the grave, and made the necessary provision for the funeral; then she hurried back to Paris. Some months later she received by post a photograph of the tomb and of Mary in widow's weeds sitting beside it. The spot can still be found in the lofty, open cemetery on Shooter's Hill; and the pilgrim, thrusting aside the overgrown shrubs which half conceal the stone, may still read the inscription which records that 'Nicholas Ogareff of Aksheno, Penza, Russia' was born on 6 December 1814 and died on 12 June 1877. Nobody knows what became of the bust of Granovsky and the pictures and photographs among which poor Nick spent his last years. They probably found their way, sooner or later, to some junk-shop in the East End.

CHAPTER 17

The Last Tragedy

THE death of Herzen had deprived Natalie of the one fixed point in her restless unhappy life. The large clan which had once gathered round them in London was altogether dispersed. The twins were dead; Olga was about to marry her Frenchman; young Alexander was now a family man in Florence; Ogarev was being cared for in Geneva by his English mistress. Natalie, Tata and Liza alone remained – two helpless women and a child – well enough provided for financially, but without home or country or fixed purpose in life. It was natural that after a few months in Geneva – the anxious months of the *affaire Nechaev* – Natalie should revive, in all seriousness, the plan which had flitted so many times during the past seven years through her distraught mind. She decided in the spring of 1871 to return to her family in Russia, taking Tata as well as Liza with her; and this narrative should end with a record of their departure. But the Russian Government once more – and for the last time – intervened fatally and effectively in the life of the Romantic Exiles. It refused, through the mouth of its consul in Geneva, to permit these dangerous conspirators to re-enter its territory.

The refusal, which was repeated in the following year, had every appearance of being final; and Natalie was thrown back on the round of aimless wandering from city to city in western Europe which had become second nature to her. We hear of her in Zürich, in Florence, in Nice and in Paris. Sometimes she lived with Tata and sometimes apart from her; but Liza was always her inseparable companion. It had at one time been Herzen's desire that the girl should be called Herzen-Ogarev and thus commemorate in her person the life-long union of the two friends. But since Herzen's death Liza had openly taken his name; and Natalie was proud when people detected her resemblance to him. Natalie was now commonly referred to as Herzen's widow; and with the death of Herzen and the disappearance of Ogarev, the embarrassments of an unconventional situation had faded away. There is no evidence that consciousness of an irregular origin played any part in Liza's abnormal development.

Liza, 'the offspring of an eagle and a serpent', inherited from her father his striking forehead and quick intelligence. It was not merely an old man's partiality for the last-born which marked her out as the most brilliant of Herzen's children. A Russian girl student, Elizaveta Litvinov by name, who met her during the winter of 1872–3 at Zürich, detected in Liza 'an exceptional mind, delicate feelings, and the beginning of lofty ambitions'. Other qualities seemed more clearly a legacy from her mother. Before she was eight, she would beg her parents not to tell the English visitors in the hotels and *pensions* where they stayed that she had been born in England, in order that they might admire the more her knowledge of English. The need for attention and admiration, carried to the point of hysteria, seems to have been implanted from her earliest years in Liza's character.

Elizaveta Litvinov has left an unforgettable picture of the external aspect of mother and daughter:

The daughter is tall and slender as a reed, dressed fashionably, elegantly, with French *chic*. The mother tiny, with short-cropped,* grey hair which, pressed down under her hat, lies in a fringe on her yellow neck. She dresses untidily, all in black, but with trimmings of contrasted colours – on the coat brown, on the hat blue, on the dress green. The daughter walks rapidly with long strides; the mother struggles after her at a little trot, swaying and stumbling as she goes. The daughter takes not the slightest notice of her mother's difficulty in keeping up with her. When she has got well ahead of her mother, she stops, poses, looks back contemptuously and gives an impatient shrug of her shoulders. You are struck at first by the irregularity of the girl's features; but a broad high forehead, intelligent, bold, light-grey eyes and an extraordinarily delicate complexion redeem the first impression. Her expression is a striking combination of imperiousness and shyness. She is very much spoilt by a projecting upper lip, of which she is evidently conscious, as she is continually biting it with her small fine teeth.

The shyness of Liza was the reserve of a proud and self-absorbed nature, disinclined to share with those around her the secret workings of her heart. Her imperiousness found an ample outlet

* Short hair in women was, at this time, the recognized uniform of radical opinions.

in her attitude to her mother. Liza had soon taken the measure of Natalie's fond, foolish and aimlessly querulous maternity; and Natalie ceased to have any influence over her daughter save as an infectious example of restless, unsatisfied indulgence in turbulent emotions. Separated from her mother, Liza could still feel and express affection for her; compelled to live with her she treated her with a tragic mixture of hostility and contempt – emotions which did not exclude a large measure of conscious or unconscious imitation. In this uneasy relationship, Tata Herzen from time to time intervened as an awkward *tertium quid*. Full of generous intuitions, floundering in a morass of chronic misunderstandings, she was alternately coaxed and abused by both sides. Of the three, Liza was the most determined and the most unscrupulous – with the naïve unscrupulousness of extreme youth; and it was she who had most of the game. Again and again she begged Tata to take her away from Natalie, and became hysterical in imitation of her mother. In the summer of 1874 the breaking-point was reached; and on the eve of her sixteenth birthday Liza declared that she could no longer live under her mother's roof. It was arranged that Tata should accompany her on a visit to Alexander and his family in Florence, the duration of which was left tactfully undefined; and in September they left Natalie alone in Zürich, and set off via Geneva for Italy.

At Florence, in the autumn of 1874, in Alexander Herzen's villa on the slopes below Fiesole, began the tragic last act of Liza's short life. The other principal actor in it was a French *savant*, Charles Letourneau by name. He was already known as the author of a work entitled *La Physiologie des Passions*, now remembered chiefly as one of Émile Zola's sources of inspiration; he published during the year 1875 a text-book of biology; and these two works were followed by numerous other treatises of scientific or philosophical character. He survived until 1902; and there was nothing either in his earlier or in his later life to suggest that his share in Liza's tragedy was anything but an incalculable and irrelevant episode in an otherwise ordinary career. He was, when he first met Liza, in his forty-fourth year. He was living with his wife and two small children at Florence, where he was engaged as a lecturer at the University; and he was an acquaintance, though not an intimate friend, of Alexander Herzen and his family.

It had been contemplated, when they left Switzerland, that Tata and Liza would spend at most two or three months at Florence and rejoin Natalie in Paris for the winter. But at the end of November a change of plan ensued, and it was arranged that they should spend the winter in Florence.

> Tata is making up her mind! [wrote Liza to her mother]. Tata has decided! God knows why we are staying, but we are staying. Human nature is strange; some secret influence impelled Tata to do what I so much wanted, and wanted twice as much since I knew that you were not opposed to it. 'We shall spend the winter here.' Do not seek any secret reasons – there are none. Don't you remember when I was at Zürich, how much I did not want to go to Paris, and how everything lured me to Florence? I must say that I have now a feeling of physical well-being which plays some part in the matter. I am no longer the 'tired creature' which you used to call me. On the contrary, I jump and shout with the children like a young child.

It may well be that the secret reasons, whose existence she so eagerly denies, had not yet emerged into Liza's consciousness. The mood of naïve exultation in which the letter was written is perhaps scarcely compatible with full self-knowledge. But the reader of the later correspondence has no difficulty in diagnosing the cause of her eagerness to remain in Florence or of the sense of physical well-being which had suddenly swept over her. Liza was in love with Charles Letourneau; and a few weeks later she had begun to write to him what must be one of the most remarkable series of love-letters ever penned by a girl of sixteen to a man almost thirty years older than herself.

The first of the extant letters* may be quoted in extenso as a specimen of the whole:

> I am sad and lonely and have no one to whom to give my hand in moments of uncertainty or despair. What can one do here on earth? Desire? Why should one for ever desire in vain? True, it kills time, but

* The letter in question, like many of the others, is undated. The letters were preserved by Charles Letourneau, and eventually returned by him to Natalie Ogarev, and were printed more than fifty years later as they were found among her papers. There is therefore a faint presumption (it cannot be called more) that the order in which they are printed is correct. Internal evidence does not help; for the tone does not perceptibly change throughout the series. The first dated letter from Liza to Letourneau bears the date 14 February 1875.

desire carries away our best years. Love? But love whom? To love for a moment is not worth while; to love for ever is impossible. Suffer? Suffer for a passion at which you will laugh as soon as you are cured of it? Shut yourself up in yourself? But our feelings are so mean and petty, our joys so trivial, our sufferings so insignificant! Observe life and not repine? Perhaps that is the best choice – not to intervene in life. But then you perceive that life is all a vulgar, stupid joke, a clumsy play on words.

Thus far the letter is a fairly accurate paraphrase of the most popular romantic lyric in the Russian language, a poem of Lermontov; and we are left uncertain whether Letourneau was intended to recognize the quotation or to suppose that he was reading the unprompted effusion of Liza's disillusioned spirit. She continues in her own person:

How true that is! I do not complain that you have shattered all my plans for the future. Once, in times past, I saw things in a better light. I said to myself: 'You will study, you are not dull, you have sufficient curiosity to take an interest in science. It is impossible for any man, whoever he may be, to love the same woman all his life, particularly if that woman is – I'. But if he loves another, what am I to do? To kill myself – the same old story. Why begin, if the best and surest solution of the problem is to end it?

In those days I naïvely imagined that children were an inexhaustible source of joy and happiness! How chimerical! Anxiety about them may drive their parents to the grave. (1) A wife no longer loves the father of her children, or he has ceased to love her; yet they must remain together and hate each other in silence for the sake of the children. (2) In infancy children are often ailing and what becomes of the mother then? It is an unbroken chain of suffering. (3) When they grow up, we are tormented by other cares – for their future: what will they become? what dangers await them? will their heart suffer, or their brain, or must they expect financial troubles? (4) The greatest grief of all still remains: your children turn away from you, they have different beliefs, different ideas, different tastes; or what if one of them has a worthless, vulgar soul or an empty place instead of a heart?

No, I do not complain of my fate. All other fates seem bad. If I had the choice between all possible existences, I should choose – guess what! To be your shadow so that I might always, always see you. I try to console myself in my sufferings with the thought that others suffer too; but if you knew how silly I am! Yesterday as I lay in bed, I imagined to myself that I was alone in the world, that nobody loved me. I felt an insensate desire to press you to me, to embrace you, to stifle you; I seized my pillow and squeezed it convulsively, biting the sheet. I do not know how it happens that when you are there I have, as you say, such a downcast look; for in your presence I not only lose my wits, but my heart leaps as if it would jump out of my breast and tell you that it loves you, that it is ready to do everything that you wish, in a word, that it is your slave. To be a torturer would become you remarkably well; I wish you would torture me a little, for there is nothing more terrible than indifference.

Au revoir!

I am afraid that Tata will make a scene. I pretended to have a headache; and here it is nearly midnight, and I am not yet in bed.

This amazing combination of furious passion and cynical reflexion cannot, it is clear, be brought within the normal and permitted limits of calf-love; and students of heredity will compare the infatuation of the sixteen-year-old Liza for Letourneau with the infatuation of the nineteen-year-old Natalie Tuchkov for Ogarev. If Liza, in the self-abandon of her passion for Letourneau, turned her back on Natalie, Natalie had in her day – and with scarcely less egoism – deserted her parents to elope with a lover twenty years older than herself. Mother and daughter are clearly of the same stock; and the greater precocity of Liza's development may be attributed to the greater freedom and the peculiar circumstances of her upbringing. Her parentage had been equivocal. Her father had, ever since she could remember, been no more than a fleeting and occasional vision. Her mother, ever since her birth, and particularly since the death of the twins, had been a pronounced hysteric; and the tense relation between mother and daughter (which clearly inspired the precocious reflexions on parenthood in the letter just quoted) had created in Liza's passionate and impressionable soul the dangerous complex of the unloved child. Finally, she had for ten years been dragged continually from country to country and from town to town; and her keen intelligence had been undisciplined by any regular education. All these conditions had made of Liza at sixteen an abnormal being. Her warm affections, hitherto untaught to fix themselves on any person or any place on the earth's surface, burst at the moment of adolescence into an uncontrollable flame of morbid sexual infatuation.

311

The literary element in Liza's passion for Charles Letourneau should, however, not be overlooked; for it has left its marks both on the course of the affair and on the romantic flamboyancy of her epistolary style. The attempts of Natalie Ogarev to direct her daughter's reading had been intermittent, naïve and pathetically ineffective:

Please do not read at random [she wrote when Liza confessed to having read George Sand's novel *Leone Leoni*]. Consult Tata. *Leone Leoni*, though very attractively written, is an unhealthy book full of unnatural passions. I told you before that you ought not to read it; but you apparently forgot.

Such exhortations could produce only one result; and Liza – perhaps one of the last victims of that strange romantic craze – lived in a world peopled by George Sand's heroes and heroines.

The other day [she wrote in one of her letters to Letourneau] they were talking about a novel of George Sand, in which the heroine makes a formal declaration of love. – * exclaimed: 'What a horror! To make a declaration of love to a man who does not love you! What lack of self-respect.' And – added something to this effect: 'Such a thing will never happen to me.' Tell me, please, why it is worse than when a man declares his love to a woman who does not love him? I do not understand.

Her limited knowledge of Russian literature was turned to equally prompt account. She not only paraphrased the romantic despair of Lermontov, she found in Pushkin's masterpiece, *Evgin Onegin*, a model for her conduct and a parallel for her situation. In *Evgin Onegin*, Tatyana, the most famous of all Russian heroines, declares her passion for Onegin who, as Liza carefully explains to Letourneau, 'after talking with her, reads her a moral lecture and takes his departure' – only to repent in vain in the last canto. The moral for Letourneau is naïvely obvious and direct. But he is not to think that he is a mere unsubstantial hero of romance.

In my eyes [she continues] George Sand and all the rest of the world together are not worth your little finger; you may not believe me, but it is true. My egoism frightens me. I am ready to say, in the words of

* Most of the proper names in these letters were erased by Letourneau before the letters were sent back to Natalie.

the Russian proverb: 'Let me only see you, and the grass may stop growing for all I care.'

She must see him – must see him every day, if only for half an hour. The only possible alternative is suicide – a threat to which she returns, in language which might well seem forced and rhetorical, in nearly every letter she writes:

> There is too little water in the Arno to drown myself; besides the whole responsibility would rest on Tata. But in Paris I can do what I like. I can only see one argument against suicide, that *then* I should not have the slightest possibility of seeing you. It may strike you as ridiculous that, if I were asked which I prefer – to die, or to suffer for twenty-three and a half hours a day but for the other half hour to be the happiest creature on earth – I should without hesitation choose the second. But if I knew for certain that I should never see you again, I should hesitate no longer.

The figure of Charles Letourneau is more commonplace and less complex than that of Liza. He was too honourable – or, perhaps, too conventional – to take advantage, in any crude sense of the term, of the infatuation he had inspired. He was shocked by it, and was vaguely conscious of its abnormality. But it does not fall to the lot of every middle-aged man to be madly worshipped by a young girl of precocious physical attractions and mental development; and although he described himself, in a subsequent letter to Natalie Ogarev, as 'one of the few Frenchmen who are devoid of vanity', Letourneau had enough of that quality – it did not perhaps require much – to be flattered by the extraordinary attentions of which he found himself the object. He preached reason to Liza; but he preached it in terms so fluent and so impassioned that the effect of his words contradicted their ostensible purpose. The author of *Les Liaisons Dangereuses* had, a hundred years before, revealed the hazards of parleying, even on the loftiest moral plane, with a passion which you seek to discourage. But Letourneau, who was merely the author of *La Physiologie des Passions*, could not be expected to penetrate the finer subtleties of the human heart.

It is difficult to determine how far we should hold Letourneau responsible for sowing the first seeds of Liza's infatuation during the winter of 1874–5. His first extant letter to her was written in

313

May 1875.* By that time Tata and Liza had already left Florence for Paris, and Letourneau and his family were preparing to follow. The moment when a skilful hand might have nipped Liza's passion in the bud was long past; and Letourneau's letter was provoked by her threat to poison herself in the event of a breach between them. This was his reply:

This is a sermon, my dear Baby, and you must read it with attention. How many divisions will it have? I don't know, but there will be several of them, and all extremely important. I suppose the title 'Baby' has already rather annoyed you. I assume that, and count on it. But how can I help calling 'Baby' one who thinks like a child and dares to communicate such thoughts to almost serious grown-ups? You have already guessed that I refer to the toxicological part of your letter. I will not dwell on this point, for I am convinced that your own common sense has already brought you to reason. But what a strange proof of devotion – to quit a man irrevocably in order to prove to him that you love him! What rampant egoism – to cause him cruel pain because you are separated from him by obstacles against which he is powerless! Think no more of these follies. Do not speak of them. Believe that I particularly esteem rational beings. Of course, it is impossible to think of any close union between us. Such a step would be ruinous for you and criminal of me. It would, apart from that, be the surest way of curing you. You do not know me. You cannot judge people by what they reveal to their best friends. There is always a certain amount of pose, and once you have attained maturity and self-control, you conceal your weaknesses, your defects, your feelings of all kinds – partly from fear of embarrassing people, partly from vanity. Whatever you may think, you have made a pretty poor choice; and it is at any rate necessary that you should have nothing to repent of, that you should be free, bound by no ties, free from secret regrets, and should have nothing serious to reproach me with, on that day when you will judge me as I judge myself, and as I am in reality. That day will come beyond doubt, whatever you may think. At your age and with your untamed nature, feelings are so passionate that the future is not taken into account; only the present seems important. But the future, which you despise, will in its turn become the present, and you must not spoil it. To risk your whole future for a few days of what now seems to you the highest happiness but would soon bore you – that would really be a reckless

* The letter is placed in the wrong order in the published collection. It is dated approximately by the reference in the last paragraph to Liza's departure for 'Babylon', i.e. Paris.

action. Yes, yes. I can see you. You are beginning to pout. I am only a cold-blooded preacher. I cannot help being a preacher, since I am writing a sermon. As far as any coldness is concerned, I am trying with all my might to achieve it. But this is not always easy; for your feeling for me, so unreserved, so complete, so care-free, always moves me and sometimes shakes my determination.

Lastly (since every sermon must have its 'lastly'), I ask you to believe that nobody takes so lively an interest in you as I. Let us remain what we have been – friends in reason. Meanwhile, I have fewer people to love me than you suppose, and none of them loves me as you do. I see that, I know it, and I shall not forget it.

Then after a paragraph of gossip about the love-affairs of some of their Florentine friends, Letourneau ends as follows:

Your departure has in fact broken up all our little colony. We scarcely see one another, and it is really quite time for us to follow you to Babylon. We shall do so probably at the end of this week. I will of course let you know the date of our departure when it is definitely fixed.

To our early, early meeting!

CH. L.

The months of June and July saw all the actors in the drama assembled in or around Paris. Natalie Ogarev had moved up from Zürich and was living in rooms. Tata and Liza installed themselves first in the apartment of Olga, who was now married and the mother of two infants, then in the *environs* of Paris, at Maisons-Lafitte. The situation thus became infinitely more complicated. Liza, the most intelligent member of the party, soon resumed her old game of playing off her mother against Tata, and fanned the flame of her mother's jealousy. When Tata, now fully alive to the danger, intercepted Letourneau's letters and refused Liza his address, Liza wheedled it out of her mother. She even dangled before Natalie the prospect of returning to live with her; and Letourneau, who was privy to the scheme, cunningly advised his young friend to insist on 'various conditions' (presumably the freedom of her correspondence with him) as the price of going to live once more under her mother's roof.

This turn of events isolated Tata, who was momentarily faced with the triple enmity of Liza, Letourneau and Natalie. Letourneau writes to Liza that his relations with Tata, formerly friendly and sincere, were now 'at the point of the thermometer where mercury freezes'; and Liza, by way of explaining the change, maliciously suggests that Tata had supposed Letourneau to be in love with her and was venting on him the bitterness of her own disillusionment. Meanwhile Natalie begins to reproach Tata with lack of frankness towards both Liza and herself, and accuses her of interfering with her efforts 'to save Liza'; and on the other hand enters herself into a friendly correspondence with Letourneau. Tata could only hold up her hands in despair and opine that 'it would end by their all going to the madhouse'.

The situation was not much relieved when Letourneau left with his family for the coast of Normandy early in August. His letters to Liza continue in the same mingled strain of rational exhortation and sentimental dalliance. But there is a new note in them of bitter hostility to Tata, 'that block of ice', who had apparently succeeded in vetoing a proposal that Liza should accompany the Letourneaus to the sea.

What a pity you are not with us! I often think of it, and regret it. It would have been so simple and easy to arrange but for the extraordinary outburst of Miss N. But never mind. You are very young, and I am not quite old; and we shall succeed in making up for it some day.

And Olga's husband, Gabriel Monod, nicknamed by Letourneau 'the archangel', receives even rougher handling for his unsolicited interference. Letourneau might himself be ready to preach reason to Liza; but he was at least resolved that nobody else should share that prerogative.

The fury of Liza's passion showed no signs of abating; but in September she consented, under Letourneau's advice, to accompany her mother to Nice. It was vaguely agreed that Tata should follow them. But Tata had tasted the embarrassments of a triangular relationship with two such hysterical beings as Natalie and Liza; and she preferred to remain in Paris. The first few days or weeks in Nice passed in relative calm. Natalie felt grateful to Letourneau, whose influence had induced Liza to return to her when all other means of persuasion had failed; and the correspondence between him and Liza was allowed to continue uncensored and uninterrupted. Natalie became convinced that the right way to handle her daughter was by indulging her every whim, and that none of this trouble would ever have happened but for Tata's wicked and ill-judged efforts to apply measures of stern repression to an innocent and affectionate child.

But letters could not long allay Liza's hunger for the presence of her lover. The life of isolation and idleness, which left mother and daughter with no other resource than their mutual society, might well have proved disastrous to their relationship even if mother and daughter had been more normally constituted. Liza's restlessness and irritability became more and more difficult to disguise. By way of a change they tried San Remo. A mild flirtation with a visitor from Corsica provided a temporary diversion. But this did not help. San Remo was merely a miniature Nice. Liza had two, and only two, desires – to be rid of her mother and to return to Florence, where Letourneau was now re-established for the winter. Natalie, weak, lonely and distracted, faltered with various schemes. Some of them were impracticable; and other were rejected outright by Liza. Finally, she offered herself to go with Liza to Florence; and Liza, seeing no other way of realizing her main ambition, consented to accept her mother's company.

It was the end of November when they moved from Nice to Florence. They stayed with Alexander and his family, and the meetings with Letourneau began again on the old basis. Liza managed her mother as easily as she had managed Tata during the previous winter, before Tata's suspicions were aroused. 'Tata and Mamma,' she gaily told a friend, 'are whipping-tops, and I am the child that whips them.' Alexander and his family reproached Natalie for her lack of authority over Liza, and Liza for her treatment of her mother; and Liza rounded on Alexander and accused him of 'taking her mother's side'. The domestic dissensions and tense atmosphere with which Natalie always managed to surround herself enveloped the tranquil Florentine household and prepared it for the culmination of the tragedy.

The events of the closing hours of Liza's life are narrated in a long letter written by Natalie some weeks after the catastrophe. From the family discussions there had emerged a proposal to send Liza to Fontainebleau to resume her neglected education. Liza wished to consult Letourneau about the plan. But he was ill in bed; and Natalie, in a last feeble attempt to impose her will, forbade Liza to visit him alone. She proposed to accompany her daughter. 'I do not want to go with you,' retorted Liza, 'but I shall pay you out.' The visit did not take place. But Liza appeared to recover her spirits, and more than once announced, with unwonted animation, that she was preparing 'a great surprise'. One evening while the children played and the others sat and talked, Liza was writing a letter and she paused in her writing to ask her mother how to spell the French words *traversée* and *fallu*. Later in the evening she told her mother that she was bored, and spoke to her 'very harshly'.

Next morning, Liza sealed the letter in the presence of her mother who supposed it to be intended for Letourneau. Then she pointed to a basket and a penknife which she had bought at Nice and said: 'This is for Letourneau and that for Lucy [Letourneau's child].' Natalie imagined she was speaking of Christmas presents.

In the afternoon Liza was left alone in the house, having refused to go with her mother into the town. When the family returned in the evening, Liza failed to appear. Her door was found to be locked, and no sound came from within. They broke it open. Liza lay on the bed with a cloth soaked in chloroform over her face – dead. They found by her the letter which her mother had seen her seal that morning and had watched her write the evening before. It was in French and ran as follows:

You see, my friends, that I have attempted to make the crossing sooner than was proper (*de faire la traversée plus tot qu'il n'aurait fallu*). Perhaps I shall not succeed – in that case, all the better! We will drink champagne in honour of my resurrection. I shall not regret it – quite the contrary. I write these lines to ask pardon for the trouble and unpleasantness which I am causing you. In addition I would ask you to arrange that those who saw us off at the station when we left for Paris should be present at my burial, if it takes place, or at the banquet in honour of my resurrection (all except the Schiffs).

(2) If I am to be buried, let it be carefully verified that I am dead, for if I wake up in my coffin it will be very unpleasant.

(3) I beg that those of my things which are fit for use should be used. I think it is stupid to preserve or to throw away things which are fit for use.

(4) I have no vote in the family council, but all the same I wish to express my opinion on money matters. Olga and Tata want for nothing; it seems to me therefore that Mamma ought to be provided

with a life-income (a more liberal one than when she was living in Paris), and that the capital and part of the income should go to Alexander. However, that is not my affair. Adieu. Greeting and fraternity.

The life that had begun, seventeen years and three months before, at Laurel House, High Street, Putney, ended at Florence in this tragic and extraordinary blend of precocious despair, adolescent defiance and childish mischief.

The romantic tragedy was played out. There were tears to be shed and agonies of self-reproach to be endured; there was another coffin to be carried to the grim vault at Nice; and there were letters of veiled recrimination to be exchanged with Letourneau. Then the childless Natalie petitioned the Tsar once more for permission to return, alone, to her own people. The authorities relented; and in the spring of 1877, while Ogarev lay slowly dying in Greenwich, she was back among her memories at Aksheno. Both Elena and Satin were dead; but her father and mother still lived on. Natalie enjoyed the longevity not seldom reserved, by an ironical fate, for those whose tempestuous emotions have wrecked the lives of weaker men. She lived with her dead; and forty years after she still dreamed of holding Lola-Boy and Lola-Girl in her arms, or of greeting Herzen on his return from a journey. She went back only once – in extreme old age – to western Europe and to her graves by the sea; and she died at Aksheno in 1913 in her eighty-fifth year.

Epilogue

THE tragedy of Liza is a fitting conclusion to the story of the Romantic Exiles. Six months later Bakunin, once nicknamed 'big Liza', died at Berne in the same stubborn lifelong refusal to compromise with reality. A year more, and the death of Ogarev at Greenwich removed the last of that brilliant generation of the forties, which had left Russia in the plenitude of faith and hope, and which now, thirty years later, found scattered and unhonoured graves in French or Swiss or English soil. Before they died the stream had already swept past them, and had left them, stranded and helpless, far away from the main current of contemporary thought. It is a commonplace to say that the generation of Herzen, Ogarev and Bakunin was – like every other generation – a generation of transition. But the transition through which this generation had to pass was bewilderingly rapid; and men like Herzen and Bakunin, coming from a country whose philosophical equipment and fashionable modes of thought were twenty years behind those of Europe, found themselves superseded long before they had completed their allotted span or their natural faculties had begun to fail. They did not, like more fortunate prophets, enjoy an honoured and admired old age. Other voices drew away their disciples even while they were preaching their gospel. The story of the Romantic Exiles ends appropriately in tragedy and – worse still – in tragedy tinged with futility. But they have their place in history. Just fifty years after his death, the Russian Revolution honoured Herzen among its great precursors by naming after him one of the main thoroughfares of its capital city, and erected monuments to him and to Ogarev, for the admiration and example of modern revolutionary youth, in the precincts of Moscow University.

Bakunin might, but for one circumstance, have taken his rightful place beside them. He might in justice have claimed a more splendid monument than they; for Bakunin was incomparably the greatest leader and agitator thrown up by the revolutionary movement of the nineteenth century. But he made one mistake. He should have died, like Herzen, or taken refuge, like Ogarev, in retirement and decrepitude. In fact, he survived to pit his enfeebled forces against the strength of the new generation, and to contest with Karl Marx, in the name of romantic anarchism, the leadership of the European revolution. In 1872 Marx secured his expulsion from the International, and thereby determined his exclusion for ever from the Marxist calendar of revolutionary saints. No memorial to Bakunin will be found within the confines of the Soviet Union.

The originality of the new revolutionary doctrine of Marx lay not, as unscrupulous adversaries have pretended, in its predatory or its destructive character – for Proudhon had already defined property as theft, and Bakunin was a far more ardent apostle of destruction than Marx – but in the essential quality of its postulates. The cause of revolution before Marx had been idealistic and romantic – a matter of intuitive and heroic impulse. Marx made it materialistic and scientific – a matter of deduction and cold reasoning. Marx substituted economics for metaphysics – the proletarian and the peasant for the philosopher and the poet. He brought to the theory of political evolution the same element of orderly inevitability which Darwin had introduced into biology. The Darwinian and the Marxian theories are strictly comparable in the ruthlessness with which they subordinate human nature and human happiness to the working of a scientific principle; and they have proved perhaps the most important and the most influential products of Victorian science.

It was indeed a new age which dawned when Karl Marx replaced Herzen and Bakunin as the most prominent figure in revolutionary Europe. The drab, respectable monotony of Marx's domestic existence already affords a striking contrast to the many-hued, incalculable diversity of the lives of the Romantic Exiles. In them Romanticism found its last expression; and though there remained a handful of dare-devil terrorists in Russia and of picturesque anarchists in western Europe, the revolutionary movement, as the years progressed, took on more and more of the grim, dogmatic, matter-of-fact characteristics of the later Victorian age. In the person of that typical Victorian *savant* Karl Marx, it entered a phase whose vitality has not yet altogether exhausted itself.

Appendices

Appendix A

ON 27 August 1870, seven months after Herzen's death, Malwida von Meysenbug, on the recommendation of Richard Wagner, wrote to Herwegh on behalf of the Herzen family asking for the return of Natalie Herzen's letters and offering Herwegh in return a 'corresponding number' of his letters to Herzen.

Herwegh replied in the following terms:

Neither now, nor later, nor ever. I have not the honour to know you personally. I know only that you have exhibited in this 'affair' – into which (as my wife said at the time) it would have been a crime to initiate anyone, except four persons, and into which on our side no one ever has been initiated – a zeal worthy of a better cause.

That you, Fräulein, who for years past have entered the Russian service and occupied yourself in hawking about Poems devoid of Truth (Dichtungen ohne Wahrheit) – and how or from whom could you learn the truth? – should now, to crown the edifice of the romantic hero, ask for the surrender of the letters of the romantic heroine in exchange for 'a corresponding number of your letters' (which the inequality of numbers would make quite impossible), passes the bounds of my comprehension.

I too have a wife and children to whom I owe it not to abandon this good weapon against possible future calumny; and these letters and other writings shall be preserved from generation to generation. That the Herzen children, whose wish I cannot therefore fulfil, need fear no misuse of them by me, is guaranteed by the attitude which I have preserved in the face of the most provocative, most scandalous, most crying brutality, seeing that I have never been induced – and shall not be induced even by your future gossipings in Florentine *salons* – to make use of a single line written by the dead woman in order to stop once for all the mouth of a band of hirelings.

I have not done it because I should thereby have been guilty of the same crime which has been committed by those who have thought any weapon good enough to use against me, including, Fräulein, your efforts to illustrate a text which was entirely unknown to you. In any case, children have no business with their mother's love-letters.

My friend Richard Wagner is one of those who have been so frequently pestered with this 'affair' by unauthorized persons that he would no doubt end by giving you any advice you wanted in order to be free from further importunities.

325

LETTER OF THOMAS CARLYLE TO ALEXANDER HERZEN

5 Cheyne Row,
Chelsea.
13 *April* 1855.

DEAR SIR,

I have read your eloquent Discourse on Russian revolutionary matters;* which manifests a potent spirit, and high talent, in various respects; and in which, especially, there is a tone of tragic earnestness not be mistaken by the reader, nor to be judged lightly by him, whatever he may think of your program and prophecy as to Russia and the world.

For my own share I confess I never had, and have now (if it were possible) less than ever, the least hope in 'Universal Suffrage' under any of its modifications: and, if it were not that in certain deadly maladies of the body politic, a burning crisis may be considered as beneficent, I should much prefer Tzarism, itself, or Grand-Turkism itself, to the sheer Anarchy (as I reckon it sadly to be) which is got by 'Parliamentary Eloquence', Free Press, and counting of heads. *'Ach! Mein lieber Sulzer, Er kennt nicht diese verdammte Race!'* said Frederick of Prussia once; and it is a sad truth he expresses there. In your vast country, – which I have always respected as a huge dark 'Birth of Providence', the meanings of which are not yet known, – there is evident, down to this time, one talent in which it has the pre-eminence, giving it potency far beyond any other Nation: the talent (indispensable to all Nations and all creatures, and inexorably required of them all under penalties), *the talent of obeying*, – which is much out of vogue in other quarters just now! And I never doubt, or can doubt, but the want of *it* will be amerced to the last due farthing, sooner or later; and bring about huge bankruptcies, wherever persevered in. Such is my sad creed in these revolutionary times.

* A pamphlet in French *On the Development of Revolutionary Ideas in Russia* which had just been published in London. Herzen had probably presented a copy to Carlyle.

In spite of all these discrepancies, it will give me real pleasure if you call some day when you are in town; nor am I myself without hope of finding out Cholmondeley Lodge in some of my walking excursions; and enjoying there once more a little talk with an estimable man of sense, which is always a pleasure to me.

With many kind regards and good wishes, I remain,

yours very sincerely,

T. CARLYLE.

Appendix C

THE following is the list of addresses of Herzen's residences in London between 1852 and 1865:

25 Aug. 1852– 20 Sept. (?)1852	Morley's Hotel, Trafalgar Square.
20 Sept. (?) 1852–31 Oct. 1853	4, Spring Gardens.
31 Oct. 1853– (?) June 1854	25, Euston Square.
(?) June 1854– 26 Dec. 1854	St. Helena Terrace, Richmond.
26 Dec. 1854–5 April 1855	Richmond House, Twickenham.
5 April 1855–5 Dec. 1855	Cholmondeley Lodge, Richmond.
5 Dec. 1855–10 Sept. 1856	1, Peterborough Villas, Finchley Rd.
10 Sept. 1856– 11 Nov. 1858	Laurel House (Mr Tinkler's), High Street, Putney.
24 Nov. 1858–25 May (?) 1860	Park House, Percy Cross, Fulham.
25 May (?) 1860–15 Nov. 1860	10, Alpha Road, Regent's Park.
15 Nov. 1860–28 June 1863	Orsett House, Westbourne Terrace.
28 June 1863–(?) June 1864*	Elmsfield House, Teddington.
(?) Sept. 1864–10 Nov. 1864	Tunstall House, Warwick Road, Maida Hill.
10 Nov. 1864–21 Nov. 1864†	11, Eastbourne Terrace, Paddington.
22 Feb. 1865–15 March 1865	6, Rothesay Villas, Richmond.

'Herzen always used to say,' remarks Natalie Ogarev in her *Memoirs*, 'that there was such uniformity about the arrangement of the rooms, and even the position of the furniture, in English houses that he could find any room or any object blindfold.'

* Between June and September 1864, Herzen, Natalie and the children were at Bournemouth and retained no house in London.

† Herzen, Natalie and the children left for Paris on 21 November 1864. Herzen returned alone on 22 February 1865.

Appendix D

BEDLAM

OR

A DAY OF OUR LIFE (1857–1858)

*

SCENE I

OGAREV (*in bed*): I suppose it's time to get up. Ugh! Another wash and brush. My feet are frozen. Why should I get up? (*Stretches himself.*)

[FRANÇOIS *brings in hot water, clothes and shoes.*]

OGAREV: What time is it, François?

FRANÇOIS: A quarter to eight. (*Exit.*)

OGAREV: Why the devil do I ask him what time it is when I know that he always comes in at exactly the same time? He has again put the shoes the wrong way round, the right one on the left, the left one on the right. What persistence in being illogical!

[*Enter* NATALIE.]

OGAREV: Good morning, Natalie. How are you?

NATALIE: Better, I think. My head isn't aching so much. I don't think I shall go to Deville.*

OGAREV: I think you had better, for I don't know what to be up to.

NATALIE: Well, wait a bit. If I can't manage without, I will go. But I think I'm better.

OGAREV: Well, we'll see. But it's no use waiting too long.

NATALIE: Get dressed and come downstairs.

OGAREV: All right. What a bore getting up is! Just five minutes more. What shall I think about for five minutes . . . Ah, I know!

* The family doctor, a French political refugee.

329

SCENE 2

At Breakfast

SASHA (*to* NATALIE): How can you eat like that?

NATALIE (*making an incoherent noise to show that she is aggrieved*): How ridiculous you are!

OLGA: I don't want any egg. (*Cries.*)

NATALIE: Well, don't eat any, nobody is making you. Aren't you ashamed of yourself? Stop crying or I'll give you an enema.

HERZEN (*to* NATALIE): Well, how are you today? Still cross? (NATALIE *frowns.*) No, just say! Are you cross or not? Oh, I can see that you are cross.

NATALIE: Why, what am I doing?

HERZEN: I can see! It is all because of what was said yesterday.

NATALIE: But I have said nothing.

HERZEN: But all the same you are cross. Listen. I didn't mean to say anything to wound you. I had nothing of the kind in my head. It was a general conversation. Why make a personal issue of everything?

NATALIE: It's all the same to me. You can keep three Marias and two men-servants if you like but it seems to me that one nurse could do the work.

HERZEN: It is extraordinary how you refuse to admit what is perfectly evident. Surely I explained to you that it is not customary here, that a nurse cannot have time –

NATALIE: All right, the house is yours. You can do what you like in it.

HERZEN: Come now! Why this tone? We are discussing how to arrange things so as to be best for everybody, and you take it all as a personal insult. What do you mean by saying the house is mine? I should have thought that, united as we are, it was impossible to take up such an attitude.

NATALIE: What slavery! Everyone has the right to his own opinion.

HERZEN: Enough, enough! Is it possible to go on discussing this one point for five days?

NATALIE: As you please. I only thought the nurse –
[OGAREV, *having finished his coffee, goes out into the garden.*]

SCENE 3

Herzen's Study

OGAREV: Listen, Herzen. Do try not to keep asking Natalie whether she is cross or not. Take no notice of her ill-humour, but carry on with the general conversation and shut your eyes to any personalities. Perhaps things will go better then.

HERZEN (*after reflexion*): Good! Believe me, I will do everything possible to calm her. An unhappy character! If she were stupid I could understand. She has intelligence and she has fine feelings, and yet she cannot for a moment take things quietly. You are right when you put it down to heredity.

OGAREV: But then again, perhaps that won't help. From what I know of the logic of illogical people, I'm afraid that, when you pay no attention to her ill-humour, that also will be taken as an insult, just as it is now an insult when you notice her ill-humour. But try all the same. We *must* save her, we *must* calm her.

HERZEN: You can trust me. Everything in my power will be done. It is really so sad. You have people marked out by destiny to love one another, and yet you have nothing but irritability!

SCENE 4

Ogarev's Room

OGAREV: Ugh! I can't write an article today. I haven't enough material. I want to go on with the poem. . . . What can I do with Natalie? God, I cannot make her out. She is suffering terribly, and she is herself to blame.

NATALIE (*entering*): I don't know what Herzen wants of one.

OGAREV: What he wants? Your eternal habit of making a grievance of everything has so poisoned relations between you

331

that he cannot help constantly suspecting you of being cross. You are jealous without any cause and you take every general remark as a personal insult.

NATALIE: I ought to take up some line of study.

OGAREV: Well, find something.

NATALIE: Tell me what. It is easy for you to occupy yourselves, but women are not prepared for any occupation.

OGAREV: I repeat once more: I cannot tell you what to study. A man must choose his own interest to suit the intellectual need which he is seeking to satisfy. How can I create this intellectual need? You are too absorbed in personalities, and for that reason cannot study.

NATALIE: When I want to study, the children prevent me.

OGAREV: By arranging a suitable time-table, you can find the time. It is inconvenient, I admit. But the point is to get over the inconvenience, to arrange everything for the best, and still have time to work.

NATALIE: But I don't know enough words.

OGAREV: You can ask or look them up in a dictionary.

NATALIE: Oh, I know perfectly well that I cannot study.

[OGAREV *shrugs his shoulders.*]

NATALIE: It is all my own fault. But really I will control myself. You will see how quiet I shall be, and how hard I will try to make everything go right.

OGAREV: So much the better. Believe me, we both love you and want terribly to see you calm and happy.

[*Exit* NATALIE. OGAREV *turns over the last stanzas of his poem, shuts the exercise book, and opens the exercise book containing the article. He shuts that too and sits down to the piano.* MARIA *calls him to lunch.*]

SCENE 5

Lunch

SASHA (*to* NATALIE): What a lot you're putting on your plate.

NATALIE (*making an incoherent noise to show that she is aggrieved*): How ridiculous you are!

OLGA: I don't want any fat. (*Cries.*)

NATALIE: I'm not giving you any fat. Aren't you ashamed of yourself? Stop crying, or I'll give you an enema.

HERZEN (*to* NATALIE): Well, how are you? Still cross, or not? Ha! You are cross. (NATALIE *frowns.*) Let us go up to London.

NATALIE: What for? We are very comfortable here.

HERZEN: Oh, enough of your ill-humour. Let us go to London. A glass of Curaçao, and everything will be as right as rain.

NATALIE: Very well, we will go.

HERZEN: Oh, no! Perhaps you don't really want to. Why force yourself? I will go for a walk, I need exercise.

NATALIE (*hurt*): As you please. (*Silence.*)

HERZEN: Well, what is decided? Are you coming or not? Or are you still cross? (*Silence.*) Well, let's go.

[NATALIE *goes to put on her things.*]

HERZEN: François!

[*Enter* FRANÇOIS.]

HERZEN: Take this letter to the post. Go at once. Yes. . . . No. . . . Wait. What did I want to ask you? Ah! Have we any red wine left?

FRANÇOIS: Certainly.

HERZEN: Then bring us a bottle. Yes. . . . but . . . Go on! go on!

[FRANÇOIS *brings a bottle.*]

HERZEN: What time is it?

FRANÇOIS: A quarter past three.

HERZEN: Ah! Missed it again. Never mind. It will go at six o'clock. Post it all the same. No! Wait. I will post it myself in London. (*Puts the letter in his pocket.*)

[*Re-enter* NATALIE *dressed.* HERZEN *goes to put on his things.* OGAREV *goes on smoking and eating the sweet.*]

SASHA: Why does Papa object to my wearing brown boots?

OGAREV: It's not done.

SASHA: But everyone does it.

OGAREV: In the first place everyone does not do it; in the second place respectable people don't do it.

SASHA: I don't understand. Everyone wears brown boots. I am going to work.

[*Takes a book and sits down to read in the garden.* TATA *and* OLGA *play near him.*]

NATALIE (*to* OGAREV): I really don't know whether to go or
not.

OGAREV: Oh, my God! Why do you suppose he doesn't want
you to go? Do take into account his manner of speaking. I am
sure there was no *arrière pensée* in what he said. Do have confidence in him.

HERZEN (*entering, dressed*): Well, you're not cross? (NATALIE
frowns.) Let us go. François, give me my hat! Where is my stick?
And my gloves?

> [*Search for hat and stick.* FRANÇOIS *brings two left-handed
> gloves of different colours.*]

HERZEN: Sasha!

> [SASHA *runs in from the garden.*]

HERZEN: Do look for my gloves.

> [SASHA *brings the gloves.*]

HERZEN: Have you no errands?

OGAREV: No!

HERZEN: Good-bye.

NATALIE: Adieu!

HERZEN: Addio!

> [*Exeunt.*]

SCENE 6

Ogarev's Room

OGAREV: They've gone. . . . They will begin a general conversation very nicely. Then Natalie will take offence at something, and they will quarrel. Then they will make it up, though
each will remain convinced that the other was in the wrong.
Generally speaking, Herzen is of course right; but he is wrong
in giving way so completely to his irritability. Ah, these
amorous-hostile relations between two beings whom I love
more than anything on earth. And then they expect me to
work! What work is my brain capable of? Pain – nothing but
pain. I must get away or I shall be stifled. The guillotine is
better than a daily succession of pin-pricks. If only there were
some physical motive at the bottom of it! But it is simply

motiveless irritability. I understand physiological excesses. Physiology never oversteps the limit. Debauchery is pathological insanity.

[*Dresses and goes out.*]

SCENE 7

*Tea**

HERZEN, *in the arm-chair;* SASHA *is drinking tea and has put his cup on the mantelpiece;* NATALIE *is lying on the couch;* OGAREV *carefully conceals that he has been drinking.*

NATALIE: Well, let us read Michelet.

HERZEN (*half asleep*): Well, give me the book. (*Takes the book and sits down at the table.*)

SASHA: Good night! I have to get up early tomorrow. (*Exit.*)
  [HERZEN *with one eye open begins to read.* NATALIE *dozes.* OGAREV *carefully conceals that he has been drinking.*]

HERZEN (*rings the bell*): Bring me some soda-water and something.

FRANÇOIS: Some sherry?

HERZEN: No, something light. Is there any red wine?

FRANÇOIS: Certainly.

HERZEN: Ah! bring me . . . some brandy. – Well, get up, Natalie. Bed-time.

NATALIE: What if it is? Why go to bed yet? There is never any time to talk. Let us lie down on the carpet and have a chat.

OGAREV (*carefully concealing that he has been drinking*): Oh, enough. Let's go to bed.
  [*In the end they manage to get up and go.*]

HERZEN (*at* NATALIE'S *door*): Well? Are you still cross? Sleep well.

NATALIE: I'm bored! Give me your hand! . . . I want some comfort.

OGAREV and HERZEN: Good night.
  [*They finally separate.*]

* Meaning, of course, the last meal of the Russian day, not the modern five o'clock variety.

SCENE 8

Ogarev's Room

OGAREV (*alone*): What a pity! Nothing left to drink. Yet somehow – the devil knows how much I might have written now,
if only there were something to drink. It's bad for me, I know
that. Yet it's good for me really. Unless I am a bit merry, I am
simply malicious, downright malicious. And that's good too;
at such moments, I could write a tragedy. . . . It's still just as
hopeless between them; and this will go on for three hundred
and sixty-five days a year, or three hundred and sixty-six days
in a leap-year. Devil take it, what a punishment! What do I
believe in? I believe that a man in his youth hesitates what bit
to take between his teeth, at a certain age he gets hold of some
bit or other, so firmly that you couldn't wrench it out with a
stake; and then for the rest of his life he gallops along with it.
This last period of life is called maturity.

> [*Undresses, lies down, takes a book, and falls into the heavy
> sleep of a drunken man. The candle burns. The dog howls.*]

Appendix E

THE *WARD JACKSON:*
FOREIGN OFFICE DOCUMENTS

THE archives of the Foreign Office contain a mass of correspondence relating to the affair of the *Ward Jackson*. It may be of interest to give some account of the more important items.

The first document is a note from the Russian Ambassador, Baron Brunnov, to Earl Russell, Secretary of State for Foreign Affairs, dated 19 March 1863. The Ambassador states, on 'trustworthy information', that 'the steamer *Gipsy Queen* is proceeding from West Hartlepool to the Thames to pick up there 200 men and cargo for an unknown destination in the Baltic'. The 'unusually large number of landing boats' which was being carried gave reason to suspect 'a destination not justified by commercial interests or by licit traffic'. He begs Lord Russell 'to consider waht measures can legally be taken to prevent an enterprise the object of which would appear to be of a character prohibited by the law in time of peace'.

On the following day (20 March) Baron Brunnov sent a further note to say that an error had been made in the name of the ship, which was not the *Gipsy Queen* but the *Ward Jackson*, that she was the property of Messrs Pile and Spence of West Hartlepool, and that she had already arrived off Tilbury.

These successive notes revealed the importance which Baron Brunnov attached to the matter; and his anxiety was still further betrayed by the sending, during these same two days, of three private letters, in his own hand, one to Lord Russell and two to Mr Hammond, the Permanent Under-Secretary of State.* 'It would really be too bad,' ran the last of these, 'if a set of $\frac{\text{Garibaldians}}{\text{Poles}}$ could start from Woolwich on a hostile expedition without any legal impediment under the eyes of the british [*sic*] authorities just as they started from Genua [*sic*] for Sicily – *coram populo.*'

---

* Baron Brunnov's official notes are in French, these private letters in English.

Copies of the official notes were sent by the Foreign Office on 20 March to the Treasury and the Home Office, and these departments were requested, in a guarded and tautological phrase, 'to take such steps as can legally be taken to prevent any infringement of the law'.

Two days later, on Sunday, 22 March, a report dated 21 March from the Surveyor of Customs at Gravesend reached the Foreign Office through the Treasury. The Surveyor reported that '50 cases entered as hardware have on examination been found to contain muskets, and that the afterhold of the ship *Ward Jackson* is fitted up with benches for troops or recruits, as the fittings are altogether unsuited for other passengers'. The Board of Customs had given orders to remove the fifty cases, but 'in the absence of any positive evidence or information beyond that furnished by the Russian Ambassador' they did not see 'sufficient grounds for detaining the ship without their Lordships' [i.e. the Treasury's] special instructions'.

This communication seems to have made, even on a Sunday, a certain impression in the Foreign Office. It was decided to consult the Law Officers of the Crown urgently on the legal position and, pending the receipt of their opinion, to request the Treasury to instruct the Customs to detain the *Ward Jackson* until further notice.

The opinion of the Law Officers, given the same day, was a model of caution. They declared that 'there was not at present any sufficient legal evidence on the whole to justify the arrest or further detention of the *Ward Jackson*,' but they wondered 'whether some risk of damages for further detention might not be run, so as to give Baron Brunnov an opportunity of supplying the requisite evidence'.

In pursuance of this opinion, Lord Russell in a note of 23 March invited Baron Brunnov 'to produce any evidence as to the purpose for which the vessel was equipped and as to her destination'.

At this point a startling development interrupts the orderly tenor of the official correspondence. The Sunday labours of the Foreign Office and of the Law Officers had been fruitless and, as the event proved, slightly ridiculous. No sooner had the note to Baron Brunnov been despatched than a letter arrived from the Treasury enclosing a report to the Board of Customs by its surveyor at Gravesend. Both these communications were dated 23 March, the day on which they reached the Foreign Office. The report from the Surveyor at Gravesend ran as follows:

Custom House,
Gravesend.
23 March, 1863.

HONOURABLE SIR,

About 7 p.m. of the 21st instant I received a telegram directing me to take out of the *Ward Jackson* for Dantzic such goods as were erroneously entered as Hardware and detain the same pending your Honor's Order.

It had been reported to me during the day that the Vessel would not sail until Monday (i.e. March 23rd). I had therefore decided to take the goods out as soon after daylight on Sunday morning as possible, it being impracticable to select those required in the dark and dangerous to take a light into the hold among the ammunition. Having been informed that the Master would be on board between 8 and 9 o'clock I went on board about that time to arrange with him as to the best method of getting the packages out some of which are very heavy, and to my surprise found the vessel was preparing to get under weigh. I found a person with the Master who said he belonged to the Broker's Office and I made them both acquainted with your Honor's Order. They replied that Steam was getting up and as soon as they could get ready the Vessel would proceed to sea at any risk, as they had arranged to take in 200 Poles at a certain time and place (neither of which were mentioned) and to do this the Vessel must leave at once, and as I had no authority to stop her and no time to get hands to take out the goods I regret to say that I was unable to carry out your Honor's Order.

I had previously placed two Officers on board and told the Master I should not withdraw them till I had got the goods and warned him not to take them out of the Port. He replied: If they do not leave when I am ready to go, I shall take them with me. I have seen the two Officers and they inform me that the Vessel left Gravesend about 11 p.m. on Saturday and arrived alongside Southend Pier about One a.m. on Sunday morning, where they landed and 200 persons said to be Poles who had arrived by special train went on board and the Vessel immediately proceeded to Sea.

On the same day, 23 March, the Home Office replied to the letter from the Foreign Office of 20 March and enclosed a report from the Chief of the Metropolitan Police. This adds nothing however to the information in our possession except the fact that the legionaries 'had left Woolwich on Saturday evening by train to London and, it is believed, went immediately to Southend' and that their pay was, for officers, seven shillings a day, for privates, threepence a day.

On receipt of these reports, Lord Russell made to Baron Brunnov, on 24 March, the communication quoted in the text (p. 210). From the practical point of view there was nothing further to be done. But the matter continued to exercise Baron Brunnov; and in further notes of 25 March and 30 March he forwarded to Lord Russell sworn affidavits by William Fox, who had watched the loading of arms and ammunition on board the *Ward Jackson*, and of William Wood, who had witnessed the embarkation of 'about two hundred persons chiefly foreigners' at Southend. The Foreign Office contented itself with acknowledging receipt of these communications.

The last document on the case in the Foreign Office archives is a letter from the Treasury to the Foreign Office of 26 May. In it was enclosed a letter from the Board of Customs reporting that the *Ward Jackson* had been sequestered by the Swedish authorities; that the master had returned to West Hartlepool on 16 April; that on 29 April he had been summoned before the Mayor and Justices of Gravesend; and that he had been fined £50 for sailing without clearance papers and £10 costs, which sums were paid.

Appendix F

NOTE ON SOURCES

A. I. HERZEN, *Polnoe Sobranie Sochinenii i Pisem*, ed. M. K. LEMKE, 22 vols. (Leningrad–Moscow, 1919–1925.)

This monumental edition of the writings and letters of Herzen, arranged chronologically, with extensive commentaries is the most important source for the greater part of the present work. Vols. XII–XIV contain Herzen's memoirs which have been (somewhat imperfectly) translated into English by Mrs Garnett under the title *My Past and Thoughts* (Chatto & Windus, 6 vols., 1924–1927).

Vospominaniya N. A. Ogarevoi–Tuchkovoi. Leningrad, 1929.

The memoirs of Natalie Tuchkov, who became Ogarev's second wife, are unreliable in statements of fact and in chronology, and hopelessly biased in their judgment of persons; but they cover the whole period and provide some vivid touches.

The following special sources have also been used in the chapters named:

CHAPTER 2

Russkie Propilei, ed. M. O. GERSHENZON, vol. I. Moscow, 1915.

Letters of Natalie Herzen to Natalie Tuchkov.

CHAPTERS 3 AND 4

Unpublished letters and papers of Herzen and Natalie Herzen, and of Herwegh and Emma Herwegh belonging to Monsieur Marcel Herwegh.

The letters and papers of Herzen and Natalie Herzen are now deposited in the British Museum.

CHAPTER 5

Mazzini's Letters to an English Family, ed. E. F. RICHARDS, 3 vols., Lane, 1920.

M. VON MEYSENBUG, *Memoiren einer Idealistin*, 3rd edition, Berlin, 1900.

CHAPTER 6

M. O. GERSHENZON, *Obrazy Proshlovo*, Moscow, 1911.
Letters of Ogarev to Maria.

M. O. GERSHENZON, *Istoriya Molodoi Rossii*, Moscow, 1907; re-issued 1913.
Letters of Galakhov to Maria.

Russkie Propilei, ed. M. O. GERSHENZON, vol. II, Moscow, 1916.
Ogarev's *Profession de Foi*.

Id., vol. IV, Moscow, 1918.
Letters of Ogarev to Natalie Tuchkov.

CHAPTER 8

Russkie Propilei, vol. IV.

CHAPTER 10

M. K. LEMKE, *Ocherki Osvoboditelnovo Dvizheniva*, Petersburg, 1910.

CHAPTER 11

Y. STEKLOV, *M. A. Bakunin*, vol. II, Moscow–Leningrad, 1927.
Foreign Office Archives (1863) in the Record Office.

CHAPTER 12

Arkhiv N. A. i N. P. Ogarevykh, Moscow–Leningrad, 1930.

CHAPTER 13

SHCHEGOLEV, *Duel i Smert Pushkina*, Moscow–Leningrad, 1927.
M. K. LEMKE, Articles in *Byloe*, February–March 1907.
M. K. LEMKE, *Nikolaevski Zhandarmy i Literatura*, Petersburg, 1908.

CHAPTER 14

Y. STEKLOV, *M. A. Bakunin*, vol. III, Moscow–Leningrad, 1927.
T. RODITCHEFF, Article in *Posledniya Novosti*, 13 Feb. 1931 (*Nechaev i Deti Gertsena*).
J. GUILLAUME, *L'Internationale – Documents et Souvenirs*, vols. I and II, Paris, 1905–1907.

CHAPTER 15

P. M. KANTOR, *V Pogone za Nechaevyni*, Petrograd, 1922.

CHAPTER 16

Russkie Propilei, vol. IV.
    Letters of Ogarev to Herzen.
Arkhiv N. A. i N. P. Ogarevykh.
A. B. BAULER, Article in *Byloe*, July 1907, *Odna iz Dorogykh Tenei*.
    Account of visit to Ogarev at Greenwich.

CHAPTER 17

Arkhiv N. A. i N. P. Ogarevykh.

An independent publishing house, Serif publishes a wide range
of international fiction and non-fiction.

If you would like to receive a copy of our current catalogue,
please write to:

Serif
47 Strahan Road
London E3 5DA

or

1489 Lincoln Avenue
St Paul
MN 55105

also published by Serif

WARRANT FOR GENOCIDE
THE MYTH OF THE JEWISH WORLD CONSPIRACY AND THE PROTOCOLS OF THE ELDERS OF ZION

Norman Cohn

The Holocaust stands out as the most barbaric episode in a century noted for its savagery. Behind Hitler's anti-semitic obsession lay an enormously influential literary forgery, the *Protocols of the Elders of Zion,* the master-plan of an alleged Jewish conspiracy to control the world.

In a fascinating work of historical detection, Norman Cohn unravels the origins of the *Protocols of the Elders of Zion.* Tracing its roots in anti-semitic mythology, Cohn pinpoints the interplay of literary hacks and secret policemen in concocting a book which, translated and published around the world, was once second only to the Bible in its circulation.

Before Hitler came to power the *Protocols* were one of the cornerstones of Nazi propaganda, and when the Second World War started they served as the principal 'justification' for the extermination of European Jewry. **Warrant for Genocide** sets the story of the *Protocols* within the broader context of the history of anti-semitism: it remains one of the key books for understanding the murderous folly of the twentieth century.

'Powerful and important ... There have been previous histories of the Protocols and the mythologies of modern anti-semitism, but this is the most lucid and ironic.'
George Steiner, *Sunday Times*

Norman Cohn is a Fellow of the British Academy and Emeritus Professor of History at the University of Sussex. His celebrated historical works include *The Pursuit of the Millennium* and *Europe's Inner Demons.*

paperback

THE STRANGE DEATH OF LIBERAL ENGLAND

George Dangerfield

At the beginning of the twentieth century Britain's empire spanned the globe, her economy was strong and the political system seemed to be immune to the ills which afflicted so many other countries. After a resounding electoral triumph in 1906 the Liberals formed the government of the most powerful nation on earth, yet within a few years the army had mutinied, industrial unrest was rife, civil war loomed in Ireland and the proceedings of 'the mother of parliaments' were reduced to little more than farce.

The Strange Death of Liberal England is the classic study of this rapid collapse of a self-confident body politic. Three factors combined to bring Liberal England to its knees. The Home Rule crisis brought Ireland to the brink of civil war and led to the mutiny at the Curragh, while the campaign for women's suffrage created widespread civil disorder and discredited the legal and penal systems, and an unprecedented strike wave swept the land.

The years before the First World War are often presented as a golden age, but this stylish and witty history shows the turbulence of an alleged *belle époque* to have been the writing on the wall for a nation which had for too long thought of itself as all-powerful

'A classic both of popular history, in the best sense of that phrase, and of good and interesting writing.'
The Irish Times

George Dangerfield was a Fellow of Princeton University and winner of the Pulitzer Prize for American History; his books include *The Damnable Question: A Study in Anglo-Irish Relations* and *The Awakening of American Nationalism*.

paperback

THE LORDS OF HUMAN KIND
EUROPEAN ATTITUDES TO OTHER CULTURES IN THE IMPERIAL AGE

Victor Kiernan

When European explorers went out into the world to open up trade routes and establish colonies, they brought back much more than silks and spices, cotton and tea. Inevitably, they came into contact with people in other parts of the world and formed views of them, occasionally admiring, more often hostile or contemptuous.

Using a stunning array of sources – missionaries' memoirs, the letters of diplomats' wives, explorers' diaries and the work of writers as diverse as Voltaire, Thackeray, Oliver Goldsmith and, of course, Kipling – Victor Kiernan teases out the full range of European attitudes to other peoples. Erudite, ironic and global in its scope, **The Lords of Human Kind** has been a major influence on a generation of historians and cultural critics and is a landmark in the study of Eurocentrism. The legacy of colonial attitudes to other cultures is an integral part of the modern world and the history of their formation is one which cannot be ignored.

'A wry delight ... brilliant, witty and humane'
Philip Toynbee, *The Observer*

Victor Kiernan is one of Britain's most distinguished historians. Emeritus Professor of History at the University of Edinburgh, he is the author of *European Empires from Conquest to Collapse, The Duel in European History* and *Tobacco*. He has written numerous other historical and literary works and is also the translator of two volumes of Urdu poetry.

paperback

THE CROWD IN HISTORY
A STUDY OF POPULAR DISTURBANCES IN FRANCE AND ENGLAND, 1730–1848

George Rudé

Who took part in the widespread disturbances which periodically shook eighteenth-century London? What really motivated the food rioters who helped to spark off the French Revolution? How did the movement of agricultural labourers destroying new machinery spread from one village to another in the English countryside? How did the *sans-culottes* organise in revolutionary Paris?

George Rudé was the first historian to ask such questions and in doing so he identified 'the faces in the crowd' in some of the crucial episodes in modern European history. An established classic of 'history from below', **The Crowd in History** is remarkable above all for the clarity with which it deals with the full sweep of complex historical events. Whether in Berlin, Beijing or Soweto, crowds continue to make history, and Rudé's work retains all its freshness and relevance for students of history and politics and the general reader alike.

'It may seem incredible that nobody tried before to discover what sort of people actually stormed the Bastille, but Rudé is the first to have done so ... Like all his work this book is concentrated, simple and clear, and admirably suited to the non-specialist reader.'
Eric Hobsbawm, *New York Review of Books*

George Rudé's numerous books include *Wilkes and Liberty, The Crowd in the French Revolution* and, with Eric Hobsbawm, *Captain Swing*. One of the most innovative social historians of the twentieth century, he died in 1993.

paperback

PLEASANT THE SCHOLAR'S LIFE
IRISH INTELLECTUALS AND THE CONSTRUCTION OF THE NATION STATE

Maurice Goldring

As Europe witnesses new states being born and clothing themselves in the symbolic apparel of nationhood, Maurice Goldring's exploration of the conscious creation of national 'traditions' could scarcely be more timely.

In this innovative survey of the interplay of literature and folklore in the building of cultural identity, Maurice Goldring makes a major contribution to our understanding of nationalism. In a penetrating and readable study of the cultural origins of Irish nationalism, he shows how Dublin intellectuals promoted the use of Galeic and concentrated their energies on idealising the life of the peasantry in the West of the country. At the same time, the Catholic clergy expanded its authority in the countryside and the power vacuum in the towns was filled by an inward-looking lower middle class. The alliance between the church and the intelligentsia which followed laid the basis for a social and moral conservatism that was used to manipulate the world-view of ordinary citizens and is only now being shaken off.

'Subtle and penetrating ... Good social criticism, and good literary criticism too'
Conor Cruise O'Brien

'Carefully wrought, subtle and intelligent'
John McGahern, *The Irish Times*

Maurice Goldring is Professor of Irish Studies at the University of Paris and author of a number of books including *Belfast: From Loyalty to Rebellion*

paperback

THE POLITICS OF ILLUSION
A POLITICAL HISTORY OF THE IRA

Henry Patterson

This is the first comprehensive study of the IRA's attempts to create a 'social republicanism', a marriage between militant nationalism and the politics of the left. From agitation amongst the peasantry in the 1920s to efforts in the 1990s to add a political dimension to purist nationalism in the form of Sinn Fein's 'peace process', Henry Patterson analyses the various failed attempts to marry two fundamentally incompatible ideologies.

Friend and foe have described the IRA as 'socialists', 'Marxists', 'fascists' or simply as militaristic and murderous thugs. In this highly praised work the author steers us through the complex, schismatic and inevitably secretive history of both the Provisional and the Official IRA, Sinn Fein and the various organisations with which they have been associated. He teases out the meaning and significance of the twists and turns in republican policy, which at different periods have involved working with trade unions, collaboration with Nazi Germany, support for tenants fighting for better housing, hunger strikes and, of course, both urban and rural guerrilla warfare.

This fully revised and updated new edition takes the history of Irish republicanism beyond Sinn Fein's best ever performance in the 1997 Westminster and Dail elections to the IRA's renewed ceasefire. Henry Patterson's conclusion is that 'physical force' or militarist nationalism and the politics of the left make uneasy and, when the rhetoric is cleared away, self-deluding and illusory bed-fellows.

'Subtle and authoritative'
New York Review of Books

Henry Patterson is Professor of Politics at the University of Ulster. He is co-author, with Paul Bew and Peter Gibbon, of the highly acclaimed *Northern Ireland 1921–1996*.

paperback